THE TYLER GENEALOGY

VOLUME II

THE
TYLER GENEALOGY

THE DESCENDANTS OF JOB TYLER, OF ANDOVER, MASSACHUSETTS, 1619-1700

BY

WILLARD I. TYLER BRIGHAM

VOLUME II

PUBLISHED BY

CORNELIUS B. TYLER, of Plainfield, N. J.

AND

ROLLIN U. TYLER, of Tylerville, Conn.

MCMXII

Another Quality Reprint of a Classic Book
by

The Apple Manor Press

2017

Markham, Virginia

Thousands of titles available at:
www.AppleManorPress.com

Book pages have been individually reproduced and processed by trained
Aritisans using uncompressed high resolution scanned images of the
original pages. Manually processing of the images allows proper attention to detail
not possible through inexpensive automated software.
Most low cost competitors use automated software with no human quality control
to process low quality compressed PDF files intended for internet viewing.

Manual processing each page allows for much better image and print quality

Volume I ISBN: 978-1-5421-0233-9
Volume II ISBN: 978-1-5421-0234-6

THE
TYLER GENEALOGY

THE DESCENDANTS OF JOB TYLER, OF ANDOVER, MASSACHUSETTS, 1619-1700

BY

WILLARD I. TYLER BRIGHAM

VOLUME II

PUBLISHED BY
CORNELIUS B. TYLER, of Plainfield, N. J.
AND
ROLLIN U. TYLER, of Tylerville, Conn.
MCMXII

CONTENTS

THE SEVENTH GENERATION

SEVENTH GENERATION

2000 THOMAS[7] TYLER (Moses[6]), born in Warren, Mass., January 26, 1787; died August 11, 1830; married, July, 1807, Susan Hodges, born in Western, Mass., September 25, 1792; died in Worcester, Mass., May 18, 1871; she survived her first husband and married (2), Timothy Bliss, of Brimfield, Mass.; she was the daughter of Daniel and Rachel (Rich) Hodges (George, William, John, William). The children were born in Warren. Children:

4263+ George W. Tyler, born Aug. 21, 1808.
4264+ Orville Thomas Tyler, born Aug. 28, 1810.
4265   Caroline Tyler, born Nov. 27, 1812; died Sept. 2, 1813.
4266+ Mary Caroline Tyler, born Feb. 10, 1815.
4267+ Alonzo Ripley Tyler, born Dec. 21, 1817.
4268   Albert Gallatin Tyler, born May 23, 1820; died Jan. 20, 1888, in Natchez, Miss.; married in 185–, Anne Nichols, of New York City; prior to 1860 she died in Natchez.
4269   Susan Augusta Tyler, born May 10, 1824; died Oct. 28, 1826.

2001 TRIPHENA[7] TYLER (Moses[6]), born in Warren, Mass., March 14, 1789; died August 11, 1829; married, March 21, 1808, Adolphus Hodges, of Warren, born in Western, now Warren, September 19, 1786; died in Warren, October 5, 1845. (*Hodges Genealogical Record*, page 224). He married (2), Charity Durfee, of Brimfield, Mass. Children:

4270+ Daniel Milton Hodges, born in Warren or Brookfield, Mass., Aug. 20, 1810.
4271   Lewis Adolphus Hodges, died unmarried, in Cincinnati, O.
4272+ Maria Louise Hodges, born in Brookfield, Mass., April 4, 1815.
4273   George Rich Hodges, died s. p. in Cincinnati, leaving a widow.

4274   John Tyler Hodges, died in New York City.
4275   William A. Hodges.

2002   SARAH[7] TYLER (Moses[6]), born in Warren, Mass., June 2, 1791; died in Cortland County, N. Y., February 7, 1856; married, December 1, 1814, Justin Morgan, of Brimfield, Mass., where the children were born.   Children:
4276   Mary Tyler Morgan, married Jeremiah Bean.
4277   Thomas J. Morgan, born Feb. 12, 1823.
4278   Jane Elizabeth Morgan, born June 29, 1825; married, Oct., 1845, Chauncey Bean, Binghamton, N. Y.
4279   Moses Tyler Morgan, born Jan. 8, 1827; died Sept., 1879, in Brimfield; he resided in Binghamton where he built a fine wall in the center of the town to reclaim lands from the river.
4280   George Byron Morgan, born Feb. 3, 1831; resided in Bunker Hill, Ill.
4281   Sarah Morgan, born Sept. 6, 1833; married Deaney Halbert and resided, in 1900, in Kansas City, Mo.

2003   MOSES[7] TYLER (Moses[6]), born in Warren, Mass., May 10, 1797; died in Vincennes, Ind., March 29, 1881; married (1), September 23, 1819, Emma Hoar, of Brimfield, Mass. (name later changed to Homer), who died there March 28, 1833, age 37; married (2), Eliza Makepeace, of Brimfield, who died in Vincennes 188—. He lived in Brimfield and then in Boston and thence moved to Vincennes. He was a dealer in hardware and agricultural implements. The eldest child was born in Warren, the others in Brimfield.

CHILDREN, by first marriage:
4282+   William Sumner Tyler, born July 16, 1820.
4283+   Sarah Tyler.
4284+   John Tyler, born Jan. 23, 1827.
4285+   Henry Tyler.

CHILD, by second wife:
4286+   Wilson Makepeace Tyler.

2004   HORATIO[7] TYLER (Moses[6]), born in Brimfield, Mass., September 7, 1800; died in Homer, N. Y., April,

1865; married, 1833 in Homer, Hannah N. Scudder born in Fairfield, N. J., October 26, 1801; died in Wautoma, Wis., 1883. His father died early and Horatio at seven years of age went to live with an uncle. At the age of fifteen he chose as guardian, Justin Morgan, of Brimfield. He became a gunsmith and moved to Homer, N. Y., where his children were born. Children:

4287+   Clement Tyler, born March 12, 1835.
4288+   Emma Tyler, born Feb. 18, 1837.
4289   Infant, died young.
4290   Infant, died young.

2008   JOHN KEYES[7] TYLER (John[6]), probably born in Bloomfield, Conn.; resided in Burns, N. Y., where a town official and died in office; thence to Weare, Mass.; moved to Burrs, Shiawasse County, Mich.; from correspondence with the clergyman of the place, nothing could be learned of the family; married Julia Miller, of Avon, Conn. Children:

4291   John G. Tyler, married Miss Risley, Rochester, N. Y., and lived in Canada, about three miles from Toronto.
4292   Julia Ann Tyler, married —— Adams; lived about ten miles west of Detroit.
4293   Timothy Tyler, lived on the homestead in Burrs, Mich.; resided in 1852 in Burns, N. Y.
4294   Edward Tyler.
4295   Olive Emily Tyler, married —— Adams, and lived near sister Julia.
4296   Sarah Tyler, married and lived in Michigan.

2009   CUTLER[7] TYLER (Isaac[6]), born in Western (Warren), Mass., November 19, 1794; died in Newbury, Ohio, April 3, 1857; estate probated in Chardon, Ohio; married, November 13 1825, Sarah Fisher, born in Canton, Mass., October 15, 1806; died in Newbury, Ohio, March 11, 1867. He bought his time from his father. Once he walked seventy miles from Western to Boston in one day and back the next. He started for Newbury Ohio, May 9, 1818, which he reached June 28. He was one of the early builders in Burton and Newbury, Ohio; was a natural mechanic. For several years was justice of the peace, and held other offices; was called " Squire Tyler " and was a friend of education and temperance. He died suddenly while driving home from Cleveland. The children were born in Newbury.

CHILDREN:

4297+ Abel Clinton Tyler, born Sept. 2, 1827.

4298 Harriet Tyler, born Feb., 1829; died 1830.

4299+ Isaac Allen Tyler, born Sept. 9, 1832.

4300+ Ruth Tyler, born Nov. 29, 1835.

4301 Daughter, born and died 1837.

4302+ Reuben Tyler, born June 11, 1839.

4303+ John Walter Tyler, born May 4, 1841.

4304 Sarah Sophia Tyler, born Jan. 9, 1846; died Jul. 27, 1873, in Cleveland.

2010 KEYES⁷ TYLER (Isaac⁶), born in Warren, Mass., September 29, 1796; married, May 19, 1822, Persis Fairbanks, of Warren, born September 27, 1797; daughter of Asahel and Diedema (Gleason) Fairbanks. He settled in Hardwick Mass., but later on the old homestead in Warren. The children were born in Warren. Children:

4305 Ruth Tyler, born Feb. 27, 1823; died in 1843.

4306+ Isaac Cutler Tyler, born Nov. 7, 1824.

4307 Charles Newell Tyler, born Jan. 3, 1827; married, Jan. 29, 1850, Augusta Clapp, of Warren; he resided in Lockport, N. Y., and elsewhere; they had one son and one daughter.

4308 Sophia Tyler, born June 10, 1829; died in 1843.

4309 Joseph Keyes Tyler, born July 18, 1831; went to Pana, Ill.; married (1), 1858, Sarah Haven; married (2), 1859, Eliza Bradley; no living children.

4310 Mary Ann Tyler, born Sept. 4, 1833; married in 1859, George Barnes, of West Brookfield, Mass., who died Feb. 20, 1874; they lived in Springfield, Mass., and then went west; they had one son and a daughter (Charles and Fannie).

4311 Lydia Paige Tyler, born Nov. 1, 1838; married (1), July 27, 1860, George H. Bacon, who died soon after marriage; married (2), March 6, 1867, Hiram L. Hugumin, of South Evanston, Ill.; they had one son (Henry).

4312+ William Alexander Tyler, born June 3, 1839.

2011   LYDIA[7] TYLER (Isaac[6]), born in Warren, Mass., February 6, 1799; died July 12, 1875; married, November 1, 1818, Timothy Janes, of Brimfield, Mass., born April 28, 1791; son of Peleg C. and Patty (Coy) Janes; he settled in Warren, where he died February 17, 1877. He also resided a while in Woodstock, Conn., where the two elder children were born; the others were born in Warren. Children:

4313   Clementine Janes, born Oct. 29, 1819; married Jeremiah Bean, of Cincinnatus, N. Y.; they lived in Bennington, Vt.; had three children (Emma, Frank, and Sumner).

4314   William C. Janes, born Sept. 16, 1821; married (1), Julia Ann Tyler, No. 2048; married (2), Martha Bliss.

4315   Sumner Janes, died Sept. 18, 1826.

4316   Reuben Sumner Janes, born Nov. 9, 1827; married, April 16, 1858, Sylvia Webster, of Bethel, Vt., born Aug. 12, 1833; had four children (Mary, Sophia, Thomas, and Tyler).

4317   Mary Elizabeth Janes, born Oct. 12, 1831; died Jan. 12, 1833.

4318   Augustus Keyes Janes, born Sept. 8, 1834; died Nov. 13, 1835.

4319   Frances Louisa Janes, born April 29, 1838; died in Warren, Jan. 20, 1883; married there, May 1, 1873, Edward C. H. Washburn; had one daughter (Minnie J.).

4320   Mary Augusta Janes, born May 30, 1842; died Sept. 29, 1864; married, Dec. 17, 1863, A. M. Hale; he died in Chicago, Sept., 1867; one child; died young.

2012   ISAAC[7] TYLER (Isaac[6]), born in Warren, Mass., June 1, 1801; died in Weld, Franklin County, Maine, October 28, 1869; married, May 3, 1827, Mary Ann Moore, of Farmington, Maine, who died May 5, 1875. (See *History of Farmington*.) He was a successful merchant in Farmington in 1820, and settled on a farm in Weld in 1835. He was county clerk and commissioner, town clerk, treasurer and selectman, and a state representative from both towns. The children were born in Weld. Children:

4321   Mary E. Tyler, born March 20, 1828; died June 26, 1847.
4322   Henry Tyler, born July 19, 1830; went to California and Australia and died.
4323   Ellen M. Tyler, born March 31, 1833; died Aug. 4, 1848.
4324   Isaac Tyler, born May 21, 1835; died Aug. 18, 1855.
4325   Nathan C. Tyler, born Jan. 15, 1837; killed, April 7, 1861, in Newton, Ga.; was unmarried.

2013   BETHIAH[7] TYLER (Isaac[6]), born in Warren, Mass., June 4, 1803; died March 2, 1893; married, January 17, 1825, Joel Chadwick, of Warren, born February 16, 1797; died September 22, 1881. The children were born in Warren. Children:
4326   Harriet J. Chadwick, born Oct. 20, 1825; married (1), April 15, 1846, Jacob Putnam; married (2), May 15, 1861, Ashel Barlow, of Warren, born in 1824; died in 1891; by her first marriage she had two daughters who died young and one son (Jacob); by her second marriage she had two sons (Herbert and Frederick).
4327   Mary Ann Chadwick, born Sept. 30, 1835; died Feb. 19, 1838.
4328   Mary Ellen Chadwick, born Nov. 11, 1842; married Henry W. Green, a manufacturer of office furniture, and lived in West Somerville, Mass.; no children.

2015   REUBEN[7] TYLER, born in Warren, Mass., February 11, 1808; died November 21, 1858; married, April 3, 1831, Elizabeth Billings, of Hardwick, Mass., where he settled, and where the children were born. Children:
4329   Reuben Cutler Tyler, born Dec. 4, 1832; died unmarried, April 25, 1865.
4330   Sarah Clementine Tyler, born July 4, 1835; resided in Hyde Park, Mass.; married ——.
4331   Elmira Elizabeth Tyler, born Aug. 15, 1838; died Nov. 12, 1865.
4332   Susan Maria Tyler, born Nov. 1, and died Nov. 14, 1847.

2016   REBECCA[7] TYLER (Isaac[6]), born in Warren, Mass., August 10, 1809; died in Farmington, Maine, September 18, 1872; married, October 25, 1829, Rial Gleason, of Farmington; born June 19, 1798; died July 15, 1858. They lived in Farmington and the children were born there. Children:

4333   Owen W. Gleason, born Jan. 11, 1832; died Aug. 8, 1858.

4334   Mary Tyler Gleason, born May 1, 1833; married Leroy Dyar, of Ontario, Cal.; she taught in Farmington, Maine, and was preceptress of the academy in Cincinnatus, N. Y. In California he was an orange and lemon raiser; they had one daughter (Helen).

4335   Sareph O. Gleason, born March 15, 1836; died Jan. 18, 1858.

4336   George S. Gleason, born March 31, 1838; died Sept. 2, 1858.

4337   Ellen M. Gleason, born Feb. 29, 1844; died Sept. 3, 1858.

4338   Sumner Austin Gleason, born Nov. 20, 1846; died in Augusta, Maine, Jan. 13, 1864; was in the Civil War one year and six months.

4339   Julia A. Gleason, born Dec. 18, 1843; married, May 26, 1866, Rollo S. Sampson, of Wilton, Maine; four children (Arthur L., Alzaleen, George C., Annie).

4340   Melvin Frank Gleason, born May 28, 1851; died Aug. 29, 1872.

4341   Ada L. Gleason, born Oct. 8, 1855; married Horace G. Staples, in Sept., 1879, of Wilton, Maine; they adopted a son.

4342   Orville Tyler Gleason, date of birth not known; married, Nov. 17, 1865, Etta M. Oakes, of Temple, Maine, where he owned a sawmill. He was town supervisor and selectman; in 1889 he moved to Farmington, Maine, where he had a fine home; no children.

2017   MARY[7] TYLER (Isaac[6]), born in Warren, Mass., November 3, 1811; died October 11, 1864; married, September

1, 1831, George Damon, of Warren, who died April 3, 1860. He settled in Madison, Lake County, Ohio, and later moved to near Madison, Wis. Children:

4343   Jerome B. Damon, born Aug. 18, 1832; died 1836.
4344   Thomas Henry Damon, born March 26, 1834; died Aug. 21, 1864.
4345   Mary T. Damon, born and died in 1836.
4346   Harrison S. Damon, born Feb. 18, 1837.
4347   Mary E. Damon, born Feb. 20, 1839.
4348   William C. Damon, born Aug. 2, 1841.
4349   Isaac Tyler Damon, born July 14, 1843.
4350   Francis L. Damon, born April 9, 1845.
4351   Edward J. Damon, born Aug. 2, 1847.
4352   John Damon, born June 4, 1850.
4353   Charles A. Damon, born Sept. 7, 1852.
4354   Martha Tyler Damon, born June 4, 1856.

2018   TRYPHENA[7] TYLER (Isaac[6]), born in Warren, Mass., February 26, 1814; died in Newbury, Ohio, November 9, 1896; married, September 11, 1833, Anson Read, of Warren, who moved to Newbury, Grange County, Ohio, and died May 9, 1859. The children were born there. Children:

4355   Carlos E. Read, born Sept. 5, 1834.
4356   Bethiah T. Read, born June 1, 1838; died April 30, 1872.
4357   Lucinda Read, born June 3, 1840.
4358   Mary R. Read, born June 21, 1842.
4359   Charles T. Read, born Sept. 20, 184—; died May 13, 1864.
4360   William Henry Read, born Aug. 21, 1846.
4361   Augusta Read, born March 20, 1849.
4362   Ella D. Read, born June 12, 1851.

2019   MOSES M.[7] TYLER (Isaac[6]), born in Warren, Mass., November 15, 1816; died in West Brookfield, Mass., November 15, 1870; married, November 25, 1851, Lucy Ann Crabtree, of West Brookfield, who married (2), Samuel M. Newton, who died s. p., 1876. They resided a while in Barrington, Ill., where the second child was born; the others were born in West Brookfield. Children:

4363   Moses S. Tyler, born Dec. 31, 1852; died Feb. 27, 1854.

4364   Isaac S. Tyler, born July 30, 1854; a schoolteacher, died unmarried Nov., 1898.

4365+ Ann Augusta Tyler, born Sept. 8, 1856.

4366   (Doctor) Albert Moses Tyler, born Oct. 18, 1858; married, June 1, 1887, Fannie Lucinda Wight, of Sturbridge, Mass.; he lived in Sterling, Mass., and in 1900 moved to Worcester; no children.

4367   Emma S. Tyler, born Dec. 12, 1861; died March 27, 1874.

4368+ Carlton P. Tyler, born March 9, 1865.

4369+ Ernest A. Tyler, born May 16, 1867.

2026 CAPTAIN JOHN[7] TYLER (Daniel[6]), born in Warren, Mass., December 4, 1803; died July 9, 1886; married, January 21, 1834, Adeline B. Coye, of Brimfield, Mass., born February 25, 1811; she was a woman of remarkable energy combined with large executive ability, happily blended with gentleness and affability. He was commissioned captain; was also justice of the peace and representative to the General Court. The male line in this family is extinct. The children were born in Warren. Children:

4370   Abbie Cutler Tyler, born Nov. 11, 1835; educated for a teacher, but decided to study medicine; was graduated from Boston Medical College and studied in New York, London and Paris. She practiced several years in Waukegan, Ill., but moved to Washington, D. C., where she now resides; is unmarried.

4371   Rhoda Jane Tyler, born Sept. 9, 1837; educated for a teacher; married, Sept. 11, 1859, Loranus Capen; resides s. p. in Washington, D. C.

4372   John Warren Tyler, born July 20, 1839; resides unmarried in Warren, where his early years were passed on a farm and where later a merchant; now a trial justice.

4373   Harriet Adelaide Tyler, born July 4, 1841; educated for a teacher of drawing and painting; studied in Boston, Dresden and Paris; in 1899 resided unmarried in Warren.

4374   Mary Augusta Tyler, born Nov. 3, 1843; educated

for a teacher in modern languages; studied in Europe; was graduated from Columbian University, Washington, D. C.; resided unmarried in Warren, in 1899.

2028 DAVID RICHARDS[7] TYLER (Daniel[6]), born in Warren, Mass., January 12, 1821; died January 22, 1881; married, December 24, 1846, Emeline A. Reed, who was living in 1897 in Brookfield, Mass. The children were born in Warren; the male line is out in this family. Children:

4375+   Julia E. Tyler, born Aug. 27, 1848.

4376   Alice Reed Tyler, born March 16, 1860; in 1897 lived unmarried with mother in Brookfield.

2034 MARY JOSEPHINE[7] HODGES (Olive[6]), born in Warren, Mass., October 11, 1817; died in Champaign, Ill., January 1, 1885; married, April 6, 1840, in Mt. Vernon, Ohio, Daniel Gardner, Jr., born in Warehouse Point, Conn., December 18, 1815; died February 13, 1883, in Champaign, Ill.; son of Daniel and Prudence (Whipple) Gardner. He was an important citizen of Champaign; state senator in 1855-1859; mayor 1860-1862; trustee of University of Illinois 1870-1882. Children.

4377   Frederick Cheney Gardner, born Dec. 25, 1841; died Oct. 20, 1842.

4378   Emily Cheney Gardner, born July 26, 1843; married, Oct. 22, 1866, Henry Swannell; they had a son and daughter.

4379   Dick Hodges Gardner, born Nov. 8, 1847; married, Feb. 8, 1871, Ella M. Angle; they had three daughters and a son.

4380   Olive Augusta Gardner, born July 25, 1852; married, March 20, 1877, N. A. Lloyd; they had one daughter.

4381   Wyllis Smith Gardner, born April 21, 1856; married, 1880, Annie Somers; they have one son.

4382   Jessie Gardner, born April 27, 1863.

2044 LUCY BROOKS[7] TYLER (Abner,[6] Jr.), born in Pepperell, Mass., December 8, 1828; married, April 22, 1857, Francis M. Bardwell, of Belchertown, Mass.; born there October 4, 1829; son of Simeon and Parthenia (Burke) Bardwell, and descended from Lieutenant Robert Bardwell, of Hatfield, Mass. In 1875 he was a manufacturer of woolen goods in Belchertown and moved to Springfield, Mass. She was educated in the academy in Leicester, Mass. The children were born in Belchertown. Children:

4383   Herbert T. Bardwell, born Oct. 27, 1859; died suddenly, unmarried, in the spring of 1907 of heart disease and other complications, in the home of his parents; was graduated from Wesleyan Academy, and the Mass. Institute of Technology in 1883; was connected with the Holyoke Water Power Company and the West End Street Railway Company in Boston, and was instructor for three years in the Mass. Institute of Technology. He was interred in Warren.

4384   Arthur F. Bardwell, born May 22, 1862; was graduated from Wesleyan Academy in 1881; thence to Harvard University and Mass. Institute of Technology; unmarried.

4385   Marian E. Bardwell, born Nov. 30, 1866; educated in Wesleyan Academy and Springfield Collegiate Institute; unmarried.

4386   Lucy L. Bardwell, born June 24, 1868; educated in Wesleyan Academy and Cowles Art School in Boston; unmarried.

4387   Louisa J. Bardwell, twin to Lucy; died June 25, 1868.

2046 MARIA S.[7] TYLER (Amos[6]), born in Warren, Mass., October 15, 1824; married, April 27, 1848, Henry Bosworth, of Warren. Child:

4388   Jennie Bosworth, born April 19, 1857; married, June 6, 1893, Frederick H. Sylvester.

2048 JULIA ANN[7] TYLER (Amos[6]), born in Warren, Mass., March 4, 1828; died in Boston, Mass., March 20, 1854; married, November 28, 1850, William C. Janes, No. 4314, who married (2), about 1860, Martha Bliss, of Brimfield, Mass., and had two daughters. He moved to East Saginaw, Mich., with his first wife, where he died December 9, 1872. Children:

4389   Frank Sumner Janes, born May 25, 1852; married,
       Sept. 2, 1873, Eva Brewer in East Saginaw, Mich.;
       resides in Springfield, Mass., and has two children.
4390   Herbert H. Janes, born March 20, 1854; died aged
       6 months.

2049   SARAH[7] TYLER (Jonas Read[6]), born in Warren, Mass., January 13, 1827; died December 28, 1890; married, May 4, 1859, John Brag, of Warren, who died February
26, 1893.   Children:
4391   Mary E. Bragg, born July 25, 1860; unmarried, lives
       with brother on grandfather's homestead.
4392   John F. Bragg, born Sept. 3, 1861; unmarried.

2051   RUTH[7] TYLER (Jonas Read[6]), born in Warren,
Mass., April 28, 1833; married, October 12, 1859, A. W.
Smith; born February 4, 1833; he settled on a large farm in
West Brookfield, Mass., where he is a very successful and in-
fluential citizen, and where his children were born.   Children:
4393   Lindsey Tyler Smith, born Nov. 28, 1863; married
       Carrie R. Ward, of North Brookfield, Mass.; he
       has a son and daughter (Lindsey and Dorothy).
4394   William E. Smith, born June 18, 1865; lives unmar-
       ried, at home.
4395   Charles W. Smith, born Feb. 6, 1867; died June 29,
       1869.
4396   Frederick G. Smith, born Nov. 23, 1868; married,
       Oct. 6, 1896, Nellie M. Lane; lives with father.
4397   Carrie A. Smith, born Oct. 19, 1870; lives at home.
4398   Windsor R. Smith, born June 11, 1872.

2052   JOHN M.[7] TYLER (John[6]), born in Tolland,
Conn., in 1806; died there October 24, 1870; married, April
30, 1848, Mary Ann Buck, of Somers, Conn.   The children
were born in Somers.   Children:
4399   Child, born March 14, 1849; died *ibid.*
4400   John B. Tyler, born June 17, 1850; resided in Spring-
       field, Mass.

2054   NATHAN[7] TYLER (John[6]), born in Tolland,

Conn.; married Lomira E. Hunn. He resided in Somers, where his children were born. Children:

4401   Dora M. Tyler, born Aug. 26, 1865.
4402   Arthur N. Tyler, born Aug. 2, 1867.
4403   Carrie Tyler, born Sept. 13, 1871.
4404   Oliver H. Tyler, born Nov. 15, 1873.
4405   Milo E. Tyler, born May 2, 1878.
4406   Ella M. Tyler, born May 17, 1880.

2056 JULIA ANN[7] TYLER (John[6]), born in Tolland, Conn., about 1816; died in North Haven, Conn., where they resided, in 1867; married Manning Bassett. The children were born in North Haven. Children:

4407   Hattie Amelia Bassett, died in New Haven, Conn., in 1867, unmarried, aged 24.
4408   William G. Bassett, a lawyer, resides in Northampton, Mass.
4409   Julia Bassett, died aged one year.
4410   Jennie Bassett, married ——; resided in Boston on St. Botolph St.; had one son.

2060 SAXTON GATES[7] TYLER (Asa[6]), born in Mexico, N. Y., August 21, 1805; died in California, in 1888; married Lucinda M. Cross, born 1812; died March 14, 1885. He was a farmer and shoemaker. He moved to Joliet, Ill., in 1835, and then to California in 1854. The two elder children were born in Mexico, the others in Joliet. Children:

4411+   Elias M. Tyler, born Feb. 25, 1831.
4412   Mary I. Tyler, born Oct. 17, 1835; died in Dixon, Cal., April 27, 1891; married in Joliet, Francis Rease, a farmer.
4413   Marcia A. Tyler, died in Dixon, Cal.; married Edward Brunkerhoff, a farmer.
4414+   Francis A. Tyler, born about 1840.
4415   Gustavus A. Tyler, resided in Jamestown, Cal.

2063 BEULAH[7] TYLER (Asa[6]), born in Mexico, N. Y., 1813; died in 1889; married in 1838, William Markham. Child:

4416   Elizabeth Markham, born 1842; married, 1861, David

Minckler; they had two sons (Gates and Charles), and a daughter (Lula).

2080 OLIVER H. P.[7] TYLER (Nathaniel[6]), born in Whitestown, N. Y., October 12, 1817; married, September 18, 1840, Elizabeth Gilson. He was a tailor. Children:
4417 Ella Jane Tyler, married —— Lafever; resides in Utica, N. Y.
4418 Mary Tyler.
4419 John Tyler, died aged about 13.

2081 MOSES MERRILL[7] TYLER (Nathaniel[6]), born in Whitestown, N. Y., July 14, 1819; died September 18, 1853; married, April 15, 1840, Ruth A. Chaplin. He was a railway conductor. He had several children and they all died young except one. Child:
4420 George Tyler, died soon after the Civil War from the effects of Libby Prison hardships.

2082 JAMES[7] TYLER (Nathaniel[6]), born in Whitestown, N. Y., April 25, 1821; died April 26, 1865; married, May 20, 1848, Ann Peacock. He was a substitute in the Civil War, going out in August, 1862; he returned in six weeks because of sun-stroke. We have the record of only one of his children, of whom there were probably three. Child:
4421 Sidney Grant Tyler, born Dec. 17, 1863; was an engineer, and resided in Rochester, N. Y.

2083 JOB[7] TYLER (Nathaniel[6]), born in Whitestown, N. Y., November 25, 1824; married, February 14, 1850, Harriet Newell Judson. He was a farmer, and in 1897 was living in Westmoreland, N. Y., where his children were born. Children:
4422 Priscilla Leoria Tyler, born Dec. 9, 1850; died Nov. 13, 1852.
4423+ Merrill Judson Tyler, born Dec. 21, 1851.
4424+ Giles Dean Tyler, born Oct. 18, 1856.
4425 Henry Addison Tyler, born Sept. 19, 1868; resided awhile in Milwaukee, Wis.

2084 JANE[7] TYLER (Nathaniel[6]), born in Whitestown, N. Y., February 2, 1827; died February 25, 1888; married, 1854, Lafayette Seeley, who resides in Yorkville, N. Y. He enlisted in the Civil War in August, 1862, and was in the army three years. Children:

4426   Ella Jane Seeley, born Dec., 1855; died Sept., 1885; married John Cole, a furniture dealer at Yorkville, N. Y.; they had one daughter (Mabel).

4427   George Seeley, is married and has two children and resides in Yorkville, N. Y.

2085   NATHANIEL[7] TYLER (Nathaniel[6]), born in Whitestown, N. Y., April 8, 1829; died in 1893; married, April 7, 1852, Julia Ann Burrows. He was in the Civil War from August, 1862; came home February, 1863, because of rheumatism. Child:

4428   Frances L. Tyler, born Sept. 25, 1855; married, Nov. 6, 1879, John Lewis, of Trenton, N. J.

2089   ISAAC NEWTON[7] TYLER (Daniel S.[6]), born in Cleveland, O., August 30, 1815; died July 28, 1891; married, September 1, 1844, Samantha Woods, who died September, 1854, in Cooper, Mich. Child:

4429   Le Grand Tyler, resided in Cooper, Mich., and had a farm there.

2093   SAMUEL S.[7] TYLER (Daniel S.[6]), born in Cleveland, O., January 9, 1823; died April 13, 1862, in Nashville, Tenn.; married, February 3, 1850, Phœbe Mott, who died in Cedar Creek, Mich., October, 1876. He resided awhile in Barry, Mich., and was a farmer. He was in the Civil War, as a private in Company A, 13th Mich. Infantry. The children were born in Barry. Children:

4430+   Charles Henry Tyler, born Aug. 5, 1853.

4431   Genevera Tyler, married —— Piper.

2094   LEWIS P.[7] TYLER (Daniel S.[6]), born in Cleveland, O., June 1, 1825; died there September 21, 1898; married, June 30, 1850, Eliza M. Butterfield, daughter of Willard Butterfield; born in Niagara, N. Y., November 12, 1830. He seems to have moved about a good deal, chiefly in Michigan. See birthplaces of the children. Children:

4432+   Mary Tyler, born in Kalamazoo, Mich., Sept. 3, 1851.

4433+   Lepha Tyler, born in Cleveland, O., Dec. 17, 1853.

4434   Sylva E. Tyler, born in Cooper, Mich., April 27, 1856; died July 8, 1856.

4435+   James W. Tyler, born in Yorkville, Mich., Sept. 26, 1858.

4436   Nettie M. Tyler, born in Galesburg, Mich., July 10, 1864; resided, unmarried, in 1898 in Cleveland.

4437   Minnie Tyler, born in Galesburg, Mich., Dec. 9, 1866; died Dec. 22, 1866.

4438   Levi Y. Tyler, born in Hope, Mich., Aug. 24, 1870.

2099   JOHN M.[7] TYLER (Isaac[6]), born in Mexico, N. Y., April 20, 1825; died in Washington, D. C., in Kalavana Hospital, April, 1863; married (1), March 26, 1853, in Coldwater, Mich., Ruth A. Sullivan; married (2), November, 1861, in Vevay, Mich., Sarah A. Miller. He enlisted in Company H, 26th Mich. Volunteer Infantry in the Civil War. The two elder children were born in Grass Lake, Mich. Children:

4439   Eugene S. Tyler, born June, 1854; married, May, 1879, Emma P. Gibbs; resided in Minneapolis, Mich.

4440   James M. Tyler, born April 2, 1856; died in Onondaga, Mich., Feb. 23, 1864.

4441   Charles E. Tyler, born in Vevay, Mich., Sept. 29, 1862; died in Mason, Mich., Nov. 23, 1863.

2100   DOCTOR DEAN M.[7] TYLER (Isaac[6]), born in Mexico, N. Y., July 5, 1828; married, 1871, Nellie L. Mathewson, of Milwaukee, Wis. He was graduated from the University of Michigan, with the degree of M. D. in 1859; was first assistant in the Insane Asylum, Kalamazoo, Mich.; was graduated from the University of Michgan, in 1875, in the Law Department; living in Ann Arbor, Mich., s. p., an invalid in 1899. Child:

4442   Ada B. Tyler, born March 21, 1874; died Sept., 1874.

2101   ASA LEWIS[7] TYLER (Isaac[6]), born in Watertown, N. Y., September 2, 1832; resided in 1899 in Portland, Oregon; married (1), August 2, 1855, Mary J. Stuart, of

Fox Lake, Wis.; married (2), 1878, Louise Boden, of Milwaukee, Mich. The male line is extinct. Child:

4443 Minnie S. Tyler, born in Milwaukee, Wis., Feb. 2, 1863.

2103 CHARLOTTE ADELIA[7] TYLER (Isaac[6]), born in Grass Lake, Mich., July 9, 1844; died in Portland, Oregon, March 14, 1898; married, in Leslie, Mich., July 9, 1868, Ebenezer Cook, a teacher of music, who moved from Michigan to Portland in 1879. Mrs. Cook was also a teacher of music. The children were born in Paw Paw, Mich. Children:

4444 Mary A. Cook, born Dec. 4, 1869; married, April 21, 1895, Trevelyan Sharp, a violinist of Portland, Ore.; they live in Cleveland, O. She studied music from an early age, and is a superior pianist; was graduated from Berlin (Germany), Conservatory in 1894, being a student of Karl Klinderworth; she gave several recitals in Berlin with success, and has made successful appearances in the United States.

4445 Dean T. Cook, born Feb. 21, and died Sept. 19, 1872.

2106 CHRISTOPHER GOULD[7] TYLER (James[6]), born in Hopkinton, N. H., July 10, 1779; killed in the battle of Little Rock, December, 1813, in the War of 1812; married ——. Children:

4446 John Tyler.
4447 James Tyler.
4448 Jeremiah Tyler.
4449 Mary Tyler.
4450 Lucinda Tyler.
4451 Candace Tyler.
4452 Anne Tyler, died young.

2108 MARY[7] TYLER (James[6]), born in Hopkinton, N. H., December 13, 1781; died November 19, 1859; married Asa Sprout, of Northfield, Vt., where they lived and where their children were born. Children:

4453 Lyman Sprout, married and had three children, all of whom died young in Northfield.
4454 James Tyler Sprout, married Nomie Powell; he died, s. p., in Boston.

4455   Lucinda T. Sprout, died unmarried, aged 29.
4456   Sarah Sprout, married and had two children, who died
         young.
4457   George W. Sprout, married, and resided in Morris-
         town, N. Y.; had two children who died young.

    2113   LUCINDA[7] TYLER (James[6]), born in Henniker,
N. H., July 18, 1791; died March 24, 1866; married, October
21, 1821, Leonard Fletcher, born in Thetford, Vt., June 10,
1798; died in West Fairlee, Vt., July 6, 1855; son of Leonard
and Grace (Benton) Fletcher; he was a farmer; she was a
school-teacher in early life.   Children:
4458   Betsey Tyler Fletcher, born Oct. 15, 1822; died Sept.
         23, 1847; married in 1841, Robert S. Holmes; they
         had a son and daughter (James and Louisa).
4459   James Tyler Fletcher, born March 12, 1824; died
         July 10, 1893; married, Sept. 10, 1846, Mary Ann
         Lane; they had three children; he was a blacksmith.
4460   Sarah Candace Fletcher, born Feb. 6, 1826; married
         (1), Sept., 1858, Henry A. Green; married (2),
         Julius F. Case; no children.
4461   Laura Ann O. Fletcher, born Jan. 28, 1828; married
         William E. Barry, a farmer; had a son (Elwyn) and
         two daughters (Eva and Hattie).
4462   Royal Benton Fletcher, born Oct. 1829; died Aug.
         17, 1831.
4463   Lucinda Fletcher, born Aug. 22, 1832; married, Nov.
         30, 1851, Lyman R. Coburn, who was in the Civil
         War; had two sons (Frank and Frederick) and a
         daughter (Nellie).
4464   Leonard Benton Fletcher, born May 13, 1838; died
         May 12, 1874; married, Feb. 5, 1862, Ann R. Ald-
         rich; he was a farmer in West Fairlee; had a son
         (Leonard) and daughter (Elizabeth).

    2114   JEREMIAH[7] TYLER (James[6]), born in Thet-
ford, Vt., September 8, 1796; died in Rockford, Ill., in 1877,
aged eighty-one; married ——; moved to Western, N. Y.,
thence to near Ionia, Mich., and thence to Rockford.   Children:
4465   Christopher Gould Tyler.

4466   Robert Smith Tyler.
4467+   James Tyler, born 1824.
4468   Jeremiah Junius Tyler.
4469   George Byron Tyler.
4470   Sarah Tyler.

2127   DOCTOR CYRIL S.[7] TYLER (Jeremiah[6]), born in Thetford, Vt., December 31, 1803; died in Hopkinton, N. H., May 27, 1865; married, May 29, 1831, Sarah Putnam, born in 1798; died in Hopkinton, April 15, 1880; daughter of Dr. Aaron Putnam, of Boston, Mass.; they are both buried in the old cemetery in Hopkinton. In 1849 he had the degree of M. D. from Dartmouth College; he studied with Dr. Muzzey and became a practicing physician in Hopkinton where he lived for over forty years, from 1823. He was an Episcopalian. The children were born in Hopkinton. Children:

4471   Isabel Putnam Tyler, born 1832; died in Hopkinton Feb. 4, 1886; buried in the old cemetery; married Lewis Evans, of Hopkinton, who was living there in 1896, s. p.; was postmaster.
4472+   Sarah Hall Tyler.

2128   DOCTOR LATIMER[7] TYLER (Jeremiah[6]), born in Thetford, Vt., October 2, 1806; died ——; married, January 8, 1834, Eliza Hall, born in Thetford, November 13, 1814; daughter of John and Hannah (Lathrop) Hall, who kept a hotel; Dr. Latimer moved to Elgin, Ill. Children:

4473+   Charles H. Tyler, born Feb. 7, 1841.
4474   Charlotte L. Tyler, born Oct. 3, 1843; died, s. p., Sept. 27, 1867.
4475   Isabella Mary Tyler, born May 26, 1846; married, Feb. 27, 1873, Edwin N. Williams, of Elgin, Ill., son of John Williams.

2129   WILLIAM MONROE[7] TYLER (Jeremiah[6]), born in Thetford, Vt.; married Mary C. Hazelton, of Orford, N. H.; daughter of Nathaniel Hazelton. He lived in Post Mills, Thetford, and probably for a time at Orford; was an old-time clothier who dressed homespun cloths; kept a store in North Andover, Mass., for a time, where "Tyler Street" (now in South Lawrence) was named for him. He also carried on a gentlemen's furnishing house in Boston. Children:

4476 Mary Hazelton Tyler, resided in Boston, and married ——

4477 Catherine E. Tyler, died in North Andover, July, 1846, aged three.

2135 LUCIUS HARVEY[7] TYLER (Simeon[6]), born in Hopkinton, N. H., November 19, 1817; in 1897 was living in Hopkinton; married (1), May 10, 1852, Mrs. Sarah Anna (Hall) Amsden, from Sherbrook, Can. (she had a daughter by her first marriage, who married Edward Tyler Buswell, No. 4490); she died April 2, 1857, aged fifty-three years, seven months, and was buried in Hopkinton; married (2), June 26, 1883, Miss Frances Eaton, of Warner, N. H. The children were born in Hopkinton. Children:

4478 Mary Jane Tyler, born Oct. 17, 1853; married, June 4, 1891, William S. Putney, a farmer of Webster, N. H.

4479+ Clara Arabella Tyler, born Aug. 3, 1855.

4480+ Bertha Scott Tyler, born May 2, 1866.

2136 NANCY[7] TYLER (Moses[6]), born in Henniker, N. H., May 4, 1799; died in Indiana, aged over eighty; married, January 6, 1828, Rev. Eber Childs, born in Thetford, Vt., July 31, 1798; son of William and Mary (Heaton) Childs. He was graduated from Dartmouth College; he taught in the academy in Groton, Mass., and studied theology in Andover, Mass.; settled as pastor in Deering, N. H., Calais, Me., and Byron, N. Y.; died in Fulton, Wis., December 15, 1847. Children:

4481 Mary Elizabeth Childs, born April 7, 1829; died 1847.

4482 William Henry Childs, born Sept. 6, 1830; died in infancy.

4483 William Henry Tyler Childs, born April 27, 1832; married, Feb. 18, 1858, Angelina Adams; was in the Civil War.

4484 Francis Brown, born Feb. 22, 1834; married, Feb., 1878, Frances M. Cheesbro; resided in Janesville, Wis.

4485 Charles Carrol Childs, born Jan. 9, 1836; died 1848.

4486   Frederick Oberlin Childs, born Dec. 15, 1838; married
        (1), Jan. 1, 1863, Maggie G. Sox; married (2),
        Sept. 19, 1870, Mary Eastman.
4487   Ellen Louisa Childs, born Sept. 14, 1844; married
        Hon. Lyman M. Ward, of Benton Harbor, Mich.

2137 SARAH[7] TYLER (Moses[6]), born in Hopkinton,
N. H., January 12, 1802; died in Tyler's Bridge, N. H., November 3, 1858; married, August 18, 1819, Aaron Wood Buswell, a farmer, of Hopkinton, born September 26, 1792; died
October 20, 1863. The children were born in Hopkinton.
Children:
4488   Caroline Wood Buswell, born Sept. 29, 1821; died
        Aug. 15, 1887; married, Jan. 28, 1844, James Per-
        kins, of Wakefield, N. H., who was in the Civil War,
        and died in 1863, in Springfield, Ill.; they had two
        sons (Albert, killed in the Civil War, and Oscar),
        and two daughters (Fannie and Florence), both of
        whom married.
4489   Jane Elizabeth Buswell, born Sept. 12, 1823; died Oct.
        18, 1859; married, April 28, 1844, Otis Prentis War-
        ren, of Laconia, N. H.; they had one son (Edward)
        and a daughter (Virginia) and other children, who
        died young.
4490   Edward Tyler Buswell, born Dec. 11, 1828; married,
        1865, Sarah A. Amsden, daughter of Mrs. Sarah
        (Hall) Amsden Tyler, who married Lucius Harvey
        Tyler, No. 2135; she died Nov. 6, 1883; resided in
        Springville, Cal. They had three sons (Mark,
        Hugh and Aaron).
4491   George Richmond Buswell, born June 21, 1833; died
        July 30, 1896; married, 1868, Helen Hallock. He
        lived in Davisville, Cal.; was in the First Ia. Cavalry
        three years, in the Civil War; they had two daugh-
        ters (Josephine and Helen), who married, and other
        children, who died young.
4492   Clara Anna Buswell, born Nov. 3, 1835; resided, un-
        married, in Springville, Cal.
4493   Helen Louise Buswell, born March 5, 1840; died Aug.
        23, 1885; married, 1866, George Whitefield Chase,
        of National City, Cal.; who died June 23, 1899;

had three daughters (Helen, Josephine, and Dido) and a son (Paul).

4494 Sarah Josephine Perley Buswell, born Sept. 10, 1842; died in Hopkinton May 25, 1861.

4495 Infant, who lived less than three weeks.

2138 CALVIN⁷ TYLER (Moses⁶), born in Hopkinton, N. H., March 11, 1806; he was an adopted son; died there April 1, 1884, aged seventy-eight; married, March 7, 1833, Silpha Hastings, born in Hopkinton February 28, 1807; daughter of Captain Heman Hastings, of Hopkinton; she was living in Hopkinton, at Tyler's Bridge, in 1896, where her husband also lived, and where the children were born. Children:

4496+ Sarah E. Tyler, born Dec. 26, 1833.

4497+ Charles Richard Tyler, born March 31, 1837.

4498 Henry Carroll Tyler, born Jan. 27, 1841; died unmarried in Hopkinton, Oct. 18, 1866; was a private in Company B, 2d N. H. Volunteer Infantry, in the Civil War; he went through the war from Sept., 1861, and was wounded at Gettysburg; he was appointed corporal in 1864, and rose to first lieutenant, but was mustered out as first sergeant, Dec. 19, 1865.

4499 Moses Cyril Tyler, born Sept. 19, 1843; married Maria Bell Cram, of Fort Wayne, Ind.; was a private in Company B, 2d N. H. Volunteer Infantry, in the Civil War; taken prisoner at Malvern Hills and was in Libby Prison several months; exchanged and re-enlisted in 18th N. H. Volunteers. Lives in Lima, Ohio; no children.

4500 Nancy Jane Tyler, born June 21, 1847; died unmarried in Hopkinton June 30, 1868.

2161 JEPTHAH⁷ TYLER, JR. (Jepthah⁶), born in Lyme, N. H., February 25, 1810; died there February 11, 1883; married Flavilla Hall. The children were born in Lyme. Children:

4501 Eli Smith Tyler, born April 2, 1835; enlisted Aug. 12, 1862, in the Civil War, as private in Company H, 11th N. H. Volunteer Infantry; wounded at

Spottsylvania, Va., May 12, 1864, and died of wounds in Washington, D. C., June 6, 1864.

4502+ Almena M. Tyler, born Sept. 10, 1837.

4503+ Mary Esther Tyler, born June 3, 1839.

4504 Henry Tyler, born 1841; died s. p.

4505 Albert Tyler, born Dec. 4, 1843; unmarried in 1898; resided in Nashua, N. H.

4506 Jason C. Tyler, born 1844; resided in Boston.

4507 David C. Tyler, born 1845.

4508 George Tyler, born 1851.

2170 MARIE H.[7] TYLER (John[6]), born in Thetford, Vt., April 27, 1803; died December 16, 1885; married there, March 11, 1823, Joseph Hoyt Quimby, born in Hopkinton, N. H., April 13, 1801; died in Thetford February 12, 1878; he was a farmer. The children were born in Thetford. Children:

4509 Maria A. Quimby, born April 18, 1825; died June 26, 1827.

4510 James B. Quimby, born June 1, 1827; resided in Lawrence, Mass.

4511 Monroe T. Quimby, born July 20, 1829; died May 2, 1893.

4512 Charles N. Quimby, born Oct. 9, 1831; died April 10, 1884.

4513 John T. Quimby, born July 19, 1834; resided in Thetford Center, Vt.

4514 Latimer A. Quimby, born Oct. 19, 1836; resided in Lawrence, Mass.

4515 Julia M. Quimby, born June 3, 1839; married —— Kimball; resided in South Fairlee, Vt.

4516 Mary A. Quimby, born April 14, 1842; died April 17, 1871.

2173 ANNIE G.[7] TYLER (John[6]), born in Thetford, Vt., July 26, 1811; died March 2, 1843; married, March 8, 1832, Hiram Bronson Sloan, born in Lyme, N. H., January 20, 1805; died June 18, 1889, in Thetford. He married (2), his first wife's sister Lucretia, who was a widow at that time. Mrs. Annie G. Sloan's children were born in Thetford. Children:

4517 Hiram Frank Sloan, born Dec. 3, 1832.

4518 Asenath A. Sloan, born Sept. 15, 1834; died in Chicago, Ill.

4519 Henry A. Sloan, born June 21, 1836.

4520 George S. Sloan, born Sept. 11, 1838.

4521 Frances M. Sloan, born July 23, 1840.

4522 Tyler G. Sloan, born Feb. 25, 1843; died June 25, 1844.

2176 LUCRETIA J.[7] TYLER (John[6]), born in Thetford, Vt., Sept. 1, 1820; married (1), Oliver Coffin Hunt, a mason; married (2), Hiram Bronson Sloan, widower of her sister, Annie G. Tyler.

CHILDREN, by first marriage:

4523 Frances A. Hunt, married —— Brown; resided in Manchester, N. H.

CHILDREN, by second marriage:

4524 Edgar Sloan.

4525 Fred Sloan.

4526 Charles Sloan.

2177 EMELINE F.[7] TYLER (John[6]), born in Thetford, Vt., May 5, 1827; married, April 2, 1850, Charles D. Lucas, born in Boston, Mass., February 11, 1827. In 1899 she resided in Thetford Center. Children:

4527 Helen D. Lucas, born in Vershire, Vt., June 3, 1851.

4528 Charles Tyler Lucas, born in Thetford May 9, 1856.

2180 ORANGE BRIGHAM[7] TYLER (James[6]), born in Thetford, Vt., March 28, 1801; died in Iberville, Can., Octo- 5, 1867; married, September 15, 1823, Marie Poutré de la Vigne, born in St. Phillips, Can., July 22, 1797; died March 16, 1878. He was a tanner and shoe manufacturer until 1838; then in Canada was a magistrate, collector of Signorial Rentes and speculator in farming properties; he resided for a time in Napierville, Quebec, where the children were born. Children:

4529+ Rosanna Tyler, born June 17, 1824.

4530 Henry Tyler, born Dec. 5, 1827; died unmarried, Sept. 26, 1852.

4531   Charles Tyler, born Sept. 2, 1829; died April 26, 1893; married April 4, 1854, Susan Caldwell; resided in Bakersfield, Cal.; had a family.

4532+   Edmond Tyler, born March 30, 1833.

4533   Oliver Tyler, born June 17, 1835; died Aug. 6, 1835.

4534+   William Tyler, born June 20, 1836.

2185 LUCRETIA AMBROSE[7] (Hannah Eastman[6]), born January 15, 1799; died December 3, 1883; married, September 22, 1823, Rev. Charles Walker, of Rutland, Vt. Children:

4535   Anne Ambrose Walker, born Aug. 5, 1827; married Rev. George N. Boardman; no children.

4536   (Rev.) George Leon Walker (D. D.), born April 30, 1830; died in Hartford, Conn., March 14, 1900; married (1), Sept. 16, 1858, Maria Williston, of Brattleboro, Vt.; married (2), Amelia Read, of Thompson, Conn., who died in 1898. Dr. Walker was of a delicate constitution, but by care he was able to live out the threescore and ten years and to attain an eminence in his church reached by but few contemporaries. He began the study of law, but on account of his health changed to the ministry; he was graduated from Andover Theological Seminary, and was chosen to such leading pastorates in the Congregational church, as Portland, Me., New Haven, Conn. (where he received the degree of D. D. from Yale University in 1870), Brattleboro, Vt., and Hartford, Conn. In 1897 he published a volume of lectures, *Aspects of the Religious Life in New England;* he was one of the commission of twenty-five which prepared the Congregational creed of 1883; he was one of the corporation of Yale University from 1887-1899; in 1888 he was made one of the continuous members of the *Board of Visitors* of Andover Theological Seminary. While visiting his only son (Prof. Williston Walker) in Brattleboro, he was prostrated with paralysis, about 1896, but he died of pneumonia four years later.

4537   Stephen Ambrose Walker, born Nov. 2, 1834; died unmarried, Feb. 5, 1893.

4538   Henry Freeman Walker, born July 3, 1836; unmarried.

2200   J. BOWMAN[7] TYLER (John, Jr.[6]), born in North Brookfield, Mass., March 5, 1822; died June 29, 1873; married, September 17, 1844, Lydia Jane Rice. He was a farmer in North Brookfield, where his children were born. Children:

4539   Sarah Jane Tyler, born July 31, 1845; married, Sept. 2, 1879, John Monroe, a farmer, of Rutland, Mass.; no children.

4540   John Henry Tyler, born Aug. 22, 1848; married, March 10, 1870, Ella Stone, of Hubbardston; he is a mechanic and auctioneer, resides, s. p., in North Brookfield.

2202   MARTHA ELIZABETH[7] TYLER (John[6]), born in North Brookfield, Mass., July 20, 1826; married, September 19, 1844, John Jay Sherman, born in Fairfield, Vt., January 22, 1826; son of Elijah and Sarah (Larkin) Sherman; he was a farmer in North Brookfield, where the children were born. Children:

4541   Myron Winslow Sherman, born July 9, 1846; died in West Brookfield, s. p., Oct. 27, 1895; married, June, 1869, Ella Thompson, of North Brookfield; he enlisted, Aug. 23, 1864, in Company E, 4th Mass. Heavy Artillery; mustered out June 17, 1865; was a corset manufacturer in Springfield, residing in West Brookfield.

4542   Mary Emma Sherman, born June 11, 1850; died March 2, 1874; married Alfred O. Stevens, of Dana, Mass.; resided in North Brookfield.

4543   George Henry Sherman, born Sept. 23, 1854; died in North Brookfield Oct. 3, 1854.

4544   Myra Eliza Sherman, born Aug. 15, 1858; died June 12, 1859.

4545   Cyrus Tyler Sherman, born Jan. 9, 1861; married, March 14, 1889, Angelia M. Carter, of Milford, Mass.; he was graduated from the Boston Dental College and resides in Quincy, Mass.; has two sons.

4546   Sidney Algernon Sherman, born April 24, 1862; was

graduated from Amherst College, 1885; married, Dec. 20, 1887, Daisy Fairfield, of Amherst; was five years principal of the Amherst High School; in 1898 assistant in the High School in Providence, R. I.; has two sons and a daughter.

4547 George A. Sherman, born June 9, 1865; married, June 12, 1890, Alberta W. Merritt, of Quincy, Mass.; was an architect and resided in Wollaston, Mass., where he died Jan. 25, 1899.

2204 THEODORE[7] TYLER (Phineas[6]), born in Brookfield, Mass., November 17, 1795; died in New Braintree, Mass., October 20, 1857; married, April 29, 1821, Abigail Gould, who died December 7, 1871. He was a tailor, and they lived in New Braintree, where the children were born. Children:

4548 Warren Tyler, born March 15, 1822; died, unmarried, May 22, 1845.
4549+ Dwight Tyler, born Dec. 7, 1823.
4550+ Susan Tyler, born Sept. 18, 1825.
4551 Sarah Tyler, born Oct. 10, 1827; married, March 20, 1866, Denison Nichols, born in Westminster, N. H., July 12, 1823; no children.
4552+ Gardner Tyler, born Feb. 2, 1829.
4553 George Tyler, born Dec. 17, 1831; died in New Braintree, Feb. 9, 1894; unmarried.
4554 Edwin Tyler, born April 27, 1835; resided in New Braintree; unmarried.

2205 FRANCIS BARNES[7] TYLER (Phineas[6]), born in Brookfield, Mass., and died in Warren, Mass.; married (1), Polly Hill, born in New Braintree in 1794; married (2), Theodosia Thomas of Brookfield. The children were born in Warren.

CHILDREN, by first marriage:
4555 Charlotte Tyler, married Cyrus Gordon, of Warren, and died in Springfield.
4556+ Frederick Tyler.

2206 ISAAC[7] TYLER (Phineas[6]), born in Brookfield, Mass., December 2, 1808; died in West Brookfield, February

5, 1886; married, 1834, Catherine Olds Gilbert, born February, 1808; died in West Brookfield, August 3, 1879. The children were born in West Brookfield. Children:

4557   James H. Tyler, born Oct. 8, and died Oct. 13, 1834.
4558+   James W. Tyler, born Oct. 16, 1835.
4559+   Sarah L. Tyler, born March 22, 1838.

2220   AVILDA BARTLETT[7] TYLER (David[6]), born in North Brookfield, Mass., March 27, 1825; died there June 17, 1896; married, October 17, 1848, William Stoddard, born in North Brookfield, February 8, 1819; died there September 9, 1865, and there his children were born. He was the son of Bela Stoddard. Children:

4560   Emma A. Stoddard, born Sept. 27, 1849; married, March 30, 1876, George M. Duncan, of North Brookfield.
4561   William Tyler Stoddard, born Oct. 17, 1851; died in North Brookfield, March 4, 1885.
4562   Mary A. Stoddard, born Aug. 23, 1856; married, Aug. 23, 1878, Lucius S. Woods, Jr., a merchant of North Brookfield.
4563   Sarah A. Stoddard, born March 8, 1864; died young.

2221   ELIZABETH R.[7] TYLER (David[6]), born in North Brookfield, Mass., December 27, 1826; married, March 22, 1843, as his second wife, Kittredge Hill, Jr., born in North Brookfield, September 29, 1813; son of Kittredge Hill (Thomas, Peter, John, of Rehoboth); he married (1), Susan H. Brimhall, of North Brookfield, who died s. p.; married (3), October 12, 1860 (his second wife having obtained a divorce), Fanny B. Sheldon, of Deerfield, Mass. He was a farmer and mason, and postmaster; in 1861 he removed to New York State, and in 1864 to Centerville, Ind. The children were born in North Brookfield.

CHILDREN, by second marriage:
4564   Lloyd Kittredge Hill, born Jan. 8, 1844; married, May 25, 1870, Louisa Pierce, of Knightstown, Ind.; had four daughters.
4565   William Tyler Hill, born Dec. 26, 1846; died Aug. 16, 1847.

4566   Albert Tyler Hill, born June 10, 1854; died April
        17, 1857.
4567   Warren Tyler Hill, born Dec. 19, 1858; died March
        6, 1859.
4568   Walter Copeland Hill, twin to Warren, died March
        25, 1859.

2230   GEORGE FRANCIS[7] TYLER (Eli[6]), born in
West Brookfield, Mass., November 13, 1820; died February 10,
1894; married, November 4, 1838, Caroline W. Pepper, of New
Braintree, Mass.   He was a farmer and lumber manufacturer.
The children were born in West Brookfield.   Children:
4569+   Abbie F. Tyler, born Oct. 10, 1853.
4570+   George Warren Tyler, twin to Abbie.
4571+   Dwight M. Tyler, born June 16, 1855.
4572   Eliza J. Tyler, born Sept. 28, 1856; in 1901 was living
        in West Brookfield.
4573+   Phebe A. Tyler, born March 19, 1858.
4574+   Hattie M. Tyler, born Aug. 19, 1861.
4575+   Orianna Tyler, born April 13, 1863.

2236   HARRIET ELIZABETH[7] TYLER (Eli[6]), born
in West Brookfield, Mass., February 20, 1831; died in Boston,
February 20, 1854; married, September 20, 1850, Captain
John W. Tuttle, a sea captain; killed on Federal Street in Boston in the great fire of 1871.   Child:
4576   William Henry Tuttle, born Dec. 25, 1851.

2237   SUSAN MARIA[7] TYLER (Eli[6]), born in West
Brookfield, Mass., February 9, 1833; married, January 27,
1848, Edward Walker Thomas, born in Leeds, England, December 18, 1828; resided in Franklin Falls, N. H.; was a needle-
maker.   Children:
4577   Edward W. Thomas, born Dec. 3, 1852; married, Nov.
        19, 1871, Ida E. Faber; they had two sons.
4578   Charles Henry Thomas, married Nov. 20, 1872, Kate
        Kilkenny.
4579   Warren N. Thomas, married, Dec. 12, 1874, Ellen
        Harrison.
4580   Joseph Francis Thomas, married, June 11, 1887, Lucy
        Montgomery.
4581   Arthur De Witt Thomas.

2240 CHARLES AUSTIN[7] TYLER (Eli[6]), born in West Brookfield, Mass., March 11, 1841; married (1), 1877, Mary B. McLoughlin; married (2), April 11, 1889, Laura E. Hayward, of East Concord, N. H. He was in the 6th Mass. Light Artillery from 1862-1865; was in New Orleans under General Butler. Employed in the Tilton Mills; resided in Northfield, N. H.

CHILD, by first marriage:

4582 Arthur Tyler, born July 2, 1879.

2241 CHARLOTTE FRANCES[7] TYLER (Eli[6]), born in West Brookfield, Mass., October 23, 1842; married, in Laconia, N. H., December 25, 1865, Walter Weston Thompson, born September 12, 1841; died in Franklin Falls, N. H., December 1, 1889; was in the sash and blind business and lived in Franklin Falls, where his children were born. Children:

4583 Frank Weston Thompson, born Oct. 16, 1869.
4584 Jennie Frances Thompson, born May 12, 1873; died Sept. 16, 1874.
4585 Cora Belle Thompson, born Dec. 25, 1874; married, June 30, 1897, Millard C. Wells, of Concord, N. H.; born Oct. 14, 1872.
4586 Mabel Thompson, born March 25, 1877; married, Aug. 9, 1898, Herbert H. Doubleday; lives in Claremont, N. H.
4587 Evelyne Tyler Thompson, born Sept. 4, 1889.

2242 DWIGHT[7] TYLER (Joshua[6]), born in Chesterfield, N. H., January 13, 1805; died 1884; married, December 30, 1832, Mary V. Fisk, born August 30, 1810; died November 20, 1884; daughter of Josiah Fisk. He lived in South Londonderry, Vt., where was town clerk for thirty-eight years. His children were born there. Children:

4588+ Harland D. Tyler, born May 8, 1840.
4589 George D. Tyler, died aged twelve.

2243 JOSHUA[7] TYLER, JR. (Joshua[6]), born in Dummerston, Vt., December 4, 1811; died in Murphysboro, Ill., July 30, 1891; married (1), 1840, Martha Jane Morgan, who died in 1849; married (2), 1850, Mrs. Nancy Northen Crilley, who died in 1860; married (3), October 12, 1863, Mrs. Esther

Wilson Marshall, who lived in Murphysboro in 1901. At the age of seventeen he left his home in Pennsylvania, where he had moved with his father, and went West and was on the Mississippi and Missouri rivers for many years.

CHILDREN, by first marriage:

4590   Joshua Tyler, born 1841; died June, 1864, in the hospital in Chattanooga, Tenn.; was a private in Company H, 27th Ill. Volunteer Infantry, and was wounded in the Battle of Missionary Ridge.

4591   Elizabeth Tyler, born 1843; died in Adams County, Neb., 1879.

4592+   Hannah Tyler, born Feb. 2, 1845.

4593+   George Tyler, born March 14, 1847.

4594   Joseph Tyler, born 1849.

CHILDREN, by second marriage:

4595+   James Tyler, born May 4, 1851.

4596+   Daniel Tyler, born Oct. 12, 1854 (or 1852).

4597   Bollin Tyler, born April 30, 1854.

4598   Julia Tyler, born Dec. 19, 1855; killed by a wild animal, July 8, 1862.

4599+   Laura Tyler, born Dec. 15, 1857.

4600+   Frances Ellen Tyler, born Nov. 18, 1859.

CHILDREN, by third marriage:

4601+   Eva Lois Tyler, born March 5, 1865.

4602   Martha Louisa Tyler, born May 7, 1869.

4603   Jesse Tyler, died in infancy.

2251   PARKMAN TYLER[7] DAVIS (Judith[6]), born in Chesterfield, Vt., June 30, 1810; died in Boston December 12, 1885; married, February 11, 1835, in South Heron, Vt., Elizabeth Clark, who died in Boston, April 19, 1885. The children were born in Burlington, Vt. Children:

4604   Fannie Elizabeth Davis, born Sept. 30, 1836; married, May 15, 1859, Alexander Stowell in South Hero, Vt.

4605+   Gertrude Maria Davis, born Feb. 28, 1847.

2252   HARRIET B.[7] TYLER (Jason[6]), born in Chesterfield, N. H., November 13, 1803; died in Fitzwilliam, N. H., February 1, 1885; married, November 15, 1827, Joseph Dyar, of Middlebury, Vt., who died February 23, 1850.   Children:

4606   Harriet Chapman Dyar, born Nov. 15, 1829; married, May 20, 1850, James Satterlee Phelps, a son of U. S. Senator Phelps, of Vermont; she died in Washington, D. C.; they lived in Keene, N. H.

4607   Julia Adelaide Dyar, born July 17, 1831; in 1899 was living in Keene.

4608   Sarah Josephine Dyar, born Aug. 2, 1834; died Nov. 17, 1835.

4609   Sarah Elizabeth Dyar, born Sept. 22, 1838; died Nov. 7, 1838.

4610   Charles Joseph Dyar, born March 11, 1840; died Sept. 15, 1840.

2255 SAMUEL KING[7] TYLER (Jason[6]), born in Chesterfield, N. H., November 3, 1810; died in West Chester, Ohio, September 20, 1866, to which place he removed from Chesterfield; married Esther Sawyer, of Swanzey, N. H.; born August, 1811; died in Hamilton, Ohio, January 8, 1899 (see Randall's *History of Chesterfield*).   Children:

4611   Selleck K. Tyler, born in Jaffrey, N. H., May 27, 1843; married, in Montgomery, Ohio, Nov. 23, 1865, Edna Crain; he resided in Hamilton, Ohio.

4612+   Dana L. Tyler, born in Keene, N. H., Sept. 1, 1845.

4613   Harriet S. Tyler, born in Fitzwilliam, N. H., July 24, 1849; married, in West Chester, N. H., Feb. 1, 1877, Z. T. Walker; lived in Hamilton, Ohio.

2256 MARY N. M.[7] TYLER (Jason[6]), born in Chesterfield, N. H., February 2, 1812; died July 26, 1897; married, 1838, Raymond Stratton, of Rindge, N. H.; they moved to Marietta, Ohio, in 1852, where he died in 1869.   After she became a widow, she moved to Harmar, Ohio.   The children were born in Fitzwilliam, N. H.   Children:

4614   Mary Elizabeth Stratton, born April 22, 1839; died Sept. 21, 1889; married, Dec. 27, 1858, Morris German Knox, born in Marietta, Ohio, June 14, 1832, where he was a steamboat builder in 1899, and where the children were born; they had two sons and three daughters (William S., Harry D., Lizzie C., died young, Esther G., died young, and Sallie A.).

4615   Esther Tyler Stratton, born 1841; married 1866, Frederick Birdsall, of Cincinnati; in 1899 they lived in Sacramento, Cal.; they had three children (Esther, Ernest, and Jennett).

2260   SARAH CHAPMAN[7] TYLER (Jason[6]), born in Chesterfield, N. H., October 22, 1821; died in Fitzwilliam, N. H., January 29, 1889; married, November 26, 1846, Charles Clinton Carter born in Fitzwilliam September 23, 1814; died January 4, 1899. For more than fifty years he was a member of the firm of E. & C. Carter, carriage-makers in Fitzwilliam; was town treasurer 1861-1862. She taught school when young in Rindge, N. H., and became a writer of children's stories, chiefly, and contributed to *Demorest's Magazine, Young America, Little Pilgrim,* and to Mrs. Lippincott's publications (Grace Greenwood). She was the author of several of the " gift " books so popular in the middle of the nineteenth century, and published these and other books under the pseudonym of " Clara Seymour." The children were born in Fitzwilliam.

CHILDREN:

4616   Emma Frances Carter, born July 29, 1845; died Dec. 8, 1851 (adopted).
4617   Harry Clinton Carter, born Jan. 23, 1853; died April 21, 1856.
4618   Anna Maria Carter, born Aug. 10, 1857; married, Dec. 24, 1890, Zenas Arthur Blodgett; lives in Fitzwilliam; two sons and a daughter.
4619   Harriet Tyler Carter, born May 17, 1859; resides in Fitzwilliam.
4620   Percy Augustine Carter, born Dec. 13, 1860; married, Sept. 17, 1889, Adebelle James; lives in South Dakota; has three sons.
4621   Wallace Charles Carter, born Aug. 8, 1862; lives in Fitzwilliam.

2261   ELIZABETH H. C.[7] TYLER (Jason[6]), born in Chesterfield, N. H., November 25, 1823; died in Cincinnati,

O., July 15, 1883; married, January 17, 1856, Captain Daniel Collier, of Avondale, Ohio, born in Adams County, Ohio, September 7, 1813; died in Cincinnati, October 14, 1887, son of John Collier. (He married (1), Lydia F. Sampson, and had two sons and a daughter.) He became a clerk on a steamer on the Ohio River, and later captain and part owner of two steamers, and finally sole owner of a third; he then built and commanded four other steamers, the last one, the *A. O. Tylor*, was purchased by the Government and made into a gunboat and used in the Civil War. He made the last trip in it from New Orleans to Cincinnati, which was made until after the Civil War. He did this with the Union flag flying, in spite of officers of the C. S. A. and mobs and threatened arrest and confiscation. He obtained a document, a quasi customs' clearance, from New Orleans, C. S. A., to Cincinnati, U. S. A., on the ground that they should give him the same privileges that they conceded to vessels of other countries. At Memphis, one man, the wharfmaster, an old friend, held the mob at bay while Captain Collier backed out with colors flying and proceeded up the river. The last of his life he was, for twenty years, of the coal firm of Collier, Budd & Co., of Cincinnati.

CHILD:

4622   Albert Tyler Collier, born in Cincinnati, Ohio, April 2, 1858; married, Dec. 15, 1886, Mary Agnes Leonard. moved to Tacoma, Wash., 1889; one son (Leonard, lives in Tacoma).

2262 CAPTAIN JOHN LARKIN[7] TYLER (Jason[6]), born in Chesterfield, N. H., June 17, 1826; married Adeline Howard, of Palmer, Mass. In 1845 he entered Norwich (Vt.) University, but leaving, he went with General Scott in the Mexican War, to the City of Mexico, where he lived for a time in the " Halls of the Montezumas." During the Civil War he was instructor in military camps, and was captain of several military companies. He was connected with the public schools of Fort Wayne, Ind., as teacher of writing, drawing, elocution and military tactics. He was, at one time, the " Champion Penman " of Ohio and Indiana. From September, 1872, he served twenty-three years as special teacher in writing in Fort Wayne.

In 1898 he lived in Rome City, Ind., retired on a pension from the Fort Wayne schools.

CHILDREN:

4623+ Julia A. Tyler, born in Springfield, Mass., Feb. 2, 1852.

4624+ Major Eugene Tyler, born in Harmar, Ohio, July 18, 1854.

4625+ Alliezuma Tyler, born in Columbus, Ohio, June 12, 1857.

4626+ Jason King Tyler, born in Dayton, Ohio, Dec. 25, 1859.

2264 CAROLINE DAY[7] TYLER (Joseph Warren[6]), born in Hinsdale, N. H., May 10, 1824; died there March 4, 1868; married, June 4, 1846, George W. Bowker, of South Royalston, Mass., a chair manufacturer of that town, where the children were born. Children:

4627 Charles W. Bowker, born March 7, 1848; died in South Royalston, June 6, 1886; he was a musician.

4628 Frederick Pitts Bowker, born May 14, 1850; died in Keene, N. H., Oct. 25, 1899; married, Feb. 14, 1877, Nellie Howard, of Troy, N. H.

4629 Addie Eleanor Bowker, born March 21, 1855; married, Nov. 30, 1876, John J. Archibald, of Hinsdale; they had two sons.

4630 Charlotte A. Bowker, born Dec. 12, 1860; married, Feb. 4, 1885, Clarence E. Barker, of Orange, Mass.; has one son.

2265 SOPHIRA SMITH[7] TYLER (Joseph Warren[6]), born in Hinsdale, N. H., October 17, 1825; died August 28, 1864; married, November 27, 1845, George H. Ide, of Hinsdale, a marble dealer. Child:

4631 Arthur L. Ide, born in Hinsdale, Oct. 20, 1857; married, Jan. 12, 1877, Annette L. Allen, of Cambridgeport, Mass.; born in Milford, N. H., March 7, 1856. They reside in West Swanzey, N. H., and have two sons and a daughter (Viola A., William I., Mahlon C.).

2266 PITTS CUNE[7] TYLER (Joseph Warren[6]), born in Hinsdale, N. H., March 17, 1827; died December 24, 1899;

married, September 14, 1853, Mary E. Ide, of Hinsdale. In 1849 he went to California as a miner; he settled in Athol, Mass., as a merchant, where the children were born. Children:

4632   Albert W. Tyler, born April 10, 1855; married, Nov. 25, 1875, Harriet Howe, of Shutesbury, Mass.; they reside in Athol, where he is a coal dealer.

4633   Edwin P. Tyler, born Dec. 12, 1856; married, Dec. 26, 1887, Katie Crawford, of North Dana, Mass., where he is a woolen manufacturer; no children.

2268   ELIZABETH A.[7] TYLER (Joseph Warren[6]), born in Hinsdale, N. H., June 17, 1830; married, April 5, 1851, Albert G. Moulton, of Athol, Mass., born in Lyman, N. H., March 20, 1813; died there September 6, 1889. He was a superintendent of railway bridges. The children were born in Athol. Children:

4634   Frank Pierce Moulton, born April 13, 1853; married, July 30, 1878, Marcia E. Atwood; lived in Bath, Me., and had four daughters and one son (Marion E., Imogene A., Shirlie L., Helen, Albert J.).

4635   Elizabeth M. Moulton, born Sept. 21, 1854; died there May 30, 1886; married, Oct. 27, 1875, Otho Amsden, of Athol; had one son (Albert W.).

4636   Arthur Woods Moulton, born Feb. 23, 1858; married, Jan. 12, 1884, Della D. Fisk; lived in Fitchburg, Mass.; had two daughters (Blanche S., Minnie E.).

4637   James Tyler Moulton, born Aug. 4, 1859; married, Aug. 18, 1878, Jessie Bedel; lived in Bath, N. H.; had one daughter (Alice E.).

2270   ORCUTT B.[7] TYLER (Joseph Warren[6]), born in Hinsdale, N. H., June 15, 1834; died there January 1, 1900; married, 1887, in Hinsdale, Clara Smith, born in Boston January 17, 1850; daughter of Charles and Martha (Huntington) Smith. He is a farmer and resided in Hinsdale. Child:

4638   Charles Tyler, born in Hinsdale Sept. 1, 1887.

2273   CHARLES H.[7] TYLER (Joseph Warren[6]), born in Hinsdale, N. H., December 19, 1838; married May 19, 1868,

Lina S. Cook, of Athol, Mass., where he is a merchant, and where their child was born.   Child:

4639   E. Warren Tyler, born Feb. 19, 1874; a merchant in Athol.

2274   ADALINE P.[7] TYLER (Joseph Warren[6]), born in Hinsdale, N. H., September 21, 1841; married, June 1, 1867, Charles F. Dennison, of Springfield, Mass., who is with the Massachusetts Life Assurance Company.   Child:

4640   Charles H. Dennison, born in Athol, Mass., Oct. 17, 1875; died in Springfield, March 28, 1883.

2278   CORNELIA EVELENA[7] TYLER (Buckley Olcott[6]), born in South Woodstock, Vt., July 26, 1829; died in Fitchburg, Mass., September 27, 1878; married, December 2, 1849, Horace Platt, of Fitchburg, Mass., who died in Pittsfield, Me., December 21, 1882.   The children were born in Fitchburg.   Children:

4641   Mary Ella Platt, born April 14, 1850; married, Aug. 14, 1883, Charles G. Hubbard; in the wool business in San Antonio, Tex.; one child (Mabel).

4642   Alvaro Horace Platt, born July 18, 1852; married, Dec. 23, 1891, Jennie F. Gramps; lives in Barre, Vt.; no children.

2279   FRANCES LESTENA[7] TYLER (Buckley Olcott[6]), born in South Woodstock, Vt., April 23, 1831; died in Worcester, Mass., April 6, 1900; married, July 11, 1859, Lorenzo D. Warren, a jeweler of Hollis, Me.   Child:

4643   Charles Eugene Warren, born in Hollis, June 19, 1864; married, Nov. 14, 1895, Nellie Maxwell Hoke, of Sullivan, Ind., where they reside; they had one daughter (Helen C.).

2280   DOCTOR ALVARO MERRILL[7] TYLER (Buckley Olcott[6]), born in South Woodstock, Vt., June 21, 1834; died February 18, 1897, in Worcester, Mass.; married, November 25, 1875, Lucie E. Lufkin, of Portland, Me.   In 1862 he enlisted in the Civil War for three years and was on the medical staff at Fort Washington, Md.   He became a merchant in Portland, Me., and in 1879 moved to Valley Head,

'Ala., where he was a fruit-grower and stock raiser; moved to Worcester in 1888; he was also a druggist at one time.   He was a Knight Templar.   Children:

4644   Dean Olcott Tyler, born in Portland Oct. 4, 1876.
4645   Ferdinand Leonard Tyler, born in Valley Head Feb. 2, 1882.

2283   GRACE ISABELLA[7] TYLER (Buckley Olcott[6]), born in Montpelier, Vt., October 13, 1853; married (1), September 21, 1876, George D. Willis, of Montpelier, who died; married (2), September 10, 1891, William G. Derry, of Boston, Mass.

CHILD, by first marriage:
4646   Mabel Willis born in Montpelier Nov. 13, 1877.

CHILD, by second marriage:
4647   Ernest E. Derry, born Dec. 8, 1895.

2284   CHARLES RUSSELL[7] TYLER (Buckley Olcott[6]), born in Montpelier, Vt., November 2, 1856; died in Burlington, Vt., September 6, 1900; married, September 19, 1891, Myra J. Bagley, daughter of William A. Bagley, a manufacturer of Warren, Vt.   Charles was a silversmith and resided in Burlington.   Child:

4648   George Goldsmith Tyler, born in Montpelier, September 25, 1895.

2285   STELLA M.[7] TYLER (Rolston Goodell[6]), born in Chesterfield, N. H., June 24, 1838; married February 2, 1862, Jonathan P. Holton, of Mount Hermon, Mass.   He was a farmer there and the children were born there.   Children:

4649   George L. Holton, born February 22, 1863; married, September 26, 1885, Fanny L. Pratt; resides, a farmer, in Los Angeles, Cal.; one son (Robert G.).
4650   William Tyler Holton, born September 18, 1864; married (1), 1888, Abbie M. Stewart, who died December, 1891; married (2), June 8, 1898, Pearl Hopkins; a farmer in Arlington, Cal.
4651   Harry Clinton Holton, born July 2, 1869; a farmer and lives in Mt. Hermon, Mass.

2291 ENOCH FRANKLIN[7] WOOD (Mehitable[6]), born in Boxford, Mass., October 17, 1832; died in Hyde Park, Mass., January 16, 1882; married (1), August 6, 1866, Adela R. Poor, who died September, 1867; an infant daughter born then died August, 1868: married (2), in South Waterford, Me., December, 1872, Louise F. Monroe. He was educated at Phillips Academy, Andover, and at the Putnam Free School, in Newburyport, where he was graduated in 1851. He became a school-master, teaching in various places, with marked results for good upon his pupils, many of whom testify to the influence for good that he brought into their lives. For 16 years he was in the Quincy School in Boston, and for 11 years was its master. He was a man of high ideals and sterling character, and he did a large work in this school among the boys of the foreign population, helping to raise their standards of living and assisting to make good citizens of them. His home was in Hyde Park, Mass., where his children were born.

CHILDREN:
4652   Annette Monroe Wood, born February 24, 1874.
4653   Louise Tyler Wood, born September 12, 1875.
4654   Franklin Tyler Wood, born October 9, 1877: he is a pen and ink artist, and his illustrations are often seen in the leading periodicals.
4655   Florence Monroe Wood, born July 6, 1879.

2296 JOSEPH C.[7] TYLER (Andrews[6]), born in Sempronius, N. Y., June 8, 1807: died in Hampshire, Ill., November 14, 1860: married, May 10, 1836, Mary Alson Dewolf, born in Lucerne, N. Y., November 19, 1814; died May 10, 1860. He lived in Beaver and Conneaut, Pa. The three elder and the 7th and 8th children were born in Beaver. Children:
4656   Charles Tyler, born March 1, 1837; died March 12, 1837.
4657   Comins Tyler, born March 26, 1838; died in Kane County, Ill., May 19, 1864, of consumption; was a contractor in the Civil War.
4658   Betsey Ann Tyler, born February 3, 1840; died in Kane County, Ill., March 18, 1858.
4659   Samuel Putnam Tyler, born January 1, 1842; killed in the Battle of Shiloh, April 6, 1862.

4660   Matilda Jane Tyler, born in Conneaut, Erie County,
        Pa., February 3, 1845; married —— Van Vleet.
4661   Ira Tyler, born in Conneaut, January 22, 1849; died
        April 3, 1872.
4662   Alexander Dewolf Tyler, born October 11, 1852; vet-
        erinary surgeon in Elgin, Ill.
4663   Melissa Arvilla Tyler, born June 12, 1854.
4664   Andrews C. H. Tyler, born September 7, 1859.

2297 NATHANIEL[7] TYLER (Andrews[6]), born in
Sempronius, N. Y., January 25, 1809; married Clarissa Harts-
horn, born in Otsego County, N. Y., April 13, 1814. He
lived in Springfield, Pa., and Richfield, Adams County, Ill.
The two elder children were born in Springfield; the third in
Clinton County, Mo., and the others in Richfield. Children:
4665   (Dr.) Alvin Willis Tyler, born July 14, 1832; mar-
        ried (1), 1866, Lucretia Williams, of Illinois; mar-
        ried (2), 1895, ——; was graduated from St.
        Louis Medical College; he crossed the plains in 1852;
        was in the Union Army in 1862-1865; moved to Tu-
        lara, Cal.; no children.
4666   George Washington Tyler, born June 25, 1835; died
        unmarried.
4667   Polly Tyler, born March 22, 1839; died in Adams,
        Ill., December 31, 1896; married, July 4, 1858,
        Hamilton Young; she had three children, all of
        whom died young. Her husband was a captain in
        the Civil War, and lost his life in the service. She
        went to the front, after his death, and rendered large
        aid to sick and wounded soldiers. Some stories are
        told of her beautiful heroism that should give her
        a lasting place in the history of the war. In 1872
        she settled on a claim in the west and began pioneer
        life. From farming she went to speculating and
        everything she touched turned into money. She
        built houses in Wichita, Kan., in the early seventies,
        which paid her well; she went to Wellington, Kas.,
        with the railroad and erected houses there which she
        rented well, and from there she went to Caldwell
        where her success was phenomenal. When Kiowa
        was started, Mrs. Young arrived on an early train

and began to put up business buildings which paid for themselves in a short time. In other western Kansas towns she was a leader in building up the places. She then went to Colorado, where her rare success attended her operations. When she entered a new town she was soon surrounded by a swarm of carpenters and builders. In Oklahoma she started in at Reno City; when El Reno became the rising star she set builders at work there. She was looked upon as a " mascot " in western Kansas, and people invested where she did, because they believed in her " luck." Although she was an eminently successful business woman, she had a sweet and sympathetic disposition and a tender heart.

4668+   Edgar Edwin Tyler, born November 27 or 29, 1842.
4669   Ira Tyler, born May 11, 1844; died March, 1845.
4670   Clarissa Adelaide Tyler, born April 5, 1847; died unmarried.
4671   William Warren Tyler, born May 10, 1849; died March 11, 1850.
4672   Ellen Tyler, born March 3, 1851; died unmarried.

2298   ALMINA[7] TYLER (Andrews[6]), born in Sempronious, N. Y., April 23, 1811; married Isaac Buhumin. The five elder children were born in Springfield, Pa.; the two younger in Provo City, Utah. Children:
4673   Andrew I. Buhumin, born August 14, 1835.
4674   Alma M. Buhumin, born March 12, 1837.
4675   Polly Buhumin, born June 10, 1838; died in Hancock, Ill., 1839.
4676   Nancy M. Buhumin, born February 8, 1840; died in Hancock.
4677   Seven M. Buhumin, born May 18, 1842; died in Hancock.
4678   Hyrum S. Buhumin, born in Iowa, April 22, 1845.
4679   Elijah C. Buhumin, born in Iowa, November 7, 1847.
4680   Almina Buhumin, born September 30, 1850.
4681   Benjamin Buhumin, born February 4, 1853; died June, 1856.

2299   WILLIAM P.[7] TYLER (Andrews[6]), born in Sem-

pronious, N. Y., October 14, 1814; married in Springfield,
Pa., March 2, 1836; Sally Dewolf. He lived in Beaver and
Springfield, Pa. Children:

4682   Orin W. Tyler, born in Beaver, Pa., April 6, 1838.
4683   Harlow H. Tyler, born in Springfield, Pa., October
        17, 1839.
4684   Frederic W. Tyler, born May 7, 1841.
4685   Lucia A. Tyler, born February 14, 1845.
4686   Ellen A. Tyler, born March 21, 1850.
4687   Eva Tyler.

    2300 DANIEL[7] TYLER (Andrews[6]), born in Sempro-
nious, N. Y., November 23, 1816; married September 11, 1836,
Ruth Welton, of Kirtland, O., who died in Beaver City, Utah,
April 14, 1897, aged 77 years and 2 months. He was in the
Mexican war. He moved to Beaver City, after having lived in
the following places: Griggsville, Ill., where his eldest child
was born; Bear Creek, Ill., where the twins were born; Council
Bluffs, Ia., where the fifth child was born; Salt Lake City, where
the next two children were born, and in Draper, U., where the
two younger were born. Children:

4688+   Perintha O. Tyler, born June 4, 1839.
4689   Mary Tyler, born September, 1843; died November,
        1843.
4690   Martha Tyler, twin to Mary, died October, 1843.
4691   Ruth Tyler, born October, 1845; died November, 1845.
4692+   Emily P. Tyler, born January 28, 1847.
4693+   Daniel M. Tyler, born January 27, 1850.
4694   Fitz Henry Tyler, born September 12, 1851; died Sep-
        tember 23, 1852.
4695+   John C. Tyler, born November 30, 1857.
4696+   Alice M. Tyler, born May 6, 1859.

    2302 LIEUTENANT IRA[7] TYLER (Andrews[6]), born
in Sempronious, N. Y., May 29, 1822; died in Richfield, Ill.,
January 12, 1901; married, February 14, 1844, Martha Ann
Cook of Adams County, Ill. As a widow, she resided in Richfield. He was second lieutenant in Company F, 118th Ill. Volunteer Infantry, from November, 1862, to October, 1865. Early
in life he moved to Illinois, and in the early forties he kept a
store near Richfield. He sold out his business, bought a farm

and lived there to the end of his life.   He was acting-captain at the close of the war, having come to the position through vacancies.   He was commissioned as captain by the Governor of Illinois, October 1, 1865, but did not receive the same until he had been mustered out of service.   His neighbors and townsmen always gave him the title, however.   He was often elected to office in his township, and was three times sent to the Legislature and it is said that he might have been elected again and again if he had not declined the honor.   He was a Master Mason.   His children were born in Richfield.

CHILDREN:

4697   Elizabeth A. Tyler, born September 6, 1846; died August 22, 1857.
4698   Martha J. Tyler, born March 21, 1850; married —— Trotter, of Missouri.
4699   Dollie A. Tyler, born March 25, 1855; married —— Rice, of Richfield.
4700   Andrew J. Tyler, born March 24, 1859; resides in Richfield.
4701   Charles William Tyler, born January 29, 1867; resides in Richfield.

2304   URIAL[7] TYLER (Andrews[6]), born in Springfield, Pa., July 6, 1826; died January 29, 1867; married February 22, 1862, Ruth Lola Young, born September 3, 1842.   He enlisted as a private in Company F, 118th Ill. Infantry, August, 1862, and was discharged for disability, December 8, 1863; he subsequently died of sickness contracted in the service.   He lived in Springfield, Pa., where the children were born.   Children:

4702   Elizabeth Marcia Tyler, born April 10, 1865; married December 30, 1884, David Piker; had two sons (Gilbert Tyler and Andrew Earle) and three children who died young.   She lives in Warsaw, Ill.
4703   Polly Ruth Tyler, born December 8, 1866; died December 7, 1867.

2306   HENRY B.[7] TYLER (Andrews[6]), born in Springfield, Pa., March 13, 1831; married (1), July 21, 1853, Mary Z. More, born September 12, 1831; died February 14, 1881;

married (2), October 25, 1884, Martha Randall. He was a farmer. He resided for a time in Liberty, Ill., and then moved to Richfield, Ill. He enlisted in the Third Missouri Cavalry as bugler of Company K; was wounded; honorably discharged in 1865. The children were born in Liberty.

CHILDREN, by first marriage:

4704   Melissa Tyler, born April 10, 1854; died August, 1855.
4705   Sarah Adeline Tyler, born July 21, 1856.
4706+   John Andrew Tyler, born July 1, 1859.
4707   Robert Franklin Tyler, born December 16, 1861; died October 12, 1881.
4708   Adelia Tyler, born December 2, 1867.
4709   William Henry Tyler, born February 2, 1870.
4710   Ida May Tyler, born October 24, 1872.
4711   Otis Joseph Tyler, born May 12, 1875.

2309   HUMPHREY PERLEY[7] TYLER (Elisha[6]), born in West Haverhill, Mass., August 1, 1813; died in Rock Island, Ill., May 17, 1893; married (1), Priscilla Thayer, of Franconia, N. H., born November 1, 1812; died in Paw Paw, Mich., February 27, 1848; married (2), Mrs. Mary Ann (Downs) Flanders, of Paw Paw. He was in the Civil war, Company I, 19th Ill. Infantry, enlisting June 12, 1861, in Galena, Ill. He was wounded while travelling on the Ohio and Mississippi Railway when the train fell through Beaver Creek bridge. He was discharged November 10, 1861, disabled. He re-enlisted September 4, 1863, in Company D, Fourth Veteran Reserve corps for three years. He moved to Rock Island.

CHILD, by first marriage:

4712   Lydia Tyler, born in Lisbon, N. H., May 1, 1839; married —— Bowen; resided in Hotel Hyser, Minneapolis, Minn.

CHILD, by second marriage:

4713   Orlean Tyler, born September 11, 1862; lived in Sand Prairie, Ill.

2311   ELISHA[7] TYLER, JR. (Elisha[6]), born in Benton, N. H., December 13, 1820; married, October 9, 1853, in

Mattawan, Mich., Emeline M. Sams, born in Richland, O., September 5, 1831. He was in the Mexican war, enlisting November 7, 1847; discharged August 20, 1848; he enlisted September 7, 1861, in Company E, 13th Mich. infantry as sergeant, then became orderly sergeant. He was detailed on Pioneer Brigade at Glasgow, Tenn., until discharged January, 1864, and he re-enlisted the same day. Was in the battles of Shiloh, Owl Creek, Farmington, Corinth, Lookout Valley, Lookout Mountain, Chickamauga, Chattanooga, Missionary Ridge, and a host of minor battles; discharged July 25, 1865. He resided in Lawton, Mich., and Paw Paw, Mich. Child:

4714   Etta Tyler, born in Paw Paw, July 30, 1858; married, July 7, 1879, Henry F. Sartore, who died November, 1899; lives in Lawton, Mich.

2316   RELIEF⁷ TYLER (Kimball⁶), born in Benton, N. H., November 2, 1805; married Rev. Horace Webber, a Baptist clergyman, who died July 31, 1899. Children:

4715   Lucy Webber, married —— Thompson; two children.
4716   George Webber, married ——.
4717   Charles Webber, a wholesale clothier in Saco, Me.; married and has a family.
4718   Susan Webber, died unmarried.
4719   Ellen Webber, married (1); —— Durgan, of New Market, N. H., and had one daughter; married (2), —— Langley; no children.

2318   KIMBALL⁷ TYLER (Kimball⁶), born in Coventry (Benton) N. H., December 9, 1808; died in Lynn, Mass., December 24, 1886; married, May 13, 1829, Charlotte Noyes, born in Haverhill, N. H., February 15, 1806; died in Lynn, November 8, 1883. He was the first male child born in Coventry. He lived for a time in Haverhill, Mass., where all his children were born except those otherwise indicated. They had thirteen children in all, of whom four died young; nine only are recorded. Children:

4720+   Elthea Harding Tyler, born Feb. 10, 1830.
4721+   Francina Tyler, born Aug. 15, 1831.
4722+   Thaddeus Warsaw Tyler, born July 16, 1833.
4723+   Mary Jane Tyler, born in Wentworth, N. H., June 25, 1835.

4724+ Harriet Tyler, born July 18, 1837.
4725+ Lydia Tyler, twin to Harriet.
4726+ Laura Ann Tyler, born May 1, 1840.
4727   Melissa Pike Tyler, born Mar. 28, 1842; died in Lynn, Mar. 3, 1880; married, Nov. 26, 1863, Webster Graffam, who died in Lynn, s. p.
4728+ George Lafayette Tyler, born in Bath, N. H., June 18, 1849.

2319 SALLY[7] TYLER (Kimball[6]), born in Benton, N. H.., May 27, 1810; died in Stoneham, Mass., October 20, 1899; married Hazen Whitcher, a carpenter. Children:
4729   Sarah R. Whitcher, born Dec. 25, 1837; married, July 1, 1861, Colonel Oliver Marston, born in Sandwich, N. H., Dec. 17, 1837. He was a manufacturer of pails in Sandwich, N. H., from 1859 to 1862; he then raised a company of which he was made captain and they served in the Civil war three years, being mustered out Aug. 1865. He attained the rank of lieutenant-colonel. He was with Sherman in his March to the Sea; at Augusta, Ga., he and his regiment guarded Jefferson Davis and members of his Cabinet through the city to the boat en route to Savannah. In 1869 he moved to Stoneham, Mass., where he was in the sewing machine and hardware business until 1897. He then invented a machine for folding druggist powder papers. Had one daughter (Mary W. who married Arthur L. Souther and has two sons).
4730   Hannah H. Whitcher, born Dec. 23, 1839; died Feb. 15, 1842.
4731   Betsey T. Whitcher, born Aug. 7, 1841; died Aug. 14, 1842.

2320 SUSAN N.[7] TYLER (Kimball[6]), born in Benton, N. H., September 14, 1812; died January 29, 1891; married Jeremiah B. Davis, a farmer, born May 7, 1803; died June 28, 1884. Children:
4732   Wesley B. Davis, born Aug. 27, 1832.
4733   Mary A. Davis, born Mar. 7, 1834.
4734   Eliza C. Davis, born Mar. 4, 1836.

4735   Laban T. Davis, born Aug. 22, 1838.
4736   Kimball T. Davis, born Sept. 5, 1841.
4737   Jeremiah B. Davis, born May 30, 1844.
4738   Sarah W. Davis, born Oct. 25, 1846; died Sept. 187-.
4739   Dennis D. Davis, born Mar. 8, 1849.
4740   George C. Davis, born July 11, 1851; died Sept. 30, 1863

2321   EDWIN[7] TYLER (Kimball[6]), born in Benton, N. H., August 20, 1814; died November 30, 1891; married (1), October 1, 1837, Charlotte Bradish, born July 19, 1820; died October 29, 1851; married (2), August 8, 1852, Mary Summers, born May 25, 1829; died January 26, 1859; married (3), January 9, 1860, Sarah Feltmore, who died July, 1885. He sold dry-goods through New Hampshire. From there he went to Iowa, and thence to Missouri, where he bought a farm. His eldest child was born in Benton.

CHILD, by first marriage:
4741+ Henry Tyler, born Dec. 14, 1842.
CHILDREN, by second marriage:
4742   John Tyler, born Mar. 31, 1854; died Aug. 21, 1855.
4743   Kate Tyler, born Jan. 10, 1855; died Oct. 17, 1855.
4744   Frederic Tyler, born Aug. 14, 1856; died Nov. 11, 1856.
4745   Edwin Tyler, born Jan. 26, 1859; moved west.
4746   Edward Tyler, twin to Edwin, died Oct. 8, 1859.

2322   ALFRED[7] TYLER (Kimball[6]), born in Benton, N. H., March 13, 1816; married Phoebe Howe. Children:
4747   Isaac Tyler, went in early life to St. Paul, Minn., where he taught school and had a store; moved to Amboy, Minn.; his health failed him; he had a son, a telegraph operator.
4748   Betsey Tyler, died.
4749   Sally Tyler, born 1842; died May 12, 1847.

2324   LABAN[7] TYLER (Kimball[6]), born in Coventry (Benton) N. H., January 26, 1819; married (1), Elizabeth J. Marden, born November 11, 1819; died 1876; married (2), November 17, 1880, Mrs. Elmira Jackson. He resided in

Lynn, Mass., and at one time was a prosperous farmer in Paw Paw, Mich. The children were born in Benton.

CHILDREN, by first marriage:

4750+   George B. Tyler, born May 29, 1841.

4751   Ezra E. Tyler, born Mar. 11, 1848; married, Nov. 18, 1868, Evaline Piper, of Kalamazoo, Mich. He early moved to Van Buren county, Mich.; in 1863 he enlisted in Company H, 3d Mich. cavalry under Sheridan; mustered out Mar. 20, 1866. He bought a farm in 1886, near Mona Lake, Muskegon county, Mich., which was platted in 1889 as " Tyler's Addition " to Muskegon, and was in the best part of the city. He became a real estate dealer and lives in Muskegon, Mich. He has one daughter (Birdie).

4752   Frank Tyler, born Nov. 19, 1851; died Aug. 21, 1852.

4753+   Frank Chase Tyler, born Mar. 14, 1854.

4754   Hazen W. Tyler, born Apr. 30, 1859; married and resides s. p. in Lynn, Mass.

4755   Elmer E. Tyler, born Feb. 24, 1864; married and lives in Lynn; has one son.

2325   ELIZA[7] TYLER (Kimball[6]), born in Benton, N. H., October 16, 1821; married (1), December 21, 1840, William Howe, a farmer of Benton, who moved to Paw Paw, Mich., where he died; married (2), October 16, 1870, William Lee, of Paw Paw, who also died. She lives in Spokane, Washington. Her children were born in Benton.

CHILDREN, by first marriage:

4756   Harry T. Howe, married Bertha Hill and lives in Fernwood, Ill.; had two sons and a daughter (Harold, Chester and Dorothy).

4757   Susan Howe, married Charles Flanders, of Paw Paw, and moved to Spokane; three sons (Fred H., Arthur C., Roscoe H), and three daughters (Nora, Bessie and Alice), and four children who died young, unnamed.

4758   Lucetta Howe, married Alvah A. Hutchins of Paw Paw; he moved to Nywot, Colo.; had three sons

(George A., Fred A. and Gilbert), and two daughters (Maude and Ella A.).

4759   Frank Howe, died young.

2326   MOSES K.[7] TYLER (Kimball[6]), born in Benton, N. H., March 14, 1823; married, March 14, 1853, Angeline Parker, born May 4, 1832; died November 14, 1895.   He went to Lacota, Mich., as a farmer, and previously was a shoemaker in Stoneham, Mass., where the children were born.   Children:

4760   Lyman Tyler, born June 16, 1854; died June 28, 1858.
4761+   Ida Tyler, born Aug. 7, 1856.
4762   Charles Tyler, born Sept. 28, 1858.
4763   William Tyler, born June 17, 1860; married, July 14, 1898, Mae Southwell; lived in Lacota, Mich.
4764   Frank Tyler, born Aug. 4, 1862; died Aug. 14, 1887; married Rose ——, who died Mar. 29, 1885.

2327   CHARLES CARROLL[7] TYLER (Kimball[6]), born in Benton, N. H., July 29, 1827; was found dead in Benton, July 27, 1878; married, January 28, 1847, Diana Bishop.   The children were born in Benton.   Children:

4765+   Lucetta Streeter Tyler, born Apr. 15, 1848.
4766+   Wilder C. Tyler, born Oct. 28, 1849.
4767+   Fred M. Tyler, born July 17, 1852.
4768+   Alfred Elmore Tyler, born Apr. 7, 1854.
4769   Hannah W. Tyler, born June 26, 1856; lives in Stoneham, unmarried.
4770+   Byron M. Tyler, born Feb. 22, 1861.
4771   Susan M. Tyler, twin to Byron; died Nov. 15, 1862.
4772   Dexter I. Tyler, born Nov. 12, 1863; died Mar. 18, 1882 .
4773+   Leslie G. Tyler, born Nov. 30, 1865.
4774+   May Tyler, born Nov. 30, 1868.
4775   Carroll B. Tyler, born June 3, 1870; a farmer and lives in Benton.

2328   GEORGE[7] TYLER (Kimball[6]), born in Benton, N. H., May 27, 1831; married Jane Siddons.   He lived in Benton; thence went to Paw Paw, Mich., where he had a farm.   His line is extinct.   The children were born in Benton.   Children:

4776   Harry E. Tyler, born 1858; died Sept. 2, 1863.
4777   Lillie M. Tyler, born 1862; died Sept. 4, 1863.

2353 WILLIAM STEARNS[7] TYLER (Abel[6]), born in Camden, Me., July 4, 1810; died in Searsmont, Me.; married ———. He was a foreman printer in the office of the *Boston Courier* for seventeen years, and was publisher of the North Bridgewater (Mass.) *Patriot*. The children were born in Camden. Children:

4778 Charles Tyler, a carpenter, unmarried, and lives near Boston.

4779 Mary Eliza Tyler, married ———; lives in Boston.

4780 Celia Tyler, died unmarried about 1890.

2354 SERENA CATHERINE[7] TYLER (Abel[6]), born in Camden, Me., September 6, 1812; died in Searsmont, September 4, 1851; married, September 1, 1831, Edmund Woodmans, Jr., born June 23, 1808; died in Searsmont, August 12, 1861, son of Edmund and Lydia (Crocker) Woodmans, of Barnstable, Mass.; he married (2), Rhoda Ann Tyler, sister of his first wife, but they had no children. Child:

4781 Adelaide Woodmans, born in Mountville, Me., Feb. 19, 1832; died, s. p., Sept. 7, 1865; married, Oct. 15, 1856, Dr. Thomas A. Foster, of Portland, Me.; she was his second wife.

2355 CHARLES AUGUSTUS[7] TYLER (Abel[6]), born in Camden, Me., October 5, 1814; died June 4, 1890; married, November 15, 1840, Eliza Keen. He lived in Searsmont, Me., where the children were born. Children:

4782 Augusta Anna Tyler, born Dec. 6, 1841; died Dec. 24, 1892; married (1), David Flavill, and had a daughter; married (2), Eustice E. Burt.

4783 Catherine Jensen Tyler, born Oct. 24, 1843; died Mar. 13, 1882; married, Jan. 12, 1867, George U. White, of Belfast, Me., no children.

4784+ Abel Merrill Tyler, born Sept. 25, 1845.

4785+ George Augustus Tyler, born Sept. 2, 1847.

4786 Charles Herbert Tyler, born Jan. 19, 1850; died Feb. 19, 1896; married, Sept. 23, 1876, Eva Young; no children.

4787+ Mary Amelia Tyler, born Jan. 10, 1852.

4788 Fanny Adelia Tyler, twin to Mary; died May 10, 1873; married, Nov. 2, 1872, James H. Foley.

4789   Elizabeth True Tyler, born July 8, 1854; died Dec. 2, 1871.
4790   William S. Tyler, born Feb. 4, 1857; married Isabel Osgood, of Abington, Mass., and lives in Pawtucket, R. I.; no children.
4791   Frank Howland Tyler, born Mar. 8, 1860; died unmarried, in Brockton, Mass., Oct. 23, 1884
4792+   Rhoda Woodman Tyler, born Dec. 24, 1862.
4793   Galen K. Tyler, born Dec. 31, 1863; married, June 29, 1884, Alma G. Edwards, of Brockton; no children.
4794+   Adelaide Foster Tyler, born July 2, 1868.

2356 ABEL DUDLEY[7] TYLER (Abel[6]), born in Camden, Me., May 7, 1817; died in 1900; married, December 25, 1839, Frances Lavan Morrow, born in Windham, N. H., born March 13, 1818. His father died when he was seven years old and when sixteen he was sent to learn the trade of a blacksmith in Searsmont, Me. He lived in Hope, Me. In 1842 he was deputy sheriff for two years; moved to Searsmont and was town clerk for five years, justice of the peace and notary public for fourteen years; moved to Camden, Me., where deputy sheriff two years; in 1859 moved to North Bridgewater, Mass. (now Brockton). He was an inventor and took out five patents on a bicycle handle and a tool handle, etc. He held the highest Odd Fellows honors in Searsmont. The second, third and fourth children were born in Searsmont; the last two in Camden.

CHILDREN:
4795+   Eugene Tyler, born in Hope, Me., Jan. 2, 1841.
4796+   Ann Sarah Tyler, born Oct. 18, 1843.
4797+   John Morrow Tyler, born Aug. 9, 1846.
4798+   Frances Lavan Tyler, born Aug. 10, 1849.
4799+   Abel D. Tyler, born May 24, 1852.
4800+   Jessie Benton Tyler, born Aug. 15, 1856.

2358 MARY ULMER[7] TYLER (Abel[6]), born in Camden, Me., March 25, 1822; married, 1843, George A. Stevens, a builder of Rockland, Me., born in Lincolnville, Me., October 12, 1814; died in Brockton, Mass., May 12, 1900. He was a good story-teller; active in business, in the church and in society. The children were born in Rockland. Children:

4801 Helen A. Stevens, born Sept. 1843; died Nov. 3, 1851.

4802 Emma C. Stevens, born 1845; died Aug. 22, 1854.

4803 Lucy W. Stevens, born Mar. 28, 1848; married, Nov. 8, 1871, Simon A. Fish.

4804 Katherine N. Stevens, born Oct. 9, 1852; married, Nov. 8, 1871, William H. Sylvester, of Brockton, Mass., two daughters (Lucia W., May W.).

4805 Roscoe Stevens, born Feb. 1855; died Sept. 1857.

4806 Edgar B. Stevens, born Apr. 14, 1858; married, Aug. 14, 1878, Florence H. Bowen, of Brockton, Mass. After his course in the High school in Brockton, he showed great proficiency in chemistry and at eighteen years of age he discovered a satisfactory process for refining crude wood alcohol, a by-product in the manufacture of acetate of lime. This discovery led to purchasing all the available supply of crude wood alcohol and to starting a new industry, now grown to enormous proportions giving employment to several thousand men. In 1881 Mr. Stevens moved his works to Buffalo, N. Y., and became associated with men whose capital and energy promoted the business rapidly. The business is done under the name of The Manhattan Spirit Company and has a capital of $3,000,000, and they supply the world with methyl alcohol. Mr. Stevens devotes much of his leisure to study and experiments in scientific lines; has a private laboratory and finds his greatest pleasure in working out scientific problems. He has given several lectures on scientific subjects before the Buffalo Academy of Science and other institutions. He is a recognized authority on many scientific lines. He has one son (Edgar A. Stevens, born in Buffalo, July 1, 1886).

4807 George E. Stevens, born January 29, 1861; married, May 12, 1886, Annie E. Curtis; had three sons (Ernest, Arthur, Raymond).

4808 Serena A. Stevens, born June 12, 1866; unmarried in 1897.

2362 BENJAMIN F.[7] TYLER (Simeon[6]), born in Camden, Me., June 2, 1814; died in Camden, June 16, 1872;

married (1), Louise Tressell; married (2), Sarah J. (Love) Howe, widow of Ephraim Howe; died March 3, 1861, aged 44 years, 3 months and 27 days. He was a joiner by trade. In the time of the gold excitement he went to California, but returned. The children were born in Camden:

CHILDREN, by first marriage:

4809 Erastus F. Tyler, died unmarried Dec. 10, 1867, aged 23 years.

4810 Lucy M. Tyler, died unmarried Sept. 6, 1862, aged 21 years and 9 months.

4811 Frances A. Tyler, died unmarried Sept. 4, 1859, aged 17 years and 6 months.

2364 THEODORE[7] TYLER (Simeon[6]), born in Camden, Me.; married Arabine Pease, of Appleton, Me.; her sister married Theodore's brother Edwin. He was a joiner and lived in East Union, Me. Child:

4812 William Tyler, born in Camden; in 1898 was in Boston in the U. S. Navy, unmarried.

2366 EDWIN[7] TYLER (Simeon[6]), born in Camden, Me.; died in Appleton, Me.; married Eliza Pease, of Appleton, sister of his brother Theodore's wife. Child:

4813 Harriet Tyler, born in Appleton, married Levi A. Oaks and lives in Charlestown, Mass., s. p.

2367 REBECCA[7] TYLER (Simeon[6]), born in Camden, Me., September 13, 1809; died September 17, 1875; married, December 23, 1833, Henry Noyes, a grocer in South Boston, Mass., where her children were born. Children:

4814 Lucy Eleanor Noyes, born Sept. 17, 1834; married, 1858, Amos M. Kidder, of New York City, who was wealthy; they had a son and a daughter (William, Lucy).

4815 Elizabeth Sophia Noyes, born Oct. 1, 1836; married, 1857, George Prescott, of San Francisco, Cal.; had three daughters and a son (Ella, Lulu, George, Alice).

4816 Henry E. Noyes, born Aug. 23, 1839; was graduated from West Point; married, July 2, 1864, Louise W.

Walker; had three sons and two daughters (Henry, Arthur, Samuel, Louise, Margaret).

4817   William Mason Noyes, born Dec. 17, 1841; died Mar. 24, 1843.

4818   Mary Catherine Noyes, born Feb. 21, 1844; married in 1864, Fred Grant, of San Francisco, had a son and daughter (Fred, Maude).

4819   Helen Agnes Noyes, born Sept. 19, 1848; married Ephraim L. Haddaway, of Malden, Mass.; had one son and three daughters (Mabel, Bertha, Helen, William).

4820+   John Albert Noyes, twin to Helen, married, 1878, Amelia C. French; lived in Frankfort, Me.

2368   HARRIET[7] TYLER (Simeon[6]), born in Camden, Me.; married, December 8, 1850, Robert Jacobs, a shipwright, who moved from Camden to Roslindale, Mass. The children were born in Camden. Children:

4821   Frederick W. Jacobs, born Dec. 8, 1851; married, Carrie J. Houghton, and was a grocer in Boston; had a daughter (Winifred); they live in Roslindale.

4822   Addie W. Jacobs, born Nov. 28, 1856; married William Swift, had one daughter (Mabel); lives in Roslindale.

2370   ALDEN LORENZO[7] TYLER (Samuel[6]), born in Belfast, Me., May 18, 1820; died July 24, 1896, in Rockland, Me.; married, June 20, 1844, Drusilla E. Packard, of West Camden, Me. He was a teacher in the public schools of Rockland for a half century; he did not teach continuously, but was connected with the schools either as teacher, or supervisor during that period. He was also connected with the city government and in that capacity promoted the welfare of the schools. At least three generations came under his personal instruction. He was a natural teacher, having a great love for the work, as well as singular ability in imparting instruction and winning the esteem of his pupils. His influence was always for the highest good. For two years before his death he was a sufferer from paralysis. A school has been named in his honor. He was clerk of Knox county courts from 1864-1868. His children were born in Rockland.

CHILDREN:

4823   Helences D. Tyler, born May 14, 1845; died in Boston, s. p. Aug. 7, 1870; married, June 1, 1865, Benjamin Trundy, of Boston.

4824+   Sarah Fidelia Tyler, born Aug. 5, 1848.

4825   Mary C. Tyler, born May 4, 1850, a teacher in Rockland; she was of great assistance to her father in his later years of teaching, especially in the preparation and examination of the many papers required by modern methods; she inherited her father's love for this vocation, and the interests of father and daughter were closely united.

4826+   John Packard Tyler, born Dec. 12, 1852.

4827+   Samuel Tyler, born Jan. 14, 1858.

4828+   Lemuel Tyler, twin to Samuel.

2371   SAMUEL HENRY[7] TYLER (Samuel[6]), born in Belfast, Me., March 4, 1824; died suddenly in 1893; married, January 24, 1850, Anginette Sylvester, who died in 1889. He moved to Hammonton, N. J., in 1865, where he was a fruit grower. Children:

4829   Frances O. Tyler, born Jan. 24, 1851; married —— Householder; lived in Philadelphia; had one daughter.

4830   Henry H. Tyler, born 1853; married —— Parker, of Thomaston, Me.; lives in Hyde Park, Mass.

4831   Samuel Alden Tyler, born Jan. 14, 1858; married —— Parker, of Thomaston, Me.; lives in Westboro, Mass.; two children.

4832   Charles Tyler, died in infancy.

4833   Elizabeth Tyler, born 1862; died about 1886; married —— Scullin; one daughter who died in infancy.

4834   Fred S. Tyler, born 1867; was graduated from Yale College.

2373   SUSAN ROSELLA[7] TYLER (Samuel[6]), born in Belfast, Me., March 26, 1816; died in Haverhill, Mass., April 28, 1902; married (1), February 27, 1834, Captain James Grover, of East Thomaston, Me. (now Rockland), who was lost at sea, December 1, 1849; married (2), November 11, 1852,

Silas Barrows, of Camden, Me., who died in 1869. She was a twin and lost her father at the early age of thirteen. Their mother then went to that part of Thomaston which is now Rockland, with her children. She and her sister twin bore a close resemblance to each other. Her children were born in Camden.

CHILDREN, by first marriage:

4835   Edmond Augustus Grover, born Sept. 25, 1836; died May 30, 1853, in Kingston, Jamaica.

4836   Samuel Alden Grover, born Nov. 18, 1838; died July 18, 1846.

4837   Lucy Fidelia Grover, born Aug. 25, 1840; died Aug. 27, 1846.

4838   Nathan Hudson Grover, born June 4, 1843; died Oct. 10, 1844.

4839   James Hudson Grover, born Sept. 4, 1845; died Oct. 3, 1864, in Petersburg, Va., from wounds.

4840   Samuel Tyler Grover, born July 1, 1848; died Mar. 22, 1850.

CHILD, by second marriage:

4841   Charles A. Barrows, born May 10, 1855; married, Nov. 24, 1881, Emma Lane, of Burnham, Me.; lives in Haverhill, Mass.; has one son (Frank).

2374 MARGARET FIDELIA[7] TYLER (Samuel[6]), born Belfast, Me., March 26, 1816; in 1896 was living with her daughter in Rockland; married, January 24, 1836, Gilman Barrows, in West Camden, Me. He was a farmer and teacher. At the death of her father when she was thirteen, her mother took her children back to Thomaston, to the part now Rockland, Me. Her sight, which had not been good for some years, came back to her in her 75th year. Her husband's cousin, Silas Barrows, became the second husband of her twin sister. Her children were born in Camden. Children:

4842,   Helen L. Barrows, born June 6, 1837; died Jan. 31, 1855.

4843   Mary A. Barrows, born Sept. 25, 1838; died Nov. 28, 1842.

4844   Rosella A. Barrows, born July 15, 1840; married, Nov. 23, 1862, Leander S. Keene, of Camden, and later of Wolfsboro, N. H., and Haverhill, Mass.; one daughter (Myra, who married Newton Osgood), and a son (Frank) who died.

4845 Beniah Barrows, born Apr. 4, 1843; died Feb. 3, 1874; married, June 23, 1866, Olive Gurney, of Appleton, Me.; has a son who was graduated from Yale College.

4846 Alden Tyler Barrows, born Nov. 14, 1847; died Dec. 1864.

4847 Juliette G. Barrows, born June 21, 1849; married, Sept. 19, 1871, Moses Smith, of Camden; lived in Haverhill and had a daughter and son (Lula and Barrows).

4848 Lucy Ellen Barrows, born Mar. 1, 1856; married, Sept. 23, 1874, John Clough, of Rockland, Me.; one daughter (Emma).

2375 LUCY ANN[7] TYLER (Samuel[6]), born in Belfast, Me., February 2, 1822; died in Kingston, Jamaica, in 1852; married Alvin Tolman, master mariner who died in the Mediterranean sea. They resided in Rockland, Me. Children:

4849 Adella Tolman, born about 1843; died in Kingston, Jamaica in 1852.

4850 John Crocker Tolman, born December 17, 1849; died January 9, 1884; married December 25, 1876, Jennie Collamore of Rockland; his widow and daughter (Laura) live in Winchester, Mass.

2377 ALONZO[7] TYLER (Coburn Jonathan[6]), born in Camden, Me.; died in Pittston, Me., 1876; married Mary Calderwood. He was a mariner of Vinal Haven, Me. Children:

4851 Julia Ann Tyler, married and lived in Vinal Haven and had a family; died there.

4852 Mary La Von Tyler, married —— Thomas, of Rockland, Me., who died; had one son.

4853 Jennie Tyler, married —— Jones, of Bay View, Mass.; one child.

2379 SIMEON COBURN[7] (Coburn Jonathan[6]), born in Camden, Me., February 12, 1836; married, April 2, 1857, Rebecca Wood Horton born in Camden, May 20, 1838; daughter of John and Mehitable (Richards) Horton. In 1897 he lived in Camden, where he was a builder, and where his children were born. Children:

4854+ Blanche Howard Tyler, born April 13, 1858.

4855+ Ralph Sumner Tyler, born July 11, 1860.

4856+ Anna Eugenia Tyler, born April 25, 1862.

4857 Winifred Kendall Tyler, born June 23, 1864; died October 29, 1876.

4858 John Coburn Tyler, born June 21, 1866; died unmarried January 31, 1890.

4859+ Berenice Antoinette Tyler, born June 21, 1868.

4860 Josephine Mehitable Tyler, born February 16, 1880.

2387 WILLIAM[7] TYLER (Daniel[6]), born in the first quarter of the 19th century, probably about 1817; name of wife unknown; resided in West Troy, N. Y. Children:

4861 Louisa M. Tyler, born in West Troy, 1845; married Levinus A. Tyler, No. 2399.

4862 Franklin W. Tyler; lives in Hudson, N. Y.

4863 Daughter, married J. Wesley Jones of Chatham, N. Y., and had two daughters; one (Carrie) married George Montague of Philadelphia.

2391 JULIA[7] TYLER (Daniel[6]), born in Bridgewater, Mass., April 5, 1825; married, October 27, 1850, in Plainfield, Ill., James Riley Ashley, born in Martinsburg, N. Y., February 3, 1825; lives in Joliet, Ill., the proprietor of the Ashley Wire Company. The children were born in Plainfield. Children:

4864 Alice Estelle Ashley, born January 27, 1854; died September 18, 1854.

4865 Julia Christina Ashley, born October 2, 1859; died September 6, 1860.

4866 Nellie Clementine Ashley, born September 28, 1861; died January 24, 1864.

4867 Ella Marian Ashley, born April 27, 1865; married November 21, 1888, George Woodruff Bush of Joliet, Ill.

2393 MARY ANN[7] TYLER (Moses W.[6]) born in Pittsfield, Mass., August 24, 1820; married in Troy, N. Y., October

15, 1838, Robert Cornell, proprietor of Farmer's Hotel in Troy until 1850, when he moved to Chatham, Pa. In his early days he went to West Troy with his father. In 1901 she resided in Chatham. They had other children than the one recorded. Children:

4868   Charles R. Cornell, born in West Troy February 6, 1840; lived in Little Marsh, Pa.; married and had two daughters (Mary and Amy).

2399   LEVINUS A.[7] TYLER (Moses W.[6]), born in West Troy, N. Y., August 25, 1839; married (1), December 22, 1863, Louisa M. Tyler of Balston, Spa, N. Y., No. 4861, who died in 1879; married (2), 1880, Emma Acley of Rondout, N. Y. He resides in Avon Park, Fla. Enlisted in April, 1861, in the 2nd infantry of New York; discharged because of disability, December, 1863.

CHILDREN, by first marriage:

4869   Charles Wesley Tyler, died in infancy.
4870   Charles Marshall Tyler, born November 25, 1865; lived in Rochester, N. Y.; had two children.
4871   Carrie L. Tyler, born October 4, 1867; married Dr. H. A. Hayes of Buffalo, N. Y.; four children.
4872   Willie G. Tyler, born 1869; died 1870.

CHILDREN, by second wife:

4873   Elizabeth Tyler, born May 3, 1882.
4874   Guy Lansing Tyler, born May 28, 1884; in 1903 was in Lake City College, Fla.
4875   Harold Hayes Tyler, born May 9, 1890; died young.
4876   Henrietta O. Tyler, born January 30, 1895; died young.

2411   ASA LADD[7] TYLER (Joseph[6]), born in Piermont, N. H., September 14, 1794; died in Monroe, Ill. October 2, 1882; married September 14, 1817, in Parishville, N. Y., Fanny Tupper, born in Bennington, Vt., March 18, 1796; died in Monroe, Ill., November 15, 1871; daughter of Silas Tupper. He was a cooper and farmer. He was in the War of 1812. (*See Pension Book, page* 64.) He lived in Lawrence and Brasher, N. Y.; went to Saybrook, O., and in June,

1854, went thence to Illinois. All the children were born in Lawrence, except the youngest, who was born in Saybrook.

CHILDREN:

4877   Freeman F. Tyler, born March 13, 1819; a farmer; has a son (De Witt C. Tyler), a physician, who lives in Norwood, Kas.

4878+   Maria N. Tyler, born April 14, 1821.

4879+   Elmira S. Tyler, born July 4, 1823.

4880   Harriet J. Tyler, born September 1, 1825; married —— Bradley; lives in Lake City, Ia., and has two sons and one daughter.

4881   Mary Tyler, born December 5, 1827; died January 19, 1833.

4882+   Silas D. Tyler, born August 1, 1831.

4883+   Horace C. Tyler, born May 3, 1838.

2414 GEORGE WASHINGTON[7] TYLER (Joseph[6]), born either in Piermont, N. H. or Waterbury, Vt. (as his father did not go to St. Lawrence County, N. Y. until 1805) March 30, 1800; died in National, Iowa, July 14, 1893; married (1), September 27, 1827, Melinda McKnight, born October 28, 1807; died December 25, 1859; married (2) ——. He was a farmer and lived in St. Lawrence County, N. Y., where his children were born, and then moved to Iowa. He had three children by his second marriage, names not known.

CHILDREN, by first marriage:

4884+   Edmond Tyler, born August 11, 1828.

4885   Edwin Tyler, twin to Edmund; died February 11, 1831.

4886   Emerson Tyler, born May 28, 1831; died December 1831.

4887+   Thirza Tyler, born January 3, 1833.

4888+   Edwin H. Tyler, born May 27, 1835.

4889+   Electa Amelia Tyler, born May 1, 1837.

4890   Maria Eliza Tyler, born June 1, 1840; died young unmarried.

2417 DOCTOR TRUMAN MURRY[7] TYLER (Joseph[6]), born in Rutland, Vt., August 30, 1804; died in

Galesburg, Ill. January 19, 1883; married, 1836, Mary Ann Cutler. He moved to Lawrence, N. Y. with his father; at the age of 20 his father gave him an ox and a year's "time." He cut cord wood to get the money for two terms of school at Dartmouth College, and then went to teaching. He moved to Ashtabula, O., where, while teaching, he was persuaded by Dr. Farrington to study medicine. In 1839 he moved in a "schooner" to Illinois City, Ill., where he practiced medicine until 1849; he then went to Edgington, Ill., until 1863, when he went to Galesburg, where he remained for 20 years. The two younger children recorded were born in Edgington, Ill.

CHILDREN:

4891+ Helen Louise Tyler, born in Illinois City March 1, 1847.

4892   Christopher Columbus Tyler, born March 13, 1850; he attended Lombard University and completed the classical course to the senior year. Taught in 1871, and was in various lines of business until 1884, when he entered the employ of the C. B. & Q. Railway, and is in their office in Galesburg.

4893   (Dr.) Franklin Pierce Tyler, born June 21, 1853; studied medicine and graduated from the Rush Medical College in Chicago; practiced ten years in Kansas and then moved to Galesburg, where he now lives.

2418 REV. RICHARD HARRISON[7] TYLER (Joseph[6]), born in Lawrence, N. Y. September 9, 1806; died early in Kenosha, Wis., married ——. Children:

4894   Loretta Tyler.

4895   Cornelia Tyler.

4896   Richard Alexis Tyler.

2420 JOHN L.[7] TYLER (Joseph[6]), born in Lawrence, N. Y., April 10, 1810; died June, 1872; married ——. He was a farmer and moved to Ohio and then to Iowa. Children:

4897   (Dr.) Josiah S. Tyler, lived in Eagle Bend, Minn.; s. p.

4898   Mary Ann Tyler, married and had three children; one is living.

4899   Almeda Tyler, s. p.

2427   EBENEZER[7] TYLER (Samuel[6]), born in Bradford, Vt. January 1, 1809; died August 27, 1872; in Richland City Wis.; married, in Ottawa, Ill., 1842, Eliza Meekham, who was born in Akron, Ohio.   The children were born in Richland City.   Children:

4900   Agnes Tyler.
4901   Tuma Tyler.

2428   MARIA[7] TYLER (Samuel[6]), born in Bradford, Vt., April 16, 1811; died in Hudson, Wis., 1890; married, in Springfield, Pa., June, 1832, John Lord, who died February 22, 1842.   Children:

4902   Edwin (or Edward) W. Lord, lived in Sextonville, Wis.
4903   Celia C. Lord, married a farmer near St. Paul, Minn.
4904   Samuel Tyler Lord, went to New Mexico.
4905   Rufus Lord, lived in Blue River, Wis.
4906   Lucy A. Lord, died.

2431   HIAL[7] TYLER (Samuel[6]), born in French Creek, N. Y., April 23, 1820; married Frederica Bernard of Ottawa, Ill.   He moved to California in 1852.   Children:

4907   George Tyler, resided in Denver, Col.
4908   Eliza Tyler, married —— Risser; lived in Serreno, Ill.

2432   ASENATH[7] TYLER (Samuel[6]), born in Springfield, Pa., January 25, 1823; married, 1839, —— Fox, of Waterloo, Ia.   Children:

4909   Benjamin Fox.
4910   Alfred Fox, lives in Denver, Col.
4911   Frank Fox.
4912   Nellie Fox, lives in Waterloo.
4913   Belle Fox, married Frank Fern of Waterloo.

2433   LYDIA[7] TYLER (Samuel[6]), born in Springfield, Pa., May 10, 1825; died in Richland City, Wis., September 23, 1868; married John Hooper of Ottawa, Ill.   Children:

4914   Lydia J. Hooper, resided unmarried in Idaho Springs, Col.
4915   Frank Hooper, went to Mexico.
4916   William Hooper, went to the Klondike.

2434 CATHERINE B.[7] TYLER (Samuel[6]), born in Springfield, Pa., September 18, 1829; married August 30, 1848, in La Salle, Ill., John Buchenan, born in Carlsbad, Germany February 3, 1817. They lived in Ottawa, Ill., St. Joseph, Mo., Wathena, Kas., and in 1900 were in Helena, Mont. The two elder children were born in Ottawa; the next three in St. Joseph and the youngest in Wathena. Children:

4917   Annah E. Buchenan, born June 3, 1849; died September, 1883, married April 5, 1865, Robert McPherson and lived in Elwood, Kas.; five children (Kate, Minnie, Bert, Elbia and James).

4918   Hial A. Buchenan, born October 1, 1851; died February 27, 1852.

4919   Ada C. Buchenan, born February 7, 1853; married, February 29, 1871, David Blacker of Helena, Mont.; five children (Muzetta, Lelia, Catherine and Jack).

4920   Alberto C. Buchenan, born April 23, 1856; died June, 22, 1897, in Twin Bluffs, Wis., unmarried.

4921   Herbert A. Buchenan, born September 26, 1859; in 1900 was living unmarried in Helena, Mont.

4922   John Leone Buchenan, born November 6, 1864; unmarried, in Helena, Mont. in 1900.

2435 ESTHER ANN[7] TYLER (Samuel[6]), born in Springfield, Pa., November 17, 1830; married, 1846, in Ottawa, Ill., —— Reed. They lived in Sextonville, Wis. The children were born in Ottawa. Children:

4923   Mary Reed, born September 17, 1849; married, May 26, 1866, ——; had two daughters and a son (Luella, Esther and Benjamin).

4924   Riley Reed, born April 18, 1851; married, July 12, 1874, Alice Hackett, and lives in South Superior, Wis.; had one son and a daughter (George and Mary).

2447 EZRA B.[7] TYLER (Amasa[6]), born in Saybrook, O., February 23, 1835; married, 30 December, 1863, Emeline Howard, who died in 1875; daughter of Arthur Howard of Plymouth, O. He was a farmer. The children were born in Saybrook. Children:

4925   Sarah Tyler, died in infancy.

4926   Fannie Tyler, died in infancy.

4927   Minnie Tyler.

2459   CLIMENIA[7] TYLER (John Howard[6]), died
April, 1876; married Eben Danforth, her second cousin. They
probably had other children than those recorded. Children:

4928   Calvin Danforth, died at the age of about 58, unmarried.

4929   Emily Danforth, married Joseph Thompson and
died s. p. in 1892.

2460   CALVIN J.[7] TYLER (John Howard[6]), died in
Ashby, Mass., March 23, 1887; married Alice Whitney who
died in Ashby September 19, 1858. They lived for a time in
Waterford, Vt., and then went to Ashby, where the children
were born. None of the family are in that town. Children:

4930   John M. Tyler, born December 20, 1838; married
July 5, 1865, in Ashby, Adelaide D. Shattuck.

4931   Sarah K. Tyler, born January 16, 1840.

4932   Willard Tyler, born August 6, 1841.

4933   Ann C. Tyler, born March 18, 1847.

4934   Alice Tyler, born October 30, 1850.

2462   ISAREL WILLARD[7] TYLER (John Howard[6]),
born March 20, 1820; died in Stewartstown, N. H., September
14, 1897; married January 27, 1847, in Pittsburg, N. H.,
Harriet Perry, born in Vernon, Vt., July 22, 1822; died in
Stewartstown, N. H., April 15, 1897. He was a farmer and
lived for a time in Pittsburg, where the two elder children were
born; in Clarksville, where the other children were born, and
finally moved to Stewartstown. Children:

4935   Lyman Tyler, born December 27, 1847; died September, 1852.

4936   Mary L. Tyler, born July 10, 1853; married December
5, 1871, Edward S. Atherton, born in Columbia, N.
H., June 6, 1839; was living in Colebrook, N. H., in
1900. Had one son (Samuel E., born April 5,
1878).

4937   John Howard Tyler, born March 15, 1855; died January 8, 1864.

4938   Harriet P. Tyler, born November 10, 1857; married

Charles Martin; had three children (Melvin Moses, Emma J. and Mary H.).

4939   Anna Tyler, born March 18, 1859; died August, 1863.

4940   Susan Tyler, born February 21, 1862; died May 6, 1864.

4941   William Tyler, born August 8, 1864; died June 22, 1865.

2489 DAMON YOUNG[7] TYLER, (Amos[6]), born in Piermont, N. H., May 15, 1827; married, June 12, 1853, in Philadelphia, Pa., Maria Jane Taylor. Between the years 1854 and 1859, he went west to Wisconsin from Canada. The two younger children were born in Merrimack, Wis. Children:

4942+   Lawrence Stewart Tyler, born in Compton, Que. August 19, 1854.

4943+   Leonora Emma Tyler, born in Newport, Wis., June 26, 1859.

4944   Lydia Irene, born July 19, 1867; married —— Seivers, and lives in Duluth, Minn.

4945   Lewis Amos Tyler, born January 8, 1870; lives in Salem, South Dakota.

2490 AMANDA MELVINA[7] TYLER (Amos[6]), born in Compton, Que., March 14, 1840; married, September 24, 1861, Chauncey K. Richardson of Newport, Wis., where their children were born. Children:

4946   Daniel Victor Richardson, born July 29, 1864; married Hattie Cowles of Leroy, Wis. He was graduated from Hillsdale (Mich.) College in 1889; admitted to practice law in Illinois in 1894; he is a practicing lawyer and the editor of the Loyal *Tribune*, in Loyal, Clark County, Wis., where he lives.

4947   Nahum Vinton Richardson, born October 25, 1865; died March 9, 1866.

4948   Verna Richardson, born November 27, 1869; is a music teacher and was graduated from Ripon (Wis.) School of Music in 1894.

2492 ROXANA CUTTING[7] TYLER (Amos[6]), born in Compton, Que., April 14, 1848; died in Pascoag, R. I., June

20, 1890; married October 5, 1881, Rev. W. E. Dennett, a graduate of Wisconsin University and the Theological department of Hillsdale College; was afterward pastor in Pascoag, R. I. She was a very precocious child finishing the common schools at twelve years of age; was graduated from Hillsdale College, Mich., and afterward a teacher there; also taught in Baraboo, Wis. A very cultured woman and an exceptional mother. The children were born in Pascoag.

CHILDREN:

4949   Tyler Wilbur Dennett, born June 13, 1883.
4950   Ransom Marion Dennett, born April 9, 1886; died September 4, 1886.
4951   Mildred Dennett, born August 26, 1888.
4952   Roxie Dennett, born June 16, 1890; died September 7, 1890.

2493 AMOS EUGENE[7] TYLER (Amos[6]), born in Compton, Quebec, March 3, 1851; married July 14, 1875, Mattie W. Thayer of Janesville, Wis.; was graduated from Whitewater Normal School, Wis., in 1882 and taught there several years; afterward going into mercantile business in Eau Claire, Wis. The three elder children were born in Whitewater, Wis. Children:

4953   Ariminta Emogene Tyler, born February 26, 1877; died November 4, 1877.
4954   Glenn Amos Tyler, born November 23, 1878.
4955   Leon Meredith Tyler, born April 26, 1882.
4956   Vida Elizabeth Tyler, born in Eau Claire, Wis., August 20, 1889; died in Getup, Ala., July 22, 1891.
4957   Pansy Amanda Tyler, born in Getup, Ala. August 19, 1892; died there August 30, 1892.

2497 JOSHUA B.[7] TYLER (Dudley[6]), born in Haverhill, Mass., November 16, 1803; died in Elkhart, Ind., February 21, 1869; married (1), Sophia L. ——; married (2), in Worcester, Mass., May 4, 1851, Caroline C. Rogers, born in Springfield, Mass., 1820. The children were born in Worcester.

CHILDREN, by first marriage:

4958   Joshua Dudley Tyler, born June 15, 1829.

4959   George Hoskins Tyler, born February 25, 1833; lived
        in 1896 in Worcester.

2498   CHARLES[7] TYLER (Dudley[6]), born in Haverhill, Mass., June 15, 1805; died in Millbury, Mass., March
21, 1841; married Laura ——; his estate was probated in
Worcester, Mass., William M. Benedict, administrator; his
widow, Laura, declined; he speaks of a brother who died insolv-
ent; was a hatter.   The children were born in Millbury, Mass.
Children:
4960+   George Tyler, born in 1837.
4961   Charles A. Tyler, born in 1841; died June 13, 1870 s.
        p..   Was probably in Civil war; resided in Deerfield
        and Lakeport, N. H.

2499   GEORGE W.[7] TYLER (Dudley[6]), born in Haverhill, Mass., October 13, 1807; died in Worcester, Mass., June
16, 1850; married (1), Clarissa P. ——; who died in Worcester,
November 7, 1832; married (2), Mary A. ——.

CHILD, by first marriage:
4962   John Augustus Tyler, born in Worcester October 24,
        1832.
CHILD, by second marriage:
4963   Henry J. Tyler, born in Millbury, Mass., 1844; mar-
        ried, October 27, 1870, Carrie A. Keith of Sutton,
        Mass., where he lives.

2501   MOSES KIMBALL[7] TYLER (Dudley[6]), born
in Haverhill, Mass., February 2, 1814; died there April 24,
1902; married, June 11, 1840, Elvira Perley who died July
14, 1867, aged 58.   He was a shoe manufacturer.   Child.
4964   Ellen W. Tyler, born in Haverhill April 20, 1842;
        married, August 8, 1866, James S. Ames who died,
        s. p. November 18, 1866.   In 1896 she lived in
        Haverhill with her father.

2503   WILLIAM WINTER[7] TYLER (Thomas[6]), born
in Haverhill, Mass., November 30, 1803; died September 26,
1838; killed on a railway while living in Boston; married September, 1835, Rebecca Cheney Searles, born in Sanbornton, N.

H. He was an employee of the Boston & Lynn Railway. Child.
4965+ Helen W. Tyler, born in Lowell, Mass., September, 20, 1836.

2504 EBENEZER BALLARD[7] TYLER (Thomas[6]), born in Haverhill, Mass., March 18, 1805; died July 18, 1880; married (1) 1831, Mary Maria Wardwell of Andover, Mass., who died about 1858; married (2) 1858, Mrs. Nancy Marie (Jones) Pierson of Andover. He was "put out" at the early age of eight years; at 16 he went to Andover.

CHILDREN, by first marriage:
4966+ Thomas Henry Tyler, born in Haverhill October 20, 1832.
4967 Edward Everett Tyler.
4968 Eben Ballard Tyler lives in Minneapolis, Minn.
4969 Herbert Tyler, lives in Milford, Mass.
4970 Sarah Maria Tyler, married David O. Clark of Haverhill.

CHILDREN, by second marriage:
4971 George A. Tyler, born January 29, 1860; married, September 28, 1887, Louisa B. Burnham of Andover, Mass.; lives in Malden, Mass.
4972 Elizabeth Tyler, born February 23, 1863; married October 11, 1888, Myron Edwards Gutterson who lives in Andover; one child, died young.

2506 THOMAS[7] TYLER (Thomas[6]), born in Haverhill, Mass., January 24, 1808; died in Meriden, Conn., December 17, 1891; married about 1829, Mehitable Yale, a member of a prominent family in Meriden who died a few years before him. When about 18 years old he moved to Meriden, where he remained the rest of his life. He was foreman in the tin factory of his brother-in-law, Samuel Yale, for many years. The children were born in Meriden. Children:
4973 Caroline M. Tyler, born July 12, 1831; married October, 1881, William B. Greene of Meriden; he died November, 1892, s. p.
4974+ William H. Tyler, born September 18, 1835.

2510 JOB[7] TYLER (Joseph[6]), born probably in Haverhill; died there 1846; married, September 4, 1827, Lucy Meady of Haverhill, who died there February 7, 1880, aged about 70. He was a shoe dealer; resided for a time in Danversport, Mass.; his estate was probated in Salem, Case 55933. In September, 1846 his wife was made administratrix of the estate. The children were born in Haverhill. Children:

4975   Franklin Tyler, born May 7, 1828; married Lydia A. Freind, who died in Salem December 5, 1893, aged 64; daughter of William Freind.

4976+   Edward Tyler, born February 6, 1830.

4977   Otis H. Tyler, born November 2, 1831; died July 27, 1833.

4978   Rachel M. Tyler, born July 25, 1833; married Alexander Creelman; one son (George Edward).

4979   Harriet M. Tyler, born December 30, 1835, died January 2, 1883; married Isaac Forbush; two children (William H. and Lottie H.).

4980+   John Otis Tyler, born November 3, 1837.

4981   Mary West Tyler, born December 18, 1839; married Thomas Kellough of East Boston, Mass.; three children (Arthur, Horace and Walter).

4982   Helen Chase Tyler, born June 23, 1843; married John Caves of Wenham, Mass.; two children (Horace S. and Lizzie W.).

4983   Caroline Little Tyler, born January 3, 1846; married Henry B. Wallis of Beverly, Mass.; four children (Frank B., Henry M., Lewis R. and John A.).

2530 JOHN ALEXANDER[7] TYLER (John[6]), born in East Canaan, N. H., December 25, 1812; died in Milldale, Ky., July 8, 1887; married (1), in 1852, Mrs. Mary Tyner; married (2), April 13, 1871, Clara B. Stallo of Cincinnati, who was residing there in 1897. He was educated at Dartmouth, N. H., and Reading, Pa. He went early to Louisiana where he studied law with Judah P. Benjamin of Jackson, Miss.; was admitted to the bar there January 13, 1838; was admitted to practice before the United States Supreme Court; moved to California in 1849 where he was a successful gold hunter.

CHILD, by first marriage:

4984   (Dr.) John A. Tyler, born in San Joaquin County,

California, November 18, 1856; married, 1880, Lee Porterfield of Hollow Rock, Tenn. He was graduated from Vanderbilt University, Nashville, Tenn., 1882; practiced medicine in Hollow Rock, in Texas and California, and in 1899 was living in Port Orford, Or.

CHILDREN, by second marriage:

4985 Lillian Stallo Tyler, born in Mulberry, Ohio, February 15, 1872; a professional pianist; was graduated from the Cincinnati College of Music in 1890 and teaches.

4986 Grafton S. Tyler, born in Mulberry, Ohio, January 23, 1875; a custom-broker in Cincinnati.

2534 ELSIE A.[7] TYLER (Job Colman[6]), born in Canaan, N. H., probably about 1845; married Isaac Davis also of Canaan, where their children were born. Children:

4987 Herbert C. Davis; lives in Mattapan, Mass.; a conductor on the N. Y. and N. H. & H. Railway.

4988 Della J. Davis; married —— Goss of Canaan, N. H., where she resided in 1901.

2536 JAMES S.[7] TYLER (James Pike[6]), born in Canaan, N. H., March 29, 1832; died March 1, 1894; married January 1857, Sophia Young who lives in Ipswich, Mass. He enlisted as a private in Company E, First Regiment of U. S. Volunteer Sharpshooters, August 19, 1861; discharged for disability in New York City September 12, 1862. Children:

4989 Carrie J. Tyler, born December 9, 1857; married 1878, Albert Dodge.

4990 Florence N. Tyler, born November 24, 1859; married 1881, W. N. Hunt.

4991 John A. Tyler, born November 9, 1861; died in Lebanon, N. H. December, 1891; married, 1883, Nancy Morris; no children.

4992 Ella B. Tyler, born December 23, 1863; died August 28, 1865.

4993 Charles S. Tyler, born March 18, 1868; married, 1895, Louisa Seaton; lives in Ipswich.

4994   James W. Tyler, born August 6, 1873; married, 1895,
—— Winters; lives in Hyde Park.

2538   DAVID MOREY[7] TYLER (James Pike[6]), born in
Canaan, N. H., May 7, 1837; died in Ipswich, Mass., September
26, 1896; married, in 1862, Harriet Willcomb of Ipswich.   He
lived for a time in Fort Payne, Ala.   Children:
4995+   Harry W. Tyler, born April 16, 1863.
4996   Emily W. Tyler, born July 26, 1865.
4997   Clara L. Tyler, born September, 1871; died November 12, 1874.
4998   Lizzie Tyler, born October, 1873; died November 26,
1874.

2540   COLMAN J.[7] TYLER (James Pike[6]), born in
Canaan, N. H., May 28, 1842; married Abbie A. Burnham.
He enlisted in 1861 in the 2nd Mass. Volunteer Infantry for
three years; he was in 18 battles.   He was a jeweler and lived
in Salem, Mass.   Child.
4999   Coleman F. Tyler, born in Ipswich July 23, 1868;
married, October 22, 1895, Mary E. White, born in
Beverly, Mass., 1869; daughter of Jeremiah and
Eunice White.

2555   JOHN LAIRD[7] TYLER (William Hunt[6]), born
in Calais, Me., June 13, 1833; died there April 17, 1896; married November 5, 1855, Georgie Brewer Simpson; in 1897 she
lived at the Maine General Hospital, Portland.   He was in the
auction and commission business, in Calais, where his children
were born.   Children:
5000   Daughter, died in infancy.
5001+   William Hunt Tyler, born March 13, 1859.

2557   DUDLEY[7] TYLER (Broadstreet[6]), born in Willington, Conn.; married Roxana ——.   The records of this
family are meager.   Children:
5002   Charles Tyler.
5003   Lucy Tyler.
5004   Thomas Tyler.

2558   PERRY[7] TYLER (Broadstreet[6]), born in Willington, Conn.; married Lucy Pink; lived in Broome County, N. Y. Little is known of this family, beyond the names. Children:

5005 Dudley Tyler, lived near Susquehanna, Pa.
5006 Nancy Tyler.
5007 Emeline Tyler.
5008 Eugene Tyler.
5009 James Tyler.
5010 Austin Tyler, married and had a family; lived in Binghamton, N. Y.

2559 SALLY[7] TYLER (Broadstreet[6]), born in Willington, Conn.; married Nathaniel Finch. Children:
5011 Vincent Finch, married (1) Flora Abel, No. 5017; married (2) —— M; had a son and daughter (Charles and Flora); lived in Binghamton, N. Y.
5012 Ruby Finch, had seven sons.

2560 ARA[7] TYLER (Broadstreet[6]), born in Willington, Conn., June 9, 1793; died in "Ferry Hill," Stafford, Conn., April 25, 1863, to which place he had moved; married March 31, 1814, Abigail Ferry, born in Stafford May 29, 1798; died July, 1874; daughter of James Ferry. The children were born in Stafford. The records of this branch are from the family Bible of Alvin Tyler. Children:
5013 William Tyler, born July 11, 1817; early sickness caused him to be weak minded; he lived unmarried in Stafford, Conn.
5014+ Alvin Tyler, born February 5, 1825.
5015 Daughter, died young.

2562 POLLY[7] TYLER (Broadstreet[6]), born in Willington, Conn.; married Peter Abel of Binghamton, N. Y. Children:
5016 Tyler Abel.
5017 Flora Abel, married Vincent Finch, No. 5011.
5018 Artlissa Abel.
5019 Burdett Abel, married ——.
5020 Oramel Abel.
5021 Son, married Helen Davis; had two daughters (Antoinette and Etta) and a son.

2563 WILLIAM[7] TYLER (Broadstreet[6]), born in Willington, Conn. (another record says Stafford), June 11, 1798; died in South Otselic, N. Y., June 6, 1876; married (1), May 26, 1824, Alemeda Beach, born in Litchfield, Conn., August 14, 1798; died in South Otselic, February 5, 1841; married (2), March 30, 1843, Almira Tallett, born October 7, 1819; died October 2, 1869, in North New Salem, Mass. At eighteen he bought his time of his father. He went to South Otselic where he was a justice of the peace many years and a large land owner and where the children were born. He was a travelling dealer in merchandise, as well as a farmer. The male line is extinct.

CHILDREN, by first marriage:

5022 William Wallace Tyler, born Apr. 3, 1827; died unmarried, Dec. 15, 1850.
5023 Samuel Beach Tyler, born Nov. 13, 1828; died in Booneville, Mo., of cholera, Oct. 4, 1850; he was unmarried.
5024+ Clarissa Helen Tyler, born Sept. 12, 1830.
5025+ Mary Ann Tyler, born Aug. 21, 1832.

CHILDREN, by second marriage.

5026+ Almeda B. Tyler, born Oct. 14, 1843.
5027+ Annette M. Tyler, born Feb. 24, 1852.

2564 ELLA[7] TYLER (Broadstreet[6]), born in Willington, Conn.; married —— Brown of North Salem, Mass. Children:

5028 Hosea Brown, married Mary Ann Tyler, No. 5025.
5029 William E. Brown, married Laura Brown.
5030 Calista Brown.
5031 Child, married —— Haskell; had three sons.

2565 LOUISA[7] TYLER (Broadstreet[6]), born in Willington, Conn.; married Joseph Eaton, of Cuyler, N. Y. Children:

5032 Louisa Eaton, married —— McLean; had two daughters.
5033 Eugene Eaton, married ——.
5034 Philetus Eaton, married ——.

2568 WILLIAM W.[7] TYLER (Asahel[6]), born in Massachusetts (probably Peru), January 14, 1797; died in Naples, N. Y., March 25, 1881; married, 1812, Theda Moulton, who died in Naples, May 27, 1873. He was a farmer and cleared his land of pines on which he lived for fifty years, going to New York state with his father, to Hamilton and Middlesex, and thence to Naples, where his children were born. He was a leading member in the Methodist church.

CHILDREN:

5035 Cynthia Minerva Tyler, married John Oakley; they had a son (Daniel), who lives in Naples, N. Y., and who owns a grape vineyard; he married twice and had one daughter (Elizabeth) who died.

5036 James Tyler, enlisted July 25, 1862, in Company D, 126th N. Y. Infantry and was in the battle of Harper's Ferry, and died in the post hospital there, Sept. 20, 1862; he was a farmer and unmarried.

5037 Delia A. Tyler, married (1), John Metcalf; married (2), 1877, Henry H. Torrey; no children.

5038+ Ashel Tyler.

5039 Edwin Tyler, a farmer; enlisted July 31, 1862, in Company D, 126th N. Y. Infantry; was a sergeant; killed at Gettysburg, July 3, 1863.

5040+ Henry Tyler.

5041 Charles Tyler, died young.

5042+ Frances M. Tyler, born Oct. 28, 1847.

2570 LUCINA[7] TYLER (Asahel[6]), born in Hamilton, N. Y., October 9, 1802; married Richard Sackett, of Rushville, N. Y. They had three sons and five daughters. The name of one only is known. Child:

5043 Mary Tyler Sackett, married L. F. Sutphen, of Rushville, N. Y.

2572 ASAHEL WATKINS[7] TYLER (Asahel[6]), born in Middlesex, N. Y., March 2, 1807; died in Cohocton, N. Y., April 9, 1876; married Cynthia Moulton, born March 22, 1809; died March 23, 1881. He was a farmer; moved to Naples, N. Y., and about 1845 he went to Cohocton, where he was a founder

of the North Cohocton M. E. church.   The children were born
in Naples.   Children:

5044   Cecelia A. Tyler, born August 16, 1835; died April,
            1863; married John Beckwith and had one son.
5045+   Byron A. Tyler, born Jan. 28, 1838.
5046   Mylon J. Tyler, born Apr. 5, 1840; enlisted in 1861,
            Company I, 161st N. Y. Infantry and went through
            the war; he is unmarried.
5047   Cynthia Arvilla Tyler, born Feb. 17, 1843; married
            Samuel Parker, of Cohocton, N. Y.; one son.
5048   Lucia J. Tyler, born Dec. 11, 1844; married Halstead
            Clayson, of Wayland, N. Y.; had one son and one
            daughter.
5409   Hermione Tyler, born June 4, 1848; died in child-
            hood.
5050+   Carnot M. Tyler, born Jan. 27, 1854.

   2573 SPEDA M.[7] TYLER (Asahel[6]), born in Middlesex, N. Y., August 24, 1810; married ―― Gilbert, a farmer
of Middlesex, who died.   When a widow she moved with her
daughter to Nebraska and took the old family records with her.
She had two sons who moved west and lived near Rock Island,
Ill.; given names not known.   Child:
5051   Lucina Gilbert, married William Wager and moved to
            Nebraska.

   2574 ROSWELL ROOT[7] TYLER (Asahel[6]), born in
Middlesex, N. Y., December 29, 1812; married Sarah Wood.
There were probably more children than those here recorded.
Children:
5052+   Harvey W. Tyler, born in Middlesex, N. Y., Mar. 25,
            1844.
5053   John Tyler, resided in Middlesex in 1900.

   2577 ASAHEL[7] TYLER (Job[6]), born in Hartland,
Vt., August 11, 1788; died in Strafford, Vt.; married May 25,
1815, Ruby White, of Strafford.   Children:
5054   Andrew J. Tyler, lives in Toledo, O.
5055   Lucinda Tyler, married Mason Harris, her sister's
            widower.

5056 Sophronia Tyler, married Rev. Eli Clark; they had a son (Lucian), who was also a minister.

5057 Sophia Tyler, married Mason Harris; they had one daughter (Chloe).

5058 Laura Tyler, died of consumption in Strafford.

2578 MERRILL⁷ TYLER (Job⁶), born in Hartland, Vt., in 1795; died in Waitsfield, Vt., August 18, 1863; married Zelinda Whitcomb, daughter of Philemon and Sarah (Brown) Whitcomb, who came from Swanzey, N. H., to Fayston, Vt. (See *History of the Brigham Family* for the Brown family.) Zelinda was lineally descended from John Whitcomb, one of the ten original grantees of the town of Lancaster, Mass.; she died in Waitsfield, Vt., May, 1884, aged 81. Merrill settled in Fayston, Washington county, and his home was on a verdant slope in the heart of the picturesque Green Mountains and there his children were born.

CHILDREN:

5059 Cyrus Tyler, born Oct. 3., 1821; died Oct. 5, 1822.
5060+ Laura Elvira Tyler, born Oct. 25, 1823.
5061+ Cyren Tyler, born Feb. 2, 1827.
5062+ Lucius Merrill Tyler, born July 27, 1832.
5063 Harriet Louisa Tyler, born June 9, 1834; died Oct. 13, 1853, unmarried.
5064 Willard Whitcomb Tyler, born July 2, 1837; went to California with Cyren and died in Sacramento, Cal., June 22, 1859, at the early age of 22.
5065+ Josephine Maria Tyler, born Dec. 3, 1840.
5066+ Sarah Eliza Tyler, born Oct. 24, 1843.

2580 HANNAH⁷ TYLER (Job⁶), born in Hartland, Vt., about 1799; died at the residence of her son, Hiram, in Manston, Wis., about 1889, aged 90; married Stephen Dana, of Poughkeepsie, N. Y. Children:

5067 Hiram Dana, went to Wisconsin; eleven children, nine daughters and two sons (Charles and William).
5068 Charles C. Dana, went to Wisconsin and died in Racine; three sons and a daughter (Rodney, Nellie, Reed and Frank).
5069 Ransom Stephen Dana, died in Poughkeepsie, 1895; married Laura Moulton, of West Randolph, who

died in 1882 in Poughkeepsie; three daughters (Ellen L., Ruth E. and L. Frances).

5070   Louisa Dana.

2581   HIAL⁷ TYLER (Job⁶), born in Hatley, Canada, 1804; died there March 11, 1878; married Mercy S. Smith, born in Bangor, Me., and died February 18, 1881.   He lived with his uncle Derias some years and became a farmer; lived for a time in Strafford, Vt., where the third child was born; and in Bernston, P. Q., where the fourth and fifth were born.   Children:

5071+   Lyman Tyler, born in Hatley, June 9, 1828.
5072   Francis Tyler, born 1830; died 1831.
5073+   Sarah Ann Tyler, born Sept. 14, 1833.
5074   Roswell Burdette Tyler, born Oct. 14, 1835; lived in Ways Mills, Quebec, and had eight children.
5075+   Sophronia A. Tyler, born Mar. 21, 1840.

2589   ROSWELL⁷ TYLER (Job⁶), born in Rumford, Me., March 14, 1814; married in Hatley, Canada, January 29, 1844, Sally Kenaston, born in Barnston, P. Q., December 28, 1817.   He was a carpenter and resided in 1897, in North Hatley, P. Q.   The children were born in Hatley.   Children:

5076+   Marion Augusta Tyler, born Nov. 10, 1845.
5077+   Ernest Albert Tyler, born Oct. 21, 1847.
5078+   Adelaide Tyler, born Dec. 20, 1848.
5079+   Caroline Ellen Tyler, born Feb. 3, 1851.
5080   Alice Jane Tyler, born Aug. 5, 1853; married, Oct. 2, 1872, Charles E. Drew, and resided, s. p. in Lawrence, Mass.
5081   Frederick William Tyler, born Mar. 14, 1855; married, Feb. 25, 1885, Elsie Bennett; resides s. p. in Lowell, Mass.
5082   Gertrude Adina Tyler, born June 11, 1857; married, Dec. 25, 1872, Monroe Demerse, from whom divorced in 1880; she lived, s. p. in 1897, in Hatley, P. Q.

2590   DERIAS⁷ TYLER (Job⁶), born in Hatley, P. Q., Canada, probably about 1816; married Mary Smith.   He was a blacksmith.   Children:

5083   Lydia Tyler.

5084   Alfonso Tyler; lived in North Derby, Vt.
5085   Alvira Tyler.

2592 SOPHIA[7] TYLER (Derias[6]), born in Strafford, Vt., May 28, 1796; married, January 23, 1817, Joseph B. Flanders, of Strafford, where the children were born.   Children:

5086   Lorenzo D. Flanders, born Oct. 14, 1820; lives in Joliet, Ill.; one son and one daughter.
5087   Emily Flanders, born Feb. 13, 1823; died September, 1894; married Newton Flanders, of South Royalton, Vt.
5088   Albert Vernon Flanders, born Apr. 26, 1826; lives in Chelsea, Vt.; two sons (Herbert A., Elmer J.).
5089   George W. Flanders, born June 2, 1829; lives in Tunbridge, Vt.; three sons and four daughters.

2594 LYMAN[7] TYLER (Derias[6]), born in Strafford, Vt., September 28, 1799, died in Sharon, Vt., November 25, 1872; married (1), September 11, 1823, Roxana Robinson, of Strafford, who died in 1843; married (2), January 5, 1846, Mrs. Harriet Barrett, who died in Strafford, 1876; estate probated in Thetford, Vt., March 5, 1877; he was a farmer; his estate was administered upon in Thetford, December 4, 1872. He moved to Sharon, where the eldest and probably the other children were born.

CHILDREN, by first marriage:
5090+   William O. Tyler, born March, 1825.
5091   Albert O. Tyler, born Apr. 1829; died in Strafford, Jan. 1874; was unmarried.
5092   Lucian C. Tyler, born Jan. 20, 1834; married, Oct. 6, 1856, Lauraitte Keith; no children; he lived in Lowell, 1856-1873, and then in Arlington, Mass.; a boot and shoe dealer.
5093   Hiram M. Tyler, born Aug. 30, 1838; died in Arlington, June 8, 1879; married twice; no children.
CHILDREN, by second marriage:
5094   Addie E. Tyler, born June, 1849; married William Spencer, of Lebanon, N. H., died Sept. 1880.

2596 ALVAH[7] TYLER (Derias[6]), born in Strafford,

Vt., February 17, 1804; died in Chelsea, Vt., October 16, 1872; married, February 28, 1832, Achsah Ordway, of Strafford, who died February 21, 1876.   He was a farmer.   The children were born in Chelsea.   Children:

5095   Stillman M. Tyler, born Dec. 23, 1832; died Aug. 5, 1875; married in Iowa, —— Davis; he was a farmer; had one daughter (Louise Mabel).

5096   Francis A. Tyler, born Jan. 6, 1837; married, Jan. 20, 1878, Julia A. Fisk, of Brookfield, Vt.; a farmer; had one daughter (Flossie A., born July 9, 1881).

2598   ZERUIAH⁷ TYLER (Derias⁶), born in Strafford, Vt., January 29, 1808; died September 3, 1847; married, January 4, 1831, Hiram Robinson, of Strafford, born December 5, 1805; died February 6, 1892.   Children:

5097   Marcia Adeline Robinson, born Oct. 26, 1831; married, May 8, 1853, Benjamin George, born Nov. 30, 1825; no children.   Mr. George owns a large stock farm in Aurora, Ill.

5098   Daniel Robinson, born Jan. 3, 1834; married, Jan. 13, 1858, Elvesa A. Fullam, born Nov. 15, 1833.   He is a farmer and lives in Strafford.

5099   Marinda Emily Robinson, born July 7, 1840; married, Sept. 5, 1864, Elliot Safford Fullam, born May 3, 1837; died Oct. 8, 1874; they had a child (George R.), who died young.   Mr. Fullam was a merchant in Burlington, Vt.   After his death, Mrs. Fullam was graduated from the Bellevue (N. Y.) training school for nurses, studied medicine at the Women's College in Chicago, and since 1886 she has practiced in Aurora.

2599   LUCIUS⁷ TYLER (Derias⁶), born in Strafford, Vt., May 16, 1810; died in Sharon, Vt., 1897; married, 1836, Sarah A. Hackett, born in Strafford, February 4, 1813; died December 24, 1896.   He was a farmer.   All but the youngest child were born in Strafford.   Children:

5100+   Mary Jane Tyler, born Mar. 12, 1838.

5101   Sarah Ann Tyler, born Dec. 13, 1841; died 1844.

5102+   Lucia A. Tyler, born May 19, 1848.

5103   Emma Sarah Tyler, born in Sharon, Vt., May 23,

1853; married Jan. 1, 1878, Edward W. Boardman, of Somerville, Mass., son of Rev. A. B. Boardman; no children.

2600 HANNAH[7] TYLER (Derias[6]), born in Strafford, Vt., November 3, 1812; living in 1896, aged 84; married, March 25, 1834, Joseph Lewis Fay, of Sharon, Vt., born March 17, 1808, in Strafford; died 1870. Children:
5104 Nomey Fay, married Alonzo Gardner of South Royalton, Vt.; three children.
5105 Susan Fay, died 1863; married (1), William Robinson; no children; married (2), Silas Preston, one son.
5106 Lewis Gilson Fay, born 1850.

2621 ABIGAIL STICKNEY[7] TYLER (Abraham[6]), born in Boxford, Mass., June 8, 1793; died April 27, 1879; married, March 24, 1833, as his second wife, Daniel Wood, No. 1114; born February 10, 1793; died August 27, 1889; he married (1), October 12, 1820, Marie Barker, and they had a son, William Hall Wood, born March 16, 1821, who married Sarah Jane Tyler, No. 5121. Abigail's children were born in Boxford. Children:
5107 Louisa Marie Wood, born March, 1833; died Dec. 21, 1834.
5108 Maria Louisa Wood, born Mar. 1835; died Nov. 23, 1835.
5109 Samuel Eaton Wood, born July 24, 1837; died Sept. 24, 1839.

2622 CAROLINE BARTLETT[7] TYLER (Abraham[6]), born in Portland, Me., 1795; died in Lawrence, Mass., July 13, 1868; married, February 5, 1824, Moses Leach, of Haverhill, Mass., where the three elder children were born; possibly the others, also. Children:
5110 Henry Leach, born Feb. 6, 1825; married Mary E. Prescott, May 1, 1849; one son (Lewis).
5111 Lewis P. Leach, born 1827.
5112 Louisa A. Leach, born Nov. 15, 1828; married Frederic Mitchell, of Haverhill, Mass., six daughters.

5113   Zelma Leach, born Oct. 3, 1830; married Isaac Emerson; two sons and two daughters.

5114   Jane Leach, born Sept. 7, 1833; married Elbridge Kimball; four sons.

5115   Lewis Leach, born Sept. 20, 1835; died in West Haverhill, at the age of six.

5116   Ann Leach, born Feb. 19, 1838; married, Aug. 6, 1859, Charles Couilliard; two sons and two daughters (Charles O., Edwin H., Minnie B., Inez F.).

2623   OSBORN HULL⁷ TYLER (Abraham⁶), born Oct. 9, 1798; died in Roxbury, Mass.; married (1), Mrs. Sally (Fiske) Gage, of Allentown, N. H.; married (2), Patience W. Cowell, born in Lebanon, Me., November 4, 1809; died in Boston, February 7, 1888. He was a printer and painter.

CHILDREN, by first marriage:

5117   Harrison Green Tyler, born 1817; went to Mobile, Ala., about 1842; last known of him he was in St. Louis, Mo.

CHILDREN, by second marriage:

5118   Charles E. Bartlett Tyler, born in Augusta, Me., Dec. 1, 1833; a scenic painter in Boston; unmarried.

5119+   Maria Amy Tyler, born Feb. 13, 1837, in Boston.

2624   PHINEAS PARKER⁷ TYLER (Abraham⁶), born in Boxford, Mass., Dec. 24, 1800; died in West Boxford, March 27, 1885; married, March 20, 1825, Sarah Ann Day, who died October 10, 1835, aged 27 years and 11 months; daughter of Joseph Day, of Bradford, Mass. He lived in West Boxford, where the children were born. Children:

5120   Son, died at birth in 1826.

5121   Sarah Jane Tyler, born Sept. 27, 1827; married, Feb. 13, 1867, William Hall Wood, born Mar. 16, 1821; died Nov. 6, 1891; son of Daniel and Marie (Barker) Wood; his father's second wife was Abigail Tyler, No. 2621; he was of Boxford; no children.

5122   Larissa Clark Tyler, born Aug. 21, 1829; married (1), Dec. 18, 1851, Orville L. Hovey, who died July 1,

1872, aged 48; married (2), Nov. 3, 1875, John I.
Ladd, who died Aug. 21, 1894, aged 78. She lives
in West Boxford. She was the inspiration to Mr.
Brigham in starting this history. She gave him
great assistance in gathering records of Boxford and
the surrounding region. To her Mr. Brigham always referred as his strong ally in the work.

5123 Charles Parker Tyler, born Jan. 1, 1832; died Sept.
20, 1834.

2626 JOSIAH GOODRICH[7] TYLER (Isaac[6]), born
July 26, 1797; died June 20, 1881; married, February 19, 1820,
Lydia Curtis, born March 18, 1791; died April 21, 1876. He
lived in Bradford, Mass. The two elder children were born in
New Rowley, Mass., now Georgetown. Children:

5124+ Leverett Winslow Tyler, born Sept. 20, 1820.
5125 Chandler B. Tyler, died Apr. 1826.
5126 Maria Ann Tyler, born in Bradford, Mass., July 11,
1828; married John H. Savory of Groveland, Mass.;
they had two sons, one of whom died without being
named; the other (Harry) survives.

2627 ORLANDO[7] TYLER (Isaac[6]), born in Rowley,
Mass., 1802; died in Salem, N. H., aged 55; married (1), May,
1832, Marie Brown, who died May, 1833, aged 28; married
(2), June, 1834, Elizabeth Emerson.

Children, by second marriage:
5127 Mary Elizabeth Tyler, born Apr. 17, 1835.
5128 Susannah Marie Tyler, twin to Mary.

2629 SARAH JANE[7] TYLER (Isaac[6]), born in Rowley, Mass.; married Isaac Braman Platts. Children:
5129 George Henry Platts, born Jan. 7, 1833.
5130 Mary Ann Platts, born 1834.
5131 Charles Braman Platts, born July 17, 1846.

2632 LAVINIA[7] TYLER (Jacob[6]), born in Atkinson,
N. H., September 27, 1797; died in Concord, N. H., August 25,
1853; married William H. Virgin, of Concord. Children:
5132 Ellen Virgin, died young.

5133   William Virgin, died in the service of the U. S. in the Civil war; married —— Sanborn; lived in Epsom, N. H.

5134   Daniel Webster Virgin, lives in California.

5135   Charlotte Virgin, married David Abbott, of Concord, N. H.

5136   John Virgin.

5137   Greenleaf Virgin, died in infancy.

5138   George Virgin.

5139   Roxie Virgin.

2633   ABRAHAM[7] TYLER (Jacob[6]), born October 22, 1799; died in Montgomery, Ala., November 20, 1844; married Susan Giddins Tyler, of Claremont, N. H., who was descended from the Tylers of Wallingford, Conn., No. 12126; granddaughter of Benjamin Tyler, of Claremont, N. H.   Children:

5140   Frederick Tyler, born Apr. 10, 1828; he died in Montgomery, Ala.; was a noted breeder of horses.

5141+   Ellen W. Tyler, born May 3, 1829.

5142   Mary Tyler, born Jan. 3, 1832; she died early; married Joseph Davis, of Montgomery, who was in the Confederate army.

5143   Caleb Giddins Tyler, died young.

5144   Kate Tyler, born Oct. 10, 1834; died in Alabama; married Joseph Barker, of Andover, Mass.; no children.

5145   Rollo Tyler, born 1840; died during the Civil war; was in the Federal army.

5146   James Edwin Tyler, born Jan. 31, 1841; died in Montgomery.

2635   CALEB GREENLEAF[7] TYLER (Jacob[6]), born October 18, 1805; died June 8, 1860; married, October 2, 1833, Rooxbee Chaplin, of Georgetown, Mass.   Children:

5147+   Chaplin Greenleaf Tyler, born in Montgomery, Ala., Aug. 10, 1834.

5148+   Charles Edwin Tyler, born in Boston, Mass., July 7, 1839.

5149+   George Prescott Tyler, born in Georgetown, Mass., Aug. 1, 1843.

2636 CATHERINE THOMAS⁷ TYLER (Jacob⁶), born in Concord, N. H., August 25 or 29, 1808; married Edward Gerald, of Concord, N. H., where the children were born. Children:

5150 Mary Jane Gerald, born May 22, 1837.
5151 Edward Gerald, born June 20, 1841; died.
5152 Solendia Gerald, born June 31, 1843.
5153 Augusta Gerald, born Apr. 14, 1845.
5154 Frank Gerald, born Jan. 14, 1847.
5155 Lizzie Gerald, born Aug. 20, 1850.
5156 Adelaide N. Gerald, born Jan. 7, 18——; married N. G. Eastman.

2645 WILLIAM G.⁷ TYLER (Job⁶), born in Boston, Mass., on Copp's Hill, May 18, 1804; died in Tylertown, Miss., November 23, 1893; married, December 28, 1837, Mary Lindsay Connally, who died May 22, 1862. At the age of three years he moved with his father to Andover, Mass.; was a blacksmith; moved south in 1837, and resided many years in Tylertown, Miss., which was named for him, and where the children were born. Children:

5157+ William Thaddeus Tyler, born Nov. 23, 1836.
5158+ Mary Elizabeth Tyler, born July 19, 1840.
5159+ Sophronia Matilda Tyler, born Sept. 11, 1846.
5160 Sarah Margaret Tyler, born in 1849; married John M. Alford, a farmer; resides in Hammond, La.
5161+ Frances Ann Tyler, born Nov. 8, 1852.

2646 HENRY⁷ TYLER (Job⁶), born in Andover, Mass., December 25, 1809; found dead in the street in Boston; married (1), Maria Richards; married (2), ——. He was in the Mexican war, where he lost his health and died soon after the close of the war. He enlisted as a private in Boston, June 4, 1846, in Company B, First Mass. infantry; his height was five feet, eight and one-half inches; complexion dark and hair black; his occupation was that of a carpenter. His company and probably those of the entire regiment were mustered out in Boston, July 24, 1848. Child:

5162+ Henry Tyler.

2649 JEREMIAH⁷ TYLER (William⁶), born in Boxford, Mass., June 21, 1800; died in Woburn, Mass., Apr. 10, 1870, of heart disease; married, July 27, 1828, Mary Ann Tyler, No. 2628, born in West Newbury, Mass., February 20, 1807. The children were born in Bradford, Mass. Children:

5163   Walter Franklin Tyler, born Apr. 24, 1829; died Jan. 4, 1832.

5164   Walter Clark Tyler, lost at sea in 1858, unmarried.

5165   Jeremiah Tyler, born Sept. 1832; died 1833.

5166+   Louise Marie Tyler, born Mar. 10, 1841.

2650 SOLENDIA[7] TYLER (William[6]), born in Boxford, Mass., July 6, 1802; died in Georgetown, Mass., February 7, 1883; married, March 20, 1826, Nelson Bodwell, born in Methuen, Mass., September 25, 1803; died in Andover, Mass., January 11, 1892; both buried in West Boxford. The fourth and fifth children were born in Rochester, N. Y. Children:

5167   Newman Bodwell, born in Methuen, Mass., Mar. 17, 1828; left home when quite young and never heard from.

5168   Leonard Warwick Bodwell, born in Boxford, Dec. 13, 1829; married, Oct. 5, 1852, Abby M. Sullivan, born Oct. 5, 1834.

5169   Sanford Bodwell, born in Perry, N. Y., Sept. 23, 1831; married (1), Helen Herbert, of Rowley, Mass.; married (2), ——.

5170   Nancy Emeline Bodwell, born July 30, 1835; married, Nov. 29, 1860, George S. Cole, of West Boxford, Mass.; he is deputy sheriff and lives in Andover; office in Lawrence; they have three daughters and a son (Rebecca, Emma, Maud and George).

5171   Eliza Ann Bodwell, born July 24, 1839; died Oct. 1841.

5172   Ellen Augusta Bodwell, born in Boxford, Mass., Feb. 24, 1846; died Feb. 1847; these two daughters are buried in West Boxford.

2651 LUCINDA[7] TYLER (William[6]), born in Boxford, Mass., November 26, 1805; married, April 24, 1825, Joseph F. Kimball, of Bradford, Mass., where the five younger children were born. They also lived in Methuen, where the elder children were born. Mr. and Mrs. Kimball and two or three of the boys are buried in Bradford, but none of the family now live there.   Children:

5173   Charles Kimball, born Mar. 5, 1826; was in Minneapolis, Minn., in 1903.

5174   William A. Kimball, born July 28, 1827; married Nancy ——, of South Berwick, Me., and lives in Hornellville, N. Y.

5175   Joseph Warner Kimball, born Oct. 23, 1828; living in 1903, in Rutland, Vt.

5176   Stillman Kimball, born Mar. 23, 1830; married Ann Rebecca Poor, daughter of Daniel Poor, of Bradford, Mass.; living in 1903.

5177   Leverett Woodbury Kimball, born Sept. 17, 1831.

5178   Sarah E. Kimball, born Dec. 22, 1832; married Daniel Poor, Jr., of Bradford, who died there, aged 71.

5179   Elbridge Kimball, born Sept. 2, 1834; married Jane Leach, of Haverhill, Mass.; they have four sons.

5180   John Kimball, died in the Civil war.

5181   Granville Kimball, died in the Civil war.

5182   Sylvester Kimball, married Martha Kimball, of Bradford, where he died.

5183   Caroline Kimball, married (1), —— Foss; married (2), Frank Ellis, of Bradford.

5184   Seth Kimball, died young.

2652   SALLY[7] TYLER (William[6]), born in Boxford, Mass., February 4, 1807; living in Lynn, Mass., in February, 1904, aged 97 years; married, January 3, 1831, Samuel Granger Robinson, No. 2620, born January 12, 1808.   He enlisted, in Newburyport, Mass., October, 1861, in the 23d Mass. volunteers, as fife major; he died in Newburyport.   Children:

5185   Charles Granger Robinson, Jr., born July 14, 1833; died May 25, 1841.

5186   William W. Robinson, born Apr. 14, 1837; died in Lynn, Mass., Apr. 11, 1892; was in the Civil war, Company I, 23d Mass. volunteers; he married in 1858, —— Beane; five children.

5187   Sarah M. Robinson, born Mar. 4, 1841; married, 1861, Charles E. Beane, who enlisted in Company I, 23d Mass. volunteers and was killed in the second Bull-Run battle, Aug. 30, 1862.

2656 HANNAH[7] TYLER (Joseph Stickney[6]), born December 27, 1800; died April 21, 1891; married, May 6, 1824, Captain Richard Spofford, of Boxford, Mass., born June 7, 1797; died February 1, 1864. He was captain of the Boxford Light infantry. Children:

5188   Mary Ann Pierce Spofford, born Sept. 5, 1825; married (1), June 22, 1845, Horace Tibbetts, of Danvers, Mass., who died in Marietta, O.; two sons (Walter and Herbert), and a daughter (Agnes); married (2), Jan. 28 1884, Isaac Atkinson.

5189   Elizabeth Foster Spofford, born July 7, 1827; married, June 11, 1861, Henry M. Doherty, of Newark, N. J.

5190   Thomas Little Spofford, born Dec. 2, 1829; married Mary G. Day; four daughters (Alice, Eva, Clara, Mary).

5191   Francis Newton Spofford, born Nov. 3, 1831; died Jan. 17, 1871; married Susie ——; had a son and a daughter (Arthur and Clara).

5192   Louisa Augusta Spofford, born Feb. 6, 1834; died unmarried, June 30, 1865.

5193   Sarah Warren Spofford, born May 18, 1836; died unmarried, Feb. 6, 1867.

5194   Abbie Nelson Spofford, born June 10, 1838; married, Apr. 27, 1859, Hiram Towne, of Boxford, Mass.; went to Lawrence, Kas., where he died Dec. 6, 1859.

2658 ABIGAIL STICKNEY[7] TYLER (Joseph Stickney[6]), born October 17, 1804; died April 26, 1895; married, April 7, 1825, Benjamin McLaughlin. Children:

5195   Walter McLaughlin, born May 31, 1826; died Sept. 29, 1894; married, July, 1848, Sophia P. Brown.

5196   Benjamin McLaughlin, born Feb. 24, 1830; died May 5, 1834.

5197   Henry Martin McLaughlin, born Mar. 16, 1832; married, Oct. 27, 1859, Martha J. Rogers; one daughter (Edith A.).

5198   Sarah Nelson Tyler, born Mar. 8, 1834; married, Nov. 29, 1855, Charles L. Carter; lives in Andover, Mass.

5199   Mary Tyler McLaughlin, born Mar. 5, 1836; married, June, 1856, George T. Wildes; lives in Andover.

5200   Benjamin Little McLaughlin, born May 24, 1839; died
        June 23, 1864, in the Civil war.

5201   Martha Carleton McLaughlin, born Aug. 15, 1842;
        died Dec. 29, 1881.

5202   Ellen Augusta McLaughlin, born Feb. 15, 1845; mar-
        ried William Chauncey Walker.

5203   Rosamond Abbott McLaughlin, born July 15, 1848;
        married, Jan. 27, 1873, Charles W. Gay one daugh-
        ter (Florence W.) ; lived in Andover.

2659 ROXANNA[7] TYLER (Joseph Stickney[6]), born
August 28, 1806; died January 12, 1871; married, December 8,
1831, Enoch Abbott, of Andover, Mass. (See *Abbott Genealogy*). Children:

5204   Charlotte Nelson Abbott, born Nov. 9., 1832.

5205   Mary Tyler Abbott, born Apr. 6, 1835.

5206   Charles Atwood Abbott, born Sept. 26, 1836.

5207   Frank Flint Abbott, born Dec. 17, 1842.

5208   George Thomas Abbott, born Sept. 6, 1849.

2660 IRA STICKNEY[7] TYLER (Joseph Stickney[6]),
born in Boxford, Mass., August 23, 1811; died in Georgetown,
Mass., February 25, 1883; married, August 2, 1836, Harriet
Esney, born July 1, 1815; died January 30, 1867. His will
was probated in Salem, April 9, 1883. The children were born
in Georgetown. Children:

5209   Roxanna Tyler, born July 31, 1838; died Oct. 1, 1838.

5210   Ann Maria Tyler, born June 26, 1839; died young.

5211   Abbie Augusta Tyler, born June 29, 1840; died unmar-
        ried, April 10, 1886.

5212   George Melvin Tyler, born July 17, 1842; drowned
        June 13, 1869, in Baldpate Pond; unmarried.

5213   Frank Henry Tyler, born Aug. 22, 1845; married,
        Aug. 20, 1868, Nellie Evangeline Strickland, of
        Groveland, Mass. He moved away from George-
        town to a residence unknown; had a son and a
        daughter (Gertrude).

5214+   Nelson Tyler, born Feb. 17, 1851.

2663 MOSES COBURN[7] TYLER (Parker[6]), born in
Andover, Mass., May 7, 1805; died Sunday, January 31, 1897,

at 12:30 P. M.; married, 1829, Susan W. Baldwin; died in Salem, Mass., October 7, 1884, aged 79. He learned the boot and shoe trade and worked with his father until he was 20, and remained in this business until 1864, when he retired. At the age of 20 he joined the Andover Light infantry, an old company said to have served in the Revolution, and also in the War of 1812, and he remained in this company eight years; by 1833 he was first sergeant; in that year the company escorted President Andrew Jackson when he went from Salem to Andover and thence to New Hampshire. Mr. Tyler voted at every presidential election since John Quincy Adams was elected, voting for McKinley in 1896. He marched in the great parade in the campaign of William Henry Harrison in Boston. He had a retentive memory and was an interesting story-teller of the times of his youth. He moved to Salem in 1842, and remained there until his death. The children were born in Andover.

CHILDREN:

5215   George Francis Tyler, born Mar. 26, 1830; died Jan. 12, 1901; married, in Salem, Mass., Nov. 22, 1853, Ann A. Sanborn, of Chichester, N. H., daughter of James and Anna Sanborn; no children.

5216+   William Baldwin Tyler, born Aug. 13, 1832.

5217+   Lydia Marshall Tyler, born Jan. 30, 1834.

5218   Moses Osgood Tyler, born Feb. 26, 1836; died Dec. 26, 1836.

5219   Louise French Tyler, born June 27, 1838; lived in Salem, unmarried.

2664   JOHN ABBOTT[7] TYLER (Parker[6]), born in Andover, Mass., October 3, 1807; died June 12, 1883; married (1), in Salem, Mass., December 18, 1831, Marion Luscomb Nichols, who was descended through Samuel Nichols from one of the original settlers of Reading, and their old homestead, known as the Kendall Parker house was on Cowdrey's Hill; married (2), Hannah Wellman Mullet. Mr. Tyler lived in Salem and removed to Andover; one record says 1840, but the records of all the children after the eldest say " born in Andover," so that the date of his removal is probably earlier.

CHILDREN, by first marriage:

5220   John Abbott Tyler, born in Salem, Oct. 29, 1832; died Aug. 28, 1848.

5221+   William Nichols Tyler, born Dec. 7, 1834.

5222+   George Leslie Tyler, born Nov. 6, 1835.

5223+   Marian Luscomb Tyler, born Mar. 8, 1838.

2666   ALEXANDER SUMNER[7] TYLER (Parker[6]), born in Andover, Mass., May 14, 1812; died in Keokuk, Ia., February 27, 1875; married, July 22, 1841, Frances Catherine Robson, of Palmyra, N. Y., born there October 19, 1815. He was named " Edward," but when he went to live with a relative in Billerica, Mr. Alexander Sumner, at the age of ten or twelve, his name was changed at his guardian's request. He went overland to Marietta, O., remaining there a few years. Then he was employed by a lumber company on Grand Island in Niagara river, N. Y. When an insurrection occurred in Canada in 1837, he assisted to raise a company of volunteers of which he was captain, and helped to fortify the Navy Island in Niagara river and to hold it against the Canadian royalists. Later, in Buffalo, he was in the clothing business, thence to New York city and in a year or two to Boston, where he opened a boat store about 1848 on Foster's wharf. In 1850 he went to California, via Cape Horn, and took a number of framed houses ready to erect on arrival. In Sacramento he kept a hotel, and was also a merchant there and in San Francisco, but in 1853 sold out and returned to Boston. Again he went to California in 1855, by way of the Isthmus, but soon returned east as far as Keokuk, Ia., where he kept a hotel and entertained many western emigrants who came in " prairie schooners," etc. He was also an active business man and took part in the Lincoln and Hamlin campaign of 1860, and in 1861 was elected captain of a home company, commanding among others, Samuel F. Miller, future chief-justice, and George W. McCrary, future secretary of war. They sent out heavy details to guard powder magazines and roads leading to Missouri, and had a prominent part in the exciting days which followed. From 1863 to 1870 he went into various kinds of business which the conditions then made profitable and was interested in petroleum. He was a prominent Odd Fellow. He had a stirring, adventurous life, with many successes. In San Francisco he was one of the famous " vigilance committee " and experienced the terror occasioned by numerous earthquakes. He was a passenger in one of the first trains running between San Francisco and Omaha, and was well acquainted with many of the large cities of his day as well as the new regions opening up to settlement.

CHILDREN:

5224+ Abigail Sumner Tyler, born in Buffalo, May 22, 1842.
5225+ Loren Sumner Tyler, born on Fort Hill, Boston, Apr. 21, 1845.
5226 Frances Catherine Tyler, born in Boston, Mar. 22, 1848; died Apr. 4, 1848.

2667 LEONARD[7] TYLER (Parker[6]), born in Andover, Mass., October 20, 1815; married (1), May 5, 1842, Abigail Nye Brown, of Salem, Mass., born July 7, 1817; died October 20, 1853; married (2), May 10, 1856, in Buffalo, N. Y., Harriet E. Mattingley, born February 26, 1831; died October 15, 1873. He was a blacksmith and lived in Lowell, Lynn, Salem and Boston, Mass., and Janesville, Wis., where the children of the second marriage were all born.

CHILDREN, by first marriage:

5227+ John Hollis Tyler, born in Lowell, Apr. 30, 1843.
5228 Susan Brown Tyler, born in Lynn, Mass., Oct. 30, 1847; died in Salem, Oct. 15, 1848.
5229+ Abby Margaret Tyler, born in Salem, Sept. 27, 1849.
5230 Abraham Tyler, born in Boston, May 7, 1852; died Aug. 4, 1852.

CHILDREN, by second marriage:

5231 Franklin Tyler, born Sept. 14, 1857; died Oct. 10, 1858.
5232+ Ellen A. Tyler, born Nov. 14, 1858.
5233 Charles H. Tyler, born June 4, 1860; died Oct. 16, 1861.
5234+ Harriet E. Johnson Tyler, born Sept. 3, 1861.
5235+ George W. Tyler, born Jan. 7, 1863.
5236+ Lucy A. Tyler, born Apr. 5, 1864.

5237   William H. Tyler, born Feb. 8, 1866; died Mar. 11, 1876.
5238   Jennie F. Tyler, born Nov. 21, 1868.
5239   Eugene W. Tyler, born Mar. 6, 1870.

2668   REBECCA[7] TYLER (Parker[6]), born in North Andover, Mass., May 24, 1818; married, June 21, 1840, William B. Harris, of Beverly, Mass., who died August 20, 1891. She was living as late as 1896. The children were born in Beverly. Children:
5240   William Sumner Harris, born Oct. 10, 1841; married, Nov. 10, 1869, Hattie Newcomb, of Salem, Mass.; they had children.
5241   Harriet Frances Harris, born Mar. 7, 1844; married Frederick Porter, of Beverly; no children.
5242   Emma Augusta Harris, born May 12, 1846; married, June 12, 1872, William H. Greene, of Beverly; they had a family.
5243   Warren Putnam Harris, born June 12, 1850; unmarried in 1896.

2669   WARREN PARKER[7] TYLER (Parker[6]), born in Andover, Mass., February 17, 1821; married in Charlestown, Mass., September 6, 1855, Harriet Ann Mulliken, daughter of John William and Sarah (Hunt) Mulliken, one of the old families of Lexington, then of Charlestown; she was long an invalid and died in Newton, Mass., November 25, 1898. When Mr. Tyler was thirteen years old he went to work on a farm in Danvers and went to school winters only for the next five years. In 1839 he went to Boston to work for Isaac Osgood, a clothier in Dock Square, who was one of the old-fashioned Boston merchants, a brother of Doctor Samuel Osgood, one of the eminent Unitarian clergymen, of Boston, and young Tyler lived in the family of his employer. At the end of seventeen years Mr. Tyler formed a partnership with a fellow-clerk and started another firm of clothiers in the Tudor building, then on the corner of Court street and Court square. In 1858 Mr. Tyler moved to Newton. With Mrs. Tyler he had joined the Harvard Church in Charlestown (Rev. Dr. George Ellis) in 1856. They now united with the Channing church in Newton and he was deacon and treasurer of the church for ten years, superintendent

of the Sunday-school five years, and chairman of the standing
committee twelve years.   He was a councilman and an alderman, and for over thirty years held many positions of trust and
importance in the interests of the city and of benevolence.   For
thirty-five years he was trustee of the oldest known institution
for the care of orphan children in Boston, " The Children's Mission to the Children of the Destitute."   In 1866 he moved into
a beautiful home in Newton, and in 1869 he adopted legally two
young girls.   After many years of active business life he retired and spent a winter and summer abroad.   He is a strong
force for good in his community.

CHILDREN (adopted):

5244   Emma Tyler, died Feb. 29, 1884.
5245   Rena Sherwood Tyler, died Mar. 3, 1886.

2670 CHARLES KIMBALL[7] TYLER (Parker[6]), born
in North Andover, Mass., September 28, 1823; married (1),
June 12, 1844, Abby E. Covil, of Boston, Mass., born in Pittston, Me.; married (2), January 30, 1872, Eunice Murray, of
Chicago, Ill.   All the children except the eldest and youngest
were born in Boston.

CHILDREN, by first marriage:

5246   Charles Henry Tyler, born in Andover, Mar. 18, 1845;
        died in infancy.
5247   Martha Jane Tyler, died in infancy.
5248   Charles Green Tyler, died, aged six years.
5249   Abby May Tyler, died, aged three years.
5250   Frank Henderson Tyler, born July, 1857; married.
5251+   George Albert Tyler, born Sept. 7, 1862.

CHILD, by second marriage:

5252   Grace Myrtle Tyler, born in Chicago, Jan. 1, 1874;
        unmarried and resides in Boston.

2671 SAMUEL FRYE[7] TYLER (Parker[6]), born in
Andover, Mass., July 3, 1826, died in Larrabee, Pa., July 18,
1882; married (1), 1853, Nancy Homer, who died November
23, 1855; married (2), Nellie Rogers; married (3), November
11, 1873, Jennie E. McMan, who survived him and married

David L. Robbins, of Eldred, Pa. Mr. Tyler was a railway engineer, and served on the Boston & Maine, the Erie, the Chicago, Burlington & Quincy, and the Pennsylvania, New York and Buffalo Railways, and lived in Lawrence, Mass., Buffalo and Hornellsville, N. Y., and Larrabee, Pa.

CHILD, by second marriage:

5253   Charles P. Tyler, born in Hornellsville; a railway engineer, of Buffalo, N. Y.

2672   MOODY[7] TYLER (Phineas[6]), born in Leominster, Mass., February 24, 1789; died July 3, 1870; married, December 9, 1819, Betsey Barker, of Stoddard, N. H., born July 4, 1795; died May 30, 1877. He was a paper-maker before the days of machinery. He lived for a time in Union and Gardiner, Me., in Leominster, Worcester and Dalton, Mass., and in Virginia. The two elder and the six younger children were born in Leominster; the second and third in Union and the fourth in Gardiner. Children:

5254   Elizabeth Tyler, born July 3, 1820; married Merrill Williams, who died in Worcester, Mass., s. p., May 5, 1844.

5255+   Sarah Tyler, born Jan. 6, 1822.

5256+   Marcus Tyler, born June 20, 1823.

5257+   Lucy Tyler, born Jan. 10, 1824.

5258+   Almira Tyler, born Apr. 18, 1827.

5259   Esther Richardson Tyler, born Nov. 11, 1828; died Sept. 13, 1848.

5260   John Barker Tyler, born June 21, 1830; lived in Breckenbridge, Mich., in 1897.

5261+   Henry Kendall Tyler, born Apr. 27, 1832.

5262+   Daniel Webster Tyler, born May 5, 1834.

5263+   D. Waldo Tyler, born June 22, 1836.

5264+   Jane L. Tyler, born Aug. 12, 1838.

2674   CATHERINE[7] TYLER (Phineas[6]), born in Leominster, Mass., January 5, 1793; died December 18, 1867; married, February 8, 1814, Nathaniel Bigelow, of Framingham, Mass., born July 26, 1789; died July 28, 1876; descended from Captain George Barbour, who was in Dedham, Mass., in 1635.

He removed in 1822 to Jaffrey, N. H., where both he and his wife died. The children were born in Leominster. Children:

5265   Nathaniel Perkins Bigelow, born Nov. 11, 1814; married, October, 1846, Ann. M. Palmer, of Zanesville, O. He moved to Mansfield, O., and was the first mayor there; was living there in 1901; one son and a daughter (N. P. and Kate).

5266   Catherine Bigelow, born Mar. 29, 1817; married, June 2, 1841, William Carter, of Jaffrey, N. H., born Aug. 1816; removed to Fitchburg in 1873, where she resided, as a widow; one son and a daughter (William and Zephyr).

5267   Joseph Tyler Bigelow, born Sept. 15, 1819; died in Jaffrey, N. H., May 18, 1892; married, Aug. 22, 1849, Mary C. Barker, born in Hancock, N. H., Mar. 13, 1826; died in Jaffrey, Mar. 22, 1896; in the seventh generation from Richard Barker, of Andover, Mass. He was a prominent man; three daughters (Carrie E., Georgia A., and Josie M.).

2675   JOSEPH[7] TYLER (Phineas[6]), born in Jaffrey, N. H., June 16, 1795; died in Irving, N. Y., March 8, 1878; married, in Greenfield, Mass., June 11, 1820, Sarah Willis Hall, born in Greenfield, November 18, 1797; died October 23, 1844, in Baldwinsville, N. Y. He was a book-binder in Greenfield, where the children were born. Children:

5268   Sarah Hall Tyler, born Apr. 25, 1821; died, s. p. July 20, 1849; married, Aug. 28, 1837, Preston Mitchell, of New York state.

5269+   Harriet Stone Tyler, born Nov. 23, 1826.

5270   Joseph Tyler, born Oct. 24, 1828; he died, s. p. in Baldwinsville, N. Y., May 28, 1896; married (1), Oct. 23, 1854, Emma S. Greenland, who died Feb. 15, 1877; married (2), 1879, Anna Pike.

5271+   George Burt Tyler, born Apr. 14, 1830.

5272   Henry Pierce Tyler, born Feb. 9, 1832; died July 1, 1832.

5273+   Cornelia Annah Tyler, born May 6, 1838.

2676   PHINEAS[7] TYLER (Phineas[6]), born in Jaffrey, N. H., January 25, 1798; died in Rockland, Me., September 28,

1856; married (1), in Union, Me., August 28, 1823, Louisa Alden, born there January 30, 1802; died in Thomaston, Me., September 29, 1827; daughter of Ebenezer Alden, son of John Alden, of Middleboro, Mass.; Ebenezer went to Union in 1795 and in 1799 married Patience Gillmor, of Franklin, Mass (See *Alden Genealogy*); married (2), May 9, 1832, Electa Parsons Robinson, of Thomaston. He moved to Leominster, Mass., thence to Union, Me., and finally to Thomaston, Me., where he was a merchant for years. The male line is extinct.

CHILDREN, by first marriage:
5274   William Parker Tyler, born Mar. 30, 1824; died at sea.
5275+   Edwin Tyler, born in Union, Oct. 25, 1826.
        CHILDREN, by second marriage:
5276+   Louisa Augusta Tyler, born in Thomaston, May 6, 1833.
5277   Julia Caroline Tyler, born May 29, 1835; died, s. p., Aug. 22, 1855; married Nathaniel F. Leeman, of Thomaston.
5278   Lucretia George Tyler, born Dec. 29, 1836; married Howard A. Field, of Portland, Me.
5279   Clara Hartwell Tyler, born in Thomaston, Me., Aug. 25, 1838; died Aug. 15, 1896; married (1), James N. Brown, of Rockland, Me.; married (2), William E. Rivers, of Thomaston; had four sons by first marriage (Clarence, Frank, Charles, John).
5280   Lucy Copeland Tyler, born July 26, 1842.

2677 LABAN AINSWORTH[7] TYLER (Phineas[6]), born in Leominster, Mass., June 8, 1800; died in Boston, Mass., December 26, 1869; married Mrs. Mary (Fellowes) Ranlet, daughter of Ephraim Fellowes, of Exeter, N. H. He was a bookbinder. He lived in Exeter, N. H., where the three elder children were born, in Methuen, Mass., where the fifth child was born, and in Boston where the fourth and sixth were born. Children:
5281   Charles Ainsworth Tyler, born Apr. 10, 1825; went to California in 1848 with Gen. Frémont's party; was unmarried.
5282   Catherine Maria Tyler, born Nov. 2, 1827; died Decem-

ber 19, 1850; married, May 14, 1848, Albert G. Lyon, of Leominster; had one son (Charles Julius).

5283   Joanna Odion Tyler, born Apr. 13, 1830; died Jan. 19, 1854.

5284   Mary Elizabeth Tyler, born October 13, 1833; married, July 19, 1862, Hannibal Franklin Ripley, who died Feb. 28, 1894; one daughter (Rena Alice) died young.

5285   Henry Rollins Tyler, born Aug. 9, 1836; died Oct. 27, 1837.

5286+   William Henry Tyler, born May 18, 1839.

2678   LUCY HARTWELL[7] TYLER (Phineas[6]), born in Leominster, Mass., Apr. 14, 1803; married, June 15, 1824, John Woodcock, of Union, Me., son of Benjamin and Affa (Peabody) Woodcock, and descended from David and Abigail (Holmes) Woodcock, of Attleboro, Mass.; he removed to Gardiner, Me., where he died in 1893, aged 93. Children:

5287   Jane Sophia Woodcock, born in Union, Me., June 27, 1825; died in South Boston, Mass.; married Charles S. Hildreth; had a family.

5288   Lucy J. Woodcock, died May 14, 1860; married Charles Osgood, who went to California and China; she was a music teacher.

5289   Ann S. Woodcock.

5290   William J. Woodcock, a merchant tailor; had a family.

2679   LUKE[7] TYLER (Phineas[6]), born in Leominster, Mass., December 10, 1805; died July 18, 1831; married March 22, 1829, Jane Sullmen Richardson, who died in Lowell, Mass. Child:

5291   Rinaldo Tyler.

2680   STEPHEN G.[7] TYLER (Phineas[6]), born in Leominster, Mass., February 25, 1809; married (1), November 12, 1833, Jane Dunster; married (2) ——. He went to St. Louis, Mo. Children:

5292   Mary J. Tyler, married a German in St. Louis.

5293   Adeline Tyler.

2685   SEWALL[7] TYLER (Simeon[6]), born in Leominster, Mass., May 3, 1799; died April 24, 1883; married, in Lancaster, Mass., October 22, 1820, Eunice Houghton, of Leominster, who died there April 25, 1883. He was a farmer near North Leominster and moved to Jaffrey, N. H. He and his wife lived together over sixty years and were buried in one grave. The two younger children were born in Jaffrey. Children:

5294   Mary Tyler, born in Leominster, Oct. 22, 1821; died in Jaffrey, Oct. 5, 1823.

5295   Mary Tyler, born Sept. 18, 1824; married (1), 1847, Peter E. Davidson, of Sterling, Mass.; married (2), G. H. Maynard, of Maynard, Mass.; by her first marriage had one daughter, who died.

5296   Charles Henry Tyler, born Sept. 24, 1832; died unmarried in Leominster, Jan. 9, 1866.

2687   THIRZA⁷ TYLER (Simeon⁶), born in Leominster, Mass., April 26, 1806; died there July 27, 1886; married, May 8, 1828, Bartimus Tenney, born September 8, 1802, in Leominster; died July 5, 1853; son of Major Joseph and Dorcas (Colburn) Tenney. He resided in North Leominster. His portrait is in the *History of Leominster*. Children:

5297   Sarah Jane Tenney, born Sept. 7, 1829; died unmarried, Apr. 7, 1862.

5298   Thirza Ann Tenney, born Oct. 9, 1830; lives on the homestead.

5299   Elizabeth Drucilla Tenney, born Aug. 17, 1835; died Sept. 15, 1838.

2689   WILLIAM⁷ TYLER (Simeon⁶), born in Leominster, Mass., August 29, 1814; died there November 3, 1854; married, April 5, 1842, Caroline Winn, born March 18, 1815; died in Leominster, December 3, 1895; daughter of Joseph Winn. He was a comb maker and lived in Leominster, where the children were born. Children:

5300   George William Tyler, born Jan. 6, 1843; lived unmarried in Leominster in 1897.

5301   Milo Hildreth Tyler, born Jan. 18, 1845; died in Leominster, Nov. 10, 1859.

2691   LEWIS⁷ TYLER (Samuel⁶), born in Leominster,

Mass., June 23, 1797; died May 23, 1865; married, October 21, 1832, Sally Symonds, of Middleton. Children:

5302   Henrietta Tyler, born Apr. 7, 1834; was unmarried.

5303   Lewis Harrison Tyler, born Sept. 4, 1835; died April, 1842.

5304   Sally Maria Tyler, born Jan. 24, 1837; died Apr. 22, 1842.

2693   FREDERIC[7] TYLER (Samuel[6]), born in Bradford, Mass., December 6, 1800; died in Northampton, Mass., September 18, 1888; married Marie Greely, of Foxcroft, Me. He is mentioned in the Penobscot County Registry of Deeds as " of Foxcroft." Children:

5305   Ellen Maria Tyler, born 1830; died in Lawrence, Mass., Dec. 25, 1849; married Rev. George H. Clark, a Universalist clergyman, of Lawrence, who died in 1851; no children.

5306   Frederic Greely Tyler, died November, 1871; married (1), Abbie Gowen, of Dover, N. H.; married (2), Zelda Tice, of Newport, Vt.; no children.

5307+   Sarah Frances Tyler, born in Foxcroft, Dec. 20, 1837.

2694   ABEL H.[7] TYLER (Samuel[6]), born in Bradford, Mass., July 2, 1802; died in Danversport, Mass., October 3, 1867; married (1), in Concord, Mass., September 24, 1834, Eliza Lawton, who died July 10, 1839; married (2), January 5, 1840, Mrs. Louisa Hall, of Lowell, Mass., who died November 23, 1867. He lived in South Danvers, Tyngsboro, Dracut and Danvers, Mass., and in the latter place the sixth and ninth children are known to have been born and perhaps some of the others whose birthplaces are not otherwise noted.

CHILD, by first marriage:

5308+   Frances Harriet Tyler, born in South Danvers, Mass., Aug. 13, 1835.

CHILDREN, by second marriage:

5309   Eliza Elizabeth Tyler, born in Tyngsboro, Mass., Oct. 17, 1840; married, June 3, 1866, William Edward Carey, of Salem, Mass.; one son (Frederick O.).

5310+   Alfred Tyler, born in Dracut, Mass., Feb. 26, 1842.

5311   Alma Victoria Tyler, born Sept. 29, 1843; married, July 30, 1862, William Mackie, of Danvers; she had a son who died young; she lived in Boston.

5312   Marietta Tyler, born Nov. 27, 1845; died in Danvers, May 15, 1846.

5313+   Abel Norton Tyler, born Mar. 2, 1847.

5314   Orrace Hardy Tyler, born Dec. 13, 1849; married Carrie Plummer, of Wenham, Mass.; in 1898, was living childless.

5315   Adelaide Tyler, born Nov. 12, 1851; married, Nov. 24, 1870, George Withey, of Danversport, Mass.; she was living in 1898; no children.

5316+   Edward Melvin Tyler, born Jan. 8, 1855.

5317   Eva Rexaville Tyler, born Nov. 26, 1856; died in Salem, Mass., July 25, 1862.

2695   SAMUEL[7] TYLER, JR. (Samuel[6]), born in Bradford, Mass., May 16, 1804; died November, 1870; married Phebe Stiles, of Middleton. Children:

5318   Rebecca Tyler, married George Stevens.

5319   Cynthia Tyler.

2698   HARRIETTE H.[7] TYLER (Samuel[6]), born in Bradford, Mass., August 11, 1810; died December 15, 1891; married Moody Elliot, of Middleton, Mass. Children:

5320   Harriet A. Elliott, married Captain George C. Johnson, of Danversport, Mass.; had a family; she died.

5321   Henry M. Elliott, married Ella Story, of Danversport; had a family.

5322   Abbie M. Elliott, married Jacob Burton, of Vermont.

5323   Helen A. Elliott, married Edwin Humphreys, of Salem; no children:

2700   ADDISON[7] TYLER (Samuel[6]), born in Bradford, Mass., August 10, 1813, died November 8, 1884; married Abigail Wilkins, of Middleton, where they resided. Children:

5324+   Ansel Peabody Tyler.

5325+   Maurice Endicott Tyler.

5326+   William Harrison Tyler.

2702   ERI BURTON[7] TYLER (Samuel[6]), born in

Bradford, Mass., May 19, 1818; married Hannah Lake, of Topsfield, Mass. Child:

5327   Hannah F. Tyler, married James Cass, of Topsfield.

2709   RUFUS H.[7] TYLER (Daniel[6]), born in Leominster, Mass., September 10, 1817; died in Windsor Locks, Conn., November 20, 1852; married, December 25, 1841, Mary Cowen, who died July 17, 1862. He was a wonderfully skilled mechanic. The children were born in Worcester, Mass. Children:

5328+   Jane Almira Tyler, born Apr. 19, 1843.
5329   Harriet M. Tyler, born Dec. 19, 1844; died Feb. 6, 1871; unmarried.
5330   Eliza A. Tyler, born June 24, 1847; died July 6, 1847.
5331+   Rufus Henry Tyler, born Aug. 8, 1849.
5332+   Mary Ellen Tyler, born June 10, 1852.

2710   ELIZABETH[7] TYLER (Daniel[6]), born in Leominster, Mass., May 22, 1818; married Captain Nathan C. Johnson, of Hopkinton, Mass., born May 23, 1815; died Feb. 3, 1856; he resided in Milford, Mass., in 1898. The children were born in Hopkinton. Children:

5333   Edward E. Johnson, born Jan. 10, 1838; married, Aug. 31, 1871, Mary A. Monroe, born May 15, 1851, daughter of Joseph B. and Sarah E. (Kenure) Monroe. He was an extensive land owner and stockman in Beverly, Lincoln county, Kansas; a scout and cavalryman in the Civil war. No children.

5334   Mary E. Johnson, born Aug. 30, 1839; married (1), Sept. 3, 1861, Almond A. Sumner, who died in Titusville, Pa., May 27, 1861, from a railway accident on a train of which he was conductor; son of Andrew Sumner, of Milford, Mass.; married (2), Oct. 28, 1868, Andrew Franklin, a farmer son of Horatio and Mary (Smith) Franklin; two sons and a daughter who died young; lived in Ashford, Conn.

5335   Alonzo W. Johnson, born July 14, 1841; married (1), Amy H. Carside; married (2), Mary L. ——, who died; he had one son (Forrest C.) by first marriage, and one son (Harry L.) and one daughter (Nellie M.) by second marriage.

5336   Ellen M. Johnson, born Jan. 5, 1845; died Aug. 3, 1860.

5337   Harriet V. Johnson, born Nov. 8, 1847; died Aug. 2, 1849.

5338   Elva E. Johnson, born July 19, 1850; died Dec. 28, 1881; married Orison Cheney, son of Dr. Cheney, of Milford, Mass.; three sons (Frank, Clinton and Bert), and three daughters (Cora, Ellen and Lottie); others died young.

5339   Rufus L. Johnson, born July 4, 1852; married (1), Emma Stacy; married (2), Eva B. Carley, of Ripon, Wis.; lived in Clear Lake, Wis.; one child by second marriage (Maggie E.).

5340   Nathan C. Johnson, born Sept. 24, 1855; died unmarried, Aug. 17, 1882.

2712 LYDIA ANN[7] TYLER (Daniel[6]), born in Leominster, Mass., January 19, 1822; married, April 11, 1843, Captain Joseph Hancock, born in Milford, Mass., December 6, 1818; son of Samuel and Submit (Bruce) Hancock. He was an enterprising man; enlisted in the Civil war, August 5, 1862; discharged June 8, 1865, in Alexandria; was in Company F, 36th Mass. Regiment. He was living in Milford in 1898, where his children were born. Children:

5341   Emeline Matilda Hancock, born Jan. 11, 1844; died June 4, 1851.

5342   Henry Joseph Hancock, born Dec. 5, 1845; died May 25, 1870; married, Dec. 6, 1866, Mary Elizabeth Baker, of East Holliston, Mass., who died July 19, 1878; he was a boot manufacturer.

5343   Waldo Hancock, born Jan. 1, 1848; married (1), May 31, 1874, Hannah Springer, who died 1882; married (2), June 7, 1891, Emma Lewis; by his first marriage he had one daughter (Ella) and two sons (Alvin and Waldo); in 1894 he was in business in Beverly, Kas.

5344   Ada Maria Hancock, born Nov. 8, 1850; married (1), Aug. 17, 1870, William H. Remington, who died in Providence, R. I., Dec. 5, 1881; married (2), May 17, 1888, Charles W. Monroe.

5345   John Hancock, born Nov. 29, 1852; married (1), July

11, 1872, Ida A. Russell; who died in Milford, Mass., Jan. 27, 1877; married (2), June 25, 1881, Ella G. Smith.

5346   Mary Ella Hancock, born Nov. 25, 1855; married, Aug. 14, 1875, Fred M. Walker, of Milford, Mass.

5347   George Elmer Hancock, born June 19, 1861; married, Apr. 13, 1887, S. Mattie Parks; in 1894 lived in Worcester, Mass.

2713   JANE MEHITABLE[7] TYLER (Daniel[6]), born in Leominster, Mass., December 5, 1823; married, April 18, 1841, Ezra Hunt, born in Milford, Mass., June 6, 1819; living there in 1898; son of Ebenezer Hunt (Daniel, Abidah, Isaac, Isaac William); a farmer and foreman in a shoe manufactory. The children were born in Milford.   Children:

5348   Eldora Jane Hunt, born Oct. 11, 1843; died Apr. 1, 1850.

5349   Lucy Hunt, born June, 1845.

5350   Caroline Maria Hunt, born Nov. 24, 1848; died Aug. 3, 1893; married, May 5, 1869, Edmund B. Blood, who died Oct. 27, 1885, in Milford; they had two daughters (Grace and Bessie) and a son who died.

5351   Bessie Hunt, born Sept. 1, 1861; died Aug. 19, 1861.

5352   Frank Lincoln Hunt, born Apr. 18, 1865; died June 28, 1865.

5353   Willie Ezra Hunt, born Mar. 9, 1868; died Oct. 26, 1876.

2715   ADOLPHUS[7] TYLER (Daniel[6]), born in Leominster, Mass., October 29, 1827; married, November 28, 1852, Roana Wilson, of Brookfield, Vt., born July 19, 1833, daughter of James and Sophia Wilson.   He was a shoe operative, and resides in Milford, Mass., where the children were born.   Children:

5354+   James Addison Tyler, born Oct. 21, 1853.

5355   Helen L. Tyler, born Oct. 4, 1859; married, Dec. 18, 1887, Clarence W. Gordon, of Phillips, Me.   She was an adopted daughter and resided in Milford, Mass., had one daughter (Edith M.).

2716 ABIGAIL R.[7] TYLER (Daniel[6]), born in Leominster, Mass., September 17, 1829; married, June 6, 1849, James Dewing Bailey, born in Milford, Mass. December 1, 1825; died December 18, 1896; son of Eliphalet Bailey, who was the son of Eliphalet, who was in the Revolution. She was living in Milford in 1898, where her children were born. Children:

5356 James Oscar Bailey, born Mar. 6, 1850; married, Oct. 20, 1875, Mary Lizzie Bowers. He was a watchmaker and jeweler and lived in Marlboro, Mass.; was for a long time head watchmaker with Palmer & Batchelder in Boston; had a daughter (Abigail R.), and a son (Alvin); the latter died young.

5357 Edgar L. Bailey, born Jan. 15, 1852; married, July 26, 1876, Eva Ellen Jewell, No. 5365. He was educated in Milford; was in the boot business, and later agent for Streator (Ill.) Coal Company; then assistant cashier in freight department of the Wabash Railway in Chicago; in 1885 with Aurora Iron Mining Company in Ironwood, Mich., as assistant manager, paymaster and bookkeeper; he showed such ability that John D. Rockefeller & Company induced him to move to Everett, Washington, to look after their interests and in 1898 he was director, secretary and treasurer of Monte Christo and Pride of the Mountain Mining Company with their smelting and reduction works; no children.

5358 Ezra Hunt Bailey, born Dec. 25, 1853; married (1), January 18, 1879, Lauretta Benson, who died July 3, 1883; married (2), Oct. 23, 1884, Gertrude E. Canfield, of Randolph, N. Y.; he lives in Streator, Ill.; one daughter (Edith L. born Jan. 19, 1881).

2717 ADDISON HARDY[7] TYLER (Daniel[6]), born in Leominster, Mass., November 30, 1831; married, in Milford, Mass., October 21, 1857; Eliza B. Parkhurst, born in Milford, October 19, 1835; died April 11, 1892; daughter of Oliver B. and Maria (Nelson) Parkhurst. He lived in Atlanta, Ga., where long a manager of the Estey Organ & Piano company for the southern states. All but the fifth child were born in Milford. Children:

5359   Frank A. Tyler, born Dec. 2, 1858; died Feb. 2, 1862.
5360   Albert H. Tyler, born Jan. 12, 1862; died June 20, 1879.
5361   Son, born Sept. 4, 1864; died Sept. 9, 1864.
5362   Charley Tyler, born July, 1867; died Sept. 1868.
5363   Harry Nelson Tyler, born in Wenona, Ill., Sept. 20, 1869; an architect in Atlanta.
5364   Oliver Parkhurst Tyler, born July 30, 1877; in 1898 was a student in the Polytechnic Institute in Worcester, Mass.

2719 ARETHUSA[7] TYLER (Daniel[6]), born in Hopkinton, Mass., March 10, 1836; married, February 12, 1853, Nathaniel Jewell, born in Winthrop, Me., November 18, 1830; son of Robert and Nicy (Grover) Jewell. He is a machinist and in 1898 was residing on the Daniel Tyler homestead on North Purchase road in Milford, Mass. The children were born in Milford. Children:

5365   Eva Ellen Jewell, born Jan. 12, 1854; married Edgar L. Bailey, No. 5357.
5366   Alvan Augustus Jewell, born in 1856; died in 1857.
5367   Alston Jewell, born in 1858; died same year.
5368   Lizzie Jewell, born in 1860; died same year.
5369   Frank Jewell, born in 1862; died in 1863.
5370   Mira Belle Jewell, born Oct. 14, 1872; married May 1, 1892, Warren H. Stevens, of Holliston, Mass.
5371   Ella Maude Jewell, born Aug. 15, 1875.

2720 ALVAN ELNATHAN[7] TYLER (Daniel[6]), born in Hopkinton, Mass. (Woodville), October 22, 1838; married (1), April 14, 1863, Eleanor A. Miller, of Randolph, N. Y., born September 4, 1839; died in Corey, Pa., February 24, 1865; buried in Kennedy, N. Y.; daughter of Asa Miller; married (2), June 4, 1866, Caroline L. Mason, of Bear Lake, N. Y., born there January 3, 1845; died suddenly of malarial fever in Streator, Ill., July 18, 1870, where she is buried; daughter of Corydon Mason; married (3), November 30, 1871, Ella L. Benson, daughter of Sylvanus L. Benson, of Blackstone, Mass., and Streator, Ill., where she died December 1, 1879; married (4), May 23, 1882, Mrs. N. Celora Arkills, of Lake Geneva, Wis., born near Richmond, Ill., November 9, 1848, daughter of Derrius P. Sampson, and widow of Charles Arkills. He is a banker and resides in Lake Geneva, Wis.

CHILD, by first marriage:

5372   Son, born in Corey, Pa.; died Feb. 24, 1865.

CHILDREN, by third marriage:

5373   Gertrude Thusa Tyler, born in Streator, Oct. 23, 1872; died in Lake Geneva, Nov. 7, 1887; buried in Streator.

5374   Howard Benson Tyler, born July 28, 1876; died Nov. 18, 1876.

2721   MIRA ELIZA[7] TYLER (Daniel[6]), born in Milford, Mass., February 28, 1841; married, May 11, 1864, James Franklin Miller, of Kennedy, N. Y., born April 25, 1829; son of Asa and Sally (Oliver) Miller. In 1898, he was residing in Kennedy, N. Y.; a lumberman and stockman. The children were born in Kennedy. Children:

5375   Ella May Miller, born Mar. 7, 1865; married Aug. 30, 1892, Ansel W. Bunce, of Kennedy, N. Y.; a miller; has two children (Clayton T. and Theo. L.).

5376   Son, born Feb. 18, 1867; died next day.

5377   Clayton Adolphus Miller, born Mar. 20, 1870; married, Oct. 17, 1894, Louise Wheedon; resides in Streator, Ill.; a bookkeeper and paymaster of extensive brick and tile manufacturers.

5378   Flossie Lucille Miller, born Apr. 21, 1882.

5379   Daughter, born July 3, 1884; died Sept. 25, 1884.

2728   ANCILL[7] TYLER, JR. (Ancill[6]), born in Lunenburg, Mass., October 10, 1810; died in Leominster, Mar. 11, 1896; married, November, 1840, Harriet Parker, who died January 30, 1890, aged 75; daughter of David and Pamelia (Dwight) Parker of Shirley. He learned the comb trade and was a skilful engraver of them; he was in business in Hudson, Mass., and then became a farmer in Lancaster. All the children were born in Lancaster, except the second. Children:

5380+   Josephine Parker Tyler, born July 15, 1846.

5381   Hattie Jane Tyler, born in Northboro, 1848; died in 1850.

5382   Annette L. Tyler, born Nov. 15, 1852; married, Oct.

19, 1872, Robert A. Hillson, a cabinet maker of North Leominster; one child who died young.

5383   Hattie Celeste Tyler, born Sept. 7, 1856; married, Mar. 31, 1897, W. G. Dudley, of Leominster; she was a teacher; was graduated from the New England Conservatory of Music in Boston; he is on the board of assessors in Leominster.

2729   MARY L.[7] TYLER (Ancill[6]), born in Lancaster, Mass.; married January 3, 1842, George Washington Allen, of Woburn, Mass., born there January 28, 1814; son of George Cheney Allen.   They lived in Woburn, where the children were born.   Children:

5384   Montressor Tyler Allen, born May 20, 1843; married, June 22, 1865, Julia Peasley, of Woburn.
5385   Mary Elizabeth Allen, born Jan. 7, 1845.
5386   George A. Allen, born Aug. 7, 1847.
5387   Marcellus Houghton Allen, born Jan. 6, 1849.
5388   Jane Tyler Allen, born June 7, 1852.
5388a   Emma Mabel Allen, born Dec. 22, 1854.
5389   Etta Josephine Allen, born July 5, 1857.

2730   ABRAHAM[7] TYLER (Ancill[6]), born in Lunenburg, Mass.; married (1), Lizzie Kendall, daughter of John and Mary Kendall, of Marlboro, Mass., married (2), January 29, 1855, Nancy E. Capen, of Lunenburg; daughter of Henry and Relief (Tyler) Capen No. 2722.   In 1898 was residing in Marlboro, where the children were born.

CHILDREN, by first marriage:
5390   Mary Elizabeth Tyler; died 1898; married Leonard Wheeler, of Hudson, Mass.; she had ten children, five sons and five daughters.
5391   Lucy Levine Tyler; married Rufus Stratton, of Hudson, Mass.; had one daughter (Mertice G.).
5392   John Tyler; died in childhood.
5393   Emma J. Tyler; married (1), Henry M. Sells, of Marlboro; married (2), William A. Heald, of Boston, Mass.   In 1898 was living s. p.
5394   Ella Ray Tyler; married Clarence Page, of Boston; had two sons (Edgar and Harry).

5395   Josephine Tyler; died in childhood.
5396+   Frederick Bates Tyler.

CHILDREN, by second marriage:
5397   Willie Tyler; died young.
5398   Frank Tyler; died young.
5399   Henry Tyler; died young.
5400   Sarah Tyler; married (1), H. Lewis Clark, of Fre-
        leighburg, Can.; married (2), Irvin Gates, of Hud-
        son; two children by first marriage (Carl A. and
        Fred).
5401   Martha Adelaide Tyler; died young.
5402   George Houghton Tyler; died young.

2731 JAMES PERKINS[7] TYLER (Ancill[6]), born in
Lancaster, Mass., 1818; died of heart disease in Woburn, Mass.,
July 19, 1881; married Louisa L. ——. Child:
5403   Henriette L. Tyler, born in Woburn, Oct. 16, 1846;
        died April 14, 1849.

2732 MOSES AUGUSTUS[7] TYLER (Ancill[6]), born in
Lancaster, Mass., 1820; died in Woburn, Mass., July 16, 1885;
married, December 8, 1842, Sarah Merrill Allen, of Woburn,
born June 27, 1824; daughter of George Cheney and Lois Allen. The children were born in Woburn. Children:
5404+   Albert A. Tyler, born Aug. 5, 1843.
5405   Daughter, born Oct. 7, 1851; probably died young.
5406+   Cora Merrill Tyler, born May 14, 1859.

2736 FRANCIS[7] TYLER (Ancill[6]), born in Lancaster,
Mass.; married, May 31, 1858, Hannah B. Tasker, of Woburn.
Children:
5407   Mary Elizabeth Tyler, born in Woburn, Mass., Dec. 3,
        1860.

2737 ELLEN L.[7] TYLER (Ancill[6]), born in Lancaster,
Mass.; married, October 8, 1860, Samuel R. French, of Woburn,
where the children were born. Children:
5408   Emma Louisa French, born June 27, 1862.
5409   Arthur French, born Jan. 6, 1865.
5410   Lewis French, born Sept. 6, 1872.

5411   Carl Clifton French, born Sept. 6, 1876.
5412   Lena French, born Aug. 29, 1879.

2738   CLARA A.[7] TYLER (Ancill[6]), born in Lancaster, Mass.; married, August 31, 1871, Charles W. Fifield, of Woburn, where the children were born.   Children:
5413   Mary Tyler Fifield, born January 6, 1873.
5414   Edith Fifield, born March 21, 1875.
5415   Gracie M. Fifield, born November 17, 1878.
5416   Gertrude Adella Fifield, born September 30, 1883.
5417   Charles W. Fifield, born November 9, 1890.

2742   DOCTOR JOHN[7] TYLER (Asa Peabody[6]), born in Rome, N. Y., November 14, 1803; died there, in November, 1867; married March 20, 1829, Catherine Sheldon, born September 11, 1807; died in 1868.   Children:
5418   Lois Cornelia Tyler; died in infancy.
5419+   Cyrus H. Tyler.
5420+   Henry H. Tyler, born August 1, 1831.
5421   Eliza Tyler; married, J. D. Ely of Rome, N. Y. and had one son who died aged about 12 years.

2744   JONATHAN WALDO[7] TYLER (Asa Peabody[6]) born in Rome, N. Y. June 25, 1807; died February 7, 1874; married, February 20, 1838, Theodosia Babcock.   He was a farmer.   Children;
5422   Caroline Tyler.
5423   Seraphine Tyler.

2746   DOCTOR ANSEL[7] TYLER (Asa Peabody[6]), born in Rome, N. Y., October 14, 1811; married November 13, 1836, Catherine C. Larkin; resided in New Hartford, N. Y. Children:
5424   Sarah Tyler.
5425   Ansinette Tyler.
5426   Clarence A. Tyler; married and has one child; resides in Alden, N. Y.

2747   ALBERT[7] TYLER (Asa Peabody[6]), born in Rome, N. Y., December 3, 1813; married April 1, 1838, Eliza

Milks, born June 19, 1818. He is a farmer; moved to Lock-port, Ill. Children:

5427   James W. Tyler, born September 21, 1839; resided in Morris, Ill.

5428   Frances O. Tyler, born February 11, 1842.

5429   Mary E. Tyler, born February 13, 1844.

5430   Asa N. Tyler, born June 10, 1847.

5431   Alice A. Tyler, born August 22, 1850.

2748   SARAH[7] TYLER (Asa Peabody[6]), born in Rome, N. Y. October 29, 1815; died May 2, 1870; married (1), December 15, 1836, James W. Cadwell; married (2), February 20, 1840, John Golly of Lee, N. Y.

CHILD, by first marriage:

5432   Julia W. Cadwell.

CHILDREN, by second marriage:

5433   Asa Tyler Golly.

5434   Ann Eliza Golly.

5435   Mary C. Golly.

5436   Henry H. Golly.

2749   DOCTOR ASA NORTON[7] (or Newton) TYLER (Asa Peabody[6]), born in Rome, N. Y., June 10, 1818; died in New Hartford, N. Y. September 15, 1889; married (1), June 22, 1848, Mary A. Richardson born in New Hartford March 29, 1829, died September 5, 1854; married (2), June 26, 1856, Jennie M. Carpenter of Huntington Center, Vt., who was living in 1899. He was a physician of the Eclectic School; practiced five years with his brother Ansel in Sauquoit, N. Y. and then went to Hartford, N. Y., where he practiced over 40 years. The children were born in New Hartford. Children:

5437   Nathan R. Tyler, born August 2, 1849; died September 12, 1849.

5438   Herbert N. Tyler, born October 19, 1850; lived in New Hartford in 1899, unmarried.

2751   MARY FOSTER[7] TYLER (Joshua[6]), born in West Newbury, Mass. January 11, 1801; died in Lowell, Mass. January 16, 1892; married, 1834, William Ross. Children:

5439   Mary Jane Ross, born June 23, 1835; married July 1, 1860, Ward S. Dudley of Lowell, who died there October 4, 1898. He was originally from Maine; in 1901 she was living in Lowell; had four children who died young.

5440   Caroline Maria Ross, born April 11, 1838; married William R. Jameson of Newburyport, born in 1830; died 1898; they lived in Lowell; had a son and daughter.

5441   Charlotte Frances Ross, born Oct. 30, 1840; married David L. Watson; they live in San Jose, Cal.; had two sons and a daughter.

5442   Child, died in infancy.

2762 CHARLOTTE AUGUSTA[7] TYLER (Bradstreet Jr.[6]), born in Boxford, Mass. December 5, 1833; died in 1867; married (1), 1857, Charles Pearl; married (2) George B. Austin.

CHILD, by first marriage:

5443   Edward Everett Pearl, born February 12, 1858; married, September, 1879, Catherine Killam; had a family.

CHILD, by second marriage:

5444   Charles F. Austin, born 1867; unmarried in 1896.

2764 ELIZA[7] TYLER (Joshua Jr.[6]), born in Leominster, Mass., October 8, 1806; died March 14, 1878; married April 8, 1830, Edward Hartwell of Leominster, Mass., born September 10, 1807; died June 3, 1873. In 1830 he removed to Blue Grass, Ill.; in 1834 to Lafayette, Ind., where he was a farmer. Children:

5445   Sarah Hartwell, born 1831; died young.

5446   Charlotte A. Hartwell, died young.

5447   Elizabeth Hartwell, born November 30, 1840; married, October 16, 1860, William McC. Tenney of Zanesville, O. He was a cattle-drover and lived in Hoopeston, Ill.; had one daughter.

5448   Mary E. Hartwell, born July 30, 1844; married, December 9, 1891, Henry T. Perry. In 1879 went as missionary and teacher to Siam and returned in 1884; lectured; in 1901 lived in Turkey in Asia.

2776 JOEL J.[7] TYLER (Thomas[6]), born in Jaffrey, N. H. June 7, 1823; married July 18, 1850, Sarah Green of Lunenburg, Mass. Child:

5449   Joel G. Tyler, born March 8, 1855; married, November 20, 1883, Alice G. Crosby.

2784 HANNAH FLINT[7] TYLER (Flint[6]), born in Bradford, Mass. June 17, 1817; died June 17, 1895; married Charles F. Kimball of West Boxford, Mass., born September 3, 1818; died July 4, 1883. The children were born in West Boxford. Children:

5450   Mary J. Kimball, born March 21, 1841.
5451   Charles N. Kimball, born September 17, 1843.
5452   Walter B. Kimball, born December 19, 1846.
5453   Ella M. Kimball, born July 7, 1849.
5454   Carrie L. Kimball, born Sept. 20, 1856.
5455   George E. Kimball, born July 28, 1858.
5456   Frank E. Kimball, born December 8, 1861.

2785 AARON PARKER[7] TYLER (Flint[6]), born in Wilton, N. H. November 9, 1819; died in Boxford, Mass., 1846; married, Susan Simonds Kimball of Bradford, Mass.; she married (2) Jacob Bartlett of Haverhill, Mass., where she died. Child:

5457+   Henry Parker Tyler, born in Boxford, Mass., February 22, 1846.

2800 PARKER[7] TYLER (Parker Jr.[6]), born in Jaffrey, N. H. July 15, 1820; died of apoplexy in Fitchburg, Mass., April 17, 1895; married, April 16, 1845, Milly Whitcomb. The children were born in Leominster, Mass. Children:

5458   Abbie Tyler, married Andrew Stetson of Whitman, Mass.
5459   John Albion Whitcomb Tyler, born July 17, 1856; married; lives in Chelsea, Mass.
5460   Wesley Whitcomb Tyler, born July 7, 1862; died in Leominster September 19, 1862.

2801 ISAAC MATSON[7] TYLER (Parker Jr.[6]), born in Jaffrey, N. H., September 8, 1822; died of apoplexy in Leominster, Mass., September 25, 1894; married (1) Susan Cranston of Cranston,, R. I.; married (2) Mrs. Mary (Sloan) Adams, born 1835; died in Leominster, Mass., December 15, 1895; daughter of Peter and Nancy Sloan. The children of the first marriage were born in Leominster; those of the second in Lunenburg, Mass. The four younger children all live in Leominster.

CHILDREN, by first marriage:

5461+ George Fontenelle Tyler, born April 25, 1849.
5462   Charles Eldores Tyler, born May, 1851; died in Leominster June 9, 1878.
5463   Emma Tyler, married George Powell of Townsend, Vt., five children.
5464   Ida Tyler, married William Pratt of North Leominster; four children.

CHILDREN, by second marriage:

5465+ Abel Nelson Tyler, born September 9, 1858.
5466   Mary Tyler.
5467   Henry Tyler.
5468   Lulu Tyler.
5469   Charles Tyler

2803   JOHN PIERCE[7] TYLER (Parker Jr.[6]), born in Jaffrey, N. H., February 18, 1826; died of blood poisoning September 7, 1857; married, May 21, 1851, Mary Antoinette Spaulding, who died February 19, 1860, aged 30. He went to California in 1849. He was a casket-maker. The eldest child was born in Townsend, Mass. Children:

5470   Eudora Imogene Tyler, born July 6, 1856; died March 16, 1858.
5471   Addie E. Tyler, married in 1871, James Gibson of Townsend, who was a farmer and cooper; no children.

2804   ALBERT[7] TYLER (Parker Jr.[6]), born Jaffrey, N. H., February 18, 1828; living in Northboro, Mass., in 1896; married (1) Sarah Livingston, who died in Leominster, Mass., October 1, 1854, aged 21; married (2), Emily Daboll of Lancaster, Mass. The children were born in Northboro.

CHILD, by first marriage:
5472 Infant, died.

CHILDREN, by second marriage:
5473 Etta Tyler, born 1857; married Sargent Faber of Northboro, Mass., who died about 1892.
5474 Elinor Tyler, born 1862; married Elmer Chase of Leominster.
5475 Harry L. Tyler, born 1870; lives in Boston, Mass.

2805 ARVILLA ANNE[7] TYLER (Parker Jr.[6]) born in Lunenburg, Mass., January 11, 1831; married, February 6, 1852, Benjamin M. Spaulding of Leominster, Mass., born 1825. He was in the Civil War four years in the 32d Mass. Ambulance Corps. They lived in Townsend, Groton and Ayer, Mass. Children:
5476 Nellie Anna Spaulding, born in Groton, Mass., April 23, 1858; married, April 4, 1878, Stephen Tyler of Townsend, No. 2841.
5477 Bertha Rush Spaulding, born in Townsend October 15, 1860; died April 3, 1862.
5478 Edith Lincoln Spaulding, born June 17, 1866; died April 19, 1892, unmarried; was an organist; attended the Lawrence Academy in Groton.

2810 JOSEPH AUGUSTUS[7] TYLER (Seth Payson[6]), born in Leominster, Mass., December 20, 1830; married, July 3, 1855, Polly N. Noyes of Leominster, born April 5, 1835, daughter of Stephen and Betsey Little of Warren, N. H. The children were born in Leominster. Children:
5479 Sarah Elizabeth Tyler, born May 16, 1856; married, November 26, 1881, Henry R. Davis.
5480 Bemis Augustus Tyler, born May 18, 1862; died February 23, 1866.
5481 Herbert H. Tyler, born February 14, 1864; died August 3, 1864.
5482+ Charles Payson Tyler, born September 5, 1865; married, Cora A. Derby.
5483 Wendell N. Tyler, born November 21, 1869; died September 29, 1870.

5484   Jennie Maud Tyler, born January 19, 1873; died March 8, 1890; an adopted daughter.

2814 MARY FRANCES[7] TYLER (Putnam[6]), born in Milford, N. H., December 12, 1845; married Frank Cram of St. Louis, Mo., who died in Carthage, Tex., February 8, 1900; he was an advertising agent in Ayer County, Lowell, Mass. The four elder children were born in Milford. Children:

5485   Stella F. Cram, married, February 7, 1888, Clarence E. Quimby, son of Professor S. E. Quimby, of Tilton, N. H.; was graduated from the New Hampshire Conference Seminary in 1886; an optician; four children (Raymond, Chester, Conrad and Christine).

5486   William E. Cram, born August 7, 1867; married, November 22, 1893, Mary H. Blick, of Roxbury, Mass.; three children (Donald, Mildred and Esther).

5487   Myrtie May Cram, born July 6, 1870; died August 4, 1871.

5488   Albert M. Cram, born June 12, 1872; married, June 20, 1894, Ada J. Eastman of Sunapee, N. H.; three sons (Earl, Frank and Neil).

5489   Edna L. Cram, born in Hillsboro, N. H., July 21, 1878.

5490   Agnes M. Cram, born in Antrim, N. H., April 4, 1884.

2815 ALMON PUTNAM[7] TYLER (Putnam[6]), born in Milford, N. H., June 27, 1847; married (1), January 1, 1870, Edna F. Cram who died March 24, 1871; married (2), December 31, 1877, Rose M. Smith. He is a farmer and resides in Sullivan, N. H., where the children of the second marriage were born.

CHILD, by first marriage:
5491   Bessie L. Tyler, born in Marlow, N. H., November 18, 1870; died August 24, 1872.

CHILDREN, by second marriage:
5492   Andrew A. Tyler, born May 20, 1879.
5493   Bessie E. N. Tyler, born November 8, 1884; died November 17, 1889.

5494   Mildred Edith Tyler, born April 28, 1886; died August 19, 1886.
5495   Willie A. Tyler, born March 20, 1889.

2816   JULIA ELLEN[7] TYLER (Putnam[6]), born in Milford, N. H., July 11, 1849; married, February 7, 1872, Austin A. Ellis a manfuacturer in Keene, N. H.   He is a member of the City Council and President of the Young Men's Christian Association.   In 1900 was Mayor of Keene; deacon of First Congregational church.   Their child was born in Sullivan.   Child:
5496   Myrtle E. Ellis, born September 14, 1875; married May 20, 1897, George B. Robertson of Keene, N. H.; entered Smith College in 1894; has one son (Ellis) and a daughter (Mary).

2821   FREDERIC CHARLES[7] TYLER (Putnam), born in Marlow, N. H. January 20, 1862; married August 4, 1892, Emma C. Pierce of Cleveland, O.   Was a machinist in a bicycle factory in Cleveland where the children were born.   Children:
5497   Leslie Pierce Tyler, born December 4, 1893.
5498   Charles Lawrence Tyler, born July 15, 1895.

2829   LEVI ANDREW[7] TYLER (Levi[6]), born probably in Wilton, N. H. April 17, 1828; died August 20, 1884; married (1), December 24, 1853, Hannah D. Curtis of Lyndeboro, N. H.; married (2), ——, Mrs. Frances A. Beales.   He lived in Lyndeboro and Wilton.

CHILDREN, by first marriage:
5499   Isabella V. Tyler, born January 27, 1855; married Jerome B. Shedd of Peterboro, N. H.; no children.
5500   Anna V. Tyler, born May 28, 1859; died February 5, 1897, unmarried.
5501+   Olivia Tyler, born in Lyndeboro July 15, 1868.

2831   EMMA F.[7] TYLER (Levi[6]), born in Wilton, N. H., June 17, 1834; married, November 19, 1854, Charles Tarbell of Wilton, and Lyndeboro, N. H., who died April 2, 1896; he was a selectman in Lyndeboro.   Children:

5502   Nelo W. Tarbell, born in Wilton October 25, 1855;
        married Anna Livermore Kimball; and has a family.
5503   Fred W. Tarbell, born July 21, 1870; married in
        Brooklyn, N. H., July 29, ——, Emma C. Foster;
        has a family.

2841 STEPHEN A.[7] TYLER (Asa[6]), born in Townsend, Mass., April 13, 1846; married (1) November 25, 1867,
Addie A. Lawrence of Fitchburg, Mass., who died December
14, 1876, aged 29 years, 5 months; married (2), April 4,
1878, Nellie Spaulding, No. 5476, of Ayer, Mass., born in
Groton, Mass., April 23, 1858; died December 25, 1883; daughter of Benjamin and Arvilla A. (Tyler) Spaulding; she was
an organist; married (3), February 21, 1885, Mrs. Harriet
Adams of Tilton, N. H.   He was a stone cutter and was in
business in Townsend, Mass., Keene, N. H. and East Pepperell, Mass.   He was in Alaska in 1898 and 1899, and then
settled in Seattle, Wash., where he pursued his trade.   All
the children were born in Townsend except the 3d.

CHILDREN, by first marriage:
5504+   Mary Gertrude Tyler, born May 25, 1868.
5505+   Alice F. Tyler, born January 14, 1871.
5506   Laura M. Tyler, born in Keene, N. H., September 14,
        1873; married, April 25, 1893, Charles Holden who
        died in North Adams, Mass., November, 1894; she
        lives in Fitchburg.
5507   Addie L. Tyler, born December 5, 1876; married Feb-
        ruary 14, 1899, Albert M. Wilder of Ashby, Mass.,
        who is a wood turner.
CHILD, by second marriage:
5508   Nellie Tyler, born November 2, 1883; died July, 1884.

2842 AARON PARKER[7] TYLER (Asa[6]), born in
Townsend, Mass., May 31, 1850; died there August 25, 1885;
married January 1, 1872, Mary F. Seva of Townsend, born
there 1850; daughter of Augustus Seva; when a widow she married (2), June 9, 1889, John W. Roush and moved to Kendrick,
Idaho.   He was a cooper and removed to Sandusky, O., thence
to Chicago, Ill., where he was in a music store; he was a musician.   Children:

5509+ Harry Asa Tyler, born in Townsend January 20, 1877.

5510 John Edward Tyler, born in Chicago, September 28, 1882.

2847 CAPTAIN PHINEAS LOVEJOY[7] TYLER, (Nathan Peabody[6]), born in Blenheim, N. Y., January 29, 1809; died at the residence of his daughter, Mrs. Colby, in Bergenfields, N. J., January 16, 1896; married, June 30, 1831, Jane Ann Waldron, of Honesdale, Pa., a great-granddaughter of Baron William von Waldron, one of the original eighteen Dutch settlers in Harlem, N. Y. In 1828 he moved to Honesdale, where he bought land and opened a lumber business. In 1836 he went to Missouri and took up 6000 acres of land. In 1836 he returned, at the urgent solicitation of his father, to assume the captaincy of the passenger and freight service between Barrytown, N. Y., and New York city, in which position he remained until 1859, when the firm of Tyler and Sons retired from active business. This business was founded in 1790 and was conducted under the name of N. P. Tyler & Sons, and they did a very large freighting business from Barrytown. Captain Tyler was widely known, the personal friend of many men who have made national history; his integrity and affability won friends for him everywhere. He was a cousin of George Peabody, the philanthropist, and was related to many of the best-known families who sprung from New England soil. He resided during the latter part of his life with his daughter in Bergenfields. The three elder children were born in Honesdale; the two younger in Barrytown. Children:

5510a Henry Oscar Tyler, born March 20, 1832, died October 16, 1840.

5510b George Calvert Tyler, born March 8, 1834: died August 5, 1835.

5510c Mary Elizabeth Tyler, born January 21, 1836; married, November 15, 1881, D. C. Whyte; no children.

5511+ George Calvert Tyler, born in Missouri, November 20, 1839.

5512 Henry Leavenworth Tyler, born in Missouri, January 8, 1843; died March 11, 1906, unmarried.

5513 Harriet Ida Tyler, born December 15, 1845; died August 19, 1876; married, December 15, 1868, D. C. Whyte; no children.

5514+ Nathan Peabody Tyler, born October 11, 1848.

2849 ISABELLA MARIA[7] TYLER (Asa[6]), born in Holland Patent, N. Y. September 25, 1816; married May, 1842, Timothy Williston.   Children:

5515   Seth Williston.
5516   Mary Williston.
5517   Melville Horn Williston; lives in Manchester, Ia.
5518   John Williston, died young.
5519   John Williston.
5520   Timothy Williston, was drowned.

2850 HELEN JENETTE[7] TYLER (Asa[6]), born in Holland Patent, N. Y., October 15, 1818; married February 15, 1837, Nathan Haskins Townsend of St. Joseph, Mich. The three younger children were born in Vienna, N. Y.   Children:

5521   Mary H. Townsend, born in Floyd, N. Y., 1840; died 1866; married, 1863, Peter F. Benson; one son died young.
5522   Nathan T. Townsend, born 1842; married, 1867, Annie Willis of St. Paul, Minn.; two sons (Nathan T. and Frank W.) and two daughters (Maud M. and Edith R.)
5523   Caroline J. Townsend, born 1846; died 1874; married, 1868, Edgar Bartlett; one son (Frederick E.).
5524   Charles H. Tyler Townsend, born 1863; married, 1889 Caroline Hesse; lives in El Paso, Tex.; one son (Carl H.) and a daughter (Helen).

2851 HARRIETTE AUGUSTA[7] TYLER (Asa[6]), born in Holland Patent, N. Y., July 27, 1821; married, November 30, 1842, Chauncey Watson of Middleburg, N. Y.

CHILDREN:

5525   Cora Watson, married Charles Chatfield; they have three sons and a daughter (Arthur, Walter, Charles and Nellie).   Her eldest son was the Yale " class baby," 1866.

5526   E. Arthur Watson, married Lottie Coney.
5527   Helen Watson, married John Cornwall.
5528   Isabella Watson.

2852   JEROME B.[7] TYLER (Asa[6]), born in Holland
Patent, N. Y., December 9, 1823; lived in Tylerdene, West Va.;
married, August 5, 1851, Mary Elizabeth Cadwell, daughter of
Daniel G. Cadwell, (descended from Thomas Cadwell, who
was in Hartford in 1652; in 1812 Daniel resided in Washington, D. C.).   Children:
5529   Frederick C. Tyler.
5530   Charles Cadwell, was graduated, A. B. Yale College;
        LL. M. Columbia Law School; collector of Internal
        Revenue under McKinley and Roosevelt; interested
        in apple orchards of " Tyderlene " the largest found
        east of the Mississippi river.
5531   Caroline C. Tyler was graduated from Wellesley Col-
        lege.

2856   FRANCES LATHROP[7] TYLER (Asa[6]), born in
Holland Patent, N. Y., August 21, 1839; died February 7,
1880; married, 1857, John Milton Holmes of Yale.   Children:
5532   Eunice Carter Holmes, lives in Oakland, Cal.
5533   Mary Bridgman Holmes, died young.
5534   John Milton Holmes, lived in Oakland, Cal., and has
        two children.

2866   WILLIAM[7] TYLER (Nathaniel[6]), born in Bethel,
Me., January 23, 1819, married (1), March 24, 1846, Sarah
Martin, who died November, 1867; married (2), March 1,
1873, Dolly Paine of Mason, Mass.; they reside in West Bethel.
The children were born in Bethel, except the youngest.

CHILDREN, by first marriage:
5535   Madison Monroe Tyler, born June 11, 1848; died
        April 18, 1874 s. p.
5536   Joseph Allen Tyler, born June 9, 1850; died April 7,
        1898 s. p.

CHILD, by second marriage:
5537   Fritz J. Tyler, born in Albany, Me., December, 26,
        1873; married November 17, 1896, Grace Bartlett.

2868 JONATHAN[7] TYLER (Nathaniel[6]), born January 1, 1822; died January 5, 1899; married in Bethel, Me., December 31, 1845, Elizabeth L. Hall, born February 14, 1829, of Denmark, Me., daughter of Kimball Hall; resides in Bethel, where the children were born.   Children:

5538   Eunice H. Tyler, born June 26, 1847; married Almon T. Littlehale who died March 24, 1890; had several children; all died but son (William) who was with‘ the Army in Cuba in the Spanish war.

5539   Delia Tyler, born March 4, 1851; married George A. Murphy; resides in West Bethel, Me.; one child.

5540   Calista J. Tyler, born October 10, 1852; died June 27, 1863.

5541   Isabella R. Tyler, born June 16, 1855; married Sewall J. Walker, who died October 13, 1891.

5542   Ammi M. Tyler, born July 7, 1857; married Annie C. Gilbert, who died December 18, 1884.

5543   Mary C. Tyler, born July 25, 1859; married Charles Walker; has a family and resides in South Paris, Me.

5544   James Grant Tyler, born April 19, 1864; married April 8, 1886, Maud Rose Verrill, born February 27, 1870; has two children and resides in Snow Falls, Me.; is a carpenter.

5545   (Dr.) John Adams Tyler, twin to James; died November 30, 1896, unmarried; in 1891 was in the University of Vermont.

5546   Almon Bert Tyler, born April 7, 1869; resides with his mother; unmarried.

2872 LEWIS[7] TYLER (Nathaniel[6]), born in Bethel, Me., November 24, 1831; married, in 1863, Ellen May Murphy; residing in 1899 in West Bethel.   The children were probably born in Bethel.   Children:

5547   Flora A. Tyler, born May 19, 1865; married Everett T. Dresser of Lyndon, Vt.; had two sons and a daughter (Elvin E., Alvah E., and Inez A.)

5548   Willard E. Tyler, born March 1, 1871; married Annie Kenerson of Albany, Me.

5549   George C. Tyler, born June 24, 1873.

5550   Bertha A. Tyler, born February 8, 1875; married
        Leonard A. Sumner of West Bethel.
5551   Alfreda M. Tyler, born September 17, 1883.

2873   SAMUEL F.[7] TYLER (Jonathan[6]), born in Windsor, Me., January 20, 1810; died in South Cushing, Me., April 13, 1880; buried in Windsor, Me.; married (1), —— Coburn; married (2), in 1850, Sarah Teel of South Cushing who survived him and married (2), Levi Seavey who administered her Tyler husband's estate.

CHILDREN, by first marriage:
5552   Clarissa Tyler.
5553   Elbridge Tyler.

2874   ASA F.[7] TYLER (Jonathan[6]), born in Windsor, Me., February 8, 1811; died there, his will dated June 3, 1859; married, January 1829, Cynthia Merrill, born February 29, 1812. The children were born in Windsor. Children:
5554   Olive Tyler, born February 23, 1839; died October 29, 1848.
5555+   Rev. Orrin Tyler, born May 15, 1841.
5556   Christiana Tyler, born November 25, 1843; died October 7, 1845.
5557   Maria Tyler, born April 6, 1846; died July 22, 1850.
5558   Olive Tyler, born August 9, 1849; died July 28, 1850.
5559   Frank Tyler, born February 16, 1853; married Ella Longfellow; they had one son (Frank).
5560   Ellen Tyler, born January 2, 1856; married George Fairfield of Fairfield, Me.; had a son and daughter (George and Ethel).

2875   JOSHUA[7] TYLER (Jonathan[6]), born in Windsor, Me., September 12, 1812; died there March 21, 1889; married, in China, Me., July 20, 1851, Elizabeth Erskins, born in China, Me., February 23, 1833; resided in China, Me. The children were born in China. Children:
5561+   Ella Maria Tyler born July 15, 1853.
5562+   Henry Johnson Tyler, born July 3, 1857.
5563   Mary Elizabeth Tyler, born June 30, 1864; married

September 12, 1883, Gilbert Herrick, a harness maker; resides in Augusta, Me.

2879   MARY[7] TYLER (Jonathan[6]), born in Windsor, Me.; married James Libby of Clinton, Me., July 29, 1841; moved in 1869 to Patten, Me.   Children:

5564   Elias T. Libby, born in 1842; resides in Patten, Me.
5565   James O. Libby, born in 1845; has a family.
5566   Hanscon L. Libby, born in 1849.
5567   Daughter.

2882   BETSEY[7] TYLER (Jonathan[6]), born in Windsor, Me., about 1824; died about 1887; married Walter Stuart. The children were born in Windsor, Me.   Children:

5568   Levi Stuart.
5569   Aurilla Stuart; married ——— Haskell; has four children.
5570   Ira Stuart; married ——— Briggs; has one child.
5571   Henry Stuart.
5572   Giles A. Stuart, born in 1850; resides in New Britain, Conn., and in 1899 was superintendent of schools; married ——— Fuller; had two children; a son (Fred E.) a sergeant at Santiago, died in 1898 in Cuba.

2883   ELEAZER[7] TYLER (Jonathan[6]), born in Windsor, Me.: died in Vienna, Me.; married (1), Wealthy Merrill of Windsor, Me.; married (2), Lydia M. Fowls of Whitefield, Me. The children were all born in China, Me., except the two eldest who were born in Windsor.

CHILDREN, by first marriage:

5573   Elias Tyler, born November 18, 1841; killed at the battle of Gettysburg, Pa., July 3, 1863; unmarried.
5574   Angie Tyler, born July 12, 1844; died May 12, 1866, s. p.; married November 18, 1863, Alonzo H. Getchell.
5575+ Annie Tyler, born February 17, 1847.
5576   Farewell Tyler, born March 25, 1850; died
5577   Russell Tyler, born March 27, 1852; died.
5578   Mary E. Tyler, born May 3, 1854; died.
5579   Elbridge Tyler, born February 7, 1856; died.

CHILDREN, by second marriage:

5580   Daughter, died in infancy.

5581   Gardiner Tyler, resides in Waterville, Me.

5582   Sadie M. Tyler; married John A. Spear; resides in
Gardiner, Me.

2885   HANNAH SLADE[7] TYLER (Ebenezer[6]), born
in Sidney, Me., May 3, 1815; died February 18, 1900; married April 23, 1840, James Madison Sinclair, born in Brent-
wood, N. H., March 26, 1814. The children were born in
Monmouth, Me. Children:

5583   Hartron Dolton Sinclair, born February 26, 1843;
died in Maryland Hospital, May 26, 1865; was clerk
in provost marshall's office, Boston; enlisted in the
2nd Mass. cavalry in Civil war.

5584   Henry M. Sinclair, born March 1, 1848; married, October 22, 1877, Abbie Proctor Norton of Essex,
Mass.; resides in Salem, Mass; a clothier; s. p. in
1898.

5585   Charles Roscoe Sinclair, born August 17, 1849, died
in Monmouth, Me., September, 1865.

5586   James Ellery Sinclair, born February 1, 1857; married September, 1877, Elmer F. Whiting of Bruns-
wick, Me.; two daughters (Florence and Pearl).

2886   REBECCA W.[7] TYLER (Ebenezer[6]), born in
Augusta, Me., July 4, 1816; died in Monmouth, Me., August
12, 1889; married (1), April 12, 1839, Joseph Sylvester, of
Turner, Me.; married (2), March 1, 1855, Daniel Weymouth
a farmer of Monmouth, Me., born in 1814; died September 12,
1887.

CHILD, by first marriage:

5587   Mary Eliza Sylvester, born in Portland, Me., May 8,
1842; died September 18, 1866; unmarried.

CHILD, by second marriage:

5588   Orra A. Weymouth, born in Monmouth, Me., August
19, 1857; married (1) Oliver H. Frost; married (2)
Warren J. Potter, a farmer; had one son (Arthur)

by first marriage and a son (Lawrence) and daughter (Ethel) by second marriage.

2899   JULIA ANN[7] TYLER (Thomas Sherlock[6]), born in Belgrade, Me., November 19, 1823; married, February 10, 1842, in Vassalboro, Me., Silas Farnham. The children were born in Hallowell, Me., except the eldest and the fifth. Children:

5589   Hiram Augustus Farnham, born in Vassalboro, Me., February 15, 1843; died January 19, 1901; a farmer unmarried.

5590   Hannah Jane Farnham, born April 28, 1845; died August 18, 1864.

5591   Vesta Boena Farnham, born May 5, 1848; married George Washington Morgan; eight children (Charles, George, Robert, Walter, Clarence, Susan, Laura, Percy).

5592   Joseph Hubbard Farnham, born December 28, 1851; died August 16, 1852.

5593   Josephine Elmira Farnham, born in Chelsea, Me., September, 1853; married (1) William Livingston who died in Milwaukee, Wis.; married (2), William Sibley of Chelsea. Me.; a daughter (Maud).

5594   Anverlene Augusta Farnham, born April 13, 1855; married Robert McKay, soldier in the Civil war; died in Chelsea, 1884; three children (Catherine, Julia and Robert).

5595   Susan Maria Farnham, born September 18, 1857; died March 16, 1879; married Patrick Hayes.

5596   Elmira Adelaide Farnham, born March 25, 1861; died October 7, 1866.

5597   Orrin E. Tyler Farnham, born October 11, 1864; married (1) Anna Barker; married (2) Mary E. Stinson; one child (Harriet) by first marriage.

2900   ELIZA ANNA[7] TYLER (Thomas Sherlock[6]), born in Sidney, Me., June 1, 1826; married, April 13, 1851, in Hallowell, Me., William S. Dorr of Gardiner, Me., born October 9, 1829; a farmer. The children were born in Chelsea, Me., except the eldest. Children:

5598   Sumner Marcellus Dorr, born in Hallowell, Me., October 26, 1851; married Maggie E. Russell; resides in Pittston, Me.; three children (Sumner O. T., Nettina E. and Lizzie I.).

5599   Eliza Violet Dorr, born November 23, 1853; married Ruell Bram; four children (Arthur, Wilford T., Alice and Nellie).

5600   Elizabeth Anna Dorr, born December 17, 1855; married John Franklin Lunt; two children (Ernest A. T., and Mertie).

5601   Caroline Chenery Dorr, born December 8, 1857; married William Henry Knox; one son (Percy T.) and two daughters.

5602   Wilson Jackson Dorr, born February 3, 1859; married Mina Moody; three children (Ernest T., Edith and Ethel).

5603   Alice Evaline Dorr, born June 13, 1861; married Albert David Wing; two children (Leon T. and Jessie).

5604   Wilford Manson Dorr, born October 15, 1863; married Katie McNulty; one child (Mary).

2903   HARRIET E.[7] TYLER (Thomas Sherlock[6]), born in Sidney, Me., May 13, 1832; died in Chelsea, Me., September 24, 1855; married, in Hallowell, Me., June 30, 1850, George Washington White. The children were born in Chelsea, Me. Children:

5605   George Albion White, born March 17, 1852; moved to Boston, Mass.

5606   Thomas Roselven White, born June 5, 1854; died April 25, 1884.

2904   ANNIE R.[7] TYLER (Thomas Sherlock[6]), born in China, Me., September 3, 1835; married (1), in Chelsea, Me., April 5, 1855, Ruel W. Keene, who died in Reach River, Me., February 21, 1875, aged 43 years; was a sergeant in the 2d Me. cavalry in the Civil war three years; married (2), in Gardiner, Me., June 5, 1880, Charles Field, born in Sidney, Me., December 10, 1822; died in Augusta, Me., Oct. 1, 1901; son of Benjamin and Nancy (Gardiner) Field. He moved to Augusta early (married (1), in 1848, Mary C. Folsom, by whom he had nine children, three of whom survived him); was a very highly respected citizen. The two elder children were born in Vassalboro, the others in Chelsea, Me. She resides in Augusta, Me. Children:

5607   Holice Ruel Keene, born January 30, 1856; died February 14, 1856.

5608   Laforest Nuel Keene, twin to Holice; died February 14, 1856.

5609   Bessie Annie Keene, born February 5, 1857; died April 21, 1868.

5610   Ziba Herbert Keene, born July 14, 1860; married Mary A. Levitt; a sergeant in the Capital Guards, Augusta, Me.; has a son and daughter (Ruel and Jessie).

5611   Twins born June 7, 1863; died same day.

2910   DANIEL WILLARD[7] TYLER (Elias[6]), born in China, Me.; married, September 11, 1853, Dolly K. Bisbee, daughter of Horatio Bisbee. He moved from China, Me., to Gardiner, Me., and afterward to Menoken, N. D. The children were born in China, Me. Children:

5612   William T. Tyler, born July 21, 1854; resides in Menoken; has one son (Frederick).

5613   John L. Tyler, born Jan. 25, 1858; unmarried.

2912   ELIZABETH (BETSEY) JANE[7] TYLER (Joseph C.[6]), married (1), John Booden; married (2), December 21, 1861, Daniel Osborn Bennett, a farmer of Gilead, Me. In 1900 she was living in West Bethel, Me.

CHILDREN, by second marriage:

5614   Eva M. Bennett, born Jan. 15, 1870; married, Oct. 6, 1895, George E. Cruse.

5615   Willie C. Bennett, born July 25, 1871; married, July 29, 1898, Nellie B. Kendall; had one daughter (Gladys M.).

2917   ALONZO CHASE[7] TYLER (Joseph C.[6]), born in China, Me., April 11, 1836; married (1), Annie Edwards who died May 16, 1869; married (2) in Boston, Mass., Elmira Emma Baylis.

CHILD, by first marriage:

5616+   Mary Elizabeth Tyler, born in Boston, Mass., July 1, 1867.

2934 WALDEN[7] SPARHAWK (Ruth[6]), born September 12, 1812; lost at sea, 1850-53, coming from California; married (1), Mercy McFarland; married (2), Margaret Maratty of Oswego. Children by first marriage:

5616a   Permelia Ann Sparhawk, born Apr. 24, 1843; married Joe. McFarland; eight children (Dora, died 1905, married —— Nickerson; Matilda, married —— Pottle, who died; Mercy, married —— Baker; three children, *Eva, Percy, Blanche*; Bell, married —— Burnham; Jennie, married —— Davis, and died; Elmer, Frank and Grace, are unmarried and live in Portland, Me.).

5616b   Daniel Walden Sparhawk, born Apr. 1, 1845; married Nancy McClure; four children (David, Maud, Mabel and William). Lives in Bowdoinham, Me.

5616c   Melville Nathaniel Sparhawk, born July 24, 1847; three children (William, Minnie and Lena). Lives in Roxbury, Mass.

CHILD, by second marriage:

5616d   Mary Ellen Sparhawk, born Sept. 10, 1849; married (1), Horace Twitchell, of Sandy Creek, N. Y.; two children (Maggie and Roy); married (2), Zeno Sanders; two children (Ladette and Zeno). Lives in Appleton, Wis.

2936 AMBROSE RUEL[7] SPARHAWK (Ruth[6]), born March 30, 1820; married (1), Maria Greely, of Augusta, Maine; served 18 months in Civil War; married (2), in 1849, Alice Elizabeth Eastwood, of Oswego, N. Y., born April 13, 1828, at Richmond, Va., and died in Oakland, Cal., Feb. 18, 1890 Children, by first marriage:

5616e   Charles Sparhawk, born 1847, died in youth.

5616f   Carrie A. Sparhawk, born November 19, 1848.

CHILDREN, by second marriage:

5616g   William Wallace Sparhawk, born July 22, 1850, in Oswego; married (1), 1873, Luetta Hutchings, of

Augusta, born February 3, 1849; (2), Nancy Mc-
Clure, born in Hallowell, Me., March 16, 1852; died
Sept. 19, 1892, in Scotia, Neb.; (3), Fanny Barnum
Day, born December 28, 1857. Lives in Sandford,
Ida. (Two children by first marriage Rosetta and
an infant, both died; six children by second mar-
riage; William Wallace, born August 15, 1880; Ada
Ann, born Oct. 1, 1884; Frank Nathaniel, born Mar.
15, 1882; Nelson Pepperell, died in infancy; Nellie
Martha, born July 9, 1888; Georgia Olie, born Mar.
16, 1890; three children by third marriage; Martha
Myrtle, born Feb. 4, 1894; Alice Goldie, born Aug.
11, 1897; Polly Barnum, born Jan. 2, 1902).

5616h Adah Ann Sparhawk was born Mar. 10, 1853 in Oswego. Taught school until 1883, then travelled
with her invalid mother; stayed two years at the
sanitarium, Battle Creek, and lived in Nebraska, and
in Oakland, Cal., where Mrs. Sparhawk died, Feb.
18, 1890. Afterwards, while teaching in a mission
school in Alaska, Adah A. Sparhawk married J. W.
Young, also a teacher there many years. His
brother, Rev. S. Hall Young, was one of the first
missionaries in Alaska, and is still there. Mr. Young
died in Oakland, Cal., September, 16, 1905. Mrs.
Young lives in Ketchikan, Alaska.

5616i Roland Ambrose Sparhawk, born May 20, 1855, in
New Haven, N. Y.; married April 13, 1884, Effie
Axtel; ten children (Mabel Alice, born 1885; mar-
ried George Phillips; one child; Pearl, born 1887,
married Ladette Sanders, Appleton, Mich.; Charles
Edgar, born 1888; Otie Roland, born 1889; Del-
bert Ceylon, born 1892; George Nathaniel; John
Coral; Lafayette Fremont, born 1903; Blanche
Elizabeth, born 1900; Shirley Pepperell, born 1908).
Lives in Stevens Point, Wis.

5616j Minnie Myrtle Sparhawk, born Feb. 6, 1857; unmarried, in Oakland, Cal.

5616k Frank Eastwood Sparhawk, born Feb. 18, 1859; died
1894; married Ella Bateman, of New Haven, N. Y.,
born Oct. 15, 1864; one child (Floyd Adelbert, born
Dec. 30, 1884).

5616l Alice Delight Sparhawk, born Nov. 18, 1860; married (1), Lewis Bussen (2), Oliver G. Hossler of San Francisco. Lives in Land Point, Ida.

5616m Lafayette Fremont Sparhawk, born Dec. 7, 1863; married Bertha Whipp, Dec. 6, 1897; at Grant's Pass, Ore. Lives in Snohomish, Wash.; seven children (Frederick Charles, born Sept. 21, 1898; Percy Nathaniel; Bertie Lafayette; Dean Ambrose; Esther Alice; Rachel Elizabeth; Adelbert C.

5616n Adelbert Ceylon Sparhawk, born June 14, 1867; died Oct. 15, 1890; was a dentist in Oakland, Cal.

5616o Charles Edgar Sparhawk, born Mar. 22, 1871; lives in Sand Point, Ida.; married, 1897, Minnie Sill, of Grant's Pass, Ore.; two children (Lynden Charles, born Sept. 16, 1898; Mildred Alice).

5616p Edward Earnest Sparhawk, married June 12, 1901, at Oakland, Cal., Martha Ann Brockhurst. He is a dentist in Oakland; was graduated from the College of Physicians and Surgeons, Dental Department, 1902, San Francisco. One child (Alvan Brockhurst, born Aug. 31, 1904).

2939 REUBEN ROLAND[7] SPARHAWK (Ruth[6]), born 1825; died 1892, in Parish, N. Y.; married (1), Apr. 27, 1851, in Augusta, Me., Rachel Billington; married (2), Jane Stevens, of Parish, N. Y. Children, by first marriage:

5616q Cynthia Sparhawk, married Perry Cole of Parish, N. Y.; three children (Daniel, Bertie, Lottie).

5616r Walden Sparhawk.

5616s Ellen Sparhawk.

Children, by second marriage:

5616t Ettie Sparhawk, married Asa Forbes; two children (Herbert and Homer died).

5616u Asa Nathaniel Sparhawk, has three children (Leo, Losena, Lester).

5616v Cora Jane Sparhawk, is deceased; married Willard Edick; two sons (Carl and Roy).

5616w Ruth Sparhawk, married, and has one child.

5616x Lillie May Sparhawk, married —— Nye; three children.

5616y   Eliza Ann Sparhawk, married —— Young; one child.

5616z   Reuben Roland Sparhawk, has two children.

5616z1   Ambrose Sparhawk, unmarried; lives in Los Angeles, Cal.

5616z2   Lottie Sparhawk, married Lyman Huntley; two children.

2947   JOHN WOODBURY[7] TYLER (John[6]), married Phoebe Thurston; lived in Albany, N. Y., where the children were born.   Children:

5617+   William Tyler.

5618   Jennie Tyler.

5619   Delia Tyler; married Thomas Paul.

5620   Lucy Tyler; died under ten years of age.

2954   JOSHUA[7] TYLER (John[6]), born in Greenbush, N. Y., died in Cleveland, O., in 1890; married Laura Burdick. Children :

5621   Oscar Tyler, born in Troy, N. Y.

5622   Allen Tyler, born in Troy, N. Y.

5623   John Tyler, born in Fall River, Mass.

5624   Laura Tyler, born in Cleveland, Ohio; died in 1877.

2958   ABBY[7] TYLER (Philip[6]), born in Charlestown, Mass., August 10, 1823; died April, 1898; married, November 16, 1845, William H. Oaks, of New York City, a printer and engraver of music.   Children:

5625   Harrison Tyler Oaks, born Nov. 9, 1846; died Sept. 5, 1847.

5626   Arthur Howard Oaks, born February, 1850; died unmarried in New York City.

2963   GEORGE EMORY[7] TYLER (Philip[6]), born in Charlestown, Mass., November 26, 1832; died October 24, 1886; married, February 20, 1857, Charlotte Augusta Cole. He enlisted in the Third Mass. Light battery in 1861 and was discharged for disability.   He was a painter.   Children:

5627   George Hunting Tyler, born July 13, 1859; died June 20, 1860.

5628+   Edith H. Tyler, born Dec. 31, 1863.

5629   Arthur B. Tyler, born Feb. 16, 1869; married (1),

Jan. 1897, Edith L. Atkins. In 1900 he lived in Somerville, Mass.

2965 THOMAS REA[7] TYLER (Philip[6]), born in Charlestown, Mass., May 6, 1837; married, September 22, 1865, Emily Francis Cole. He enlisted in the 2d Mass. Light battery, 1862-1865; was a ship carpenter, sailor and bookbinder. In 1900 he lived in College Point, L. I. Children:

5630   Harry I. Tyler, born in Lynn, Mass., June 22, 1867; died May 19, 1888, unmarried.

5631   Philip E. Tyler, born Aug. 7, 1870; was unmarried in 1900; in the rubber business.

5632   Grace May Tyler, born Oct. 1, 1872; unmarried in 1900.

2966 GEORGE SPAULDING[7] TYLER (William[6]), born in Billerica, Mass., March 20, 1830; died in South Framingham, Mass., December 22, 1891; married in Nashua, N. H., June 5, 1854, Mary Livermore Bateman Hay. The second and third children were born in Lowell, Mass. He was a locomotive engineer. Children:

5633   Emily Justina Tyler, born in Nashua, N. H., May 27, 1855.

5634   George Albert Tyler, born April 17, 1858; died in Lowell, Mass., July 7, 1863.

5635   Edmund Hay Tyler, born Jan. 8, 1865.

5636   Mary Eliza Tyler, born in Fitchburg, Mass., July 27, 1868; died in Lowell, Mass., Aug. 27, 1889; unmarried.

2967 WILLIAM[7] TYLER (William[6]), born in Billerica, Mass., February 28, 1833; married (1), in Aurora, Ill., July 23, 1861, Fannie Scott, who died in Peterboro, N. H., August 29, 1884; married (2) in Birmingham, Alabama, Sallie Haynes; may have resided in Peterboro, N. H. The children were born in Aurora.

CHILD, by first marriage:

5637   Fannie Jane Tyler, born Sept. 14, 1863.

CHILDREN, by second marriage:
5638   George Tyler.
5639   Sarah Tyler.

2976   HON. ARTEMAS STANLEY[7] TYLER (Silas[6]),
born in Middlesex Village, Mass., November 2, 1824; died in
1901; married (1), October 12, 1854, Angeline Cushing, born
January 10, 1832; died September 12, 1860; married (2), July,
17, 1862, Ethalinda Cushing, born August 14, 1834; his wives
were sisters and daughters of Stephen and Ethalinda (Edwards) Cushing, of Lowell, son of Joseph Cushing (descended
from Matthew, who emigrated to America, who was the son of
Peter and descended from Thomas of Hardingham, Norfolk
county, Eng.).   Mr. Tyler was educated in the public schools
of Lowell and became a clerk in the counting-room of a manufacturer.   After four years he went to Taunton and finally became a clerk to the cashier in the Railroad bank in Lowell.   In
five years he, with others, started the Prescott bank as a state
bank and Mr. Tyler became its first cashier.   In 1854 he started
the Five Cents Savings bank and was made its first treasurer.
For seventeen years he had charge of both banks, when he resigned the Prescott bank duties and remained with the Savings
bank until March, 1894, when he retired after a banking expe-
rience of forty years.   In 1873 he was a member of the common
council of Lowell and in 1874 and 1875 he represented the city
in the Legislature.   He was a lieutenant in the " National
Highlanders," a military company organized in 1841; the members dressed in Scotch uniform and were young men of standing
in the community.   Mr. Tyler was an excellent conversational-
ist and had a fine memory.   The children were born in Lowell.

CHILDREN, by first marriage:
5640+   Stanley Cushing Tyler, born June 4, 1857.
5641+   Artemas Lawrence Tyler, born Sept. 7, 1860.

CHILDREN, by second marriage:
5642   Fanny Maria Tyler, born July 11, 1867; died May 21,
         1882.
5643   Ethalinda Tyler, born Sept. 10, 1871; died July 19,
         1872.

2978   JULIA ANN⁷ TYLER   (William⁶), born in Chelmsford, Mass., March 12, 1851; married Charles Ernest Carter, of Lowell, Mass., where the children were born.   Children:

5644   Juliette Butterfield Carter, born Apr. 12, 1876.
5645   William Tyler Carter, born Apr. 17, 1877; died Sept. 13, 1879.
5646   Edward Ernest Carter, born Apr. 26, 1879.
5647   Joseph Warren Carter, born Jan. 21, 1882.
5648   Edith Adele Carter, born Mar. 20, 1885.
5649   Ruth Carter, born June 29, 1888.
5650   Charles Ernest Carter, Jr., born Oct. 18, 1893.

2980   FRANK IGNATIUS⁷ TYLER (Ignatius⁶), born in Lowell, Mass., August 29, 1835; married Helen E. Appleby. He is a bookkeeper and lives in Brockton, Mass.   Child:

5651   Frederick Ignatius Tyler, born in Burlington, Vt., Aug. 7, 1871; died in Lowell, unmarried.

2981   GEORGE OTIS⁷ TYLER (Ignatius⁶), born in Lowell, Mass., September 18, 1838; married Elizabeth H. Patten, of Charlestown, Mass.   He lived in Burlington, Vt.; was educated in the military academy in Norwich, Vt.; learned the lumber business; about 1880 became a member of the firm of Rolfe, Tyler & Company, of Burlington; after six or eight years he became the superintendent of the outside Burlington branch of the Shepherd Lumber Company, of Boston.   Children:

5652   Jennie Wilder Tyler, born Aug. 15, 1862; was educated in a convent in Canada; a bookkeeper in Burlington.
5653   Ignatius Tyler, born July 16, 1865; is with the Grand Trunk Railway, in Montreal, Canada.
5654   George Otis Tyler, born Aug. 10, 1867; died July 23, 1868.
5655   May Belle Tyler, born Oct. 5, 1869; a stenographer in Burlington.
5656   Bessie Maud Tyler, born July 18, 1872; married Dr. George F. Cahill, of Arlington, Mass.
5657   Roy G. Tyler, born April 26, 1874; in business in Burlington.

2995 ABRAM⁷ TYLER (James⁶), born probably in Freedom, N. H., July 6, 1818; married Mary Ann Lovering. He lived on the " Sweat " road in Freedom, N. H. Children:
5658   James Tyler.
5659   George Tyler.
5660   Martha Tyler, married Dana Allard.
5661   Eliza Tyler, married Augustus Miller.

2996 JOHN L.⁷ TYLER (James⁶), born probably in Freedom, N. H., February 19, 1821; married Hannah Harmon. He lived on "Great Hill" about one mile from Freedom Village. Child:
5662   Edson Tyler.

2997 WENTWORTH⁷ TYLER (James⁶), born probably in Freedom, N. H., October 16, 1823; married Mary Andrews of Buxton, Me., daughter of Ezekiel and Sally (Bradbury) Andrews. He lived about one mile from Freedom Village, N. H., and was a man of marked ability, a selectman, good farmer and respected citizen. Children:
5663   Franklin Tyler, married Laura Libby.
5664   Joseph H. Tyler, married Mary E. Young.
5665   Nellie J. Tyler; married Ansel Alley.
5666   James Tyler, married Rhoda Libby; lives in Boston, Mass.

2999 JAMES⁷ TYLER (Abraham⁶), born in Saco, Me., November 6, 1815; died August, 1894, aged 79 years; married Julia Ann Sawyer, born in Parsonsfield, Me., December 25, 1818; died January, 1892. They resided in Westbrook, Saco, Buxton and Hollis, Me. The third and fourth children were born in Buxton and the three youngest in Hollis. Children:
5667   Abraham Tyler, born in Westbrook, Me., December 21, 1840; married Elizabeth Crockett; he was in the Civil war; resides in North Chatham, N. H., and had two sons and one daughter.
5668   Charles Henry Tyler, born in Saco, Me., Oct. 4, 1842; married Etta Hasly; resided in Arapahoe, Neb.; s. p. in 1900; was in the Civil war.
5669   George S. Tyler, born Feb. 27, 1844; died Dec. 13, 1862, from effects of a wound in Civil war; married

Malissa Towle; had three daughters; resided in North Chelmsford, Mass.

5670+   Lucette S. Tyler, born Apr. 23, 1845.

5671   Margaret Tyler; died young.

5672   Nathaniel S. Tyler, born Mar. 4, 1849; married Ella Elden; resided in Buxton Center, Me.; has one son and one daughter.

5673   Franklin Pierce Tyler, born Nov. 2, 1852; married Abby York; resides in Buxton, Me.; two daughters.

5674+   James Tyler, born Aug. 29, 1854.

5675   Fred Dean Tyler, born Oct. 14, 1855; married Harriet Sweetzer; resides in Hollis, Me., s. p. in 1900.

3001 ANDREW[7] TYLER (Abraham[6]), born in Saco, Me., March 16, 1822; died suddenly, September 30, 1870; married, December, 1847, Margarette W. Beckmore, of Bangor, Me. He came into possession of his father's farm at the " Heath "; the place is now deserted. The children were born in Saco, Me. Children:

5676   David L. Tyler, born Nov. 15, 1848; a farmer residing in Rochester, N. H., with his wife ———; had three wives; s. p.

5677+   Louise S. Tyler, born Mar. 30, 1850.

5678   Elizabeth S. Tyler, born Sept. 11, 1851; died June 7, 1869, of consumption s. p.; married Feb. 17, 1869, Frank Tarbox, of Hollis, Me.

5679+   Emma E. Tyler, born Mar. 29, 1853.

5680   Abram Tyler, born Sept. 10, 1854; a farmer; resides in Rochester, N. H.; unmarried.

5681+   Luella P. Tyler, born Nov. 7, 1858.

3002 LYDIA S.[7] TYLER (Abraham[6]), born in Saco, Me., October 15, 1828; married (1), William Henry Libby, of Saco, born April, 1825; died January 30, 1862; married (2), February 18, 1868, George E. Johnson. She continued living at the old homestead in Saco, after her second marriage. Her children were all born there.

CHILDREN, by first marriage:

5682   George Libby, born June 18, 1849; died 1851.

5683   Sarah Ann Libby, born July 29, 1850; died 1851.

5684   Georgianna Libby, born Mar. 29, 1852; married Albert Robinson.
5685   Sally Libby, born Nov. 9, 1854; married Robert Graffam.
5686   Eunice Buzzell Libby, born Mar. 16, 1861.

3003   ANN ELIZA[7] TYLER (Andrew[6]), born in Frankfort, Me., April 5, 1833; married, December 31, 1851, Captain Robert Crosby Treat, Jr., born in Frankfort, Me., Nov. 24, 1829; died in Bangor, Me., October 4, 1867; son of Colonel Robert Treat (descended from Richard of Weathersfield, Conn.). He was a sea-captain and a merchant. The children were born in Frankfort. Children:
5687   Florence Evelyn Treat, born June 10, 1855; died unmarried, Oct. 7, 1867.
5688   Marion Hubbard Treat, born Jan. 4, 1857; married, in 1878, Gordon McKay, of Newport, R. I.; had a son (Robert G.) and daughter (Marion V.).

3028   ANDREW[7] TYLER (Allison[6]), born in Prospect, Me., August 11, 1838; died in Winterport, Me., October 20, 1874, intestate; married, January 1, 1867, Caroline Celeste McDermott, daughter of Capt. J. B. McDermott, of Frankfort, Me. His estate was probated in Belfast, Me.; was a mariner. He was Allison's last male descendant. The children were born in Winterport. Children:
5689   Blanche T. Tyler, born Jan. 6, 1871; died June 5, 1896, with infant child; married Charles W. Everett of Pittsfield, Me.
5690   Florence P. Tyler, twin to Blanche; married, Mar. 10, 1891, William Belcher, of Winterport; one daughter (Blanche M., born Jan. 4, 1893).

3059   ALBION P.[7] TYLER (Benjamin[6]), born in Maine; name of wife unknown. He had six girls and four boys; only the names of the boys are known. Children:
5691   Freeman Tyler, lived in Greenville, Me.
5692   Eugene Tyler, lived in Greenville, Me.
5693   Clarence Tyler, lived in Greenville, Me.
5694   James B. Tyler, is in the U. S. army.

3063 JOSEPH CURRIER[7] TYLER (William[6]), born in Pownal, Me., July 9, 1814; died in Durham, Me., October 22, 1882; married in Pownal, Esther J. Watts, born 1819; died March 1, 1891. He was a musician and organized and led one of the earliest bands in Maine, at Pownal, in 1842, and he led the Durham band, which succeeded his first band, for 30 years. His sons, Irving and Joseph, were associated with their father, inheriting his musical talent. He played the violin, bugle and clarionet; was a singing-school master, and a chorister, many years. He was Annie Louise Cary's earliest teacher. Became a colonel in the Maine militia. (See Stackpole's *History of Durham*). The children were doubtless born in Pownal, but in the absence of data this is uncertain.

CHILDREN:

5695 Lauraette Tyler.
5696 Helen Tyler, married Doctor Darius F. Drake, who died; has one daughter and resides in Chicago.
5697+ Irving W. Tyler, born 1842.
5698+ Joseph Tyler.
5699 William Tyler, died aged about fifteen years.
5700 Howard Tyler, lives in Ohio.
5701 Laura Tyler, married (1), ——; married (2), William Beals.
5702 Edward Everett Tyler, married, has a family and lives in Oak Dale, Deering, Me.

3064 MARY ANN[7] TYLER (William[6]), born in Pownal, Me., May 29, 1816; married, October 14, 1838, Elisha Strout, of Durham, Me., who died. The children were born in Durham. Children:

5703 William J. Strout.
5704 Emma Rebecca Strout, married (1), Stephen Sibley; married (2), Sylvanus Lewis, of Porterville, Cal.; one son (William) and one daughter (Angie) by first marriage.
5705 Margaret Hasty Strout, born June 7, 1850; married Westley H. Day, of Durham, Me.; s. p.

3068 IRENE GRAVES[7] TYLER (William[6]), born in Pownal, Me., August 10, 1825; married (1), November 2, 1845,

William D. Miller, of Durham, Me., married (2), Rufus Ficket of Auburn, Me.; a farmer; died s. p.   The three eldest children were born in Durham; the next two in Bangor and the others in Kenduskeag and South Dover, Me.   Children:

5706   Sarah Folansbee Tyler Miller, born Nov. 6, 1846; married Lavator O. Morse; resides in Auburn, Me. s. p.

5707   Luella French Miller, born Aug. 4, 1848; married Frank Clark; resides in Lynn, Mass.; two sons (Ernest and Raymond).

5708   Abby Menelva Miller, born Aug. 12, 1850; married Samuel C. Jackson, of Haverhill, Mass.; had three children (Louis, Irene and Lulu.)

5709   Franklin Peirce Miller, born Jan. 31, 1853; married Matilda Jury, of Freeport, Me.; had seven children.

5710   Frederick Augustus Miller, born February 1, 1854; married Susie Libby, of Scarboro, Me. s. p.

5711   Alberton Miller, born Dec. 19, 1855; died unmarried.

5712   William Melburn Miller, born Apr. 18, 1857; married Josephine S. McConkey.

3070   EMELINE ELIZABETH[7] TYLER (William[6]), born in Pownal, Me., September 20, 1829; died October 11, 1897; married, May 25, 1851, Joseph Henry Davis, of Pownal, where the children were born.   They live in Auburn, Me.   Children:

5713   Clara Emma Davis, born Feb. 21, 1852; married Orlando S. Keith, of West Auburn, Me.; no children in 1896.

5714   Cora A. B. Davis, born June 14, 1853; not married in 1896.

5715   Ella Maria Davis, born June 17, 1856; married Nov. 3, 1875, George T. Wilson, of Auburn, Me.; had a son and daughter, who died.

5716   Mary W. Davis, born Jan. 26, 1861; died in Auburn, Oct. 14, 1861.

3078   ZEBULON[7] TYLER, JR. (Zebulon[6]), born in Durham, Me., March 6, 1824; died there; married, in Mercer, Me., in 1849, Julia F. Riggs.   The children were born in New Sharon, Me., except the eldest.   Children:

5717   Elizabeth Ferguson Tyler, born in Chesterville, Me., Jan. 19, 1850; died aged three years.

5718   Llewellyn Starbard Tyler, born May 24, 1851; in Marshfield, Wis.; died May 12, 1881, unmarried.

5719+   George H. Tyler, born Mar. 2, 1853.

5720+   Sarah Elizabeth Tyler, born Oct. 23, 1854.

5721+   Minnie A. Tyler, born Mar. 28, 1858.

5722   Eliza A. Tyler, born Feb. 29, 1860; unmarried.

5723+   Joseph A. Tyler, born May 3, 1862.

5724   Frank P. Tyler, born Jan. 30, 1865; a farmer, and resides on old homestead; unmarried.

5725+   Hattie Zora Tyler, born Sept. 11, 1867.

3080   LUCY T.[7] LIBBY (Eveline[6]), born in Scarboro, Me., May 30, 1823; died January 9, 1901; married, December 9, 1841, John S. Larrabee, of Scarboro. Children:

5726   Theresa E. Larrabee, born Sept. 1842; died Feb. 16, 1857.

5727+   Philip J. Larrabee, born Apr. 12, 1844.

5728   Lucy Maria Larrabee, born Dec. 26, 1846; married William D. Libby; had two sons and two daughters.

3081   ZEBULON TYLER[7] LIBBY (Eveline[6]), born in Scarboro, Me., January 23, 1825; married, April 18, 1850, Mrs. Charlotte (Libby) Moody. He was a farmer and lived on the homestead. Children:

5729   Anna Maria Libby.

5730   Charles Zebulon Libby, lives on the old homestead.

5731   Phebe Ellen Libby.

5732   George Osgood Libby.

3084   JOHN TYLER[7] LIBBY (Eveline[6]), born in Scarboro, Me., April 29, 1832; died 1895; married, February 17, 1856, Ellen C. Rich, daughter of Rushworth and Mary (Harmon) Rich. He is a contractor and builder in Portland, Me. Children:

5733   Henry Sylvester Libby.

5734   Fred Williston Libby.

5735   Herbert Johnson Libby.

5736   Mary Ellis Libby.

3090   MORSEEN G.⁷ TYLER (John⁶) born in Pownal, Me., February 1, 1841; married, January 4, 1870, Stewart Russell, of East Deering, Me. He was a school teacher. Children:

5737   Maud A. Russell; a school teacher.
5738   Perly Russell, died, aged fifteen years.

3117   GEORGE L.⁷ TYLER (Orville⁶), born in Unity, Me., January 27, 1837; married September 22, 1861, Ann S. Cook, of Troy, Me., born January 9, 1841. He resided in Troy, Me., where he was selectman twelve years; in 1897 was town treasurer; justice of the peace ten years; a farmer. The children were born in Troy. Children:

5739   Annie R. Tyler, born in 1866; married —— Whitney, of Troy, Me.
5740   George L. Tyler, Junior, born in 1873; married —— Woods, of Troy, Me.

3142   MARY C.⁷ TYLER (John⁶), born in Hartford, Me., April 27, 1839; married (1), 1860, Augustus Reed, of Hartford; married (2), Fulton Corbett, of Cambridgeport, Mass., who died in 1877. Children:

5741   Freeman Reed, born in Hartford, 1861; died aged about four years.
5742   Emma H. Reed, born Sept. 5, 1867; married, Mar. 15, 1884, Carroll H. Fogg, of Hartford; they have a son (Albert H.).

3143   DORCAS L.⁷ TYLER (John⁶), born in Hartford, Me., April 26, 1840; died May 1, 1896; married (1), 1861, Edwin Andrews, of Paris, Me., who died, s. p., in the Civil war; married (2), 1863, C. C. Fletcher, of Hartford, where the children were born.

CHILDREN, by second marriage:

5743   John A. Fletcher, born Jan. 28, 1865; died unmarried Apr. 2, 1890.
5744   Nettie J. Fletcher, born Oct. 31, 1866; died Oct. 15, 1892; married 1883, George W. Brown, of Upton, Me.; had one son (Edwin).
5745   Annie Y. Fletcher, married, June, 1889, Frank Allen, of Canton, Me.

5746   Bertha M. Fletcher, died May 17, 1891, aged sixteen
        years and four months.

    3144   JOHN F.⁷ TYLER (John⁶), born in Hartford,
Me., July 31, 1842; married, 1867, Viola A. Parsons.   He is a
farmer and in 1899 lived in Hartford, where the children were
born.   Children:
5747   Clara S. Tyler, born Mar. 1, 1868; married, Jan. 17,
        1887, Caleb E. Mendall; no children.
5748+   Letitia M. Tyler, born Apr. 19, 1872.
5749   J. Alton Tyler, born Oct. 15, 1881.
5750   Arthur N. Tyler, born Oct. 22, 1887.
5751   Marion C. Tyler, born Nov. 20, 1893.

    3151   GILBERT⁷ TYLER (James Josse⁶), born   in
Hartford, Me., February 5, 1832; married, July 20, 1862,
Martha H. Lennell, of Grafton, Me.   He was a lumberman and
farmer and lived in Grafton, Me., in 1899, where the children
were born.   Three infants died after the birth of son Fred.
Children:
5752   Annette Desire Tyler, born March, 1865; married, Oct.
        1888, David Fleet; they adopted a boy.
5753+   Arthur Ulysses Tyler, born Feb. 1868.
5754+   Addie May Tyler, born Feb. 1870.
5755   Fred Warren Tyler, born May, 1878; lived with father
        unmarried in 1899.

    3153   MARY EMERY⁷ TYLER (James Josse⁶), born
in Hartford, Me., Jan. 27, 1842; married, April 14, 1863, Asa
B. Jones, of Turner, Me., who died April 15, 1888; a mill owner
and farmer.   The children were born in Turner.   Children:
5756   Hartwell Munroe Jones, born Dec. 5, 1865; died 1878.
5757   Harriet Bisbee Jones, born Feb. 27, 1867; died 1878.
5758   Almon Asa Jones, born Feb. 13, 1870; unmarried,
        1899, in Boston
5759   Mabel Idella Jones, born Sept. 12, 1871; died 1878.
5760   Embert Howard Jones, born Oct. 6, 1874; lived with
        mother, unmarried in 1899.

    3165   ABRAHAM⁷ TYLER (Benjamin⁶), born in Limington, Me., October 4, 1817; married, May 12, 1843, Mary E. McDonald, and lives in Gorham, Me.   Children:

5761   Alice Tyler, died young.
5762   Alice Tyler.
5763   Alonzo Tyler, May 7, 1857.
5764   Mary Tyler, born Oct. 22, 1862.

3166   JAMES EDWIN[7] TYLER (Benjamin[6]), born in Limington, Me., December 3, 1819; married (1), 1849, Mary Ann Jewell; married (2), Mary Jane Sanborn, who died January 27, 1868.

CHILDREN, by first marriage:

5765   Nancy H. Tyler, born Jan. 1, 1850; died; married Alonzo Cook.
5766   Charles E. Tyler, born Apr. 14, 1852; died.
5767   Mary A. Tyler, born Dec. 9, 1853; died.

3171   BENJAMIN FRANCIS[7] TYLER (Benjamin[6]), born in Limington, Me., January 19, 1834; married, April 26, 1863, Harriet Beck Sanborn.   He is a miller, and a grain and coal dealer; lives in Hyde Park where the children were born. Children:

5768   Frank Herbert Tyler, born Dec. 5, 1867.
5769   Susie Eunice Tyler, born May 17, 1870; died June 22, 1876.
5770   Hattie Louise Tyler, born July 26, 1877.

3187   FREEDOM[7] TYLER (Joseph[6]), born in Limington, Me.; died in Baldwin; married Anna Manister, who died in New Bedford, Mass.   The children were born in Gorham, Me. Children:

5671   John Tyler, born Jan. 25, 1834.
5672   Andrew Tyler, born Mar. 31, 1839.
5773   Georgia Ann Tyler, born May 27, 1843.
5774   Joseph F. Tyler, born Feb. 27, 1845.
5775   Rodney Tyler, born Mar. 1, 1847.

3188   ROYAL[7] TYLER (Joseph[6]), born in Limington, Me., in 1817; married, December 29, 1844, in Sebago, Me., by Rev. Samuel Tyler, Elizabeth Bickford, No. 3183.   In 1896 he was living in South Windham, Me., and was of great help in the work of tracing "Captain Abe's " line. Children:

5776 Melville H. Tyler, lives in Muncie, Ind.

5777 Charles Royal Tyler, also lives in Muncie.

5778 Eloise Tyler.

3189 HENRY L.[7] TYLER (Joseph[6]), born in Sebago, Me., July 26, 1821; died in Detroit, Mich., November 6, 1879; buried in Hopkinton, Mass.; married, in Milford, Mass., June 15, 1845, Alberona Strout, No. 3206, born in Raymond, Me., March 27, 1829. The children were born in Milford. Children:

5779 Eldora Tyler, born Mar. 11, 1846; married, Feb. 1, 1872, J. W. Messerre, of Milford.

5780+ Charles H. Tyler, born Apr. 30, 1848.

5781 James W. Tyler, born Mar. 20, 1850; died in Hopkinton, May 25, 1854.

3191 SYLVESTER[7] TYLER (Joseph[6]), born in Baldwin, Me., March 14, 1827; married (1), November 29, 1854, Anna Miller, who died February 18, 1867; married (2), June 2, 1873, Marion F. Crosby. He was a real estate broker in Boston.

CHILDREN, by first marriage:

5782 Ida Melissa Tyler, born Dec. 16, 1855; married Charles H. M. Bartlett.

5783+ Wesley Tyler, born Nov. 26, 1857.

5784 Leslie Tyler, twin to Wesley; married, June 7, 1886, Harriet L. Maybee; no children.

5785 Anna Tyler, born 1861; died, aged six weeks.

3192 WILLIAM R.[7] TYLER (Joseph[6]), born in Baldwin, Me.; died in Pleasant Hill, Mo., February 4, 1894; married, in Cleveland, O., September 21, 1854, Harriet M. Lappens. In 1857, he moved to Decatur, Wise County, Tex., then on the frontier; in 1868 he moved to Pleasant Hill, Mo. Children:

5786+ Ada L. Tyler, born in Cleveland, May 17, 1856.

5787+ Layton James Tyler, born in Decatur, Tex., May 10, 1861.

5788 Clinton Lot Tyler, born in Pleasant Hill, Aug. 2, 1872; unmarried in 1896; a provision dealer.

3209   JAMES LIBBY[7] TYLER (Abraham[6]), born in Limington, Me., August 14, 1825; died in Somerville, Mass., June 13, 1896; married, September 22, 1850, Elizabeth W. Wardell, born in Newcastle-on-Tyne, Eng., November 17, 1819; daughter of Robert and Jane (Lishman) Wardell, who was the son of Colonel Jacob Wardell, of England. She came to Boston with her parents from England in 1834. In 1848 Mr. Tyler was in Boston on Union street as a trunk manufacturer, later moved to Devonshire street, where he was burned out in the great fire in 1872; thence he moved to Avon street, where he continued until his building was absorbed in the progress of a large retail department store. After this he did a wholesale business. He lived in Somerville where he was chairman of the building committee which constructed the Franklin street Congregational church. The three younger children were born in Somerville.

CHILDREN:

5789+   James Libby Tyler, Jr., born in Chelsea, Mass., Dec. 10, 1851.
5790   Arthur W. Tyler, born Apr. 11, 1853; died unmarried July 27, 1896.
5791   Elizabeth W. Tyler, born Jan. 18, 1855, unmarried.
5792+   Cora L. Tyler, born May 30, 1857.

3211   CHARLES ABRAHAM[7] TYLER (Abraham[6]), born in Limington, Me., January 22, 1834; died in Farmington, Ill., September 14, 1892; married (1), in Upton, Mass., February 6, 1858, Eunice Horton, born in Medfield, Mass., August 5, 1838; died in Farmington, July 13, 1873; married (2) in Peoria, Ill., Helen Francis. He was a farmer and prominent granger. From Newton, Mass., he went west to Peoria, in 1878. The second and third children were born in East Randolph, Mass., and the sixth and seventh in Farmington. Children:

5793   Charles Harmon Tyler, born in Milford, Mass., Mar. 29, 1859; residence unknown.
5794+   William Sumner Tyler, born Apr. 14, 1861.
5795   Harriet Minnie Tyler, born May 5, 1863, lives in Davenport, Ia.
5796+   Royal Harrison Tyler, born in Newton, Mass., Nov. 23, 1864.

5797+ Joseph Elmer Tyler, born in South Weymouth, Mass., Aug. 11, 1867.

5798+ John March Tyler, born Jan. 6, 1870.

5799 Caroline Eliza Tyler, born Sept. 2, 1872; a school-teacher; lives in Cedar Rapids, Ia.

3221 REV. CHARLES MELLEN[7] TYLER, D. D. (Daniel[6]), born in Limington, Me., 1831; married (1), 1857, Ellen A. Davis, of New Haven, Conn., who died in 1890; married (2), 1892, Kate E. Stark, formerly professor of music in the Syracuse (N. Y.) University. Dr. Tyler was graduated at Yale College in 1855; afterwards received the degree of A.M and in 1892 was given the degree of D. D. He was a member of the Massachusetts Legislature in 1861. He was with the 5th Army corps under General Warren, and a member of the Loyal Legion. He was a minister in Natick, Mass., nine years, and in Chicago six years. He went to Ithaca, N. Y., in 1872, and in 1891 resigned the pastorate of the First Congregational church there, having preached in that pulpit nineteen years. He was then appointed professor of history and philosophy of religions and Christian ethics (a chair founded by Henry W. Sage) in Cornell University, where he had long been one of the trustees. He has been a voluminous literary contributor.

CHILDREN:

5800 Effie Dunreath Tyler, married James Fraser Gluck, of Buffalo, N. Y.

5801 Beatrice Desaix Tyler, lives in Ithaca, N. Y.

3264 JOHN MILTON[7] TYLER (John[6]), born in Pelham, N. H., July 20, 1816; died January 9, 1886; married (1), June 11, 1840, Betsey C. Gage, who died August 26, 1847; married (2), May 30, 1848, Mercy Ford, who died January 4, 1872; married (3), February 11, 1873, Lucy Cross Tenney, who died July 2, 1880. He moved to Cambridge, Mass., in 1855. He was a member of the common council in 1865 and served on the board of aldermen in 1866 and 1867; was also on the cemetery commission sinking fund, and was president of the Cambridge Gas Light company. He was a coal merchant in Boston.

CHILD, by first marriage:

5802+ Daniel Gage Tyler, born in Pelham, N. H., Feb. 28, 1844.

CHILD, by second marriage:

5803 John Ford Tyler, born in Cambridge, Nov. 18, 1856; married, Sept. 21, 1901, Mary Osgood Stevens, of North Andover, Mass., daughter of Hon. Moses Tyler Stevens, ex-member of Congress, and a woolen manufacturer. Mr. Tyler was graduated from Harvard University in 1877; is a lawyer in active practice in Boston and lives in North Andover.

3266 JOSEPH HOWE[7] TYLER (John[6]), born in Pelham, N. H., February 11, 1825; died in Winchester, Mass., July 11, 1892; married November 4, 1858, Abigail Little Hitchcock, born in Pembroke, Mass., July 11, 1830; daughter of Charles and Abigail Little (Hall) Hitchcock (Gad, Gad, Ebenezer, Luke, Luke); (see *Hitchcock Genealogy*.) He fitted for college at the Phillips Academy in Andover, and was graduated from Dartmouth College in 1851; he studied law and practiced in Cambridge, Mass., from 1854-1870, when he moved to Winchester. He was register of probate in Middlesex county for 34 years; a member of the common council in Cambridge, 1862-1868; on the board of aldermen 1864 and 1865; and on the school committee 1868, 1869, and 1870. In Winchester he was chairman of the school committee; for many years he was one of the trustees of the library and was one of Winchester's most prominent and respected citizens. In 1894 a memorial window was placed in the public library in Winchester, a gift of Mr. Tyler's wife and children, with an inscription. The window was accepted by the town in some highly eulogistic resolutions. It is an epitome of the art of book-making. The children were born in Cambridge.

CHILDREN:

5804 Charles Hitchcock[8] Tyler, born Oct. 11, 1863; was graduated from Harvard University in 1886; lives in Boston, where he is a lawyer and a lecturer in the law school of the Boston University, and in active practice in his profession. He is unmarried.

3805   Gertrude Eliza[8] Tyler, born Oct. 3, 1866; was gradu-
        ated from Harvard Annex (now Radcliffe Col-
        lege) in 1887; married, Nov. 25, 1896, Robert Pear-
        sall Morton, Jr.; she lives in Boston.

    3267 DOCTOR HENRY MARTYN TYLER SMITH,
(Sally[6]), born in Winchester, Vt., February 4, 1822; died in
Dunkirk, N. Y., September 24, 1878; married, December 12,
1849, Helen E. More; daughter of Jonas More (John, John);
she was living in Buffalo, N. Y., in 1901. He was graduated
from Hamilton College and studied medicine in New York City
and in the Albany Medical school, where he was graduated in
1848. They lived in Ludlow and Chicopee, Mass., two years,
and then moved to Dunkirk, N. Y., where he practiced medicine. In 1856 he established a wholesale and retail drug store
there. He was an elder in the Presbyterian church for thirty
years, and several times was elected a member of the common
council of the town. He was prominent in political affairs.
The children were born in Dunkirk.

CHILDREN:

5806   Roderick Henry Smith, born Oct. 15, 1860; on the
        death of his father he took charge of his wholesale
        and retail drug business for five years, when he sold
        the business. He has published " Science of Busi-
        ness," Putnam, N. Y., 1885; " Art of Speculation,"
        " A New Business in Wall Street," and he has writ-
        ten much upon the silver question and against im-
        peralism. He is a broker in Buffalo.
5807   Willard Payson Smith born Sept. 20, 1866; was grad-
        ated from Amherst College in 1888; LL. B. Colum-
        bia College, 1891; A. M. Amherst College, 1900; he
        is a lawyer in Buffalo, N. Y.

    3269 SARAH ELIZABETH[7] TYLER (Varnum[6]),
born probably in Methuen, Mass., Sept. 23, 1835; married, April 5, 1865, Leverett Swan, of Methuen. Children:
5808   Charlotte Tyler Swan, born April 2, 1868; married
        Sept. 27, 1893, Edward Lyons of Brooklyn, N. Y.,
        where he is a real estate and insurance business
        man; had a daughter who died young.

5809	Bessie Maria Swan, born Jan. 21, 1870.
5810	Marion Towne Swan, born Oct. 31, 1873; died July 15, 1874.

3275 APHIA ANN RUSSELL[7] TYLER (William[6]), born in Georgetown, D. C., November 22, 1820; married, September 18, 1843, Benjamin A. Follansbee, who moved from Pittston, Me., to Amesbury, Mass., where the children were born.   Children:
5811	William Tyler Follansbee, born Apr. 18, 1848, married July 8, 1879, Annette L. Pettingill; they had one daughter (Helen L.).
5812	Alice Cushman Follansbee, born Sept. 18, 1858; lives in Amesbury.

3288 CATHERINE B.[7] LOCKE (Fanny[6] Tyler), born in Ashby, Mass., December, 1827; married, 1852, Leonard H. Truax, who died in St. Johnsbury, Vt., in 1881.   They resided in Oxford, Mass.   Children:
5813	George L. Truax, died suddenly in Bennington, Vt.; married Ella Spencer; one son and two daughters.
5814	Harriet E. Truax; married Rev. C. M. Carpenter, who was a pastor in Oxford, Mass.
5815	Harry Truax; married Flora Smith, of Bennington, they resided in Grant Pass, Oregon, where he had charge of a large store of a lumber company; three children:

3297 GEORGE WASHINGTON[7] TYLER (Jonathan, Jr.[6]), born in Newburyport, Mass., November 14, 1812; died in West Newbury, Mass., June 19, 1863; married, August 23, 1836, Fannie B. Ordway, of Sutton, N. H., who died June 19, 1885.   He was a comb-maker.   His estate was administered upon in Salem, Mass., April 5, 1864.   The children were born in West Newbury.   Children:
5816	Mary F. Tyler, born Mar. 23, 1839; lived in Haverhill, Mass.
5817+	Eugenia Tyler, born Jan. 19, 1843.
5818+	George Gardner Tyler, born Oct. 1, 1844.

3298 CAPTAIN CHARLES[7] TYLER (Jonathan[6]),

born in Newburyport, Mass., October 29, 1814; died February 13, 1849; married, November 28, 1837, Evaline Hickman, of Newburyport, who died July 9, 1895. He was a sea-captain. His estate was administered upon in Salem, Mass., March 27, 1849 (*case* 55925.) Child:

5819+   Mary H. Tyler, born in Newburyport, Nov. 17, 1839.

3300   ALBERT MOSES[7] TYLER (Jonathan[6]), born in Newburyport, Mass., November 18, 1818; died in Iowa, December 22, 1902; married, October 26, 1845, Abbie M. Bean, who died in Lowell, Mass., August 22, 1896, where the children were born. Children:

5820+   Charles A. Tyler, born Nov. 7, 1846.
5821   Julia Huntington Tyler, born Aug. 10, 1861; married, October 29, 1890, Asa Radcliffe; she died in Lowell, Mar. 13, 1900.
5822   Abbie Tyler died, aged six weeks and three days.

3302   OSGOOD[7] TYLER (Jonathan[6]), born in Newburyport, Mass., May 6, 1822; died in Bradford, Mass., March 30, 1861; married, September 18, 1850, Mary Lewis, of Boothbay, Me.; she married (2), February 22, 1865, Edwin E. Chase of Bradford, Mass. The children were born in Bradford. Children:

5823+   Ida Florence Tyler, born May 4, 1855.
5824+   Clarence Edward Tyler, born Feb. 16, 1857.

3303   HANNAH[7] TYLER (Jonathan[6]), born in Newburyport, Mass., August 14, 1824; married, April 3, 1853, John B. Libbey, of Parsonfield, Me., born June 12, 1822; died May 23, 1865; he was a market-gardener. Child:

5825   Jennie Wadsworth Libbey, born in Bradford, Mass., Mar. 26, 1862; married, Oct. 23, 1889, Arthur A. Ingersoll treasurer of the Academy of Music, Haverhill, Mass.

3320   EMELINE BRIDGE[7] TYLER (Benjamin Franklin[6]), born in Charlestown, Mass., November 7, 1847; married, December 30, 1869, Calvin Simonds, Jr., of Charlestown, where the children were born. Children:

5826   Emma Louise Simonds, born Sept. 26, 1870; married,
            Feb. 24, 1895, ———.
5827   Thomas Greenleaf Simonds, born Aug. 30, 1873; died
            Apr. 28, 1874.
5828   May Elizabeth Simonds, born Dec. 24, 1877.
5829   Ethel Ruhama Simonds, born Mar. 24, 1886.
5830   Calvin Walker Simonds, born Feb. 12, 1889.

3323   JOHN H.[7] TYLER (Benjamin Franklin[6]), born
in Charlestown, Mass., April 12, 1860; married, February 24,
1882, Mary Russell McClellan, of Bath, Me. He lives in
Beachmont, Mass.   Child:
5831   Franklin Kendall Tyler, born in Charlestown, Apr. 16,
            1891.

3331   JOHN[7] TYLER JR. (John[6]), born in Warren,
R. I.; his tombstone says, " died November 12, 1834, aged 36
years "; buried in " Tyler's Point "; (but another record says,
born March 29, 1802); married in Barrington, R. I., October
23, 1827, Eliza Martin, born 1801; " died October 2, 1866, in
her 65th year."   He was a tanner in Boston, Mass., where he
was town clerk, 1827-1838, and representative to the General
Court, 1832-1833.   The child was born in Barrington.
Child:
5832+   Mary Elizabeth Tyler, born in " Tyler's Point " July
            28, 1828.

3335   EDWARD LUTHER[7] TYLER (Edward[6]), born
in Boston, Mass., August 5, 1806; died in Lexington, Mass.,
March 23, 1864; married (1), April 16, 1832, Rachel Stevens,
who died April 3, 1839; married (2), November 13, 1839,
Martha T. Savage, of Orford, N. H., who died January 6, 1890.
He left home soon after his father's death and learned the carpenter's trade; about 1828 he bought a farm in Lexington,
where he resided the rest of his life, and where the children
were born.

CHILDREN, by first marriage:
5833   Edward F. Tyler, born Nov. 13, 1834.
5834+   Mary S. Tyler, born Feb. 7, 1838.

CHILDREN, by second marriage:

5835+ Henry H. Tyler, born Nov. 22, 1840.

5836+ Arthur Fitz Tyler, born Mar. 12, 1852.

3336 ALMA ELLERY[7] TYLER (Edward[6]), born in Harvard, Mass., January 5, 1815; married, September 20, 1849, Dr. Jacob S. Eaton, of Bristol, N. H., who died in Harvard, September 5, 1888. He was graduated from Dartmouth College; also attended lectures in Philadelphia; he practiced in Alexandria, N. H., Stow and South Deerfield, Mass., and finally settled in Harvard, where the children were born. Children:

5837 Lucien Kimball Eaton, born Nov. 7, 1850; died in Elkhart, Ind., March, 1888; married, April 6, 1878, Mary E. Titus.

5838 Harriet Frances Eaton, born Mar. 11, 1852; died July 8, 1863.

5839 James Ellery Eaton, born July 10, 1855; married, July 27, 1889, Flora K. Timpany; he is a merchant in Toledo; has one son (Ellery Tyler).

5840 Alma Tyler Eaton, born Nov. 13, 1858, married, June 19, 1889, Dr. Herbert B. Royal, who was graduated in 1887 from Bowdoin Medical School; lives in Harvard, Mass.; two sons (Kent Tyler and Ellery Eaton).

3337 SUSANNAH[7] TYLER (Edward[6]), born in Harvard, Mass., July 30, 1816; died March 7, 1839; married, November 23, 1836, Luke[6] Pollard, Jr. (Luke[5], Thaddeus[4], John[3], Thomas[2], William[1]), born in Harvard, August 13, 1813; died January 22, 1906; he married (2), November 25, 1841, Elizabeth Tyler, No. 3341, sister of his first wife.

CHILD, by first marriage:

5841 Charles Henry Pollard, born in Harvard, Oct. 4, 1837; died December 5, 1838.

3339 HARRIET NEWELL[7] TYLER (Edward[6]), born in Harvard, Mass., May 29, 1820; died April 20, 1881; married, March 5, 1845, Dr. S. B. Kelley. Children:

5842 Edward Samuel Kelley; a druggist in Boston.

5843 Harriet S. Kelley, died.

3341 ELIZABETH[7] TYLER (Edward[6]), born in Harvard, Mass., June 21, 1823; died June 7, 1887; married, November 25, 1841, Luke[6] Pollard, Jr., widower of her sister Susannah, No. 3337. The children were born in Harvard. The three elder daughters live in Harvard on the old homestead built by their grandfather, Luke[5], about 1806, in the center of the town overlooking the common. Mr. George F. Pollard makes it his summer home. The house is built in the colonial style, of brick and is double with a front door on each angle. Was remodelled a few years ago, the old style being preserved.

CHILDREN:

5844   Susan Estelle Pollard, born Nov. 14, 1842.

5845   Mary Caroline Pollard, born Nov. 8, 1846.

5846   Sarah Elizabeth Pollard, born July 23, 1848.

5847   George Fisher Pollard, born May 8, 1851; married, September 21, 1876, Katherine Louise Sykes, daughter of Joseph Sykes, of Hyde Park. Mr. Pollard is in the wholesale dry goods business. They have a son and daughter (Harold Stanley, a graduate of Harvard College, and Bessie Louise, who married D. McK. Morris of Pittsburg).

5848   Frederic Ellery Pollard, born June 10, 1853; an architect in Brooklyn, N. Y.

5849   Charles Newton Pollard, born Apr. 2, 1856; married, Oct. 10, 1894, Margaret Lowell Richardson; daughter of Charles L. Richardson, of Manchester, N. H.; she died in 1895. He is an organist and has resided in Berlin, Ger., of late years.

5850   Frank Bowdoin Pollard, born Nov. 16, 1865; went to California several years ago.

3349 GEORGE[7] SUMNER (Molly[6]), born in Pomfret, Conn., December 13, 1793; died February 20, 1855; married Elizabeth Putnam, born September 24, 1794; died 1844; daughter of Daniel Putnam. The children were born in Pomfret. Children:

5851   Elizabeth Sumner; married Myron Nelson.

5852   Catherine R. Sumner; died Feb. 20, 1865; married, Sept. 25, 1856, Hezekiah Huntington.

5853   Mary Sumner; died in Burlington, N. J., Oct. 7, 1866;

married (1), Oct. 20, 1858, Joseph Warren Newcomb; married (2), C. M. Bidwell.

5854 George Sumner.

5855 Harriet G. Sumner; married (1), William Chipman;
married (2), —— Hazzard.

3353 SAMUEL PUTNAM[7] SUMNER (Molly[6]), born
in Pomfret, Conn., February 8, 1807; died October 2, 1880;
married, April 19, 1830, J. Ann Goffe, of Pomfret, who died
February 7, 1875. The children were born in Pomfret. Children:

5856 Samuel Sumner, born Apr. 24, 1831; died June 19,
1852.

5857 George Sumner, born Mar. 1, 1833.

5858 Joseph Sumner, born July 12, 1836.

5859 Edward Tyler Sumner, born Mar. 11, 1839; died in
Pomfret, Aug. 13, 1884; was a sergeant in the 11th
Conn. volunteer infantry in the Civil war.

5860 Joseph Putnam Sumner, born Jan. 20, 1842; died in
Belle Isle, Va., Feb. 13, 1864; a prisoner of war.

5861 Charles Sumner, born Feb. 19, 1845; died May 23,
1852.

5862 Mary Elizabeth Sumner, born Mar. 27, 1847; married,
Mar. 17, 1869, Albert E. Potter.

3355 CAROLINE ELIZABETH[7] TYLER (Pascal
Paoli[6]), born in Brooklyn, Conn., April 24, 1802; married, No-
vember 24, 1824, Hulings Cowperthwait, of Philadelphia.
Children:

5863 Elizabeth Cowperthwait.

5864 Ellen Cowperthwait, married James Perry Brown.

5865 Caroline Cowperthwait, married and had one child.

5866 Joseph Cowperthwait, married Mary Brown.

5867 Mary Cowperthwait.

5868 Hulings Cowperthwait.

5869 Henrietta Cowperthwait.

5870 Emily Cowperthwait.

3356 MARY BAKER[7] TYLER (Pascal Paoli[6]), born
in Brooklyn, Conn., August 17, 1812; died July 3, 1893; married, June 9, 1833, James Holbrook, of Brooklyn. Children:

5871   James Holbrook, married and had a son (Harry).

5872   Mary Holbrook, married Byron Bingham, and had a daughter (Mary).

5873   Corinne Holbrook, married B. Salisbury, and had three daughters (Mabel, Grace and Corinne).

3358   MARIA CORDELIA[7] TYLER (William P.[6]), born in Warren, Vt., September 3, 1811; died in Brooklyn, Conn., March 1, 1882; married, September 11, 1832, John Gallup, born in Sterling, Conn., April 9, 1807; died in Brooklyn, Conn., December 16, 1881; son of David Gallup, descended from John[1], (see *Gallup Genealogy*). He held many important places of trust in his town and county and was president of the Windham county bank for several years. The children were born in Brooklyn. Children:

5874   Henry Tyler Gallup, born Dec. 11, 1834; married, Dec. 8, 1860, Mary Ann Harrison, of Brookline, Mass., born in Halifax, N. S., in 1830; died s. p. in Boston, Dec. 2, 1890. They lived in Boston and he was general superintendent of the Boston and Albany railway.

5875   Ellen M. Gallup, born May 4, 1838.

5876   Edward Gallup, born Aug. 24, 1842; died in Cleveland, O., Oct. 22, 1888; married, Dec. 26, 1865, Maria Louise King, of Monson, Mass., born there in 1843; daughter of Amasa and Adaline King. He was assistant general manager of the Lake Shore and Michigan Southern railway.

3360   WATY WILLIAMS[7] TYLER (William[6]), born in Brooklyn, Conn., August 27, 1814; died May 25, 1895, in Hudson, N. H.; married, May 30, 1842, Rev. Benjamin Howe, of Ipswich, Mass., born there November 4, 1807; died in Hudson, N. H., October 18, 1883; son of Joseph and Mehitable (Stickney) Howe. He was graduated from Amherst College 1838; from the Theological Seminary in Hartford, Conn., in 1841; acting pastor in Coventry, Conn., 1833-34; in Wells, Me., 1844; ordained and installed there November 5, 1845; dismissed in 1849; teacher and preacher in Brooklyn, Conn., 1850-1855; acting pastor in Meredith, N. Y., 1855-1860; without a charge and living in New Hampshire, 1860-1866; acting pas-

tor in Hudson 1866-1867; in Lempster, N. H., 1867-1870; settled at the Linebrook church in Ipswich, May 3, 1871. A man
of force and character, highly respected wherever he lived.

CHILDREN:

5877   Homer Howe, born in Wells, Me., Aug. 16, 1848; lives
        unmarried in Hudson, N. H.
5878   Cecil Putnam Howe, born in Meredith, N. Y., Nov. 8,
        1857; died Feb. 13, 1866.

3379   SARAH SOPHIA[7] TYLER (Frederic[6]), born in
Brooklyn, Conn., June 29, 1820; died in Hartford, Conn., June
24, 1887; married, in Hartford, June 10, 1840, Sidney Joseph
Cowen, born in Saratoga, N. Y., November 20, 1815; died at
sea, September 10, 1844; son of Judge Ezekiel Cowen, of New
York Court of Appeals. The children were born in Saratoga.
Children:

5879   Katherine Berry Cowen, born Feb. 17, 1841; died in
        New York City, Feb. 27, 1883; married, in Hart-
        ford, Conn., June 20, 1860, Henry Cleveland Pratt,
        of Hartford, born in Brooklyn, N. Y., September 25,
        1838; died in Rosebank, S. I., N. Y., September 23,
        1894; had two sons (Henry E. and Sidney C.) and
        a daughter (Kate C.).
5880   Sophia Tyler Cowen, born July 29, 1843; married in
        Hartford, Feb. 9, 1876, Judge Elisha Carpenter, of
        Hartford, Conn. (his second wife), born in that part
        of Ashford, Conn., now known as Eastford, Jan. 14,
        1824; died in Hartford, Mar. 22, 1897; (he mar-
        ried (1), Harriet Grosvenor Brown, of Brooklyn,
        Conn., and his four elder children, one son and three
        daughters, are of this marriage). He was the son
        of Uriah B. Carpenter, descended from William, the
        immigrant of 1642. He was a judge of the Supe-
        rior and the Supreme Courts of Connecticut for
        about 28 years; retired from the Supreme bench in
        1894, and began the practice of law, and in 1895
        the General Assembly elected him one of the state
        referees. They had a son (Sidney C.) and a daugh-
        ter (Helen E.).

3380   GEORGE FREDERICK[7] TYLER (Frederic[6]), born in Brooklyn, Conn., August 4, 1822; died in Philadelphia, Pa., September 24, 1896; married in Brooklyn, N. Y., August 26, 1845, Louisa Richmond Blake, of Brooklyn, born in Concord, N. H., February 2, 1822; died in Philadelphia, November 26, 1883; only daughter of Rev. John Lauris Blake, D. D. (Jonathan) and Mary (Howe) Blake, his wife. Mr. Tyler was one of the founders of Anniston, Ala.; was first president of the reorganized Norfolk and Western railway; an extensive coal dealer in New York; thence he moved to Phialdelphia in 1847; connected with many large industrial and financial enterprises. The children were born in Philadelphia.

CHILDREN:

5881   George Frederick Tyler, Jr., born Aug. 1848; died Aug. 22, 1850.

5882+   Sidney Frederick Tyler, born Dec. 21, 1850.

5883+   Harry Blake Tyler, born Nov. 20, 1852.

5884+   Mary Louise Tyler, born July 5, 1857.

5885   Helen Beach Tyler, born May 26, 1859.

3384   EDWIN S.[7] TYLER (Frederic[6]), born in Hunter, N. Y., October 10, 1834; died in Hartford, Conn., October 3, 1900; married in Farmington, Conn., May 8, 1860, Camilla Augusta Treadwell, born in New York City, October 27, 1840. The children were born in Hartford. Children:

5886+   Robert Ogden Tyler, born Apr. 18, 1861.

5887   Edwin S. Tyler, born July 17, 1862; married, in Akron, O., Apr. 21, 1900, Nora Lee Wilson, born in Rochester, Minn., September 23, 1874.

5888+   Sarah Sophia Tyler, born May 26, 1865.

5889   Julia Treadwell Tyler, born May 21, 1869; died unmarried in New York City, Jan. 18, 1895.

5890+   Camilla Matilda Tyler, born Nov. 18, 1870.

5891   Louise Blake Tyler, born Oct. 23, 1876; married, in Hartford, Oct. 6, 1903, Harold Roberts Tyler, born in Westfield, Conn., May 24, 1871.

3385   ALFRED LEE[7] TYLER (Daniel[6]), born in Norwich, Conn., May 19, 1834; married, May 25, 1859. Annie E.

Scott, of Macon, Ga. He lives in Anniston, Ala., where he is
president of the Anniston Manufacturing company. Children:
5892   Emily Caroline Tyler, born 1860; married, 1891, Wil-
        liam Darrah Kelley; they have one son (William
        Darrah, Jr.).
5893+   Alfred Lee Tyler, Jr., born 1866.
5894   Emily Lee Tyler, born 1875.

3386   GERTRUDE ELIZABETH⁷ TYLER (Daniel⁶),
born in Farrandsville, Pa., February 14, 1836; died in Turin,
Italy, April 26, 1896; married, June 8, 1859, Charles Carow,
of Norwich, Conn., born in New York City, October 4, 1825;
died there March 17, 1883. Children:
5895+   Edith Kermit Carow, born in Norwich, Aug. 6, 1861.
5896   Emily Tyler Carow, born in New York City, Apr. 18,
        1865.

3387   EDMUND LEIGHTON⁷ TYLER (Daniel⁶),
born in Farrandsville, Pa., May 2, 1838; married, in Washington, D. C., March 16, 1892, Belle Alston Webb, of Washington.
He is a graduate of West Point; lives in Anniston, Ala., and
New London, Conn. The two elder children were born in Atlanta, Ga. Children:
5897   Lucy Mason Tyler, born Mar. 26, 1893.
5898   Nellie Osgood Tyler, born Mar. 13, 1895.
5899   Elizabeth Leighton Tyler, born in New London, Conn.,
        Oct. 13, 1896; died Oct. 15, 1896.

3388   MARY LOW⁷ TYLER (Daniel⁶), born in Norwich, Conn., March 2, 1841; married, April 1, 1875, Colonel
Alexander Moore, U. S. A., born in Ballymoney, County Antrim, Ire.; lives in New York City. Child:
5900   Daniel Tyler Moore, born in Montgomery, Ala., Feb.
        9, 1877.

3389   COLONEL AUGUSTUS CLEVELAND⁷ TYLER
(Daniel⁶), born in Norwich, Conn., May 2, 1851; married, in
Norwich, January 3, 1878, Cornelia Osgood, born there August
31, 1856; daughter of Dr. Charles and Sarah (Larned) Osgood of Norwich. He was graduated from West Point in 1873
and was assigned to the 4th cavalry. He served on frontier

duty at Fort Clark, Tex., until 1874; then went on scouting duty; was afterward sent on an expedition to the Indian Territory; then was on duty in various frontier forts until he resigned July 1, 1878. He is commander of the 3d regiment C. N. G. and lives south in the winter, and in New London, Conn., in the summer. During his absence, one winter, his beautiful residence in New London was destroyed by fire, to the foundation walls. The loss on the house and furnishings was large; a beautiful elm tree, said to be the finest in New England, was injured at this time. The house has been rebuilt.

CHILDREN:

5901   Edna Leighton Tyler, born in Norwich, Conn., Jan. 13, 1879.
5902   Sarah Larned Tyler, born in New London, June 22, 1880; married in New London, Oct. 5, 1904, Edward Everett Marshall, born in Philadelphia, July 3, 1877.
5903   Frederick Osgood Tyler, born Nov. 14, 1883.

3390 CARLEY[7] TYLER (Asahel[6]), born in Brookfield, Vt., February 7, 1792; died in Comanche, Ia., July 21, 1878; married in 1820, Elizabeth Simcox, born in Ohio, November 19, 1796; died in Yuma, Col., February 6, 1890. He rafted lumber on the St. Lawrence river; was in the War of 1812 (at the battles of Plattsburgh and Lundy's Lane) until 1818; was an active A. F. and M. Mason in Utica, N. Y. In 1819 moved to Shalorsville, O., where he lived and farmed for 22 years, clearing and selling in that time nine farms and in 1842 moved to Comanche. The children were born in Shalorsville.

CHILDREN:

5904+   John Asahel Tyler, born May 21, 1821.
5905   George Tyler, born Mar. 9, 1822; married Jane Waters and resides in Iowa.
5906   Royal Tyler; married and resides in Kansas; has three sons and two daughters.
5907+   Polly Rahama Tyler, born Dec. 27, 1829.
5908+   Nancy Tyler, born June 8, 1835.
5909   Weaver Tyler; died in California; married twice and had children by both marriages.

5910   Jerome Tyler, scalded to death in a hot grease vat in St. Louis; left three children (Rahama, married ——Walrod, of Syracuse, Neb., Jerome, Estella).

5911   Stearns Tyler; died in St. Louis, Mo.; has one daughter (Mrs. Lafayette Hopkins, residing in Jefferson, Ill.); has one son.

5912   Chauncey Tyler; married (1), ——, who left him taking their son and daughter; married (2), ——; had a family and resides in California.

3391 ASAHEL[7] TYLER (Asahel[6]), born in Brookfield, Vt., July 31, 1794; died in Shalorsville, O. (estate probated in Ravenna, O.) March, 1832; married Maria Barnard, who died in Ravenna where her estate was probated, October, 1843. He lived in Canandaigua, N. Y., Ravenna and Shalorsville, O. The three elder children were born in Canandaigua. Children:

5913   Barnard Tyler.

5914   Charles Royal Tyler, born March, 1821; married in Green Bay, Wis., Sept. 10, 1846, Elizabeth Arnot Cotton; daughter of Captain John W. Cotton; had three children (Augusta, Lewis and Deane).

5915+   Sarah Drusilla Tyler, born May 18, 1823.

5916   Elizabeth Tyler; married Charles Lewis; one son.

5917   Asahel Tyler; probably died unmarried.

3394 JOHN HAZEN[7] TYLER (John[6]), born in Randolph, Vt., November 30, 1793; died in Yates, N. Y., August 1, 1856; buried in Lyndonville cemetery; married (1), in Ridgeway, N. Y., 1819, Selina Gilbert, who died October 27, 1842; daughter of Simeon Gilbert; married (2), February 15, 1843, Mrs. Salome (Gates) Noble, born in Gaines, N. Y., August 13, 1814; died in Yates, February 14, 1881; daughter of Daniel and Anna (Anderson) Gates. In early life he settled in Ridgeway. He attended Randolph Academy; moved to Massena, N. Y., in 1810; was a corporal in the War of 1812 and later a captain near Ogdensburg, N. Y. (See *Pension Book*, page 67, No. 8). He took 176 acres of land in Yates in 1817 on Johnson's Creek. He was supervisor 1828-1831 and 1833-1837; was justice of the peace; a member of the State Assembly 1830-1831. The children were born in Yates.

CHILDREN, by first marriage:

5918   Tamma Tyler; married —— Walters, of Delaware, O.,
        who died soon; resided in 1898 with her sister in
        Kenton, O., s. p.
5919   Allen Augustus Tyler; died while attending College in
        Louisville, Ky., about 1848, aged about 22 years.
5920+   Ruby Tyler.

CHILDREN, by second marriage:

5921+   Laura Emma Tyler, born Mar. 7, 1846.
5922+   Lydia Ella Tyler, born Aug. 29, 1847.
5923+   John Jay Tyler, born Mar. 2, 1850.

3409 DANIEL[7] TYLER (Perley[6]), born in Northfield,
Vt., August 2, 1812; died March 1, 1891; married Eliza Buck,
born October, 1812; died April 1, 1875. He was a farmer and
wool-grower. The children were born in Northfield. Children:

5924   Azaro Tyler, born Jan. 1836; died unmarried in North-
        field, June 11, 1856.
5925   Nelson W. Tyler, married Oct. 24, 1894, Catherine E.
        McCarthy of Northfield, where he is a farmer.
5926   Wilson D. Tyler, married Orrie McAllister; he is a
        farmer and lives in Northfield; has one daughter
        (Emelia, born April 16, 1871).
5927   Emeline Tyler, born Nov. 30, 1841; died unmarried
        Apr. 19, 1872.
5928   Edwin Tyler, born 1853; died Aug. 22, 1869.

3410 ROYALL[7] TYLER (Perley[6]), born in East Randolph, Vt., November 30, 1815. He moved to Wisconsin, where
he died. He was twice married. He had other daughters besides the one named herewith, but their names and residences
are unknown. Children:

5929   John Tyler, is a merchant in Goldfield, Ia.
5930+   D. Alonzo Tyler, born in Lake Mills, Wis.
5931   Frank Tyler, lives in Valisea, Ia.
5932   Eliza Tyler, married —— French, and lives in Hum-
        bolt, Ia., and has children.
5933   E. S. Tyler, a farmer and harness-maker in Nebraska.

3415 JOHN ALFRED⁷ TYLER (Perley⁶), born in
Northfield, Vt., July 25, 1827; married November 14, 1852,
Mary E. Brown, born May 6, 1833. The children were born
in Northfield. Children:

5934+ Marosie F. Tyler, born Sept. 10, 1853.
5935 Chester F. Tyler, born Feb. 6, 1855.
5936+ Della May Tyler, born Nov. 8, 1858.
5937+ Frank E. Tyler, born Jan. 4, 1862.

3417 CLARISSA⁷ TYLER (Orris⁶), born in East Randolph, Vt., January 30, 1813; died there April 19, 1874; married, February, 1834, Edward Sprague, of Randolph. Children:

5938 Jane Sprague, born Dec. 1, 1834; married, in 1854,
William F. Whitney, a farmer in Tunbridge, Vt.,
in 1898 she was residing in Dorchester, Mass., a
widow with five children.
5939 Helen M. Sprague, born in East Randolph, Vt., June
19, 1837; married, May 25, 1858, Dr. Granville P.
Conn, of Hillsboro, N. H. He is one of the leading
physicians in Concord, N. H., and noted throughout
the state and his profession; two sons (Frank W.
and Charles F.).
5940 Tyler E. Sprague, born Dec. 21, 1845; was in Civil
war; resides in Alta, Ia.; three children.
5941 Walter C. Sprague, born Sept. 17, 1850; resides in
East Randolph, Vt.; two children.

3419 SUSAN⁷ TYLER (Orris⁶), born in East Randolph, Vt., December 29, 1819; married there, June 9, 1845,
Joseph Johnson, of Stratford, N. H., later of East Randolph,
born August 15, 1807; died February 6, 1898. He was a tanner, currier and shoemaker. The children were born in Stratford. Children:

5942 Henry Johnson, born Feb. 22, 1848; married, in Saratoga, N. Y., Jan. 7, 1874, Alice Rebecca Newell,
born in Jay, N. Y., Sept. 7, 1850; died Apr. 10,
1882; two sons (George Newell and Harry).
5943 Clara Adelle Johnson, born May 31, 1850; married,
November 17, 1878, John Baldwin; resides in Morgan Park, Ill.; one daughter (Myra Belle).

3420 SOPHIA[7] TYLER (Orris[6]), born in East Randolph, Vt., October 29, 1821; died in St. Albans, Vt.; married in 1856, Jacob Orcutt of Randolph, Vt., who died in Barre, Vt., May 3, 1893. The child was born in Randolph. Child:
5944   Perley Nathan Orcutt, died July 8, 1887, in Derby, Vt.; married June 4, 1878, Margaret S. Sirright; two daughters (Sarah S. and Margaret E.).

3422 HAZEN[7] TYLER (Orris[6]), born in East Randolph, Vt., July 13, 1826; died in Strafford Hollow, N. H., October 16, 1852; married Elvira J. Crown, born in Stratford, N. H. Child:
5945+   John B. Tyler, born in Strafford Hollow, 1850.

3423 MELISSA[7] TYLER (Orris[6]), born in East Randolph, Vt., March 12, 1828; married Hiel O. Hatch, of Barre, Vt. The children were probably born in Barre. Children:
5946   Ella Hatch; married —— Ryder, of Barre, Vt.
5947   Elgi Hatch; married —— Gale, of Barre, Vt.
5948   Daughter; married George Neill, of Burlington, Vt.

3425 ELISHA[7] TYLER (Moses[6]), born in Griswold, Conn., November 2, 1794; died in 1857; married March 9, 1830, Mary Greene, daughter of Dr. Rowland Greene, of Plainfield, Conn., and Cranston, R. I. He lived in Griswold, and in Burlington and Detroit, Mich. His desire for college and a professional career was overruled by his parents who desired their only son to be with them at home. He was in the War of 1812 (See *Pension Book*). He was fond of books and music, was a good singer and a student of science, particularly of geology, a merry companion and a true friend. Though of a Federalist family he was inclined to radicalism. He entered into the anti-masonic and anti-slavery movements. In 1835, appreciating the opportunities offered by the west, he moved to central New York and thence, in 1837, to Michigan. His plans for business were baffled by the financial panic of 1837. In Michigan he was active in aid of fugitive slaves, his own house and a fleet horse ever at their service. One of his sons has collected his letters and in them may be seen abundant proof of his intellectual sympathies, insight, hopefulness, enthusiasm and a quaint humor. He would have made his mark in literature. He was a devout man and faithful to every duty. The four elder children were born in Griswold, the sixth and seventh in Burlington and the two younger in Detroit, Mich.

CHILDREN:

5949+   Charles Coit Tyler, born Dec. 30, 1830.

5950   Rowland Greene Tyler, born Jan. 4, 1832; married, Sept. 27, 1870, Mary H. E. Thomas, of Caroline County, Va.; in 1843 he went with his family to Detroit, Mich., where he was in the grocery business for nearly thirty years, retiring in 1882 to a large farm in King William county, Va., which he purchased in 1867, and where he became a planter. In 1898 he was living in Mangohick, Va.; no children.

5951   Susannah Greene Tyler, born May 24, 1834; died in Warwick, R. I., Aug. 28, 1865, unmarried; she lived the most of her life in Michigan; passed two years in Europe.

5952+   Moses Coit Tyler, born Aug. 2, 1835.

5953+   Olive Coit Tyler, born in Marshall or Burlington, Mich., July 3, 1837.

5954   Edward Scott Tyler, born Sept. 1, 1839; died Aug. 25, 1840.

5955+   John Tyler, born July 19, 1841.

5956   Samuel Coit Tyler, born Nov. 9, 1846; died July 10, 1847.

5957   Harris Greene Tyler, born Nov. 5, 1852; died in 1856.

3435 WILLIAM BELCHER[7] TYLER (James[6]), born in Preston, Conn., January 3, 1792; died in Roxbury, Vt., April 14, 1870; married, December 30, 1819, Mary Hall, of Tunbridge, born June 5, 1797; died, in Tunbridge, July 12, 1858. He moved to Tunbridge, Vt., about 1810, then to Warren, Vt. He was a bee hunter, a notary public and held town offices in Roxbury. Was justice of the peace in Windsor county, Vt., in 1848. The children were born in Tunbridge. Children:

5958   Amos Tyler, born Aug. 31, 1820; died July 2, 1822.

5959   Henry H. Tyler, born Nov. 18, 1821; died Dec. 12, 1894, in Danville, Vt.; had a family; lived also in Warren, Vt.

5960+   Mary Jane Tyler, born Mar. 19, 1823.

5961   James Tyler, born Apr. 18, 1825; died Jan. 16, 1855, in Eureka, Cal., where he went for gold.

5962+   George W. Tyler, born Jan. 16, 1827.

5963+   Susan Tyler, born Apr. 9, 1829.

5964+   Marcia Tyler, born Sept. 18, 1830.

5965   John Tyler, born Sept. 2, 1836; died in Preston, Conn., March 3, 1847.

3436   SARAH⁷ TYLER (James⁶), born in Preston, Conn., January 16, 1794; married (1), —— Cushman; married (2), April 25, 1822, Adin Cook, of Preston, Conn. The children were born in Preston. Children:

5966   Adin Tyler Cook; died in Haverhill, Mass., in 1855; married Jane Chase, of Haverhill, Mass.; has one daughter.

5967   Henry Eckford Cook, died young.

5968   Mary Ellen Cook; died young.

5769   Rosalthea Adelaide Cook; married Isaac E. Smith, of Haverhill, Mass., a pioneer shoe manufacturer; she resides in Haverhill, s. p.

5970   James Albert Cook; married and resides in Preston, Conn., on part of old homestead.

3438   JOHN B.⁷ TYLER (James⁶), born in Preston, Conn., May 21, 1798; died in Bainbridge, Mich., November 7, 1878; married in Ashtabula, O., December 19, 1819, Eliza Buffum, born in Charlotte, Vt., October 12, 1804; died in Bainbridge, Mich., February 21, 1877. He was a farmer; resided in Liverpool, O., and in Michigan. The children were born in Liverpool. Children:

5971   James Tyler, born Oct. 18, 1822; married in Bryant, Ill., has five or six children.

5972   Maria Tyler, born Oct. 18, 1825; married —— Robinson; resides in Benton Harbor, Mich.

5973   Sarah Tyler, born Aug. 30, 1827; married —— Peck, of Alton, Tenn.

5974   John Brown Tyler, born June 26, 1829; died young.

5975   Stephen Buffum Tyler, born Nov. 11, 1832; resides in Twelve Corners, Mich.

5976   Eliza Ann Tyler, born Nov. 29, 1835; died in 1900; married —— Worth; resides in Hartford, Mich.

5977+   William Barney Tyler, born Feb. 20, 1840.

5978   Charles James Tyler, born Oct. 2, 1844; died young.

3441   BENJAMIN[7] TYLER (James[6]), born in Preston, Conn., March 3, 1805; died in Tunbridge, Vt., December 26, 1866; married, February 2, 1831, Jane Demmon, who died February 14, 1868. He was a musician and played the bass viol in the Congregational church. The children were born in Preston. Children:

5979+   Emily Jane Tyler, born Sept. 2, 1835

5980+   Levi Eckford Tyler, born June 13, 1837.

5981   Ellen Altheda Tyler, born Nov. 11, 1844; died Sept. 30, 1896; married John Stanton, of Bozrahville, Conn.

5982   Edward Clarence Tyler, born Nov. 11, 1851; moved to New Mexico.

3444   ALICE AUGUSTA[7] TYLER (Bishop[6]), born in Preston, Conn., September 12, 1804; married, January 13, 1828, Henry A. Morgan, a distant relative of her mother, and a descendant of James Morgan who went from Wales to New London, Conn., in 1640. Her husband was a farmer and they moved to St. Charles, Kane County, Ill. Children:

5983   Samuel Tyler Morgan, born Sept. 16, 1828; married November, 1849, Mary Avery of Griswold, Conn.

5984   Joseph Tyler Morgan, born May 31, 1830; died Sept. 9, 1846.

5985   Eliza Tyler Morgan, born Dec. 3, 1831; married, Nov. 28, 1850, Moses Morse, of Griswold, Conn.; they had a son and a daughter (William H. and Mary E.).

5986   Henry W. Morgan, born Sept. 2, 1833; married, June 16, 1856, Sarah Geer, of Griswold.

5987   Dwight R. Morgan, born January 15, 1835; married, Jan. 1, 1863, Lucy Haskill.

5988   Mary Jane Morgan, born June 16, 1837; in 1869 was living in St. Charles, unmarried.

5989   Mary Elizabeth Morgan, born Dec. 14, 1838; died Dec. 1842.

5990   Daniel W. Morgan, born Oct. 5, 1844; married, Nov. 5, 1867, Sarah Atkinson.

5991   Julia Ann Morgan, born Jan. 5, 1846; in 1869 was liv-
         ing in St. Charles, unmarried.

    3457 MARY AMY[7] TYLER (John Brown[6]), born in
Preston, Conn., October 15, 1804; died October 10, 1853; married, February 24, 1825, Billings Brown, of Poquetannoc,
Conn., born September 17, 1794; died in Groton, Conn., April
6, 1883.   Children:

5992   John Tyler Brown, born in Poquetannoc, November 22,
         1825; died July 18, 1851; was unmarried.
5993   Edward Alexander Brown, born June 24, 1832; died
         Sept. 15, 1832.
5994   (Hon.) Henry Billings Brown, born in South Lee,
         Mass., Mar. 2, 1836; was graduated from Yale Uni-
         versity in 1856; studied law in a private office and
         attended lectures at Yale and at Harvard and was
         admitted to the bar of Wayne county, Mich., July,
         1860; was appointed deputy marshal of the United
         States in the spring of 1861 upon the election of
         Mr. Lincoln to the presidency, and was subsequently
         assistant United States attorney for the eastern dis-
         trict of Michigan; in 1868 he was appointed judge
         of the state circuit court of Wayne county; in a few
         months he returned to active practice and formed a
         partnership which continued until 1875 when Presi-
         dent Grant appointed him district judge for the
         eastern district of Michigan; in December, 1890,
         he was appointed associate justice of the Supreme
         court to succeed Justice Miller; received the degree
         of LL. D. from the University of Michigan in 1887
         and from Yale University in 1891.   He has no chil-
         dren.
5995   Mary Stewart Brown, born May 12, 1846; died May
         2, 1851, in Griswold.

    3458 SAMUEL   ALEXANDER[7]   TYLER   (John
Brown[6]), born in Preston, Conn., November 13, 1809; died in
Marshall, Mich., February 4, 1877; married, July 30, 1846, in
Geneva, N. Y., Caroline Halsey, of Lodi, N. Y.   Began his
education in the Plainfield Academy. and went into a store at
the age of sixteen in Norwich, Conn.   His father gave him

$500, and he went to New York to seek his fortune. He took passage in a sailing vessel for South America, and after a five months voyage, arrived at Buenos Ayres in 1828; thence he went to Callao and thence to Lima, where he was employed as a bookkeeper by a large English house. In 1834 he became a member of the firm of Sellure, Reed & Company and went to Sierra Pasco to take charge of silver mines; in 1840 he sold out and came back home. The next four years he spent in travel in the United States. In 1845 he drove a team from Connecticut to Michigan and settled on 300 acres in Marengo township, near Marshall. Here he built a nice house surrounded by a fine park; also built tenements and had a fancy farm. In 1857 he met with an accident and sold his farm and removed to Marshall, where he lived until his death. He gave large aid to the cause of the north in the Civil war, and the " Tyler Guards," Captain Crittenden, were named in acknowledgment of this. He was generous to the poor and a man of high moral principles. He was a Republican in politics. His wife was a lady of talent and intellectual abilities.

CHILDREN:

5996   Son, died young.
5997   Sarah Frances Tyler, married Lieutenant-Commander John P. Merrell of the U. S. Navy, of Portland, Ore.; in 1897 he was Light House Inspector; they had one daughter (Dorcas).
5998   Frederick Halsey Tyler, was graduated from Annapolis Naval Academy; died in Norfolk, Va., s. p. in 1895; was a lieutenant in the U. S. Navy; married Josephine English, of Crosswick, N. Y.
5999   John Brown Tyler, lives in Detroit, Mich.; has no family.

3468 FRANCES MARY[7] TYLER (Joseph Coit[6]), born in Preston, Conn., July 8, 1811; died in Norwich, Conn., May 8, 1900; married, December 25, 1833, Hezekiah Lord Morgan, born January 5, 1809; died in Griswold, Conn., January 1, 1854; son of Major Daniel and Susanna (Lester) Morgan, and descended from James Morgan of New London, Conn. (See *Morgan Genealogy*.) He lived in Griswold, and the children were born there. Children:

6000   Sarah Morgan, born Jan. 29, 1835; died in Griswold, Aug. 1, 1844.

6001   Daniel Morgan, born Sept. 22, 1837; died in Griswold, May 4, 1849.

6002   Frances Morgan, born Aug. 18, 1840; died in Griswold, unmarried, Aug. 23, 1892.

3469 ELIZABETH[7] TYLER (Joseph Coit[6]), born in Preston, Conn., December 31, 1815; died November 24, 1846; married, November 6, 1833, William Huntington, born July 9, 1812; he married (2), November 17, 1847, Eunice Avery, who died March 3, 1850, in her 38th year. Elizabeth's children were all born in Griswold, Conn. Children:

6003   Sarah Huntington, born Oct. 4, 1836; died unmarried September 25, 1862.

6004   Hannah Huntington, born Mar. 21, 1840; married, Apr. 29, 1873, James P. Boutwell, a wool dealer living in Winchester, Mass., in 1896; had one daughter.

6007   Daniel Huntington, born July 31, 1844; married (1), Martha Smith, who died s. p.; married (2), Helen Dolbere; they live in Norwich, Conn.; had one son.

6008   George Huntington, born Sept. 6, 1846; died Dec. 6, 1846.

3470 FREDERICK WILLIAM[7] TYLER (Joseph Coit[6]), born in Griswold, Conn., April 17, 1817; died in Norwich, Conn., December 22, 1875; married (1), Jane Elizabeth Pratt, of Westport, Conn., born August 1, 1820; died October 10, 1854; married (2), Elizabeth Campbell, of Griswold, born June 25, 1823; died February 1, 1893. He was a farmer. The children were born in Griswold.

CHILDREN, by first marriage:

6009+ Josephine Tyler, born February 11, 1841.

6010   Fred Tyler, born Mar. 25, 1844; married, Oct. 30, 1877, Mary Stanton; of the firm of Stanton & Tyler, dealers in spices; lives in Norwich; no children.

6011   Sarah Tyler, born Nov. 27, 1845; died Jan. 20, 1846.

6012   Jeannette Tyler, born Apr. 10, 1847; married, June 25, 1884, Irving N. Gifford, of Norwich, Conn., where he is city clerk; no children.

6013   Jane Tyler, born July 15, 1853; died July, 1854.

CHILDREN, by second marriage:

6014+ Frank Tyler, born May 7, 1856.

6015 Jane Tyler, born Feb. 11, 1859; died in Norwich, May 27, 1872.

6016 George Tyler, born Mar. 5, 1862; died Jan. 28, 1871.

3485 ANN MERCY[7] TYLER (John[6]), born in Griswold, Conn., December 23, 1819; died February 27, 1847; married, July 2, 1838, Joseph Gilbert Deane of Plainfield, Conn., born May 20, 1816; died May 3, 1891. Children:

6017 Annie Tyler Deane, born June 15, 1839; married (1), Dec. 31, 1862, Oliver S. Bradley, who was lost at sea, March, 1867; married (2), Angus Arkins, of New Haven, Conn.

6018 Albert Deane, born July 23, 1841; married, Apr. 18, 1867, Harriet E. Wilford.

6019 Mary Elizabeth Deane, born Dec. 23, 1843; married John J. Southworth, of South Ashburnham, Mass.

6020 Edwin Deane, born Sept. 14, 1846; married Mary A. Bennett; lives in Westminster, Conn.

3487 MARY ESTHER[7] TYLER (John[6]), born in Griswold, Conn., February 5, 1824; died there May 23, 1895; married, March 20, 1845, Andrew Edmond, born in Griswold, June 20, 1814. The children were born in Griswold. Children:

6021 Mary Frances Edmond, born Dec. 19, 1845; married (1), Dec. 25, 1873, Frederick Brewster, No. 3506, who died Mar. 6, 1875; married (2), May 10, 1883, George Loring, of Central Village, Conn.

6022 John Tyler Edmond, born Mar. 15, 1848; married, Nov. 16, 1875, Mary J. Arnold; lives in Westerly, R. I.

6023 Abbie Cogswell Edmond, born Jan. 24, 1851; married, Sept. 28, 1871, William C. Lillibridge, of Griswold.

6024 Jane Elizabeth Edmond, born Apr. 12, 1854; married, Dec. 1872, Erastus W. Babcock, of Stonington, Conn.

6025 Hetta Coit Edmond, born Jan. 3, 1857; married, Feb. 26, 1879, George F. Champlin, of Avondale, R. I.

6026   Andrew Edmond, born Sept. 4, 1859; married, Dec. 13, 1879, Ida May Rix; lives in Westerly, R. I.

6027   Ann Tyler Edmond, born Dec. 7, 1861; died Apr. 22, 1891; married, Mar. 23, 1880, George F. Palmer.

6028   Nellie Edmond, born Mar. 29, 1864; married, Mar. 22, 1885, George E. Terrell, of Waterbury, Conn.

6029   Samuel Stewart Edmond, born Mar. 2, 1869; married, Feb. 11, 1890, Lucy I. Rude, of Griswold, where they live.

3488   LUCY BELCHER[7] TYLER (Henry Coit[6]), born in Griswold, Conn., February 5, 1824; married, April 9, 1852, Joseph Gist, of Lisbon, Conn., born March 27, 1824, in Nudlinger, Bavaria. She was living in 1896 in Lisbon, where her children were born. Children:

6030   Harriet Tyler Gist, born June 1, 1855; married Rufus Bailey, of Stonington, Conn., and lives in Lisbon; she had a daughter (Mary) and two children who died young.

6031   Anna Keisel Gist, born May 15, 1858; married Paul Gist and lives at home of her father; has a daughter (Dora).

3489   JOHN SPAULDING[7] TYLER (Henry Coit[6]), born in Griswold, Conn., November 23, 1826; moved to Dubuque, Ia., in 1857, and thence to Fairview, Kas.; married, June 21, 1866, Harriet Chace, of Leavenworth, Kas. He was a farmer. The children were probably born in Fairview. Children:

6032   Son, born Mar. 28, 1868; died next day.

6033   Augustus Hubbard Tyler, born Feb. 12, 1869.

6034   James Chace Tyler, born July 5, 1871.

6035   Lois Tyler, born July 7, 1873.

6036   John Hyde Tyler, born Jan. 1, 1881.

3494   HARRIET[7] TYLER (Henry Coit[6]), born in Griswold, Conn., June 8, 1834; married, June 17, 1856, Edwin Morgan, of Griswold, born April 26, 1811; son of Major Daniel Morgan; he died September 23, 1888 (his first wife was Alethea Frazier, and by that marriage he had seven children). Harriet's five elder children were born in Griswold, where, in 1896, she was living.   Children:

6037   William Moss Morgan, born May 13, 1862; living in Boston, a lawyer, unmarried.

6038   Edwin Tyler Morgan, born Feb. 16, 1864; married, Feb. 22, 1887, Minnie Kelly, of Rockland, Me.; and lives in Boston.

6039   Frank Cheseborough Morgan, born Mar. 11, 1865; died Oct. 17, 1865.

6040   Jesse Moss Morgan, born Sept. 19, 1868; lives in Boston, unmarried.

6041   Fanny Morgan, born Apr. 23, 1869; a nurse.

6042   Daniel Morgan, born in Plainfield, Conn., July 20, 1871; lives on the home place.

6043   Frederick Lester Morgan, born in Canterbury, Conn., Nov. 19, 1876; a lawyer.

3497   MARY ELIZA[7] TYLER (Dwight Ripley[6]), born in Griswold, Conn., April 23, 1847; married, March 4, 1869, Thurston Browning Barber, born in Norwich, Conn., February 14, 1842; died July 3, 1908; son of Rowland R. and Mary (Browning) Barber, of Norwich.   He was a farmer and they resided in Norwich.   Mr. Barber was a horse and cattle expert; understood animals and their ailments, and knew how to subdue them by kindness and consideration.   He was always a very powerful man, physically, and in his youth a noted athlete.   He was widely known and highly regarded for his integrity and kindness of heart.   He was thrown from a hay tedder on the first day of July, and died from the effects of the accident.   Mrs. Barber is greatly interested in the revolutionary history of her distinguished ancestor, General John Tyler, and has made much laborious research to verify records.   She caused the revolutionary marker to be placed at the general's tomb in Pachaug cemetery.   She has given great assistance to the author and editor of this work.

CHILDREN:

6044   Charles Tyler Barber, born and died in Sprague, Conn., Oct. 16, 1872.

6045   Mary Johnson Barber, born in Sprague, Conn., July 20, 1875; died in Norwich, Feb. 13, 1881.

3498 JOSEPH COGSWELL[7] TYLER (Thomas Spaulding[6]), born in Griswold, Conn., February 9, 1827; died March 12, 1907; married (1), January 14, 1851, Huldah Ann Gallup, born December 26, 1830; died in Griswold, March 26, 1873; daughter of John and Matilda (Kinne) Gallup, of Sterling, Conn. (See *Gallup Genealogy*); married (2), May 24, 1881, Betsey Cook, born December 9, 1844; daughter of " Squire " Clark and Sally (Kinne) Cook, of Griswold. In 1896 he was living in Griswold, where the children were born.

CHILDREN, by first marriage:

6046+   Joseph Tyler, born May 20, 1852.
6047   Martha Ann Tyler, born Feb. 1, 1860; died Feb. 6, 1894, unmarried.

3500 DWIGHT RIPLEY[7] TYLER (Thomas Spaulding[6]), born in Griswold, Conn., December 25, 1831; married (1), March, 1851, Emily Dawman Green, born in Griswold, April 14, 1816; died July 9, 1873; married (2), August 24, 1874, Alice Forney, born in Waltons Mills, O., January 13, 1855. He moved to Ohio and resided near Uhrichsville, where the children by the second marriage were born.

CHILD, by first marriage:

6048+   Emma Isora Tyler, born in Cleveland, O., Oct. 5, 1855.

CHILDREN, by second marriage:

6049+   Edward Dwight Tyler, born June 8, 1875.
6050+   Florence Irene Tyler, born May 22, 1878.

3502 GEORGE[7] TYLER (Thomas Spaulding[6]), born in Griswold, Conn., February 22, 1841; died in Waltham, Mass., November 3, 1889; married, August 27, 1862, Isabella Johnson, of Griswold, born January 23, 1842; died December 2, 1907; daughter of Henry L. and Almira Desire (Browning) Johnson. He resided in Griswold until 1882 when he removed his family to Waltham. He was deeply interested in agriculture and owned the Tyler homestead in Griswold and adjoining property comprising above 1000 acres besides extensive holdings in Ohio and California. After 1880 until his death his energies were devoted to the manufacture of agricultural implements in which he was very successful, his product being widely known and extensively used. The family continued to reside in Waltham until 1898, when they removed to the Aberdeen district of Boston where the widow died. Her interment was in the Pachaug cemetery of Griswold. The fourth child was born in Norwich, Conn.; the others were born in Griswold.

CHILDREN:

6051+ Frank Johnson Tyler, born July 7, 1863.

6052 Alfred Cogswell Tyler, born Oct. 22, 1866; married, Dec. 31, 1896, Mary Elizabeth Shannon, of Chicago, Ill., born May 31, 1871.

6053 John Browning Tyler, born Oct. 11, 1868; died Feb. 1, 1871.

6054 Kate Browning Tyler, born May 17, 1871.

6055 Lucius Spaulding Tyler, born Aug. 1, 1873; unmarried.

6056 Charles Thomas Tyler, born Dec. 10, 1875; died July 17, 1882.

6057 Florence Larned Tyler, born May 13, 1878.

6058 Warren Hull Tyler, born Jan. 23, 1882; died Aug. 3, 1882.

3520 ELIZABETH[7] TYLER (Joseph[6]), born in Preston, Conn., January 13, 1828; died in Norwich, July 31, 1897; married, May 17, 1852, Henry Bartlett Cruttenden, who died in Norwich, December 9, 1898. He was the founder of Crescent Beach, Conn. The children were born in Norwich. Children:

6059 Joseph Tyler Cruttenden, born Oct. 17, 1854.

6060 Edwin Cruttenden, born Jan. 23, 1868.

6061 Henry Cruttenden, born Apr. 24, 1870.

6062 Tyler Cruttenden, born Feb. 15, 1872.

3534 JOSEPH EDWIN[7] TYLER (Daniel Meech[6]), born in Baltimore, Md., June 25, 1835; died February 17, 1893; married, November 20, 1873, Alice Virginia Norris. The children were born in Baltimore. Children:

6063 Joseph Edwin Tyler, born Sept. 14, 1874; died Nov. 7, 1878.

6064   Charles Norris Tyler, born Apr. 20, 1876; died Feb. 25, 1877.

6065   Albert Edward Tyler, born Jan. 5, 1880; died June 5, 1880.

3535   JOHN ALPHA[7] TYLER (Daniel Meech[6]), born in Baltimore, Md., September 11, 1837; married, February 15, 1866, Kate Logue; he lives in Baltimore, where the children were born. Children:

6066   William Bancroft Tyler, born Dec. 7, 1866.

6067   Mary Logue Tyler, born May 28, 1868.

3538   MARTHA ELIZABETH[7] TYLER (Daniel Meech[6]), born in Baltimore, Md., June 20, 1844; married, May 17, 1866, Nehemiah Breed Shorey, Jr., born January 30, 1835, son of Nehemiah and Annie S. (Chase) Shorey. Children :

6068   Emma Tyler Shorey, born Mar. 1, 1867; died Nov. 27, 1874.

6069   George Alpha Shorey, born Mar. 6, 1869; died Nov. 29, 1874.

6070   Alice Anna Shorey, born Feb. 1, 1872.

6071   Olive Foss Shorey, born Dec. 20, 1875; died Nov. 21, 1886.

6072   Mattie Stevens Shorey, born May 28, 1878; died Nov. 27, 1886.

6073   Nellie Shorey, born Dec. 23, 1881; died Nov. 21, 1886.

6074   George Bancroft Shorey, born Oct. 9, 1883; died Nov. 21, 1886.

6075   Mabel Shorey, born Feb. 4, 1886.

6076   Frank Ellis Shorey, born Mar. 25, 1888.

3547   LUCY ANN[7] TYLER (Oliver Spicer[6]), born in Poquetannock, Conn., in the old " Punderson house," November 15, 1831; married, December 12, 1855, Malcolm Forbes, of New York City, son of Colonel John Forbes; he died, but she was living in Norwich, Conn., in 1896. Child:

6077   Oliver Tyler Forbes, born in New York City, Jan. 5, 1857; married, July 14, 1891, Lila Pendleton Nash, of Philadelphia; daughter of Austin B. and Ann Eliza (Pendleton) Nash.

3553 CHARLES[7] TYLER (Guerdon Kimball[6]), born in Baltimore, Md., July 4, 1836; married (1), September 11, 1862, Sallie Hoopes, who died June 12, 1871, in her 29th year; she was a Quakeress; married (2), April 30, 1873, Virginia Poulson. He was living in Baltimore in 1899, where the children were born.

CHILDREN, by first marriage:

6078   Clara Virginia Tyler, born Oct. 19, 1863.

6079   Susie Estelle Tyler, born Aug. 5, 1865; married, Oct. 31, 1895, W. M. McCormick.

6080   Gurdon Kimball Tyler, born May 21, 1867; died Sept. 10, 1867.

6081   Charles Edwin Tyler born Nov. 8, 1868; died July 4, 1869.

6082+   Walter Bancroft Tyler, born Mar. 1870.

6083   Sallie Tyler, born May 26, 1871; died Sept. 10, 1871.

CHILDREN, by second marriage:

6084   Florence Virginia Tyler, born Jan. 24, 1874; died June 26, 1874.

6085   Edith Hall Tyler, born Oct. 19, 1875.

6086   Grace Tyler, born Jan. 5, 1879; died July 30, 1880.

6087   Jessie Thomas Tyler, born Feb. 20, 1882; died Aug. 12, 1886.

3554 LUCY BANCROFT[7] TYLER (Guerdon Kimball[6]), born in Baltimore, Md., August 15, 1838; married, November 20, 1862, Edwin Davis Hoopes, of Arlington, Baltimore County, Md. The children were born in Baltimore, Md. Children:

6088   Frank Guerdon Hoopes, born Oct. 13, 1863; married Sept. 14, 1886, Millie Kennon; has one son (Guerdon K.).

6089   Susan Tyler Hoopes, born Oct. 24, 1865; married, Apr. 7, 1897, Benjamin F. Dickerson, of Charlottesville, Va.

6090   Edwin Hoopes, born Apr. 6, 1870.

6091   Lucy Bancroft Hoopes, born July 3, 1877.

3555 GEORGE GUERDON[7] TYLER (Guerdon Kimball[6]), born in Baltimore, Md., November 23, 1840; married,

October 18, 1865, Sophia Williams Goodenow, of Bangor, Me. Children:

6092   Harry Guerdon Tyler, born July 31, 1866; married, Nov. 1898, Susan Harvie Douthat, of Weyanoke, Va.; is a lumber and box dealer and resides in Norfolk, Va.

6093   Helen Bruce Tyler, born Mar. 9, 1869; married, Nov. 20, 1888, M. B. Sayre, of Baltimore, Md., one child (Dorothy Britain, born June 23, 1895).

6094   George Arthur Tyler, born May 23, 1873.

6095   Bessie Appleton Tyler, born Nov. 16, 1874; married, Apr. 7, 1896, Samuel Edwin Edgerton.

6096   Alice Louise Tyler, born Mar. 2, 1877.

6097   Sophia Ruth Tyler, born Mar. 4, 1882.

6098   John Goodenow Tyler, born Nov. 9, 1883.

6099   Stephen Bancroft Tyler, born Apr. 19, 1887.

6100   Frances Goodenow Tyler, born July 2, 1891.

3557 JAMES EDWARD[7] TYLER (Guerdon Kimball[6]), born in Baltimore, Md., March 21, 1845; married, Nov. 10, 1870, Ida Hamer. He is of the firm of Kimball, Tyler & Company, barrel manufacturers of Baltimore, where he resides. The children were born there. Children:

6101   William Guerdon Tyler, born Aug. 25, 1873.

6102   Eleanor Justis Tyler, born Mar. 7, 1877.

6103   Susan Bancroft Tyler, born Nov. 7, 1878.

6104   James Edward Tyler, Jr., born Sept. 12, 1880.

3558 SUSAN[7] TYLER (Guerdon Kimball[6]), born in Baltimore, Md., December 30, 1847; married, December 15, 1870, James Pollard, of Baltimore, born in King and Queen county, Va., and son of John Pollard; he is a lawyer and moved to Baltimore in 1871, where the children were born. Children:

6105   Lucy Kimball Pollard, born Dec. 9, 1871; married, Oct. 31, 1893, Rev. Henry M. Wharton, D. D., of Baltimore, Md.; one daughter.

6106   Susie May Pollard, born May 12, 1875; died Dec. 23, 1876.

6107   Juliette Jeffries Pollard, born Aug. 11, 1877.

6108   Guerdon Tyler Pollard, born Jan. 20, 1880.

3560 FRANK KIMBALL[7] TYLER (Guerdon Kimball[6]), born in Baltimore, Md., June 12, 1851; married, September 4, 1877, Julia M. Rivers. The children were born in Baltimore. Children:

6109   Frank Rivers Tyler, born July 12, 1878.
6110   Eva Bancroft Tyler, born Feb. 28, 1880.
6111   Julia Antoinette Tyler, born Feb. 5, 1882.
6112   Sarah Bancroft Tyler, born Feb. 14, 1884.
6113   Susan Rivers Tyler, born Aug. 6, 1886.
6114   Lucilla Dix Tyler, born Feb. 14, 1892; died July 17, 1892.

3561 JOSEPH HENRY[7] TYLER (Guerdon Kimball[6]), born in Baltimore, Md., June 8, 1855; married, September 2, 1885, Florence R. Land. The children were born in Baltimore. Children:

6115   Robert Land Tyler, born Nov. 5, 1888; died June 8, 1890.
6116   Rose Bancroft Tyler, born Aug. 31, 1891.
6117   Grace Kimball Tyler, born Aug. 11, 1895.
6118   Katherine Douglas Tyler, born Jan. 9, 1897.

3576 MARY THERESA[7] TYLER (George Washington[6]), born in Cranston, R. I., October 30, 1823; died August, 1884; married, March, 1864, W. S. Fifield. Child:
6119   George Washington Tyler Fifield, born Mar. 13, 1867; married; resides in New Haven, Conn., s. p.

3580 ABBY WATSON[7] TYLER (George Washington[6]), born June 16, 1834; married, September 13, 1854, Fayette Putnam Brown, who died May 21, 1885; resides in Providence, R. I. The children were born in Providence. Children:
6120   George Tyler Brown, born Nov. 29, 1855; died Mar. 17, 1856.
6121   Fayette Williams Brown, born Oct. 8, 1857; married June 9, 1886, Elizabeth Leighton; has two daughters.
6122   Mary Theresa Brown, born June 6, 1862; died May 18, 1868.
6123   George Tyler Brown, born July 15, 1864; married

Aug. 1889, Katherine Kinne Cronyn; has one
daughter (Barbara).

6124   Elizabeth Tyler Brown, born Oct. 14, 1870.
6125   Royal Tyler Brown, born Sept. 6, 1874; died Mar. 18,
       1875.

3592 CLAYTON⁷ TYLER (Benjamin S.⁶), born in
Royalton, O., in 1855; married Ella Poe, of Brooklyn, O.   He
studied law; carries on a fruit farm; resides in Lakewood, O.,
where he has been mayor.   Children:

6126   Clayton Tyler.
6127   Estella Tyler.
6128   Molly Tyler.
6129   Esther Tyler; died young.
6130   Child; died young.

3594 HELEN MARIA⁷ TYLER (Benjamin S.⁶), born
in Royalton, O., January 25, 1860; married, December 25,
1880, William R. Mallo, who died in Cleveland, O., November 1,
1894, aged 35 years.   He was a contractor and owned a glue
factory in Cleveland, where she lived after his death and where
the children were born.   Children:

6131   Bessy Marr Mallo, born Jan. 28, 1883; died May 2,
       1883.
6132   Helen Lulu Mallo, born Apr. 21, 1884.
6133   William Tyler Mallo, born Sept. 27, 1885.
6134   Olive Lydia Mallo, born Nov. 19, 1887.

3596 MARY ADELIA⁷ TYLER (Gideon Wells⁶), born
in Granger, O., April 1, 1844; married, September 2, 1869,
Rev. Russell Thaddeus Hall, D.D., born in Richmond, Vt., October 6, 1844; a descendant of the emigrant —— Hall, Cambridge, Mass., 1631, and son of Joseph A. Hall.   He was graduated from Oberlin College in 1865; D. D., in 1895; was graduated from Union Seminary, N. Y., in 1870; in the Civil war,
1862-1864; has served churches in Pittsford, Vt., Mount Vernon, O., Tavans and Jacksonville, Fla.; pastor of the (Wilson)
Mission church, St. Mark's Place, New York City, and the Second Congregational church in Greenwich, Conn., residing there
since May, 1892.   She was graduated from Oberlin College in
1865; taught three years in Mansfield, O., and Rutland, Vt.

The two elder children were born in Pittsford and the two younger in Mount Vernon.

CHILDREN:

6135 Edith Bronson Hall, born Mar. 1, 1877; was graduated from Oberlin College in 1899.

6136 Richard Tyler Hall, born July 9, 1879; died in Mount Vernon, O., August 18, 1880.

6137 Arthur Benedict Hall, born Mar. 27, 1881; was graduated from Yale College in 1902.

6138 Walter Grant Hall, born Dec. 10, 1884; died in Greenwich, Conn., Aug. 12, 1895.

3600 GEORGE WELLS[7] TYLER (Gideon Wells[6]), born in Medina, O., August 1, 1859; married Merion McIntosh of Bay City, Mich. He is connected with the " *Beacon*," a publication in Boston, Mass.; resides in Hyde Park, Mass. Child:

6139 Paul McIntosh Tyler, born April 18, 1889.

3609 PARKMAN TYLER[7] DENNY (Anna Sophia[6]), born December 20, 1851; married (1), November 22, 1881, Cora J. Monroe, born April 18, 1858; died May 17, 1882; married (2) December 13, 1887, Grace L. McIntosh of Mattapan, born January 22, 1858; died January 9, 1890; married (3), July 5, 1894, Cora B. Knight, of Leicester, Mass., born August 5, 1864. He was cashier of Leicester National bank 1890-1904; treasurer of Leicester Savings bank, 1890 to present time. Children:

6140 Ruth Parkman Denny, born Dec. 8, 1899; died Dec. 12, 1899.

6141 Parkman Knight Denny, born Feb. 20, 1903.

3626 FISHER AMES[7] TYLER, JR. (Fisher Ames[6]), born in Cincinnati, O., December 3, 1847; married, June 2, 1880, Eva May Hudson, born in Gainesville, Tex., December 3, 1862; daughter of General William Hudson. He was a private in Company A, 3d Miss. cavalry under General Forrest till the close of the Civil war. At 18, he was a clerk in Memphis, Tenn. He went to Gainesville, Tex., in 1879, where he lived in 1900, and where his children were born. Children:

6142 Lelia May Tyler, born April 22, 1881.

6143   Ethel Ames Tyler, born July 31, 1883.
6144   William Hudson Tyler, born July 19, 1888.
6145   Ruth Tyler, born May 31, 1898.

3651   NATHAN[7] TYLER (Elijah[6]), born in Chesterfield, Mass., in 1812; married Lydia White, of Cheshire, Mass.
He resided the most of his life in Hawley, Mass., but in 1897
was residing in Easthampton, Mass. The children were born
in Hawley. Children:
6146   Hattie Tyler, married Edward Willcutt, of Florence,
        Mass.
6147   Henry Tyler, resides in Easthampton.
6148   Herbert Tyler, resides in Smith Ferry, Mass.; unmar-
        ried in 1897.
6149   Frank Tyler, a carpenter and resides in Amherst,
        Mass.
6150   Fred Tyler, resides in Hawley, Mass.
6151   Ellen Tyler, was residing in Easthampton, Mass., in
        1897; unmarried.
6152   James Tyler, a farmer and resides in Plainfield, Mass.
6153   Ida Tyler, married William Clapp, of South Deerfield,
        Mass.
6154   Charles Tyler, a farmer in Readsboro, Vt.
6155   Walter Tyler, resides in West Brattleboro, Vt.

3653   ELIJAH[7] TYLER (Elijah[6]), born in Chesterfield, Mass., February 24, 1816; married, April 22, 1847, Lucina S. Tower, born in Chesterfield 1825; died in Conway, Mass.
February 8, 1892. He resided in Conway from about 1853 to
1884 when he moved to Leeds, Mass., and in 1900 was residing
with his daughter, Isabella, in Haydenville, Mass. The two
elder children were born in Savoy, Mass. Children:
6156   Ella Adelaide Tyler, born Feb. 14, 1849; died Nov. 3.
        1879; married Wilmot L. Clark, of Williamsburg,
        Mass., one son (Frank Elijah).
6157+   Luther E. Tyler, born Dec. 31, 1851.
6158   Isabella Lucina Tyler, born in Conway, Mass., Dec.
        25, 1853; married Martin L. Sornborger, of Wil-
        liamsburg; four children (Lindell M., Burt T., Ray
        N. and Ella L.).

3654 NANCY A.[7] TYLER* (Elijah[6]), born in Chesterfield, Mass.; died November 3, 1874; married December 7, 1842,
Ezekiel Noble, born in Castleton, Vt., May 31, 1816, son of
Ezekiel and Hannah (Gates) Noble, of Pittsfield, Mass.   They
moved to Afton, Ill.   (See *Loomis Genealogy.*)   Children:

6159   Harriet Joanna Noble, born July 24, 1844; died 1850.
6160   Emma Lolette Noble, born June 23, 1846; married
          Jan. 20, 1869, Varnum A. Glidden.
6161   William Marvin Noble, born July 10, 1848; married
          December 25, 1873, Sarah Seaborn.
6162   Caroline Nancy Noble, born Apr. 25, 1850; died 1852.
6163   Arthur James Noble, born Mar. 17, 1853.
6164   Inez R. Noble, born Mar. 24, 1855; died 1872.
6165   Charles Freemont Noble, born Aug. 3, 1857.
6166   Caroline Noble, born July 9, 1859; died 1864.
6167   —— Lillie Alice Noble, born June 20, 1861.
6168   Homer Bennett Noble, born Sept. 7, 1863.
6169   Mirtie Noble, born Dec. 5, 1868.

3655 HENRY P.[7] TYLER (Elijah[6]), born in Chesterfield, Mass., in 1820; died in Sandy Hill, N. Y., about 1895;
married Frances Edwards, of Savoy, Mass.   He was a farmer
and resided in Savoy, where the children were born.   Children:

6170   Jane Tyler, married (1), —— Joslyn; married (2),
          Horace Polly, of Savoy; had five children and lives
          in Pittsfield, Mass.
6171+ William Henry Tyler, born in 1845.
6172   George Tyler, married Emma ——, who was divorced
          and died; he lives in Sandy Hill; has a son (Harry)
          who lives in Savoy.
6173   Alonzo R. Tyler, married Carrie Jenkins and lives in
          Conway, Mass.; has a daughter (Jessie).
6174   Amelia Tyler, married (1), Frank Lincoln; married
          (2), Truman McAuley; has three children and lives
          in Sandy Hill.

3661 HON. BENJAMIN O.[7] TYLER (Ephraim[6]), born
in Wilmington, Vt., September 7, 1820; died September 2,
1880; married (1), July 31, 1849, Huldah Mather, of Marl-

* This record is given as a *probable* line from Elijah.[6] So marked in
Mr. W. I. T. Brigham's notes.

boro, Vt., who died July 12, 1865; married (2), November 12, 1867, Rosabel M. Wright, of Shelburne Falls, Mass., who died November 2, 1893.   All the children but the eldest were born in Trenton, N. J.   Mr. Tyler was educated in the academy in Brattleboro, Vt.; he was a man of fine ability and was a lawyer in Winchendon, Mass.; Wilmington, Del., and Trenton, N. J., and judge of the Court of Common Pleas of Mercer county five years.

CHILD, by first marriage:

6175   Phinehas Mather Tyler, born in Winchendon, Mass., May 31, 1851; died Sept. 12, 1854.

CHILDREN, by second marriage:

6176   Mary E. Tyler, born Feb. 3, 1869.
6177   Frank W. Tyler, born Sept. 3, 1872; died Jan. 3, 1885.
6178   Gertrude Tyler, born July 1, 1874; died Oct. 8, 1874.

3662   HON. ANSEL L.[7] TYLER (Ephraim[6]), born in Wilmington, Vt., October 11, 1822; married, September 7, 1847, Lucy A. Richardson, of Brattleboro, Vt., who died September 26, 1893.   He was educated at the academy in Brattleboro and became a merchant in Charlemont, Mass., to which place he went in 1846; he was town clerk eight years, justice of the peace and moderator for more than thirty-nine years; chairman of the board of selectmen eighteen years; county commissioner nine years; a member of the Legislature 1855, 1885; state director in the Western, now Boston & Albany Railway; assistant assessor of Internal Revenue, six years; postmaster, 25 years.   In 1887 he was chosen president of the Old Folks association and held the position many years.   His children were born in Charlemont.

CHILDREN:

6179   Mary Stewart Tyler, born Nov. 30, 1859.
6180   Fred Lyman Tyler, born July 21, 1862.

3663   D. CLINTON[7] TYLER (Ephraim[6]), born in Wilmington, Vt., October 10, 1825; died May 23, 1890; married, May 21, 1862, Martha R. Howard.   He was a farmer and lived in Guilford, Townshend, Wilmington and Brattleboro, Vt.

He never sought office; he was highly esteemed for integrity, kindness and social qualities.   Child:

6181   Minerva A. Tyler, born in Townshend, Mar. 22, 1863.

3666   HON. JAMES M.[7] TYLER (Ephraim[6]), born in Wilmington, Vt., April 27, 1835; married (1), December 11, 1861, Ellen E. Richardson, of Brattleboro, Vt., who died January 22, 1871; married (2), September 1, 1875, Jane P. Miles, of Brattleboro.   He was educated in the academy in Brattleboro; was graduated from the law department of the University of Albany, N. Y.; practiced law four years in Wilmington and in Brattleboro from 1865 to 1877; was state representative from Wilmington in 1863 and 1864 and in the special session of 1865; state attorney, 1866, 1867; member of the 46th and 47th Congress from the second Vermont District in 1887; appointed by the Governor to draft the new common school law, which he resigned to accept an appointment of judge of the Supreme Court of Vermont, which he has held since September, 1887. Since 1874 he has been a member of the board of trustees of the insane asylum in Vermont, now known as the " Brattleboro Retreat."

CHILD:

6182   Appleton Tyler, died in infancy.

3672   OSCAR STEPHEN[7] TYLER (Chester Grennell[6]), born in Whitingham, Vt., January 20, 1828; died in Princeton, Mass., January 22, 1897; married, November 22, 1855, Louisa W. Rollins, born July 11, 1826; died April, 1886. The children were born in Whitingham.   Children:

6183   Alfred Oscar Tyler, born May 22, 1859; married Oct. 24, 1896, Helen W. B. Dake, born Oct. 24, 1861, daughter of John Dake; resides in East Princeton, Mass.

6184   Elbert Ellsworth Tyler, born Mar. 10, 1861; died Sept. 4, 1866.

3675   HENRY CLAY[7] TYLER (Chester Grennell[6]), born in Bennington, Vt., in 1835; married (1), May 18, 1862, Marian L. Pierce, born April 18, 1842; died December 19, 1863; married (2), November 29, 1866, Almira Bishop, of

Hinsdale, N. H. He was in the Civil war; a farmer and resides in Dana, Mass.

CHILD, by first marriage:

6185   Edwin O. Tyler, resides in West Boylston, Mass.

CHILDREN, by second marriage:

6186   William Bishop Tyler; resides with his father.

6187   Carrie Bishop Tyler; died in infancy.

3718   AMANDA R.[7] TYLER (Simeon[6]), born in Dimmock, Pa., February 10, 1823; died January 2, 1884; in Friendsville, Pa.; married, February 12, 1845, John Foster, of Great Bend, Pa., born in Orange County, N. Y., September 15, 1817; lived in Dimmock; thence in 1884 to Friendsville. The children were born in Dimmock. Children:

6188   Jane Foster, born Dec. 5, 1846; died June 22, 1854.

6189   Eliza Foster, born April 30, 1849; married, April 12, 1870, Dr. Eben P. Hines, of Great Bend, Pa., a graduate of University of Michigan and Jefferson Medical College, had five children (Carrie, John, Lillian, Daisy, James).

6190   Margaret J. Foster, born Feb. 8, 1851; died Feb. 1875; married Charles Glidden, of Friendsville.

6191   Wealthy C. Foster, born Feb. 3, 1853; died June 22, 1854.

6192   Frank Foster, born Feb. 27, 1855; died Jan. 25, 1857.

6193   Frank L. Foster, born July 27, 1857; a lumberman; lived in Fosston, Minn.; unmarried.

6194   John H. Foster, born June 20, 1859; unmarried, a merchant in Great Falls, Montana.

3719   ELIZA O.[7] TYLER (Simeon[6]), born in Dimmock, Pa., July 9, 1825; died in Philadelphia, Pa., December 4, 1893; married, September 30, 1845, Orlando G. Hempstead, of Philadelphia, a custom house broker. Children:

6195   Delos Balch Hempstead, born May 21, 1846; lives in Philadelphia.

6196   Frederick D. Hempstead, born July 30, 1849; died June 21, 1851.

6197   Ernest Alexis Hempstead, born Dec. 15, 1851; married, Aug. 5, 1875, Annie M. Warner, daughter of Gilbert Warner, of Montrose, Pa.; lives in Meadville, Pa.; three daughters (Marguerite, Louise, Helen).

6198   William Orlando Hempstead, born Mar. 3, 1855; married, 1874, Viny Patton; he is a custom house broker in Philadelphia, where he lives; has a son and daughter (William O. and Florence).

6199   Minnie Eliza Hempstead, born July 31, 1859.

6200   Harry Newton, born June 25, 1868; married, Oct. 10, 1894, Nellie Brush, daughter of John Brush, of Indianapolis, Ind.; lives in Meadville.

3720   COLONEL CASPER W.[7] TYLER (Simeon[6]), born in Dimmock, Pa., March 6, 1837; married, March 14, 1864, Lucy T. Warner, daughter of Gilbert Warner, of Montrose, Pa. He was apprenticed at eleven years of age in the newspaper office of his brother-in-law; was educated in McGrawville College, McGrawville, N. Y.; was admitted to the bar in 1860. He helped to raise and was captain of Company H, 141st Pa. volunteers in 1862 in the Army of the Potomac; was severely wounded at the battle of Gettysburg, but joined his regiment during the holidays of the same year, was major and also Lieutenant-colonel in 1864. Was appointed assistant assessor of Internal Revenue after the war and held that office until he moved to Meadville in 1867 where he bought half an interest in the Meadville *Republican* which was later sold; he then bought the Crawford *Journal* which he held until 1872; he began to practice law in 1874. Was in the Pennsylvania Legislature in 1876 and 1882. Was secretary of the board of trustees of the Meadville Theological Seminary. The children except the eldest were born in Meadville.

CHILDREN:

6201   Elizabeth Reed Tyler, born in Montrose, Pa., Aug. 7, 1866.

6202   Mabel Louise Tyler, born Oct. 9, 1868; married Mar. 1894, Rev. Ural Sumner Hughes and was divorced; resides in Chicago, Ill., s. p.

6203   Guy Watkins Tyler, born June 18, 1870, and died next day.

6204   Grace Tyler, born Aug. 2, 1873; died Dec. 5, 1876.
6205   Dorothy Tyler, born Aug. 30, 1887.
6206   Annie Tyler.

    3723   LEANDER ANSEL[7] TYLER (Ansel[6]), born in
Dimmock, Pa., February 23, 1836; married February 23, 1865,
Mary J. Dowlin of Downington, Pa. He lived in Oil City,
East Bridgewater and Brooklyn, Pa., from 1864-1871; thence
to Easton, Pa., in 1879; in the Life Insurance business in Philadelphia, since 1870.   The two elder children were born in Oil
City; the next two in East Bridgewater.   Children:
6207+   William Dowlin Tyler, born June 24, 1865.
6208   Ada Isabella Tyler, born Nov. 22, 1867; died Nov. 12,
        1880.
6209   (Professor) Ansel A. Tyler, born Mar. 7, 1869; un-
        married in 1899; was graduated from Lafayette Col-
        lege in 1892; A.M. 1895; assistant in the biological
        department, Lafayette College, 1892-1894; Ph. D.
        Columbia, 1897; instructor in biology, Union Col-
        lege, Schenectady, N. Y., 1897-1898; instructor in
        botany, Syracuse University, 1898-1899; assistant
        in biology, 1900, University of Arizona.
6210   Mary Anna Tyler, born Dec. 31, 1870.
6211   Brewster Phillips Tyler, born in Brooklyn, Pa., Sept.
        17, 1874; B. S. Lafayette College, 1897.
6212   Sarah Belle Tyler, born in Easton, Pa., Nov. 7, 1881.

    3724   DUANE LEGRANGE[7] TYLER (Ansel[6]), born in
Montrose, Pa., July 26, 1837; married, March 30, 1870, Emma
R. Buchanan, of Ithaca, N. Y.   A carpenter and resided in
Kansas City, Mo.; he has resided in Florida, Pennsylvania,
Delaware and Connecticut.   Was in Company M, 2d Pa. Heavy
artillery, Civil war, 1862-1865.   Children:
6213   Grace Ella Tyler, born in Harford, Pa., Jan. 25, 1871,
        married, Sept. 6, 1894, Victor E. Hunter; has two
        children (Malcolm Tyler, born Feb. 17, 1896; Har-
        old H., born Jan. 26, 1898).
6214   Rose Frances Tyler, born in Walcottville, Conn., Oct.
        26, 1875.
6215   Arthur Duane Tyler, born in Kansas City, Mo., Nov.
        17, 1885.

3725 ELLEN LUCENIA⁷ TYLER (Ansel⁶), born in Dimmock, Pa., September 8, 1839; married Jason F. Whitney, of Farrington, Conn.; resides in Tiffany, Pa. Children:

6216   Ernest Whitney, married ——.

6217   Clarence Whitney; residing in Conn. in 1899; married and had four children; wife deceased.

6218   Winona Whitney; married; residing in Conn. in 1899.

3727 CLARK LEWIS⁷ TYLER (Ansel⁶), born in Bridgewater, Pa., February 20, 1842; married, October 17, 1871, Ellen Burk; is a carpenter and resides in Scranton, Pa.; the children were born there. Children:

6219   Ellen Tyler, born Sept. 9, 1872.

6220   Agnes Tyler, born Mar. 1, 1874.

6221   Lewis Tyler, born Dec. 31, 1875; is a brass finisher in Philadelphia.

6222   Florence Tyler, born Apr. 21, 1878.

6223   George L. Tyler, born Nov. 19, 1879.

6224   Ansel Tyler, born Nov. 7, 1881.

6225   Richard Tyler, born Oct. 18, 1883.

6226   Elizabeth Tyler, born July 13, 1886.

3728 MARTHA⁷ TYLER (Ansel⁶), born in Bridgewater, Pa., March 5, 1844; married May 10, 1872, Hermann Otto, of Hartford, Conn.; resides in East Bridgewater, Tenn.; the children were born there. Children:

6227   Charles Tyler Otto, born Feb. 14, 1874.

6228   Hermann Otto, Jr., born Nov. 2, 1877.

3733 GEORGE W.⁷ TYLER (Harvey⁶), born November 16, 1850; married, November 11, 1878, Emilie Brown. In 1870 he moved to Minnesota, and became a railway engineer, living in Willmar, Minn.; also car inspector on the Great Northern Railway. Child:

6229   George Harvey Tyler, born in Willmar, July 30, 1881.

3744 FRANK M.⁷ TYLER (Hiram Ward⁶), born April 25, 1843; married, October 16, 1867, Ellen Marie Taylor; resides in Grand Rapids, Mich., where the children were born. Children:

6230   Hiram Walter Tyler, born Mar. 7, 1870.

6231   Edgar Malette Tyler, born July 8, 1872; married, Jan. 3, 1898, Emma Marie Snyder, of South Bend, Ind.; resides in Grand Rapids, Mich.

3759   ALBERT WINSLOW[7] TYLER (Sophia[6]), born in Townsend, Mass.; died in Washington, D. C., March 6, 1892; buried in Arlington; married, in Boston, Mass., Tamar M. Dempster. He went through the Civil War with the Boston Lancers, Company D, 1st Mass. cavalry; then became director of Heald's American band in Washington, D. C.; was employed in the Treasury department; then held an important post with the National Bank of Redemption agency; was president of Washington Musical association No. 4; a good musician and very popular. The male line is extinct. Children:
6232+   Albert Winslow Tyler, probably born in Washington, D. C.
6233   Elizabeth Tyler, resides in Washington, D. C.; is a contralto church and concert singer; a stenographer, teacher and writer.

3761   WILLIAM P.[7] TYLER (Sylvanus[6]), born in Dimmock, Pa., July 14, 1836; died there April 26, 1877; married (1), February 21, 1853, Miranda Compton, born in New Jersey, September 26, 1836; died in Dimmock, April 26, 1877; married (2), March 11, 1878, Lucinda Taylor Newman, born in Springvale, Pa., April 14, 1844. He lived in Dimmock until 1867, running a steam mill; then went south for three years; then removed to Springvale, Pa. The elder children were born in Dimmock.

CHILDREN, by first marriage:
6234+   C. W. Tyler, born Aug. 2, 1861.
6235+   Edith Tyler, born July 9, 1863.

CHILD, by second marriage:
6236   Pearl H. Tyler, born in Springvale, Apr. 24, 1882.

3765   HENRY H.[7] TYLER (Sylvanus[6]), born in Dimmock, Pa., January 18, 1843; married (1), April 20, 1867, Mary E. Carlin, born February 18, 1847; died June 16, 1884; married (2), August 7, 1886, Sarah Mitchell, born May 18, 1856; died March 18, 1893. He lived in Elk Lake, Pa.

Children, by first marriage:
6237 Nathan Southwick Tyler, born Nov. 8, 1867; died
Apr. 2, 1883.
6238 Byron H. Tyler, born May 30, 1869; married, Jan. 1,
1901, Tillie Smith.
6239 Frank C. Tyler, born Feb. 21, 1873; died July 2, 1887.

Child, by second marriage:
6240 Gettie C. Tyler, born Apr. 8, 1890; died July 28, 1893.

3783 EMMA L.[7] TYLER (Royal[6]), born in Oak Valley, Kas.; married George Gardner, a farmer, who lives in the state of Washington. Children:
6241 Isabell Gardner, married Jesse D. Miller, a farmer in
Iowa; has two sons and a daughter (Earl E., Eymons H., Mary J.).
6242 Caleb Gardner, married Ethel ———; is a farmer and
lives in Washington; has one son (Hiram).
6243 Nora Gardner, married Edgar Thompson, a baker in
Washington; they have a son and daughter (Frank, Emma).
6244 Jessie Gardner.
6245 Nannie Gardner.
6246 Iven Gardner.
6247 Ivie Gardner.

3785 JAMES[7] TYLER (Royal[6]), born in Oak Valley, Kas.; married Jennie Atcherson. Children:
6248 Lena Tyler.
6249 Mamie Tyler.

3788 EDGAR[7] TYLER (Royal[6]), born in Oak Valley, Kas.; married Ellie A. Bond. He is a farmer. Children:
6250 Marshall Tyler.
6251 Rollie V. Tyler.

3789 ORATAS[7] TYLER (Royal[6]), born in Oak Valley, Kas.; married Mora Pock; lives in Oklahoma, a farmer. Children:
6252 Ortor Tyler.

6253   Dalia Tyler.
6254   Mary E. Tyler.

3795   BYRON⁷ TYLER (William H⁶), born near Williamsport, Ind., April 24, 1849; married (1), August 30, 1869, Laura Moore, of Time, Ill.; married (2), Mrs. Emma D. McWilliams.   In early life he was a school-teacher and a telegraph operator; since 1879 has been in grain commission business and a member of the board of trade in Kansas City.   When he moved to Kansas the county was full of game and he shipped the first car of buffalo meat to the Chicago market; he then went into the business of shipping of buffalo hides and wolf pelts; after his marriage he settled in Wilson, Kan., and took up 160 acres of land which he sold for town lots; he is a Knight Templar; was a delegate to the St. Louis convention in 1896 that favored Bryan's free silver policy.   The child was born in Time, Ill.

CHILD:

6255   Charles B. Tyler, born July 11, 1871; is a telegraph operator, stenographer and accountant; resides in Terre Haute, Ind.; unmarried in 1897.

3796   GEORGE BRIER⁷ TYLER (William H.⁶), born in Williamsport, Ind., March 10, 1851; married (1), in 1872, ——, who died soon; married (2), ——, who died about 1886. He was a street commissioner and was residing in Osawatomie, Kan., in 1897.   He was first a farmer; went to Kansas with his father, and then was teamster between the Missouri River and interior Kansas; returned to Indiana in 1872 where he injured his knee with a sickle in the cornfield and was made a cripple for life.   Children:

6256   Albert Tyler, born in 1882.
6257   Ora Tyler, born in 1884.

3798   SAMUEL⁷ TYLER (William H.⁶), born in Williamsport, Ind., February 24, 1855; married, September 27, 1882, Winnie Vallandingham.   He went to Kansas with his parents in 1868, then to Indiana in 1875, thence to Illinois in 1881.   Was residing in Rossville, Ill., in 1898, where the children were born.   Children:

6258   Anna Tyler, born July 23, 1883.

6259   Cyrus Tyler, born March 5, 1885.

6260   Alice Tyler, born Sept. 6, 1887.

3808   ELLA[7] TYLER (George Clinton[6]), born in Marshfield, Ind., March 21, 1857; married, April 12, 1876, Robert A. Chandler, of Marshfield, where the children were born.   Children:

6261   Robert A. Chandler, born June 26, 1880.

6262   Ray Chandler, born Oct. 4, 1882.

6263   Hal Chandler, born Dec. 24, 1884.

3809   JULIA[7] TYLER (George Clinton[6]), born in Marshfield, Ind., March 22, 1859; married, August 29, 1878, Charles E. Winks, of Frankfort, Ind.   The children were born in Frankfort.   Children:

6264   Alma Winks, born June 12, 1879.

6265   Elma Winks, born April 26, 1891.

6266   Charles Winks, born May 1, 1894.

3826   ANN MARIAH[7] TYLER (Benjamin[6]), born in Wadsworth, O., Nov. 4, 1843; died in East Wrightstown, Wis., July 17, 1876; married, November 5, 1858, Nathaniel Gilman Grant, of East Wrightstown, born in Antwerp, N. Y., March 31, 1834; he married (2), February 22, 1877, Susan C. Gifford.   He was on the U. S. ironclad *Pittsburg* from 1864-1865; postmaster since 1867; superintendent of schools and held many town offices; was a Republican and a Baptist.   The children were born in East Wrightstown.   Children:

6267   Minnie Mariah Grant, born Jan. 10, 1860; married, Nov. 28, 1878, Henry Priest; has two daughters (Grace M. and Rose V.), and resides in Chili, Wis.

6268   Rosina Elvira Grant, born Aug. 1, 1861; married, April 13, 1879, Melvin Phillips, of Snyderville, Wis.; has one son and one daughter (Arthur E. and Nina M.).

6269   Edith Remina Grant, born April 27, 1866; married, June 25, 1889, Elmer Brown, of Christie, Wis.; has one daughter (Nina M.).

6270   Victor Freeman Grant, born Aug. 14, 1867; married (1), April 18, 1890, Emma Baetz; married (2),

April 12, 1893, Emma Gustman; has one son by second marriage (Ernest E.); resides in Snyderville.

6271   Elmer Ellsworth Grant, born June 25, 1874; married, Jan. 5, 1897, Bertha Maves; resides in East Wrightstown.

3827   WILLIAM HENRY[7] TYLER (Benjamin[6]), born in Wadsworth, O., January 8, 1845; died in East Wrightstown, Wis., April 10, 1878; married, August 28, 1872, Jennie Sandeborg. He served three years in the Civil War in Company H, 20th Wisconsin Infantry. The children were born in East Wrightstown.   Children:

6272   Effie Charlotte Tyler, born Nov. 3, 1873; married, Dec. 22, 1892, Hubert Ellis, of Greenleaf, Wis.; had one daughter (Jennie Evalyn).

6273   Albert William Tyler, born May 5, 1876; was at Fort Logan; colonel in 1897 in Company H, 7th Infantry, in which company he enlisted in 1895, in Indianapolis, Ind., for three years.

6274   Clara Olive Tyler, born Aug. 15, 1878; married, March 30, 1896, Charles Baetz, of Wrightstown.

3830   ELLA BERTHA[7] TYLER (Benjamin[6]), born December 22, 1867; married, September 5, 1882, Willard H. Russell, born in New York, December 6, 1862; a hotelkeeper in Nickerson, Minn.   Children:

6275   Rud Arthur Russell, born Dec. 6, 1883.
6276   Franklin Benjamin Russell, born Jan. 24, 1886.
6277   William Murl Russell, born May 10, 1888; died June 27, 1893.
6278   Carl Henry Russell, born Dec. 11, 1889.
6279   Mildred May Russell, born Oct. 22, 1893.
6280   Roland Leroy Russell, born Oct. 31, 1895.

3832   RUSH S.[7] (or H.) TYLER (Joseph[6]), born in Wadsworth, O., October 15, 1851; married (1), July 1, 1875, Laura T. Stannard, who died in Wadsworth February 21, 1893; married (2), December 18, 1895, Emma F. Long, of Guilford, O.   The children were born in Wadsworth.

CHILD, by first marriage:
6281+ Winnifred Pearl Tyler, born June 21, 1876.

CHILDREN, by second marriage:
6282 Josie R. Tyler, born Aug. 2, 1897.
6283 Son, born Feb. 12, 1901.

3833 JESSIE R.[7] TYLER (Joseph[6]), born in Wadsworth. O., September 17, 1856; married, March 13, 1877, John W. Culbertson born November 11, 1854. He lived for a time in Chippewa Lake, O., where the eldest child was born; then was an engineer on the C. L. W. Railway; then a hardware dealer in Lorain, O., where the two younger children were born. Children:
6284 Guy Wilber Culbertson, born Sept. 26, 1878.
6285 Joseph Ray Culbertson, born March 21, 1883.
6286 William Leo Culbertson, born June 1, 1889.

3841 MARTHA[7] TYLER (Albert[6]), born in Oxford, Mass., May 5, 1853; married, December 31, 1873, Edson Francis Estabrook, of Paxton, Mass., born November 7, 1851; son of Dwight and Mary B. (Rogers) Estabrook. He is a mill superintendent in Worcester, Mass., where they live, and where the child was born. Child:
6287 Alice Louisa Estabrook, born Jan. 4, 1875.

3844 WALTER DRURY[7] TYLER (Albert[6]), born in Granby, Conn., April 6, 1860; married, October 21, 1879, Christina Caroline Forrest, daughter of William S. Forrest; she died in 1899. He was of the firm of A. L. Joslin & Co., boot and shoe manufacturers, in Oxford, where the children were born; but in 1901 he was living in Yarmouth, N. S. Children;
6288 Mabelle E. Tyler, born Feb. 5, 1881.
6289 Gladys Wealthy Tyler, born Feb. 15, 1895; died Oct. 3, 1895.

3848 SARAH FRANCES[7] TYLER (Charles E.[6]), born in Oxford, Mass., October 20, 1856; married (1), August 2, 1875, Orrin Johnson, of Oxford, Mass.; married (2), February 7, 1889, Charles Combs. She lived in Sutton where her children were born.

CHILDREN, by first marriage:
6290   Alfred Orrin Johnson, born Dec. 18, 1876.
6291   Edgar Johnson, born July 11, 1879.
6292   Martha Johnson, born Aug. 9, 1881.
6293   Flora Johnson, born July 9, 1884. ·
6294   Ida Johnson, born Jan. 28, 1887.

CHILD, by second marriage:
6295   Joseph Combs, born Dec. 10, 1889.

3853   ALICE AUGUSTA⁷ TYLER (Lemuel⁶), born August 7, 1871; married, May 29, 1892, Christopher H. Vick, of Chicago, Ill., who moved to Rensselaer, Ind., where he held a county office.   Children:
6296   Harry C. Vick, born Feb. 19, 1894.
6297   Clara Vick, born Jan. 17, 1897.

3898   CLARA CATLIN⁷ TYLER (John, Jr⁶), born in Harford, Pa., April 9, 1810; died June 8, 1890; married, by Rev. Lyman Richardson, June 7, 1836, William Metcalfe Clarke of Syracuse, N. Y., born April 3, 1800; died December 23, 1884. She was highly educated for the period of time and part of the world in which she lived and was preceptress of Cazenovia High School 1832-1833 and of the Manlius Academy 1834-1835.   They resided in Syracuse, where the children were born.   There she was a prominent church-worker, leader in the choir and faithful in charitable work.   The world was her field and she reached out to the poor of her own city and the negroes in the South as well as to the work of the missionaries in foreign lands.   She received a shock of paralysis some years before her death, but the unselfish devotion for others' welfare which characterized her whole life, did not abate during her invalidism.

CHILDREN:
6298   Henry Wadsworth Clarke, born Nov. 6, 1837; married
         (1), Oct. 15, 1867, Ellen Amanda Clarke, born May
         6, 1842; died Feb. 23, 1871; married (2), June
         30, 1887, Mrs. Mary Maria (Daniels) Chase, born

Jan. 5, 1836. He is a city engineer in Syracuse; has one son (Theodore W.).

6299 Frances Amelia Clarke, born Dec. 6, 1839; an invalid.

3899 HARRIET ANN[7] TYLER (John[6]), born in Harford, Pa., April 27, 1817; married, May 25, 1840, Rev. Willard Richardson, of Houston, Del., born May 23, 1815. He was the youngest of three members of the Richardson family who were famous educators in northeastern Pennsylvania. His eldest brother married Charlotte Sweet, No. 3894. In 1901 Mrs. Richardson was living in Harford. Children:

6300 Thomas Sweet Richardson, born June 16, 1845; died Feb. 23, 1846.

6301 William Tyler Richardson, born April 12, 1847; died Feb. 28, 1850.

6302 Thomas Sweet Richardson, born Nov. 23, 1848; died Feb. 28, 1876; unmarried.

6303 Oscar Wadsworth Richardson, born April 7, 1851.

6304 Clara Richardson, born Dec. 9, 1852; married, Oct. 16, 1884, William Nutter Pierce, born Jan. 21, 1847; lives in Harford.

3900 NANCY[7] TYLER (Job[6]), born in Harford, Pa., April 12, 1804; died September, 1874; married, July 19, 1821, Francis Moxley, of New Milford, Pa., born April 11, 1798. The children were born in New Milford. Children:

6305 Adaline Moxley, born March 24, 1823; died Oct. 28, 1863; married, Dec. 23, 1857, Rev. Edwin A. Francis.

6306 William Tyler Moxley, born Feb. 16, 1826; married (1), Nov. 20, 1848, Sophia Roe born Dec. 7 1826; married (2), Jan. 31, 1854, Mary E. Woodmancy.

3901 DEACON JARED[7] TYLER (Job[6]), born in Harford, Pa., April 21, 1806; died July 7, 1877; married, January 30, 1831, Sarah Hartt, born May 20, 1809; died October 16, 1874. He lived in Harford and in New Milford. The children were probably all born in Harford, except the second. Children:

6307+ Henry Judson Tyler, born Feb. 24, 1832.

6308+   John Wadsworth Tyler, born in New Milford, Pa.,
        July 6, 1834.
6309   Mary Emeline Tyler, born Dec. 23, 1838; died Feb.
        5, 1840.
6310+   Edward Job Tyler, born April 13, 1841.
6311   Jared Hartt Tyler, born Sept. 17, 1846; died unmar-
        ried, Oct. 7, 1874.
6312   Nancy M. Tyler (adopted), born March 7, 1842; mar-
        ried, June 3, 1868, Lewis Wilson.

3907   PROFESSOR WILLIAM SEYMOUR[7] TYLER,
D. D., LL. D. (Joab[6]), born in Harford, Susquehanna County,
Pa., September 2, 1810; died in Amherst, Mass., November
19, 1897: married, September 4, 1839, Amelia Ogden Whiting,
born in Binghamton, N. Y., March 4, 1819; and died in
Amherst, Mass., August 4, 1904; daughter of Mason and Mary
(Edwards) Whiting. Mason Whiting, a leading early member of the bar in Binghamton, and a prominent abolitionist,
was the son of Doctor William Whiting, of Great Barrington,
Mass. (an army surgeon in the Revolution, rendering also great
service by successful experiments in manufacturing gunpowder),
and his wife, Anna Mason, who was descended from the *Mayflower* pilgrim, Governor William Bradford; Major John
Mason, one of the patentees of the royal charter of Connecticut, commander-in-chief of the colonial forces and the
hero of the Pequot war; and through Elizabeth St. John, wife
of Samuel Whiting, D. D., from the royal families of England,
Scotland, Normandy, Spain, and Russia. Mary Edwards was
a granddaughter of the Rev. Jonathan Edwards, and was also
a descendant of Captain Thomas Willet, first mayor of the
city of New York, 1665; thirteen of Mrs. Tyler's New England
ancestors were Puritan ministers.

Professor Tyler prepared for college " by snatches as I (or
rather my father), could pick up a teacher in the vicinity or
hear of one at a distance." In the fall of 1827 Professor Tyler
entered Hamilton College in the Junior Class, but owing to
dissensions between the faculty and trustees, he left at the
end of his first term, as did most of his class. During 1828
he taught in Norwich and Binghamton, New York. His attention was directed to Amherst College and his father took him
there in midwinter " in a cutter," and he was admitted in the

same standing in which he left Hamilton, the second term of junior year. While in college, he writes: " I boarded at a Club at Mr. Green's, and it never cost me more than seventy-five cents a week." " All the cloth that I wore in college was homespun, made from the wool of sheep raised on the farm, spun in the house, and for the most part by my mother's own hands, woven in a hand-loom, and dyed and dressed in Harford." Although only a year and a half at Amherst, he received the degree of A. B. in the class of 1830, and the Salutatory or second scholarship appointment at commencement. He taught 1830-31 in Amherst Academy the Mathematics and English branches. " It was," he writes, " at Andover Seminary and during my tutorship in college that I came to prefer the department of languages." 1831-32 and 1834-35 he spent at Andover Theological Seminary, and from 1832-34 was a tutor in Amherst College where he boarded in the same family with Miss Mary Lyon, founder of Mt. Holyoke, of which institution he was made a trustee in 1862, and from 1874 to 1894 was the honored president of the board. In 1835-36 Professor Tyler studied in New York under Rev. Thomas H. Skinner, D. D., LL. D., in a class that became the nucleus of the Union Theological Seminary. He was licensed by the Third Presbytery of New York, February 29, 1836. On leaving New York in the spring of 1836, he writes, " it had been my expectation to ' go West,' either as a professor in some western college or as a home missionary," but " I found the roads were in such a state that the stage agents would not undertake to carry me." For a time he was a tutor in Amherst College. In the fall of 1836 he was appointed Professor of Latin and Greek at Amherst College, and in 1847 Samuel Williston Professor of the Greek language and literature, which position he held until he was made Professor Emeritus in 1893, after having been engaged actively as a full professor for *fifty-seven* years, during the incumbency of five of the college presidents. The Amherst College *Obituary Record* for 1898 says: " No officer in Amherst College has ever done so much as Professor Tyler for the individual improvement of the students, morally and religiously, and to a great many he has been a spiritual father."

On October 16, 1859, he received ordination at North Amherst. In 1857 Harvard University conferred upon him the degree of D. D., and he was given the degree of LL. D. by

Amherst in 1871 and by Columbia in 1887. Harvard University again selected him as one of those to be honored at the celebration of its two hundred and fiftieth anniversary in 1886, conferring upon him the degree of LL. D. It is a singular honor that he should have received from Harvard, although it was not his *alma mater*, both the degree of D. D. and LL. D. In only two other instances had that university honored one man with both degrees. He twice visited the old world in 1855-56, traveling especially in Italy, Greece, Egypt, and Palestine, and in 1869-70 studying in Athens and Egypt. He was a trustee of the Pittsfield Young Ladies' Institute, founded by his brother Wellington; he prepared the constitution and did much of the work of organizing Williston Seminary, founded by Samuel Williston in 1841; was active in co-operating with Miss Sophia Smith in the founding of Smith College; was many years a trustee, and for a time president of the Board of Trustees of this institution. He was acting president of Amherst College during the latter part of President Seelye's administration.

For years his salary was $500, but in the early days when the college faced financial ruin, he was one of the first to agree with his fellow-teachers to take each year only so much as the college could afford. The Springfield *Republican* of November 20, 1897, says: " Prof. Tyler had been identified with Amherst College; its life was his life, and he gave as much to its character, its scholarship and its great success in education as any one man, and was indeed the essential representative of its fundamental Christianity and its careful scholarship upon the long-established lines. He was often called ' the Amherst Socrates,' and this indicates his familiar method in the classroom, where his keen inquiry and his shrewd wit and occasional dry humor illuminated many a scholastic examination of texts and hard questions. He was somewhat given to sarcasm, for he was a master of that method of expression; but it never exceeded the reasonable bounds of his teaching. Perhaps there was never a college professor whose personality and individual ways counted for more." Rev. R. S. Storrs, D. D., says of him in the Introductory Note to the *History of Amherst College*, 1895, " However long the college may continue, however far its influence may reach, and howsoever rich it may become, in accumulating funds, in a generously enlarged physical equipment, in the men who as teachers give it grace and renown, in the fame which shall draw to it students from afar, it may safely be predicted that none will ever have done more to determine its character, to invigorate its life, or to give tone to its widening influence, than did those who were early associated in it as teachers and guides; and it may with equal assurance be added that of all those thus associated none will be remembered with a more affectionate honor than will be given to him who came to the college in his young manhood, and who faithfully wrought in it till fullness of years gave him right to retire." Mr. H. L. Bridgman, one of his students in the class of 1866, said of him: "He aimed to make and did make not only scholars, but men. Greek art and letters were to him but the fruit and the evidence of Greek character, and that not as an intellectual exercise, a printed page or an inscribed tablet, to be studied and literally acquired, but an inspiration to duty, manhood and clear-eyed progress." Rev. C. R. Bruce, Amherst '79, says of him: "What Arnold was to Rugby, Tyler was to Amherst, both in mental and spiritual influence. He will continue to live in the multitude he has inspired to a stronger, better life, and this shall be the truest monument to his memory."

Dr. Tyler was a frequent contributor to current periodicals, and wrote numerous articles for encyclopedias. Many of his occasional discourses and memorial addresses were also published. In addition to these his published books are:

The Germania and Agricola of Caius Cornelius Tacitus, with life of Tacitus, introductions and notes; Editions of 1847, 1852, 1878; *The Histories of Caius Cornelius Tacitus, with introductions and notes for colleges,* 1849, 1851; *Plutarch on the Delay of the Deity, etc.,* 1867; *The Theology of the Greek Poets,* 1867; *Plato's Apology and Crito, with notes,* 1859, 1873; *The De Corona of Demosthenes,* 1874, 1876, three editions; *The Phillippiacs and Olynthiacs of Demosthenes,* 1875; *The Iliad of Homer, Books XVI-XXIV, with explanatory notes,* 1886; *History of Amherst College during its first half-century,* 1873; *History of Amherst College during the administrations of its first five Presidents,* 1895; *Prayer for Colleges* (a premium essay), 1854, 1877; *Memoir of Rev. Henry Lobdell, M. D., missionary to Assyria,* 1859.

The children were born in Amherst. Children:

6313+   Mason Whiting Tyler, born June 17, 1840.

6314+   William Wellington Tyler, born Oct. 14, 1841.

6315+   Henry Mather Tyler, born Nov. 18, 1843.

6316   George Seymour Tyler, born Jan. 24, 1850; died Feb. 7, 1850.

6317+   John Mason Tyler, born May 18, 1851.

3908   WELLINGTON HART[7] TYLER (Joab[6]), born in Harford, Susquehanna County, Pa., October 14, 1812; died in Labrador, August 19, 1863; buried in Pittsfield; married, March 8, 1838, Caroline Eliza Carpenter, born August 21, 1809; died September 8, 1873; daughter of John Carpenter, of Hoosick, N. Y.   He entered college at the junior year in 1829 and was graduated from Amherst A. B. 1831, A. M. 1834. He spent three years in studying theology chiefly at Andover, and was licensed to preach by the Hampshire association in 1839.   He intended to become a minister and preached a few months in Hadley, Mass., but a throat difficulty compelled him to desist.   He devoted full twenty years to the work of teaching.   He was teacher in Mercer County, Ky., 1832-1834; tutor at Amherst College, 1834-1836; was principal for a time of an academy in Manlius, N. Y., and principal of the South Carolina Female Collegiate Institute, Columbia, S. C.; then he founded the Pittsfield Young Ladies' Institute, and was its principal and proprietor twelve years and a half, and which under his administration became one of the most successful of the female seminaries in New England; he left on account of impaired health; afterward, for the year 1862 he was principal of the Cincinnati Female Seminary at Cincinnati, O.   He then went to reside in New York; he joined a company of gentlemen in the summer of 1863 in an excursion to Labrador on account of ill health and was benefited on the voyage out; but at the furthest point of the excursion, and just as they were returning, he suddenly died.   Mr. Tyler proved himself to be always equal to great undertakings and to every emergency.   His influence is felt all over the land in the lives of the cultivated women whom he educated.   He performed a leading part in the efforts which have resulted in giving larger breadth and depth to female education, in reducing it to unity, system, and adaptation to the wants of woman in society.   As his school became popular, he invested his increasing income in improvements till, as the creation of his individual energy, the institution became collegiate in all its appointments. Says Rev. John Todd, D. D.: "Many men have indomitable energy to execute; some have far-reaching sagacity to contrive. In him they were wonderfully blended. You were never surprised, to hear of a plan far in advance of all others, and you were sure that whatever obstacles were to meet it, they would be overcome. . . . For conscious power, creating hopefulness and action, I have never yet seen the man to be compared to him. . . . He wore in his face, showed in his style, and evinced in his life, a rare combination of qualities." The children were born in Pittsfield.

CHILDREN:

6318   William Carpenter Tyler, born March 18, 1839; died Aug., 1840.
6319+   Arthur Wellington Tyler, born March 14, 1842; died March 27, 1906.
6320+   Caroline Carpenter Tyler, born Feb. 15, 1844.
6321   Anna Howard Tyler, born May 20, 1846; lives in Plainfield, N. J.; unmarried.

3909   EDWARD GRISWOLD[7] TYLER (Joab[6]), born in Harford, Susquehanna County, Pa., July 23, 1816; son of Joab and Nabby (Seymour) Tyler; died of pneumonia, April 21, 1891; married, October 1, 1844, Mary M. Carpenter, born February 1, 1825; died January 29, 1899; daughter of Hon. Morgan Carpenter, of Poughkeepsie, N. Y. He entered the freshman class of Amherst College in 1834 and maintained a standing as a scholar scarcely second to any; on account of ill health, in the second term of his sophomore year, he left college for three years, which he spent on his father's farm in Pennsylvania. Returning to college in 1839 he entered the junior class and was graduated A. B. in 1841 with the salutatory oration as his appointment at Commencement. In 1844, when his class received the degree of A. M., he delivered a "Master's Oration." Immediately after his graduation, he entered on his life-work as a teacher, beginning in the Young Ladies' Institute at Pittsfield, where he was associate principal from 1841-1845; was principal of Pittsfield Gymnasium or Boys' Boarding School, 1845-1848; principal and proprietor of Ontario Female Seminary, Canandaigua, N. Y., 1848-1861; on account of ill health he gave up teaching and engaged in business, mainly in real estate and banking, first as vice-president of the First National Bank of Canandaigua from 1864-1872, then as president after 1872. He was pre-eminently a scholar and a teacher, and his influence has always been in support of the soundest learning and the most thorough instruction, and he was especially interested in the religious education of our youth. The two elder children were born in Pittsfield.

CHILDREN:

6322   Maria Seymour Tyler, born Feb. 3, 1846; unmarried.
6323   Morgan Carpenter Tyler, born Dec. 22, 1847; married, Nov. 20, 1874, Virginia Osborn Chamberlain, who died Feb., 1889. They have one son (Edward Griswold, born Aug. 17, 1876).
6324   Mary Catherine Tyler, born Dec. 31, 1856; married, April 26, 1900, Charles Wesley Robson.

3914   HARRIET WADSWORTH[7] TYLER (Jabez[6]), born in Ararat, Pa., December 19, 1820; died April 3 (or 4), 1864; married, January 4, 1840, Albert Bushnell, born December 30, 1815; died February 6, 1861. Children:

6325   Newton Wadsworth Bushnell, born May 23, 1841.
6326   Lucy Maria Bushnell, born Oct. 1, 1843; married, April 22 (or 27), 1862, Lewis E. Shutts, born Dec. 18, 1831. They lived in State Line, N. Y.; two children (Albert Morgan and Harriet Louisa).
6327   Payson Kingsbury Bushnell, born June 3, 1845; married, April 20, 1871, Olive Elizabeth Bryant, born Nov. 1, 1845; he lives in Oswego, N. Y.; five children (Belle L., Jessie L., Albert E., William H., and Gertrude).
6328   Mary Emily Bushnell, born April 17, 1847; married, May 29, 1878, Fletcher Gustavus Warner, born Jan. 25, 1837. They live in Montrose, Pa.; one child (Louise B.).
6329   Horace B. Bushnell, born May 6, 1850; married, April 22, 1877, Frances Etta Whitney, born Nov. 23, 1857. They live in Nineveh, N. Y.; four children (Fanny L., Francis H., Arthur B., and Laura).

6330   Harriet Ann Bushnell, born May 16, 1852; died, un-
        married, Oct. 29 (or 30), 1872.
6331   Jane Louisa Bushnell, born May 25, 1856.

3916   EBENEZER DENISON⁷ TYLER (Jabez⁶), born
in Ararat, Pa., February 6, 1828; married, May 12, 1868,
Lucy Ladd, of Forest Lake, Pa., born January 10, 1843.   He
was in the Civil War, 13th Pa. Regiment and was in Libby
Prison; in 1899 was residing in Scranton, Pa.   Children: -
6332+   Mary Ella Tyler, born Feb. 26, 1869.
6333   Harriet Eva Tyler, born Jan. 9, 1871; a teacher since
        1891; unmarried in 1899.

3923   WILLIAM EBENEZER⁷ TYLER (William⁶),
born in Attleboro, Mass., April 20, 1822; married, July 10,
1856, Lurana Wilmarth, of Attleboro, who died in Northboro,
Mass., November 9, 1886.   He was graduated from Amherst
College; was professor for seven years in a deaf and dumb
institute in Columbus, O.; traveled abroad; was in the real
estate business; edited a trade paper and in 1897 was a journalist in Boston.   Children:
6334   Bessie Hersey Tyler, born April 15, 1859; died June
        19, 1859.
6335   Rebecca Stanley Tyler, born June 14, 1862; died July
        8, 1899; was a librarian in North Carolina and a
        writer of both prose and verse.
6336   Frederick William Tyler, born Feb. 2, 1869; married
        Sarah Esther Blalock, and lives in Morgantown,
        N. C.

3926   ANNA NEWELL⁷ TYLER (William⁶), born in
Weymouth, Mass., February 1, 1828; married, October 27,
1859, President Newton Bateman, LL. D., of Springfield, Ill.,
born in 1822; died in Galesburg, Ill., October 21, 1897.   He
was graduated from Illinois College in 1843; taught school in
Illinois and Missouri.   In 1858 was elected superintendent of
public instruction in Illinois.   From 1874 to 1892 he was
president of Knox College, Galesburg, when he was made president emeritus and professor of Mental and Moral Philosophy.
He was a warm personal friend of President Lincoln, whose
career was the subject of his last lecture.   He was one of the

founders of the Illinois State Normal School and State Teachers' Association.

CHILDREN:

6337   Elizabeth Newell Bateman, born Oct. 3, 1864; married Wiley K. Wright.

6338   Annie Tyler Bateman, born Aug. 21, 1869; married J. Y. Ewart, of Pittsburg, Kas.

3928   EVARTS CORNELIUS⁷ TYLER (William⁶), born in South Weymouth or South Hadley, Mass., February 10, 1832; married (1), March 25, 1858, Eliza Frances Tafft, who died November 18, 1874; married (2), February 11, 1880, Mary Cushman Ballou, born in Cumberland, R. I., September 25, 1839. He lives in Pawtucket, R. I., and is an accountant.

CHILDREN, by first marriage:

6339   George Maurice Tyler, born Aug. 18, 1859; married, Nov. 17, 1880, Clara Jennette Smith, daughter of Captain Robert and Harriet Smith; no children; they live in Pawtucket.

6340   Arthur Baldwin Tyler, born Nov. 20, 1860; lived in Pawtucket.

6341   Alfred Evarts Tyler, born Aug. 10, 1864; died March 13, 1883.

6341a   Maud Eliza Tyler, born Oct. 13, 1865.

6342   William Newell Tyler, born Aug. 6, 1868; died Aug. 26, 1869.

6343   Agnes Winifred Tyler, born Oct. 11, 1869; died Aug. 4, 1890.

6344   Annie Taft Tyler, born Oct. 14, 1870; died Nov. 23, 1872.

6345   Henry Walton Tyler, born Feb. 4, 1872; died Nov. 29, 1872.

3932   FRANCIS MAURICE⁷ TYLER (William⁶), born in Amherst, Mass., May 27, 1843; married, August 21, 1866, by his father, Delia Maria Wells, daughter of Rev. Elias and Eliza Wells, of Sandwich, Mass. The child was born in Auburndale, Mass. Child:

6346   William Wells Tyler, born July 28, 1876.

3945 RALPH[7] TYLER (Samuel[6]), born in Marcellus, N. Y., September 23, 1810; died in Perry, O., November 17, 1871; married, December 15, 1831, Maria Gordon. He was a farmer and moved to Mayfield, O., where the children were born. Children:

6347+ Malvina Tyler, born June 16, 1833.

6348 Mary J. Tyler, born Sept. 2, 1835; married, Sept. 26, 1865, John D. Thompson, a farmer; s. p. 1897.

6349 Alphonso M. Tyler, died in infancy.

6350+ Anna O. Tyler, born Dec. 25, 1843.

6351+ Jared H. Tyler, born Aug. 31, 1847.

3946 DOCTOR JOHN[7] TYLER (Samuel[6]), born in Marcellus, N. Y., April 22, 1813; died in Amber, N. Y., September 28, 1845; married, January 1, 1835, Laura A. Whitney, who died in Marcellus, May, 1895; daughter of Ira Whitney; she married (2), Mr. Dada. Child:

6352 Giles Tyler, born in 1838; died in Amber Sept., 1855.

3947 JARED WHITING[7] TYLER (Samuel[6]), born in Marcellus, N. Y., April, 1816; died in Jordan, N. Y., September 15, 1898; married (1), February 12, 1840, Grace L. Whitney, who died October 10, 1865; daughter of Ira Whitney; married (2), July 11, 1867, Julia A. Perrine, of Ira, N. Y. He moved from the old farm in " Tyler Hollow," the last of the Tylers to leave the place, in 1884, to Jordan; he was buried in Marcellus, where four generations of Tylers sleep. He was justice of the peace in Marcellus in 1853-54. He was an upright and sturdy character. The children were born in Marcellus. Children:

6353 Alvaretta Tyler, born June 18, 1842; died unmarried Sept. 13, 1865; educated in Munro, N. Y., Collegiate Institute.

6354+ John H. Tyler, born Dec. 5, 1846.

6355+ George S. Tyler, born Aug. 17, 1851.

3950 CAPT. JAMES MEAKLE[7] TYLER (David[6]), born in " Tyler Hollow," Marcellus, N. Y., March 15, 1817; died in Vicksburg, Miss., in 1861, a few days before Fort Sumter was fired upon; married, in Vicksburg, in 1852, Mary Jane Wilder, born there November 24, 1829, daughter of Stephen and Edna (Nelson) Wilder. He was interested in the steamboat business. The male line is extinct. The children were born in Vicksburg. Children;

6359+ Kate Virginia Tyler, born in 1853.

6360 Blanche Emma J. Tyler, born in 1855; died in 1856.

6361 Mary Bell Tyler, born in 1857; died in 1866.

3948 GEORGE[7] TYLER (Samuel[6]), born in Marcellus, N. Y., April 23, 1818; died in Colon, Mich., November 17, 1890; married (1), December 30, 1840, Cynthia M. Rust; married (2), December 27, 1854, Livona Bartholomew, of Perry, O. He moved to Ohio in the early fifties and went to Michigan in 1855. Children:

6356 Cynthia Tyler, married —— Danby.

6357 May Tyler, married —— Danby.

6358 Fanny Tyler, married —— Foster.

3951 CHARLES ROLLIN[7] TYLER (David[6]), born in "Tyler Hollow," Marcellus, N. Y., October 6, 1820; died in Bay City, Wis., January 19, 1896; married, in Saline, Mich., July 5, 1845, Juliette Amantha Phillips, who died in Bay City, December 28, 1882; daughter of Lyman Phillips, of Columbia, Mich. He was a fine trombone player, and played in his own band on boats between Buffalo and Detroit in his early days. In 1851 he went to California by way of the Isthmus and two years later returned East. In 1854 he went to Bay City, Wis., from Ann Arbor, Mich., where he built a sawmill and owned the land where Bay City now stands, and which he lost through a sharper. He was postmaster in Bay City. Later he made an overland trip to the Pike's Peak country. He was a naturalist and taxidermist and prepared about a thousand specimens of birds, reptiles, and fish of the northwest. The children were born in Bay City except the two elder, who were born in Ann Arbor.

CHILDREN:

6362 Charles Dwight Tyler; died aged one year.

6363 Charles William Tyler, born May 9, 1848; died May 13, 1861.

6364+ Clarence Rollin Tyler, born July 5, 1859.

6365 Mary Eloise Tyler, born June 3, 1863; married Eugene Sherburne; three children (Claude, Charles, Guy).

6366+   Willard Greenfield Tyler, born Sept. 7, 1865.

6367   Jessie Rowena Tyler, born Feb. 28, 1867; married Fred A. Young, of Bay City; three children (Ray, Maudie, Jessie Lea).

6368   Leaffie Pauline Tyler, twin to Jessie; married John F. Moran; had four children (James Tyler, Mary, Juliette, Charles).

6369   Claro Phillips Tyler, born Jan. 26, 1869; married Grace Doughty; two children; one died young (Comfort Tyler, the survivor).

6370   Genevieve Helen Tyler, born in 1871; died aged nine months.

6371   Charles Dwight Tyler; died aged one year.

3952   CORNELIA M.[7] TYLER (David[6]), born in "Tyler Hollow," Marcellus, N. Y.; married Dr. Willard Greenfield; in 1898 was residing in Edinboro, Pa. Children:

6372   Frank Greenfield; resides in Edinboro.

6373   William Greenfield.

6374   Minnie Greenfield; married ——; resides in Chicago, Ill.

6375   Catherine Greenfield; married —— McLaucklin; resides in Chicago, Ill.

3953   CATHERINE ELIZABETH[7] TYLER (David[6]), born in "Tyler Hollow," Marcellus, N. Y.; died in Morgan Park, Chicago, Ill.; married Newton Boutwell, who died in Chicago. Children:

6376   Emma Boutwell; died about 1895; married in Morgan Park, Ill., Charles Kopf.

6377   Catherine Boutwell, married Frank Newell; resides near Rosebud, Ore.; has four children.

6378   Clara Boutwell, resides near Rosebud, Ore.

6379   James Boutwell, died.

6380   Son, died.

3957   MARY ANN[7] TYLER (Job[6]), married, April 28, 1842, Rensselaer Cutler, born in Greenwich, Mass., May

29, 1813; settled in 1837 in Nottawa, Mich. The children were born in Nottawa. Children:

6381   Maria Cutler, born Aug. 25, 1843; died in 1846.

6382   Henry S. Cutler, born June 3, 1845; died June 7, 1879; married Rhoda Skinner and had a family.

6383   Mary J. Cutler, born April 16, 1856; died same year.

3973 HON. CORNELIUS TYLER[7] LONGSTREET (Deborah Wemple[6]), born in Onondaga, N. Y., April 19, 1814; died July 4, 1881; married (1), May 19, 1837, Mary S. Barlow, who died September 16, 1846; married (2), September 9, 1847, Mrs. Caroline (Redfield) Sanford, daughter of Levi H. Redfield, who died in Syracuse, N. Y., October 12, 1900. An orphan at twelve, apprenticed to a tailor, at seventeen Mr. Longstreet became a merchant tailor in Syracuse, N. Y., for ten years; in 1846 he established the first wholesale clothing house in New York city; after six years returned to Syracuse. In 1855 he went to New York to establish his son Charles in business and remained until 1862 when he retired. Was one of the board of trustees of Mechanics' and First National Bank in Syracuse and had investments in manufacturing enterprises. The children were born in Syracuse.

CHILDREN, by first marriage:

6384   Charles Augustus Longstreet, born Dec. 18, 1838; died in Los Angeles, Dec. 7, 1877; married; left three sons.

6385   Mary Julietta Longstreet, born May 13, 1840; died Feb. 1, 1842.

6386   James Longstreet, born June, 1843; died Sept. 7, 1847.

6387   Edward W. Longstreet, born April 20, 1845; died Aug. 28, 1875.

CHILDREN, by second marriage:

6388   Cally Redfield Longstreet, born June 7, 1848; died Jan. 23, 1852.

6389   Cornelia Tyler Longstreet, born Dec. 14, 1849; married, Sept. 27, 1871, Charles H. Poor, of Washington, D. C.; one daughter and two sons.

6390   Alice Meta Longstreet, born June 14, 1851; died
        May 17, 1854.
6391   Comfort Tyler Longstreet, born Nov. 6, 1857; died
        Dec. 21, 1858.
6392   Cornelius Tyler Longstreet, born May 8, 1860; died
        Aug. 4, 1860.

3985 ELLEN[7] TYLER (Oren[6]), born in Onondaga,
N. Y., July 21, 1823; married (1), John Thompson; married
(2), Nahum B. Cole. She lived in later life in San Francisco,
Cal.

CHILD, by first marriage:

6393   Celia Jane Thompson; died 1895; married Captain
        John F. Mound, U. S. A., who died; had four chil-
        dren, among them a son (John), who died in early
        manhood, and a daughter (Lily).

3986 CELIA DEBORAH[7] TYLER (Oren[6]), born in
Onondaga, N. Y., October 12, 1826; died in Albany, N. Y.,
May 25, 1895; married, June 12, 1850, Colonel Frank Chamberlain, of Albany, born December 4, 1826, son of Jacob Payson Chamberlain. The children were born in Albany. Children:

6394   Eugene Tyler Chamberlain, born Sept. 28, 1856; he
        was graduated from Harvard College in 1878, with
        honors in metaphysics. He began work on the
        Albany *Journal* as local correspondent for leading
        New York, Boston, Washington, and Philadelphia
        papers; was editor of the Albany *Argus* from 1891-
        1893; was appointed U. S. Commissioner of Navi-
        gation by President Cleveland, Dec., 1893.
6395   Elizabeth Longstreet Chamberlain, born Oct. 14, 1858.
6396   Mary C. Chamberlain, born Sept. 13, 1861.

3987 DARWIN[7] TYLER (Oren[6]), born in Onondaga,
N. Y., September 15, 1831; died November 6, 1888, in Albany,
N. Y.; married, February 12, 1863, Ann Eliza Sherman.
Children:

6397   Ellen Mary Tyler, born July 20, 1864; married, Oct.
        14, 1896, Byron Crowell, of Seneca Falls, N. Y.
6398   Sherman Tyler, born May 12, 1866; died Nov. 7, 1869.

6399   Bertha Bliss Tyler, born May 4, 1870.

6400   Edwin Sherman Tyler, born April 10, 1873; died March 14, 1893.

3990   MARY ELIZABETH[7] TYLER (Oren[6]), born in Onondaga, N. Y., December 2, 1835; died in Oil City, Pa., October 10, 1899; married, May 17, 1855, Charles W. McClintock, of Oil City. Children:

6401   Fanny Bliss McClintock, born May 24, 18—;

6402   Charles Tyler McClintock, born March 18, 18—; married, Aug. 6, 1892, Marion Boughton; lives in Oil City; has one daughter (Gladys E.) and one son (Tyler B.), who died young.

3999   ASHER[7] TYLER (Chauncey[6]), born in Seneca Falls, N. Y., August 6, 1831; married (1), November 27, 1855, Elizabeth Hawley, of Chicago, Ill., who died July 1, 1871; married (2), in 1873, Harriet L. Johnson, of Berlin, Wis. He went to Fon du Lac, Wis., in 1846; became acquainted with the language and habits of the Indians and was an interpreter; he was with Shelly in the Northwest quelling the Indian outbreak; was on the survey of the Northwest Railway and later on the Government survey in Wisconsin, Minnesota, and the Dakotas. He enlisted August 1, 1861; was commissioned first lieutenant in Major Berrie's battalion cavalry attached to the 13th Mo. Volunteers; mustered out February 1, 1862, having been in Battle of Lexington, Va.; was commissioned captain and put in command of the transportation train between Forts Snelling and Abercrombie; in 1862 he was transferred to General Sibley's expedition against the Sioux, and in command of pontoon and pioneer transportation trains. Was a gold miner and resided in 1899 in Portland, Ore.

Children:

6403   Laura Elizabeth Tyler, married B. F. Wright, of McMinniville, O.; had three children; two died young (son, Clarence Eugene).

6404   Minnehaha Eloise Tyler; died in 1900; married J. J. Johnson; had one son and two daughters (Clifton, Hattie, Alice); resided in Jackson, Cal.

4000 HELEN MARY⁷ TYLER (Chauncey⁶), born in
Seneca Falls, N. Y., December 14, 1833; married, February 18,
1863, Samuel Adams, of Waupun, Wis.; he moved to Graham,
Mo.; resides in Hiawatha, Kan., with his daughter, Jessie.
The two younger children were born in Graham and the eldest
in Waupun. Children:
6405 Jessie Adams; married Edward Kennedy, of Hiawatha,
       Kan.
6406 Ruth Adams; married George Huffman.
6407 George Adams, born April 1874.

4001 LORA ELIZABETH⁷ TYLER (Chauncey⁶), born
in Seneca Falls, N. Y., April 5, 1837; married, October 20,
1857, Nelson Utley, of Waupun, Wis. The children were born
in Waupun. Children:
6408 William H. Utley, born Aug. 24, 1858; married, July
       21, 1889, Pruda Bowers; a farmer s. p.
6409 Harriet Amy Utley, born Oct. 17, 1860; married, Feb.
       17, 1886, W. C. Hammill, of Winfield, Kan.; has
       one son (William N.) and two daughters (Nellie
       and Bertha).
6410 Bertha M. Utley, born May 17, 1862; unmarried.
6411 Charles H. Utley, born April 12, 1873; married, Sept.
       8, 1897, Rose Bowers; had one child; died young.

4002 WILLIAM HENRY HARRISON⁷ TYLER
(Chauncey⁶), born in Seneca Falls, N. Y., March 26, 1840.
He enlisted in 1861 as a private on first call, in Colonel Daniel's First Wis. Cavalry, Company B, and went through the war
rising to the rank of sergeant; was at Chickamauga and with
Sherman in his " March to the Sea "; had no wounds; was
once taken prisoner, but escaped at night and crawled into the
Union lines; re-enlisted at the end of three years in Hancock's Veteran Corps. A marble-cutter and miner, and resides
in Victor, Colo. Children:
6412 Effie Roselia Tyler; married Willard Franklin Dalbee,
       of Denver, Col.
6413 Pearl Tyler, born in Denver, Col., in 1891.

4005 HERBERT MILTON⁷ TYLER (Chauncey⁶),
born in Seneca Falls, N. Y., August 25, 1848; married, Novem-

ber 2, 1871, Harriet G. Ayshford. He is a farmer and ranchman and resides in Buena Vista, Colo., in 1899. Children:

6414   Earl Tyler, born in 1876.
6415   Coral Tyler, born in Skidmore, Mo., in 1880.
6416   Celia Tyler, born in Glendive, Mon., in 1883.
6417   Myrtle Tyler, born in Buena Vista, Colo.

4006   MARY JANE[7] TYLER (John[6]), born in Tolland, Conn., November 11, 1838; died in 1872; married, in 1860, Edward Westcott, of Lynn, Mass. In 1896 he lived in Fitchburg, Mass. The children were born in Lynn. Children:

6418   Durand R. Westcott, born July 26, 1863; died Feb. 1, 1891; unmarried.
6419   Mary E. Westcott, born 1865; in 1896 was living in Fitchburg.

4010   GEORGE DE WITT[7] TYLER (George[6]), born in Munson, Mass., May 2, 1841; married in Union City, Mich., December 10, 1863, Sophie Dennison. He is a farmer in Union City, where the children were born. Children:

6420   Frank E. Tyler, born May 12, 1875; died Nov. 11, 1881.
6421   Kate Tyler, born Jan. 9, 1888.

4013   GILES MERRILL[7] TYLER (George[6]), born in Union City, Mich., April 18, 1851; married, December 1, 1891, in Kalamazoo, Mich., Lulu Bowers, of Richmond, Va. He is a farmer in Union City, where the children were born. Children:

6422   Louise Elizabeth Tyler, born Oct. 20, 1892.
6423   Lynn Merrill Tyler, born Nov. 19, 1894.

4014   CLARA ZERUIAH[7] TYLER (George[6]), born in Union City, Mich., July 18, 1854; married there, January 27, 1885, Charles H. Sheltus, of Jonesville, Mich., later of Kalamazoo. The two elder children were born in Jonesville. Children:

6424   Winifred Grace Sheltus, born March 29, 1886.
6425   J. Irving Sheltus, born Dec. 22, 1888.
6426   Marjorie Norine Sheltus, born in Union City, Sept 21, 1891.

4015 JOHN E.⁷ TYLER (George⁶), born in Union City, Mich., November 2, 1856; married (1), in Dysart, Ia., January 1, 1879, Lorena L. Horton, who died in Union City, Mich., November 11, 1882; married (2), September 28, 1885, Mary Dodge, of Union City, where all the children except the eldest were born.

CHILD, by first marriage:

6427   Pauline Tyler, born in Onawa, Ia., Aug. 28, 1881; died in Union City, Jan. 10, 1882.

CHILDREN, by second marriage:

6428   George E. Tyler, born Sept. 26, 1886.
6429   Grover Converse Tyler, born March 9, 1888.
6430   Daughter, born June 2, 1893; died June 9, 1893.
6431   Neva Tyler, born July 8, 1894.

4017 MARY ELIZABETH⁷ TYLER (Augustus⁶), born in Middlebury, now a part of Akron, O., December 4, 1834; married in Hazel Green, Wis., October 4, 1854, Henry D. York, born in Oxford, N. Y., March 25, 1823; son of Jeremiah and Catherine (Pendleton) York. The children were born in Hazel Green. Children:

6432   Dwight Sutphen York, born Nov. 21, 1855; married in Boston, Mass., June 26, 1888, Mrs. Edith (Fisher) Mills; has two children and resides near Hazel Green.
6433   Ruth Aruba York, born June 16, 1861; a teacher in the schools of Evanston, Ill.

4019 FLORA A.⁷ TYLER (Augustus⁶), born in Notawa Prairie, Mich., November 20, 1839; married in Platteville, Wis., June 2, 1860, Charles H. Nye, born in Fairfield, Me., October 20, 1834. He was in the Civil War. The second, third, and fourth children were born in Platteville. Children:

6434   Augustus Tyler Nye, born in Hazel Green, Wis., June 25, 1862; died in Mississippi, March 22, 1905; married, May 10, 1887, Nellie Campbell; had two daughters.
6435   Ellen F. Nye, born Feb. 22, 1866; married, Nov. 24, 1887, Falcon Woodhouse; resides in Lawrence, Okla.; has three sons.

6436   Mary Jalana Nye, born Dec. 9, 1868; married Doctor John Chase, of Viroqua, Wis., and has one daughter.

6437   Charles Nye, born Feb. 17, 1876; married, July 30, 1903, Zelma Schmezer. He was in the Spanish War; resides in Viola, Wis., and has one son.

6438   Evans M. Nye, born Jan. 17, 1879; is in business in Chicago, Ill.

4020 ADALINE M.[7] TYLER (Augustus[6]), born in Notawa Prairie, Mich., September 20, 1841; died in Ashland, Ore., June 21, 1893; married in Scott River, Cal., in 1878, Warren G. Holmes, of Massachusetts. They lived in Scott River, where the children were born. Mr. Holmes now lives in Holmes, Mont. Children:

6439   Charles H. Holmes, born 1879; a ranchman in Montana.

6440   Augustus Tyler Holmes, born 1881; an engineer on the eastern coast of Texas.

6441   George W. Holmes, born June 6, 1883; died in Ashland, Ore., Dec. 21, 1887.

4022 KATE[7] TYLER (Augustus[6]), born in Notawa Prairie, Mich., June 4, 1845; married in Platteville, Wis., in 1868, James L. Nye, born in Fairfield, Me., May 31, 1842. He was in the Civil War. Children:

6442   George Nye, born June 25, 1869; married in Dixon, Ill., Nov., 1895, Susie Arn. He is a railway mail clerk from Chicago to Omaha; a son was drowned when in his tenth year.

6443   Mabel Nye, born in Platteville, Wis., March 20, 1871; married William Yearsley, of Toronto, Can., and resides in Waterloo, Ia. They have one son.

6444   James L. Nye, Jr., born Sept. 8, 1883.

6445   Bernice Nye, born Aug. 20, 1887.

4024 GEORGE HIRAM[7] TYLER (Augustus[6])), born in Hazel Green, Wis., June 14, 1849; married (1), Mahala Willis, who died in Ashland, Ore., December 30, 1892; married (2), Mary Gunton; resides in Los Angeles, Cal.

CHILDREN, by second marriage:

6446   Augustus Tyler, born about 1899.

6447   George O. Tyler, born about 1901.

4026 GENEVIEVE[7] TYLER (George[6]), born in Burr Oak, Mich., August 8, 1856; married, in 1881, Rev. Elliott Lawrence Dresser. He was graduated from Princeton College in 1876 and from the Theological School. He became a home missionary in South Dakota, where he remained eleven years, going thence to Oberlin, O., for the purpose of educating their children. Later they bought a place in Ithaca, N. Y., to be near their children in Cornell University and those in the preparatory schools. For a number of years Mr. Dresser has been pastor of the Presbyterian church in Geneva, N. Y., with his home in Ithaca. Mrs. Dresser gained a wide reputation as a highly successful concert and oratorio singer before her marriage, and afterward as a teacher of the pipe organ and voice, but of late has given up professional work. The eldest child was born in Wisconsin; the second and third in Artesian, S. D.

CHILDREN:

6448 Lawrence Tyler Dresser, born Sept. 11, 1882; a student in Blackburn University two years; then in an art school in New York, where his work has had honorable mention in competition with five hundred others, who did not receive this honor. In 1907 he opened his own studio and his future as an artist is full of promise.

6449 Genevieve Dresser, born May 12, 1886.

6450 Eloise Dresser, born May 11, 1889.

6451 Marie Dresser, born in Canton, S. D., Dec. 9, 1891.

6452 **Ivan** Chandler Dresser, born in Flandrean, N. D., July 3, 1896.

4033 ALONZO[7] TYLER (John[6]), born in Providence, R. I., January 4, 1846; died there, March 30, 1900; married Harriett Newell Brown, of Boston, Mass., born June 18, 1852, daughter of Roswell R. and Betsey M. Brown. Children:

6453 Anna Louise Tyler, born in Taunton, Mass., Sept. 11, 1875; married, Oct. 6, 1897, William Albert Boutelle.

6454 Arthur Brown Tyler, born in Providence, R. I., Sept. 19, 1879.

4035 JAMES R.[7] TYLER, JR. (James R.[6]), born in

Providence, R. 1., August 27, 1847; died ——; married, October 22, 1874, Elmira Gelina, born July 20, 1856. The children were born in Providence. Children:

6455   Walter S. Tyler, born June 26, 1875.
6456   Martin W. Tyler, born Dec. 15, 1879.
6457   Irving C. Tyler, born Feb. 15, 1882.
6458   Amelia A. Tyler, born Dec. 9, 1889.

4039   EBENEZER C.[7] TYLER, JR. (Ebenezer C.[6]), born in Providence, R. I., May 19, 1843; died April 29, 1895; married, October 27, 1863, Susan Gerald, who died February 21, 1900. The children were born in Providence. Children:

6459   Charles Henry Tyler, born Nov. 26, 1864.
6460   Abby Ann Tyler, born Feb. 26, 1866.
6461   Anna Maria Tyler, born Oct. 29, 1867.

4040   JOHN H.[7] TYLER (Ebenezer C.[6]), born in Providence, R. I., December 23, 1844; married, July 8, 1867, in Salem, Mass., Maria O'Hare. Children:

6462   Jennie P. Tyler, born Dec. 15, 1867; died Sept. 8, 1868.
6463   Frank A. Tyler, born Nov. 18, 1868; is married.
6464   Flora B. Tyler, born March 23, 1872.
6465   John H. Tyler, born Oct. 28, 1874.
6466   Lewis W. Tyler, born Nov. 27, 1876; is married.

4042   OLIVER C.[7] TYLER (Ebenezer C.[6]), born in Providence, R. I., April 22, 1853; married (1), June 9, 1871, Emma L. Dean; married (2), November 23, 1885, Carrie Hugh. The children were born in Providence.

CHILDREN, by first marriage:
6467   George F. Tyler, born April 27, 1872.
6468   Arthur H. Tyler, born Sept. 15, 1875.

4045   ALBERT D.[7] TYLER, JR. (Albert D.[6]), born in Providence, R. I., April 27, 1848; married (1), August 1, 1869, Sarena M. Mott, of Scituate, R. I.; married (2), January 1, 1876, Olive B. Tanner, of Warren, R. I. The children were born in Providence.

CHILD, by first marriage:

6469   Nellie L. Mott Tyler, born Aug. 5, 1870; died young.

CHILDREN, by second marriage:

6470   Evelyn F. Tyler.

6471   Mabel C. Tyler, born Jan. 14, 1880; died Jan. 10, 1881.

4047   EDWIN F.⁷ TYLER (Albert D.⁶), born in Providence, R. I., November 20, 1854; died September 9, 1882; married, July 17, 1878, Anna C. Otten, of New York. The children were born in Providence. Children:

6472   Edna E. Tyler, born Nov. 20, 1880; died April 10, 1881.

6473   Florence L. Tyler, born May 6, 1882.

4057   DEACON DANFORD⁷ TYLER (Moses⁶), born in Richmond, N. H., October 2, 1812; died in Warwick, Mass., August 19, 1870; married, May 18, 1843, Emily Reed, born March 1, 1821; daughter of Stephen Reed, of Warwick (Rev. Samuel, descended from William of Weymouth). Mr. Tyler was early a teacher; then a railway ticket agent in Boston; from 1837 he kept store in Richmond at "Four Corners" in company with Daniel Bassett, Jr., and his own brother David; he was postmaster, superintendent of schools and held various town offices. In 1852 he moved to Warwick where he was a deacon in the church, superintendent of schools, parish clerk, etc. The children were born in Richmond, except the youngest.

CHILDREN:

6474   Emelie Jane Tyler, born Dec. 18, 1844; married, June 1, 1876, William Lawson, of England, born Aug. 24, 1836; son of Sir Wilfrid Lawson, Bart., of Brayton Hall, Carlisle, England. She was private secretary to Dr. Samuel Howe, of the Blind Asylum, Boston, and was afterward in the Boston Public Library. She and her husband are abroad, traveling, nearly all the time.

6475+   James D. Tyler, born June 15, 1848.

6476   Moses Reed Tyler, born June 19, 1850; married, Oct.

6, 1886, Mary Catherine Mayo, born June 18, 1860; daughter of Hon. E. F. Mayo, of Warwick. He was a student in Chauncey Hall School, Boston, and went to Colorado as an assayer; returning, became a farmer in Berlin, Mass.

6477   Mary Abby Tyler, born in Warwick, April 26, 1852; was educated at Wellesley College; at one time was in the Boston Public Library; traveled abroad two years; in 1899 lived in Warwick.

4058   DAVID[7] TYLER (Moses[6]), born in Royalston, Mass., January 24, 1815; died in Dedham, Mass., February 2, 1867; married (1), May 24, 1842, Clara Bullard Allen, of Boston, daughter of Thaddeus Allen; married (2), Helen Maria Broad, of Dedham, born November 19, 1833; daughter of Horace and Maria Broad. He kept store in Richmond at "Four Corners" with his brother Danford, then moved to Boston, where he was treasurer of the Boston and Providence Railway Company. He lived in Dedham, where his children were born and where his estate was probated.

CHILD, by first marriage:
6478   Clara B. Allen Tyler, born March 28, 1851; died March 27, 1861.

CHILD, by second marriage:
6479+   George Wendall Tyler, born April 10, 1857.

4060   PATIENCE A.[7] TYLER (Moses[6]), born in Richmond, N. H., June 11, 1820; died in Berlin, Mass., June 13, 1880; married, December 13, 1846, Hon. William Bassett, born in Richmond, October 5, 1819; died in Berlin November 26, 1896; son of Daniel Bassett. He was a farmer and currier in Richmond; thence moved to Worcester, Mass., in 1852; thence to Berlin in 1857, where he was a teacher and agriculturist; was selectman, town clerk and treasurer of Richmond; selectman, assessor and on school committee in Berlin; senator in the legislature for the east district of Worcester in 1864; wrote the *History of Richmond, N. H.* The two elder children were born in Richmond; the two younger in Berlin.

CHILDREN:

6480 Mary A. Bassett, born July 21, 1848; teacher; resides in Berlin.

6481 Laura E. Bassett, born Sept. 5, 1850; died Nov. 10, 1852.

6482 Julia Ida Bassett, born in Worcester, Oct. 28, 1854; married Charles M. Sawyer, of Berlin; three daughters (Florence, Hazel, Marjorie) and two sons (one Hermon).

6483 Florence May Bassett, born April 1, 1858; married (his third wife) Edward F. Fletcher, of Worcester; she was educated in Oberlin College; is an artist.

6484 Helen E. Bassett, born Feb. 17, 1860; died Dec., 1893; married, Jan. 12, 1887, Edward F. Fletcher, who also married her sister Florence; she had two sons, who died young.

4062 LAURA J.[7] TYLER (Moses[6]), born in Richmond, N. H., December 23, 1823; died in Waltham, Mass., July, 1860; married, March 29, 1846, David Randall, who married (2); born in Richmond, N. H., February 24, 1819; died in Waltham Mass., November 27, 1887, son of Levi Randall, of Richmond. He moved to Waltham, Mass., and was a merchandise broker in Boston; was president of the Waltham Loan Association, trustee of the Waltham Savings Bank, representative of the General Court three years and senator two years. Children:

6485 David Byron Randall; married and was in business with his father; resided in New York city, then went to California, where he died s. p.

6486 Laura Eva Randall; married William Hawley, of Newton, Mass.

6487 Addie Randall; married —— Weeks, of Waltham, Mass.

6488 Daughter; died young.

4063 RHODA GALE[7] TYLER (Moses[6]), born in Richmond, N. H., April 1, 1827; died in Hudson, Mass., July 12, 1880; married, November 26, 1857, Stephen Chandler Reed, son of Stephen Reed (Rev. Samuel), of Warwick, Mass.

They moved to Hudson, Mass. He was a teacher and farmer. The two elder children were born in Warwick and the youngest in Hudson. Children:

6489   Eva May Reed, born Aug. 21, 1859; was a student at Wellesley College and became a teacher in the High School, Framingham, Mass.

6490   Clara Tyler Reed, born Oct. 4, 1861; died in Warwick, Feb. 7, 1864.

6491   Charles Lincoln Reed, born April 15, 1868; married, December 29, 1897, Rosa A. Nichols, daughter of Rev. A. R. Nichols, of Monson, Mass. He was graduated from Tufts College; a teacher in Boston and principal of High School, Hudson, Mass.; has one daughter (Constance Tyler).

4064   JUDA ANN[7] TYLER (Moses[6]), born in Richmond, N. H., July 8, 1829; died in Keene, N. H., September 10, 1887; married, May 3, 1850, Ephraim Farnum Taft, of Winchester, N. H. He is a carpenter and resides in Keene, N. H. The children were born in Keene. Children:

6492   Lorin Taft; married; telegrapher in Pennsylvania.

6493   Warren S. Taft, born July 21, 1859; a machinist.

6494   Abbie Tyler, married, Sept. 1, 1897, Charles Wilder Clark; was a teacher before her marriage; resides in Keene, N. H.

6495   Maud Emilie Taft, born Aug. 21, 1874; a medical student in Philadelphia, Pa.

4067   OSCAR[7] TYLER (John[6]), born in Liberty, Ky., April 26, 1825; died in Washington, Utah, November 20, 1871; married, April 13, 1854, in Lehi City, Utah, Harriet A. ———; born in Andover, Vt., December 20, 1835; in 1901 she was living, a widow, in Thatcher, Ariz. The children were born in Washington. Children:

6496+   Frank N. Tyler, born Aug. 26, 1860.

6497+   Oscar Tyler, born May 22, 1870.

6498   Orson Tyler, born Feb. 8, 1872.

4076   MARY WHITE[7] TYLER (Simeon Stillman[6]), married, 1865, William F. Shepard, of Maine. Children:

6499   Myra Isabelle Shepard, married Kenreth Haynes.

6500   Margaret Isabelle Shephard, married Wallis Tresback; had a son and daughter.
6501   Charles Edwin Shepard.
6502   Harriet Myra Shepard.

4077 WILLIAM LEIGH RICHMOND[7] TYLER (Simeon Stillman[6]), born in Coliton District, S. C., in 1838; married in 1872, Margaret Cornelia Dye, of Georgia. He is superintendent of the City Cemetery in Jacksonville, Fla.; he was in the Confederate Army, second sergeant, Company A, 10th Fla. Infantry. The children were born in Jacksonville. Children:
6503+   Wilfred Richmond Tyler, born in 1873.
6504   Frank Newton Tyler; died young.
6505   Edmond Marshall Tyler; is a traveling salesman.
6506   Leroy Herbert Tyler; died young.
6507   Herbert William Tyler; died young.
6508   Harris Simeon Tyler; died young.
6509   Harold Charles Tyler.
6510   Ernest Watson Tyler.
6511   Sollis Stillman Tyler; died young.
6512   Ralph Sinclair Tyler.
6513   Dorothy Cornelia Tyler; died young.

4080 JOHN FLETCHER[7] TYLER (Simeon Stillman[6]), married, 1874, Georgia Virginia Smith, of Alabama. Children:
6514   John Fletcher Tyler.
6515   Morris Philip Tyler.
6516   Grace Mitchell Tyler.
6517   Blanche Fletcher Tyler.

4081 EDMOND MARSHALL[7] TYLER (Simeon Stillman[6]), married, 1880, Ida May Burnes. He was lieutenant of the police in Jacksonville, Fla. Children:
6518   Orville Zelotes Tyler.
6519   Mary Elizabeth Tyler.
6520   Georgia Virginia Tyler.
6521   Ida May Tyler.
6522   Edna Marshall Tyler.
6523   Gladys Deen Tyler.

4082   ORVILLE ZELOTES[7] TYLER (Simeon Stillman[6]), married, 1875, Frances Xavier Farar. He lived in Jacksonville, Fla.   Children:

6524   Mary Oak Tyler, born in Jacksonville; married Tilden Rouse, of Jacksonville; they had one son (Oliver Alonzo).
6525   Jessie Gertrude Tyler.
6526   Frank Neil Tyler.
6527   Edna Francis Tyler.
6528   Leo Orville Tyler.

4084   MARY JOSEPHINE[7] TYLER (Orville[6]), born February 6, 1835; married Edwin L. Howard, of Boston, Mass.   Children:

6529   Emma G. Howard, born Oct., 1859; married J. Frank Kimball, of Cambridge, Mass.
6530   Annie Louise Howard, born May, 1862.

4086   GEORGE LE VAN[7] TYLER (Orville[6]), born October 23, 1841; married, June 14, 1863, Emma A. Peak; resides in Mount Vernon, Me.   Children:

6531   Marie Winslow Tyler, born Dec. 11, 1867.
6532   Emma Josephine Tyler, born June 2, 1871.
6533   Allston Whitney Tyler, born June 25, 1876.

4088   CHLOE IRENE[7] TYLER (Daniel[6]), born in Essex, Vt., in 1827; died April 13, 1859; married, in 1855, Alanson W. Farnsworth, son of Lyman Farnsworth, of Milton, Vt.   The children were born in Essex.   Children:

6534   George Farnsworth, born in 1857.
6535   Milton Farnsworth, born in 1859.

4091   CHARLOTTE ELIZA[7] TYLER (Rodney[6]), born in Essex, Vt., October 23, 1825; died there December 25, 1893; married there, June 1, 1851, Wilson Morse, born in Haverhill, N. H., September 14, 1815; died in Essex, Vt., June 3, 1873, son of Daniel and Sarah Morse.   The children were born in Essex.   Children:

6536   Mary Almira Morse, born April 18, 1852; married in Essex, Vt., May 12, 1874, George Wilton Lewis, of

Fredonia, N. Y., son of George W. and Eliza (Wheelock) Lewis.

6537 Francene Eliza Morse, born April 11, 1854; married, Sept. 4, 1888, Alfred Alder Doane, born in Argyle, N. S., April 20, 1855; son of Israel and Louisa (Kenney) Doane.

6538 Wilson Jenness Morse, born Feb. 15, 1859; died Aug. 20, 1871.

6539 Elsie Jane Morse, born Oct. 19, 1863; married, Sept. 15, 1892, Arthur W. Huntley, of Burlington, Vt., born in Ferrisburg, Vt., Sept. 10, 1865; died in Essex, Vt., Sept. 26, 1895.

4092 MARY ELECTA⁷ TYLER (Rodney⁶), born in Essex, Vt., March 7, 1827; married in Westford, Vt., October 16, 1851, James Hurvey Rogers, born in Westford, December 17, 1823; died there, December 17, 1892, son of Thomas and Hannah (Rice) Rogers. They resided a while in Franklin Falls, N. Y., but returned to Westford, where she was residing in 1899. The two elder children were born in Franklin Falls and the two younger in Westford. Children:

6540 Helen Maria Rogers, born March 16, 1855; married, 1878, Chester D. Morey, of Keeseville, N. Y., son of Andrew J. and Elvira (Allen) Morey.

6541 Kate Alena Rogers, born Sept. 23, 1856; married in Denver, Colo., Oct. 4, 1891, Otis A. Ware, son of Leonard and Adelaide (Moore) Ware.

6542 William Arthur Rogers, born Oct. 1, 1860; married in Franklin, Mass., Oct. 26, 1898, Annie C. North, born in Annapolis, N. S., April 17, 1865; daughter of Daniel and Amanda (Caldwell) North, of Medway, Mass.; resides in Franklin.

6543 Frank Wilbur Rogers, born June 10, 1866; married, Oct. 30, 1895, Jennie Farnsworth, born in Essex, Vt., Feb. 6, 1866; daughter of George O. and Mary (Keeler) Farnsworth.

4093 JULIA PIERCE⁷ TYLER (Rodney⁶), born in Essex, Vt., May 1, 1830; died in Saratoga, N. Y., January 10, 1902; married in Essex, May 5, 1853, Rev. Edward Newton Howe, born in Ticonderoga, N. Y., October 12, 1827; died in Saratoga Springs, August 13, 1894, son of Cyrus and Loraine (Coats) Howe. He was educated at Fort Edward Institute; admitted in 1851 to the Troy Conference; was pastor in Milton, Georgia, Enosburg, Hinesburg, and Williston, Vt., and Greenfield, Clifton Park, and Cambridge, N. Y. Children:

6544   Son, born in East Pittsfield, Vt., July 11, 1857; died July 25, 1857.

6545   Ella Persis Howe, born in Essex, Vt., June 25, 1858; died June 15, 1866.

6546   Edward Summerfield Howe, born in Benson, Vt., Feb. 11, 1860; married in Omaha, Neb., Jan. 8, 1892, Agnes Meek, daughter of John and Mary (Williams) Meek; born Dec. 25, 1873.

6547   Annie Eliza Howe, born in Starksboro, Vt., Oct. 23, 1861; married in Cambridge, N. Y., Feb. 18, 1885, George L. Burch, born in South Cambridge, Jan. 20, 1861; son of David and Sarah J. (Dennis) Burch.

6548   Arthur Cyrus Howe, born in Williston, Vt., Aug. 28, 1863.

6549   Lily Emma Howe, born in Hinesburg, Vt., March 26, 1867; died June 11, 1868.

6550   Austin Simpson Howe, born in Saratoga Springs, N. Y., June 6, 1872.

4095   SARAH JANE[7] TYLER (Rodney[6]), born in Essex, Vt., March 26, 1835; married in Essex, July 15, 1853, William Greene, born in Essex, October 13, 1832, son of Dr. Mathew and Mary (Glennan) Greene. He is a builder and resides in Dickinson, N. Y. The two elder children were born in Essex, the next three in Stockholm, N. Y., and the two younger in Dickinson, N. Y. Children:

6551   Maria Georgianna Greene, born Feb. 12, 1855; married (1), July 4, 1871, Charles LeFlesch, of Dickinson, N. Y.; married (2), in Westford, Vt., Aug. 17, 1875, David Garrow, born Jan. 19, 1849.

6552   Harriet Electa Greene, born Oct. 16, 1857; died March 9, 1883.

6553   Ellen Eliza Greene, born Oct. 10, 1859; married in 1879 Lyman Davidson, of Dickinson, N. Y.

6554   William Henry Greene, born Aug. 10, 1861; married,

July 3, 1884, Alpha J. Graves, born in Lawrence, N. Y., daughter of David and Esther Graves; resides in Dickinson, N. Y.

6555   Charles Robert Greene, born April 23, 1864; married in Dickinson, N. Y., Dec. 16, 1887, Minnie F. Graves, daughter of David and Esther Graves.

6556   Claude Winfield Greene, born April 13, 1871; married, June 18, 1895, Daisy E. Anderson, born in Grand Isle, Vt., May 24, 1877; daughter of Carl J. and Hattie (Iby) Anderson; resides in Dickinson, N. Y.

6557   Mary Jane Greene, born May 8, 1873; died Oct. 15, 1879.

4096   HANNAH MARIA[7] TYLER (Rodney[6]), born in Essex, Vt., March 2, 1837; died in St. Armand, N. Y., September 16, 1898; married in Essex, July 4, 1860, Don Carlos Wood, born in Jay, N. Y., February 27, 1821; son of Sarell and Huldah (Palmer) Wood; resides in Franklin Falls, N. Y. The two elder children were born in Franklin Falls and the three youngest in St. Armand. Children:

6558   Mary Idella Wood, born May 14, 1861; married in Vermontville, N. Y., Nov. 27, 1878, Frank B. Stickney, born in Houghton, Mich., May 24, 1855; died Nov. 22, 1898; lost in the Klondyke, Alaska; son of Edward and Delia (Stone) Stickney.

6559   Carrie Huldah Wood, born March 27, 1866; married, Oct. 24, 1892, Elmer E. Lobdell, born in Saranac Lake, N. Y., Dec., 1866; son of James and Jane (Knapp) Lobdell.

6560   Rodney Sarell Wood, born Feb. 9, 1869; married, Feb. 18, 1897, Minnie Irene Cooper, born in Wilmington, N. Y., Dec., 1868, daughter of Minor and Jennie (Musgrow) Cooper.

6561   Lillian Sabra Wood, born March 1, 1872; died March 10, 1872.

6562   Helen Sabra Wood, born Oct. 16, 1873; married (1), July 3, 1893, Franklin E. Morehouse, son of Warren and Mary (Kenedy) Morehouse; was divorced; married (2), in Plattsburg, N. Y., Nov. 21, 1896, Charles A. Tomkinson, who was killed July 1, 1898, in the battle near Santiago de Cuba; son of Henry

C. and Sarah (Allsop) Tomkinson, of Ashton, Birmingham, Eng.; she resides in St. Armand, N. Y.

4097   JOHN HARVEY[7] TYLER (Rodney[6]), born in Essex, Vt., February 26, 1839; married in Moira, N. Y., February 22, 1868, Lucy A. Bradley, born in Dickinson, N. Y., May 12, 1848; daughter of Charles B. and Almira (Kingsley) Bradley. He is a farmer and has resided in Franklin, Mass., since 1894, coming from Dickinson, N. Y. The children were born in Dickinson. Children:

6563   Mary Irene Tyler, born March 26, 1870; married in Boston, Mass., May 2, 1899, Fred Wesley C. Handy, born March 2, 1877; son of Daniel A. and Jennie A. (Rayworth) Handy.
6564   Rodney Charles Tyler, born July 21, 1872.
6565   Edward Jackson Tyler, born May 29, 1875.
6566   Flora Belle Tyler, born June 23, 1877.
6567   Orlin Elwood Tyler, born Dec. 31, 1881.
6568   Grace Myrtle Tyler, born May 31, 1883.
6569   Jesse James Tyler, born July 6, 1885.
6570   Edith Alice Tyler, born March 25, 1890.
6571   Ray Alton Tyler, born Jan. 24, 1894.

4098   BETSEY E.[7] TYLER (Rodney[6]), born in Essex, Vt., May 13, 1841; married (1), in Potsdam, N. Y., April 17, 1865, Dr. Gilbert J. Cheney, born in Lawrence, N. Y., November 22, 1843; died in Lehigh, Ia., January 4, 1883; son of Lorenzo and Lucina (Moffitt) Cheney; married (2) in Ganesvoort, N. Y., April 17, 1884, Reuben R. McClellan, a widower, born in Rutland, Vt., May 8, 1831; died in Cambridge, N. Y., February 7, 1890; son of Charles and Sally (Randall) McClellan. He was a builder. The child was born in Dickinson, N. Y.

CHILD, by first marriage:
6572   Maora Elna Cheney, born Aug. 14, 1870; died in Cambridge, Oct. 1, 1891.

4099   HARRIET SABRINA[7] TYLER (Rodney[6]), born in Colchester, Vt., June 27, 1843; married in Essex, Vt., July 4, 1865, Solomon Caswell Rogers, born in Westford, Vt., October 3, 1839, son of Marshall and Sophronia S. (Caswell) Rogers. He is a farmer and resides in Westford, Vt.; a private in Company A, 1st Cavalry, from January 4, 1864, to May 22, 1865. The children were born in Westford. Children:

6573   Homer Brayton Rogers, born April 12, 1866; married in Westfield, Mass., Sept. 5, 1894, Harriet E. Kittridge, born in Westfield, Mass., Aug. 8, 1865; daughter of Benjamin L. and Harriet A. (Merrill) Kittridge; resides in Westfield.

6574   Hobart Clifton Rogers, born Oct. 23, 1867; married in Burlington, Vt., May 6, 1891, Rose Buxton, born in Jericho, Vt., April 7, 1870, daughter of George and Martha (Conklin) Buxton.

6575   Sarah Sophronia Rogers, born Sept. 23, 1869; married in Montreal, Que., May 2, 1889, Wallace Clifton Hale, born in Underhill, Vt., May 3, 1869; died in Chatham, N. Y., Oct. 15, 1899; son of Samuel A. and Sarah (Edwards) Hale.

4109   LEWIS ORLIN[7] TYLER (Orlin[6]), born in Essex, Vt., September 19, 1829; married, 1855, Susan Abernithy, daughter of Calvin Abernithy, of Madrid, N. Y.; she died March, 1891. He lives in Farmingdale, L. I. Child:

6576   Mary Tyler, born in Burton, Wis., 1859; married, 1878, Walter L. Warner born in Tarrytown, N. Y.; died in Farmingdale, L. I., June, 1892; three sons (Edward L., Walter P., and Lewis G.).

4110   ALLEN ZURIEL[7] TYLER (Orlin[6]), born in Essex, Vt., June 6, 1832; died in Joliet, Ill., July 29, 1900; married, October 16, 1851, Caroline Morey, born in Moira, N. Y., February 4, 1837; daughter of Thompson and Nancy (Burdick) Morey. Children:

6577   Eugene Tyler, born April 29, 1854; married Lillian Hayes; lives in Morristown, Vt.

6578   Franklin Clifford Tyler, born March 22, 1858; died July 10, 1859.

6579   George Willard Tyler, born Oct. 21, 1860; married Josephine Lewshy.

6580   Mary Edith Tyler, born Nov. 4, 1862; married Leslie Polhamus, and lives in Joliet, Ill.

6581   Franklin Clifford Tyler, born Dec. 19, 1864; married
        Marcella Clark and lives in Joliet.
6582   Nancy Jane Tyler, born April 19, 1866; married
        Alonzo Lombard and lives in Joliet.
6583   Charles Newton Tyler, born May 9, 1869; married
        Minnie Smith and lives in Ottawa, Ill.
6584   Carrie Lavinia Tyler, born Dec. 31, 1875; married
        George Hansmann; lives in Joliet.

    4111   EDWARD JUDSON[7] TYLER (Orlin[6]), born in
Essex, Vt., February 2, 1837; died in Enosburg Falls, Vt.,
December 28, 1874; married Mary Woodman Pixley, born in
Fairfax, Vt., September 12, 1836; died in Essex, Vt., February
13, 1876; daughter of Albert and Elizabeth (Kimball) Pixley. The children were born in Enosburg Falls. Children:
6585   Helen Tyler, born Nov. 1, 1871.
6586+   Edward Judson Tyler, born Oct. 30, 1873.

    4112   WILLARD ADEN[7] TYLER (Orlin[6]), born in
Essex, Vt., January 4, 1839; married, August 21, 1861, Jane
Wallace, born in Willsboro, N. Y., February 24, 1841; died
in Burlington, Vt., October 18, 1869; married (2), December
23, 1873, Carrie E. Wallace, born in Willsboro, March 20,
1849. He lives in Burlington, Vt., where the children were
born.
                CHILDREN, by first marriage:
6587   Willie Wallace Tyler, born June 7, 1864; died Aug.
        10, 1865.
6588   Jessie Barnes Tyler, born Nov. 11, 1865; married, in
        Burlington, April 19, 1893, Walter R. Brown.
6589   Jennie May Tyler, born Aug. 26, 1869; died May 4,
        1870.
                CHILDREN, by second marriage:
6590   Walter Wallace Tyler, born Aug. 9, 1875.
6591   Roy Willard Tyler, born March 26, 1878.
6592   Florence May Tyler, born Nov. 13, 1879; died Dec.
        25, 1879.
6593   Merton Griswold Tyler, born Oct. 25, 1881.
6594   Harold Douglas Tyler, born June 17, 1893.

    4153   FREDERICK C.[7] TYLER (David[6]), born in

Essex, Vt., July 3, 1848; married June 20, 1882, Caroline Clarrissa Farewell, born in St. Paul, Minn., July 9, 1862; daughter of James L. and Elizabeth (Edmundson) Farwell, from Liverpool, Eng. (half-brother of Governor Farwell, of Wisconsin). Mr. Tyler resided early in St. Charles, Ill., and went to Chicago before the fire of 1871; was with Field & Palmer some years, then on the board of trade. Was president of the Western Paper Stock Company which was burned out in 1898; rebuilt. He had a stroke of paralysis and, though disabled, still attended to business. The children were born in Chicago.

CHILDREN:

6595   May Tyler, born July 9, 1883.

6596   Clarice Caroline Tyler, born Dec. 30, 1885.

4163   GEORGE W.⁷ TYLER (Erastus⁶), born in Lima, O., May 31, 1839; married, July 3, 1863, M. E. Orrell, of Quincy, Ind. In 1887 he moved to Granite, Colo., where he is a builder, miner, and hotel man. Children:

6597   Harry M. Tyler, a railway agent in South Platte, Colo.; has one child.

6598+   Leon F. Tyler, born in Licking County, O., Jan. 2, 1869.

6599   Pearl Tyler, born in 1880; unmarried and lives at home.

4167   ANDREW JACKSON⁷ TYLER (Erastus⁶), born in St. Albans, O., September 12, 1852; married, February 12, 1879, Martha Malinda Dixon, born in Burlington, O., May 23, 1862. They reside in Alexandria, O. The two elder children were born in Alexandria. Children:

6600   Clyde Lorena Tyler, born Nov. 5, 1880; died Nov. 22, 1888.

6601   Lulu Oulerette Tyler, born June 28, 1883.

6602   Chloe Lenora Tyler, born in Johnson City, Kan., Oct. 6, 1888.

6603   Goldie May Tyler, born in Garden City, Kan., March 25, 1890; died June 12, 1890.

6604   Baly Tyler, born in Garden City, Kan., June 13, 1892; died July 28, 1892.

4171   BEULAH ELIZABETH⁷ TYLER (Lorin⁶), born in Essex, Vt., August 5, 1833; married, August 14, 1860, Willard Flagg Bliss, a farmer, of Pana, Ill. He was graduated from Harvard University, spent a year abroad, and taught in St. Louis, Mo. In 1868 he was appointed to a professorship in Illinois Industrial University, now University of Illinois. He retired to a country estate in 1870. Child:

6605   George Willard Bliss, born in Bunker Hill, Ill., June 12, 1862; married; resides in Bremen, Ga.; has two sons (Norman Willard and Loren Wallace).

4177   FRANCES ESTHER⁷ TYLER (Lyman Early⁶), born in Harlem, O., June 17, 1837; married, March 25, 1863, Elijah B. Adams. He was captain of Company I, 32d O. Volunteer Infantry; recorder of Delaware County, O., from 1870-1879; resided in Delaware. In 1898 was residing in Columbus, O.; a lumber dealer. The three youngest children were born in Delaware. Children:

6606   Herbert Kelton Adams, born in Columbus, O., March 16, 1864; died May 15, 1880.

6607   John Beatly Adams, born in Harlem, O., March 20, 1868; married March 31, 1898.

6808   Lyman Bradley Adams, born Dec. 18, 1870.

6609   Edgar Tyler Adams, born Oct. 19, 1874; died Dec. 6, 1876.

6610   Nellie Josephine Adams, born March 2, 1878.

4178   LOUISA EMELINE⁷ TYLER (Lyman Early⁶), born in Harlem, O., June 9, 1839; died in Columbus, O., March 7, 1895; married Norman T. Heddon, of Columbus, O., a traveling salesman. The children were born in Harlem. Children:

6611   Frances Caroline Heddon, born March 1, 1859; died in 1873.

6612   Frederick Heddon, born Sept. 11, 1860; a foreign missionary in Africa.

6613   Robert Heddon, born Sept., 1862; married 1893 in Columbus.

6614   Jennie Eloise Heddon, born Oct. 18, 1866; married in Columbus in 1892.

6615   John Taft Heddon, born June 21, 1875.

4180 JOSEPHINE AMELIA⁷ TYLER (Lyman Early⁶), born in Harlem, O., January 11, 1846; married, January 26, 1867, John Adams. Moved to Auburn, Placer County, Cal., where he is now county assessor; also has been county recorder and abstractor of titles. The two younger children were born in Auburn, Cal. Children:
6616   Frederick Adams, born in Harlem, Feb. 26, 1868; a paralytic; unmarried.
6617   Eugene Adams, born Feb. 1, 1871; married in 1892.
6618   Clayton Adams born June 9, 1884.

4181 JANE ADELAIDE⁷ TYLER (Lyman Early⁶), born in Harlem, O., August 6, 1849; married, September, 1870, B. H. Merriott, a real estate dealer in Columbus, O. The children were born in Harlem. Children:
6619   Harry Montford Merriott, born Oct. 18, 1871.
6620   Wade Merriott, born Sept. 8, 1877.

4182 GEORGE EDGAR⁷ TYLER (Lyman Early⁶), born in Harlem, O., June 13, 1852; married, September 19, 1878, Alice Lumbert. He is a farmer in Columbus, O. The children were born in Harlem. Children:
6621   Jessie Louise Tyler, born Dec. 15, 1879.
6622   Raymond Tyler, born Oct. 17, 1881.

4183 HENRY⁷ TYLER (Cassius⁶), born in Jersey, O., October 3, 1846; married, January 23, 1879, Sarah A. Davison, born near Alexandria, O., November 26, 1850. He is a farmer and stock dealer and owns 150 acres. Child:
6623   Fred Cassius Tyler, born June 7, 1881.

4186 WILBUR⁷ TYLER (Cassius⁶), born in Jersey, O., December 16, 1856; married, March 27, 1881, Lillie E. Goddard, born near Alexandria, O., March 25, 1856. He is a farmer and stock dealer and lives on the old homestead. The children were born in Jersey. Children:
6624   Bertha M. Tyler, born Aug. 13, 1882.
6625   Minnie R. Tyler, born Nov. 26, 1886.
6626   Joa Ruth Tyler, born June 6, 1890.

4187 DOUGLAS S.⁷ TYLER (Cassius⁶), born in Jersey, O., August 1, 1860; married, November 20, 1884, Louie May Webb, born October 21, 1866. He is a farmer in Jersey, where the children were born. Children:

6627   Ethel May Tyler, born Nov. 2, 1885.

6628   Hugh Arlington Tyler, born Feb. 28, 1887.

4193   EMMA EDNA[7] TYLER (Foster[6]), born in Alexandria, O., June 13, 1854; died February 12, 1882; married, March 27, 1878, Alfred D. Osborn, who died October 8, 1886. The children were probably born in Alexandria. Children:

6629   Harry Foster Osborn, born July 19, 1879; resides in Gallipolis, O.

6630   Emma Edna Osborn, born Jan. 10, 1882.

4195   REUBEN FOSTER[7] TYLER (Foster[6]), born in Alexandria, O., September 15, 1858; married (1), April 10, 1884, Phoebe A. Jones, of Granville, O., who died November 20, 1896; married (2), August 10, 1898, Anna Jones, of Granville, born September 15, 1860; daughter of Hiram Jones. He is a farmer and stock raiser and resides in Alexandria, where his children were born. Children:

6631   Asa Edward Tyler, born March 1, 1885.

6632   Reuben Foster Tyler, born Nov. 23, 1892.

6633   Ruby Jones Tyler, born Nov. 20, 1896.

4199   FIDE L.[7] TYLER (Joel L.[6]), born in Ohio August 21, 1857; married, December 26, 1878, Robert Carlisle, wholesale hardware dealer, with his brother-in-law Tyler in Cleveland, O., where the children were born. Children:

6634   Cora L. Carlisle, born Oct. 11, 1880.

6635   Waite Carlisle, born Sept. 22, 1885.

6636   Robert Stanley Carlisle, born July 29, 1888.

4202   JOEL CLAVERLY[7] TYLER (Rufus[6]), born in Au Sable Forks, N. Y., August 26, 1857; married, August 30, 1882, Mary Emma Farrand, of Port Huron, Mich., born June 24, 1849; was graduated from Michigan University in 1877, Ph. B., and in 1878 Ph. M. He was graduated from Michigan University in 1880 and later received the degree of M. A. He was instructor in English Literature in the Michigan State Normal School 1879-1880; principal of the Somer-

ville school in St. Clair, Mich., 1881-1882. Became lumber
dealer in Kalamazoo, Mich., and then moved to Knoxville,
Tenn., where he is a member of the firm of Savage & Tyler,
making a specialty of flour and mill machinery. Children:

6637   Hugh Claverly Tyler, born May 22, 1884.
6638   Laura Whitman Tyler, twin to Hugh.
6639   Paula Tyler, born 1893.

    4206 WILLIAM F.[7] TYLER (Samuel[6]), born in New-
port, N. Y., June 7, 1824; married, August 22, 1849, Hannah
Pratt, born in Burlington, N. Y., October 19, 1826; died October 24, 1895; daughter of Elisha and Sarah (Smith) Pratt.
He went early to Mansfield, O., where he became a successful
merchant, and was residing there in 1899.   Child:

6640+   William Dexter Tyler, born in Mansfield, O., Feb-
        ruary, 1852.

    4213 BENJAMIN FRANKLIN[7] TYLER (Benjamin
Brown[6]), born in Newport, N. Y., July 12, 1835; married,
April 12, 1869, Ella A. Roberts, of Parkersburg, W. Va.   He
enlisted July, 1861, in the 26th O. Volunteer Infantry, and
served three years; was wounded September 19, 1863, at Chickamauga, and taken prisoner; was paroled later; mustered out
July 24, 1864.   He returned home and remained there until
1867, when he moved to Parkersburg, W. Va., and engaged in
oil refining; in 1899 was a foreman for the Standard Oil Company; resides in Parkersburg.   The children were born there.
Children:

6641   Carrie Tyler, born March 10, 1870; died Feb. 22,
        1894.
6642   Mabel Tyler, born Dec. 12, 1873.

    4214 WILLIAM HENRY[7] TYLER (Benjamin
Brown[6]), born in Newport, N. Y.; married, January 8, 1863,
Hannah M. Sifrit.   He was in the Civil War; a farmer, and
living, in 1900, in Walnut Run, O.   Children:

6643   Minnie G. Tyler, born Oct. 29, 1865; married C. B.
        Shough, of London, O.
6644   Owen D. Tyler, born Sept. 22, 1870; married Mary
        Withrow.
6645   Kate Tyler, born May 5, 1875; died Sept. 1, 1879.

6646   William Henry Tyler, born June 5, 1879.
6647   Mary E. Tyler, born Dec. 25, 1883.

4215   MARY AMELIA[7] TYLER (Henry[6]), born in
Adams, Mass., March 15, 1826; married, September 27, 1846,
Edmond D. Foster, of Cheshire, Mass., who died September 9,
1894. She lived in Cheshire in 1898, and the children were
born there.   Children:
6648   Henry E. Foster, born Jan. 31 1847; married, June
            20, 1877, Edna R. Brown, of Cheshire.
6649   William Calvin Foster, born May 18, 1849; married
            (1), Dec. 2, 1873, Sarah A. Slade, of Cheshire, who
            died August 19, 1878; married (2), June 8, 1892,
            Elizabeth M. Saul. He lived in Thomaston, Conn.,
            and had one son by first marriage (George).
6650   Frank Tyler Foster, born Nov. 28, 1855; married,
            June 5, 1883, Elizabeth E. Petitclen; he lives in
            Cheshire and has a son and daughter (Robert
            Wolcott and Helen Rena).

4223   JOHN BROWN[7] TYLER (Duty Sayles[6]), born
in Adams, Mass., October 3, 1826; married in North Adams,
Mass., November 18, 1846, Harriet A. Tinker; was residing in
North Adams in 1897, where the children were born.   Children:
6651   Willie R. Tyler, born July 25, 1848; died Sept. 10,
            1848.
6652   Edward Duty Tyler, born Dec. 22, 1850; died Dec.
            31, 1890.
6653   Elizabeth Louise Tyler, born Sept. 7, 1859.
6654   John Tyler, born May 30, 1862; died Sept. 23, 1862.

4225   MARIE LOUISE[7] TYLER (Duty Sayles[6]), born
in Adams, Mass., February 21, 1834; married in North Adams,
Mass., May 3, 1855, George Bulkley Perry, born in Stock-
bridge, Mass., July 7, 1828. He was a lumber dealer and
resided in North Adams. The children were born in Geneseo,
Ill., except the eldest.   Children:
6655   Cornelia Tyler Perry, born in North Adams, Mass.,
            Oct. 29, 1856; unmarried in 1897.
6656   (Rev.) Alfred Tyler Perry, born Aug. 19, 1858; mar-

ried in Hartford, Conn., April 13, 1887, Anna Morris. He was graduated from Williams College, and in 1885 from Hartford Theological Seminary; settled in Ware, Mass., over the Congregational church in 1886; has two sons (Alfred and Edward).

6657   Annie Louise Perry, born April 30, 1860; married in New Hampshire, April 18, 1888, Arthur Daniel Cady; has a daughter (Louise), born in Springfield, Mass., July 25, 1890.

4258 HATTIE ELIZABETH⁷ TYLER (Humphrey M.⁶), born in Grafton, Mass., October 28, 1849; married, October 13, 1880, Willard Mason Broad, born in Canton, O., June 17, 1852; died June 29, 1889, in Denver Colo.; son of Lewis and Martha (Sawin) Broad, of Natick, Mass. He was a stone contractor and put in the first filling of the Back Bay district in Boston; he was also a railway contractor and a musician. The children were born in Denver. Children:

6658   Mason Lasall Broad, born July 9, 1886; died Oct. 28, 1886.

6659   Ruth Broad, born Sept. 2, 1888.

4261 SAMUEL WILLARD⁷ TYLER, JR., (Samuel Willard⁶), born in Clinton, Mass., February 11, 1866; married, October 27, 1892, Carrie E. Willard, daughter of James A. and Leafy M. (Billings) Willard. In 1898 he was residing in Clinton, where he owns a music store and was town clerk from 1894-1899. The children were born in Clinton. Children:

6660   Dorothy Tyler, born Aug. 11, 1895.

6661   Samuel Willard Tyler, born May 4, 1898.

EIGHTH GENERATION

4263 GEORGE W.[8] TYLER (Thomas[7]), born in Warren, Mass., August 21, 1808; died March 29, 1850; married, October 25, 1831, Clarissa Patch, who died November 7, 1832. Child:

6662+ John Augustus Tyler, born in Warren, Oct. 24, 1832.

4264 HON. ORVILLE THOMAS[8] TYLER (Thomas[7]), born in West Brookfield, Mass., August 28, 1810; died in Belton, Tex., April 18, 1886; married, December 26, 1850, Caroline Childers, daughter of Captain Goldsby Childers, a captain in the Black Hawk War and an old Texan pioneer. Judge Tyler immigrated to Texas in 1834 when it was a part of Mexico, doing business in Houston in 1837 when that city was first laid out. From 1840 to 1848 he raised cattle in Austin County. In 1849 he settled in the present county of Coryell and at its organization was elected its first chief justice, from which circumstance he was ever afterwards called "Judge" Tyler though he was not a lawyer. In 1862 he was elected a member of the House of Representatives of the tenth legislature of Texas. He moved to Salado in 1864 and in 1884 moved to Belton, where he now lies buried in the north cemetery. He was a sturdy, indomitable pioneer, a successful man of business, progressive and very modern in his ideas. He exercised a generous hospitality and always showed a liberal public spirit. He was a member of the Baptist church and a free mason. The two younger children were born in Salado; the others in Coryell County.

CHILDREN:

6663+ George W. Tyler, born Oct. 31, 1851.

6664 Frances Minnie Tyler, born Feb. 1, 1853; died March 8, 1862.

6665 William Worth Tyler, born Feb. 11, 1855; died Oct. 26, 1864.

6666 James Albert Tyler, born Dec. 23, 1856; died Jan. 3, 1857.

6667+   Orville Thomas Tyler, born March 9, 1861.

6668+   Annie Caroline Tyler, born Jan. 31, 1864.

6669   Louis Hodges Tyler, born Sept. 15, 1866; married, April 10, 1895, Lela Erwin. He lives in Dallas, Tex., where he is a paying-teller in the American National Exchange Bank.

6670+   Louine Childers Tyler, twin to Louis Hodges.

4266   MARY CAROLINE[8] TYLER (Thomas[7]), born in Warren, Mass., February 10, 1815; died in Worcester, Mass., about 1870; married (1), —— Patch; married (2), John Temple, who died in Worcester in the seventies. The children were probably born in Worcester.

CHILDREN, by first marriage:

6671   Mary C. Patch, died in Worcester, 188—; married Charles A. Bigelow, a merchant of Worcester, who died there April, 1885; they resided in Belton, Tex., from 1858-1868; had three children (Charles F., Frank A. and Mary C.).

6672   Frank Patch, died.

6673   Ellen Patch, died in Worcester about 1870.

4267   ALONZO RIPLEY[8] TYLER (Thomas[7]), born in Warren, Mass., December 21, 1817; died in Natchez, Miss., September 13, 1887; married Miss Quarterman, who died in Natchez. Child:

6674   Caroline Tyler, married, in 1887, Barney J. O'Neal; they live in Natchez.

4270   DANIEL MILTON[8] HODGES (Triphena[7]), born in Warren or Brookfield, Mass., August 20, 1810; died in New York City, January 23, 1862; married, November 29, 1832, 'Adelaide Marcy, born in Sturbridge, Mass., October 22, 1810; died in Webster, Mass., March 29, 1881; daughter of Morris and Sally (Morse) Marcy. The children were born in Buffalo, N. Y. Children:

6675   Edward Milton Hodges, born Oct. 14, 1838; married, Feb. 9, 1878, Harriet Lucy Moon, born Nov. 2, 1851; no children.

6676   Charles Adolphus Hodges, born June 18, 1843; died

Dec. 27, 1887; married, Jan. 1, 1874, Alice Bartlett, born Dec. 16, 1847; no children.

4272   MARIA LOUISE[8] HODGES (Triphena[7]), born in Brookfield, Mass., April 4, 1815; died in Philadelphia, Pa., August, 1889; married in Buffalo, N. Y., Samuel Lyon Fiske, born in Southbridge, Mass., 1814; died September, 1869; son of Major Samuel and Sally (Lyon) Fiske. See (*Fiske Genealogy*, p. 386, and *Hodges Genealogy*, p. 352). He was a highly successful mill agent in his early life, conducting with marked ability the Hamilton Woolen Company; he suffered from ill health at a critical period and his business career was turned into other channels. He resided in Southbridge. Children:

6677   Arthur Tappan Fiske, died in Philadelphia in 1866, unmarried.
6678   John Quincy Fiske, died young.
6679+   Louis Samuel Fiske, born February 14 or 15, 1844.
6680   Frank Fiske, died young.
6681   Sally Fiske, died young.
6682   William Fiske, died young.

4282   WILLIAM SUMNER[8] TYLER (Moses[7]), born in Warren, Mass., July 16, 1820; died in Adrian, Mich., December 28, 1867; married, in Boston, May 13, 1845, Sophronia White, born in Dixfield, Me., May 21, 1821; in 1897 she was living in Adrian. He lived in Boston, where his eldest child was born, and thence went to Adrian, where the second child was born. Children:

6683   Frank Woodworth Tyler, born Sept. 14, 1848; died Sept. 24, 1868, unmarried.
6684   Florence E. Tyler, born June 27, 1854; in 1897 was a teacher in the High School in Toledo, O.

4283   SARAH[8] TYLER (Moses[7]), born in Brimfield, Mass.; died in Springfield, Mass., 188—; married in Brimfield, September 1, 1846, Hudson L. Whitney. Two infants died young. Children:

6685   Etta Whitney, died 189—, s. p.; married in Springfield, Mass., James Butterworth.
6686   Daughter, married ——.

4284 JOHN TYLER[8] (Moses[7]), born in Brimfield, Mass., January 23, 1827; died in Palmer, Mass., November 8, 1885; married, March 28, 1849, Mary Eliza Lumbard, of Brimfield, who died in Palmer in 1894. Child:

6687+ Emma Augusta Tyler, born in Detroit, Mich., Dec. 29, 1850.

4285 HENRY[8] TYLER (Moses[7]), born in Brimfield, Mass.; married, 1854, in Adrian, Mich., Kate Donovan. He lives in Titusville, Pa. Children:

6688 William Tyler.

6689 Mary Tyler.

4286 WILSON MAKEPEACE[8] TYLER (Moses[7]), born in Brimfield, Mass.; died in 189—; married in Vincennes, Ind., Maggie Eastham; she is living in Vincennes, where the children were born. He was a banker there and died following reverses in business. Children:

6690+ Frank Eastham Tyler, born Jan. 25, 1859.

6691 Alice Tyler, born Nov. 5, 1863; married, Oct. 9, 1887, Frank L. Rice, of Chicago, and died s. p., Feb., 1888.

4287 CLEMENT[8] TYLER (Horatio[7]), born in Homer, N. Y., March 12, 1835; married, February 1, 1862, Esther Topping, born in Homer, March 30, 1837; died in Wautoma, Wis., April 17, 1887; daughter of William and Eunice (Clark) Topping. In 1899 he was living in Wautoma, Wis., where a farmer. The children were born in Homer. Children:

6692 William Scudder Tyler, born Jan. 23, 1863; married, June, 1893, Kate Moriarty; he is of the firm of Tyler & Edwards, dealers in farm machinery and buggies, etc., in Wautoma.

6693 Kittie Marie Tyler, born Nov. 16, 1864; was graduated from the Battle Creek Sanitarium; is a nurse.

4288 EMMA[8] TYLER (Horatio[7]), born in Homer, N. Y., February 18, 1837; married, 1856, Curtis I. Case, of Fon du Lac, Wis. In 1899 she was in the asylum in Oshkosh, Wis. Children:

6694   Frank E. Case, killed himself about 1896, leaving a wife and little daughter in Fon du Lac.

6695   Edward W. Case, born in 1865; a printer; was unmarried in 1899; probably lives in Fon du Lac.

4297   ABEL CLINTON[8] TYLER (Cutler[7]), born in South Newbury, O., September 2, 1827; died in Wyoming, O., December 20, 1899; married (1), June 28, 1855, Mary Elizabeth Vantuyl, born December 28, 1836, in Franklin, O.; died November 3, 1872, in Glendale, O.; married (2), May 20 ,1874, Caroline White, born March 9, 1841, in Glendale, O.   He did business in Cincinnati, but resided in Wyoming, the latter part of his life.   The children were born in Glendale.

CHILDREN, by first marriage:

6696   Lida Tyler, born Aug. 30, 1862; died Sept. 10, 1862.

6697   Sarah Elsie Tyler, born July 21, 1865; was graduated from the Cincinnati College of Music and became a teacher of instrumental and vocal music; lives in Athens, Ga.

6698   Arthur Vantuyl Tyler, born May 5, 1869; died Sept. 1, 1870.

6699   Albert Clinton Tyler, born Jan. 4, 1872; was graduated from Princeton University in 1897; was a competitor at the Grecian games in Athens, Greece, 1896, and won the second prize for pole vaulting; he was on both the football and track teams at Princeton and his specialties in study were mathematics and art.   In 1897 he coached the football team of Amherst College, and began the first year in the School of Mines, Columbia University, which he completed in 1898.   Then he began to teach and went to Lawrenceville, N. J., one of the largest secondary schools in the country, and there had charge of athletics.   In 1899 his purpose was to finish the architectural course, in a few years, teaching in the interval.

CHILDREN, by second marriage:

6700   Edith Carrie Tyler, born July 14, 1878; studied vocal music and elocution.

6701   Frank Sumner Tyler, born Feb. 18, 1881.

4299   ISAAC ALLEN⁸ TYLER (Cutler⁷), born in South Newbury, O., September 9, 1832; married (1), March 31, 1859 Catherine Hetzler, born October 9, 1830; died in New Paris, O., August 17, 1877; married (2), July 20, 1879, Louisa Jane Downing, born November 29, 1843. In 1898 he lived in Campbellstown, O. The children were born in New Paris.

CHILDREN, by first marriage:
6702   Samuel Cutler Tyler, born July 8, 1861.
6703   John William Tyler, born Aug. 25, 1866.

4300   RUTH⁸ TYLER (Cutler⁷), born in South Newbury, O., November 29, 1835; married, October 29, 1856, John Baker Watertown, born in England, March 12, 1829. They lived in South Newbury on her father's homestead and the children were born there. Children:
6704   Daughter, born and died Nov. 27, 1859.
6705   Sarah Elizabeth Watertown, born Dec. 19, 1860; died unmarried, Jan. 27, 1895, in Cleveland, O.
6706   Robert Cutler Watertown, born June 10, 1864; died in Phoenix, Ariz., March 3, 1894; married Oct. 10, 1893, Carrie Blackstone, of Jamestown, N. Y.
6707   William Reuben Watertown, born Sept. 6, 1867; lives in Colorado Springs, Colo.
6708   George Wright Watertown, born May 20, 1871; died Jan. 17, 1872, in Newbury.
6709   Ruth May Watertown, born Dec. 26, 1873.

4302   REUBEN⁸ TYLER (Cutler⁷), born in South Newbury, O., June 11, 1839; married (1), December 24, 1867, Emily Louise Stone, born in Albany, N. Y., May 23, 1844; died in Wyoming, O., March 20, 1879; daughter of Francis M. Stone, a merchant of Cincinnati; married (2), October 14, 1880, Alice H. Hurin, born in Cincinnati, O., July 14, 1846; daughter of James K. Hurin, of Cincinnati. He was for several years a student at Oberlin College in the summer, teaching during the winter months. In November, 1861, he enlisted in the 69th O. Volunteer Infantry, and served several months as color sergeant, and for the remainder of the term of three years in the quartermaster's department in his regiment and elsewhere on detached service. In October, 1865, he entered the Cincinnati Law School and was graduated in 1867; he began the practice of his profession in the office of Judge Hoadley, and continues in it in Cincinnati; his home is in Wyoming, O. He is a prominent Presbyterian, having been three times commissioner to the General Assembly for the Cincinnati Presbytery. He has been commander of his G. A. R. Post in Cincinnati. The two elder children were born in Cincinnati, and the others in Wyoming.

CHILDREN, by first marriage:

6710   Alice Emily Tyler, born Dec. 21, 1868.
6711   Wilfred Marshall Tyler, born Jan. 23, 1871.

CHILDREN, by second marriage:

6712   Arthur Hurin Tyler, born Aug. 12, 1883; died Sept. 2, 1895.
6713   Agnes Ruth Tyler, born April 6, 1886.

4303   JOHN WALTER[8] TYLER (Cutler[7]), born in Newbury, O., May 4, 1841; married, December 29, 1875, Mary Eliza Higgins, born in Perry, N. Y., October 13, 1855. He is a lawyer in Cleveland, O., where the children were born. Children:

6714   John Walter Tyler, Jr., born Oct. 10, 1876.
6715   Paul Wygant Tyler, born Oct. 31, 1878.
6716   Florence Sophia Tyler, born Dec. 17, 1880.
6717   Ruth Sarah Tyler, born Dec. 24, 1882.
6718   Frederick William Tyler, born Dec. 26, 1885; died March 19, 1888.
6719   Marie Sophronia Tyler, born Dec. 16, 1892.
6720   Son, born Feb. 1, 1897.

4306   ISAAC CUTLER[8] TYLER (Keyes[7]), born in Warren, Mass., November 7, 1824; died in Westfield, Mass., January 10, 1890; married (1), November 11, 1853, Mary Bacon, of Warren, who died in 1855; married (2), April 28, 1859, Sarah Sessions, who lives in Westfield.

CHILDREN, by first marriage:

6721   Charles Tyler, lives in Abington, Mass.
6722   Mary Tyler.

4312   WILLIAM ALEXANDER⁸ TYLER (Cutler⁷), born in Warren, Mass., June 3, 1839; married (1), 1866, Minnie L. Beman, who died in Chicago, Ill., 1871; married (2), ———, a widow with children.   In 1903 he was living in Idaho Falls, Ida., and was in the hardware business.   He had one child by second marriage, but no data has been furnished.

CHILD, by first marriage:

6723   Charles W. Tyler, born in Chicago, April 28, 1869; married, June 18, 1896, Modelle Miller, of New Carlisle, Ind., where they lived in 1899, and where he was manager of the Postal Telegraph Cable Company's office; also a jeweler.

4365   ANN AUGUSTA⁸ TYLER (Moses M.⁷), born in West Brookfield, Mass., September 8, 1856; married Samuel G. Cushing, of Ottumwa, Ia., where the children were born. Children:

6724   Fannie N. Cushing, born 1883.
6725   William Tyler Cushing, born 1886.
6726   Albert A. Cushing, born 1890.
6727   Edward R. Cushing, born 1893.
6728   Charlotte E. Cushing, born 1896.

4368   CARLTON P.⁸ TYLER (Moses M.⁷), born in West Brookfield, Mass., March 9, 1865; married, October 25, 1893, Minnie F. Barrett, of Welton, Conn.   He lives in West Brookfield on the old homestead, where the children were born. Children:

6729   Emma Barrett Tyler, born Nov. 25, 1894.
6730   Stella Tyler, born April 22, 1896.

4369   ERNEST A.⁸ TYLER (Moses M.⁷), born in West Brookfield, Mass., May 16, 1867; married, October 10, 1893, Flora I. Cutler, of West Brookfield, born December 17, 1864. He lived for a time in Wolfboro and then moved to Claremont, N. H.   Child:

6731   Erving Leslie Tyler, born in Wolfboro, June 7, 1895.

4375   JULIA E.⁸ TYLER (David Richards⁷), born in

Warren, Mass., August 27, 1848; married Jerome Gould, a miller of Warren.   Child:
6732   Nina A. T. Gould, born in Warren, Aug. 4, 1872.

4411   ELIAS M.⁸ TYLER (Saxton Gates⁷), born in Mexico, N. Y., February 25, 1831; married (1), 1853, Harriet N. Cassedy, of Illinois, who died January 16, 1876, in Willows, Cal.; married (2), April, 1879, Helen H. Jeffries, born in Maryland in 1852.   He enlisted in the Federal army in 1861 and served one year.   He moved to California in 1869, where he lived in Auburn.   The two elder children were born in Illinois; the others in Willows.

CHILDREN, by first marriage:
6733   Lillie A. Tyler, born July 27, 1858; married, Oct. 14, 1874, James Eike, a farmer; they live in Willows.
6734   Mary J. Tyler, born April 29, 1869; married, Sept. 13, 1885, John Dugan, a merchant; they live in Dixon, Cal.

CHILDREN, by second marriage:
6735   Nelson G. Tyler, born March 20, 1880.
6736   Horace Upton Tyler, born Aug. 4, 1882.

4414   FRANCIS A.⁸ TYLER (Saxton Gates⁷), born in Joliet, Ill., about 1840; married, in Binghampton, Cal., August 14, 1868, Ida A. Bentley, born in Madison, Wis., May 29, 1852.   He moved with his father from Joliet to California in 1854, and in 1899 he was living in Auburn, Solano County, where the children were born.   Children:
6737   Frank Alvin Tyler, born Sept. 5, 1871.
6738   Maltby A. Tyler, born March 14, 1876.
6739   Ida A. Tyler, born April 8, 1880.

4423   MERRILL JUDSON⁸ TYLER (Job⁷), born in Westmoreland, N. Y., December 21, 1851; married, May 29, 1875, Minnie Ewland.   Children:
6740   Claude Tyler, born March 15, 1878.
6741   Tirzah Tyler, born June 6, 1883.
6742   Harriet J. Tyler, born Dec. 18, 1886.
6743   Charles Henry Tyler, born Nov. 15, 1888.

6744   Eugene Tyler, born July 18, 1890.
6745   Nat Tyler, born May 21, 1893.

4424   GILES DEAN⁸ TYLER (Job⁷), born in West-moreland, N. Y., October 18, 1856; married, November 3, 1881, Emma Turner. In 1897 he was living in Minneapolis, Minn., a railway engineer. Child:
6746   Hazel Caroline Tyler, born Aug. 2, 1895.

4430   CHARLES HENRY⁸ TYLER (Samuel S.⁷), born in Barry, Mich., August 5, 1853; married, in Baltimore, Mich., December 23, 1876, Susie A. ——, born September 26, 1856, in Indiana. He lived for a time in Hope, Mich., where the children were born; later he went to Rodney, Mich.; was a farmer. Children:
6747   Bessie A. Tyler, born Jan. 8, 1877.
6748   Edmond A. Tyler, born June 18, 1885.

4432   MARY⁸ TYLER (Lewis P.⁷), born in Kalamazoo, Mich., September 3, 1851; married, January 1, 1871, A. B. Morse, born June 20, 1849; died in Kalamazoo, November 18, 1891; son of Benjamin Morse. They lived in Cleveland, O. Children:
6749   Laura Morse, born Nov. 18, 1871; died July 8, 1872.
6750   Harry G. Morse, born Sept. 22, 1872; married, June 26, 1894, Esther Houseley; has one son (William Augustus).
6751   Clara L. Morse, born July 18, 1877.

4433   LEPHA⁸ TYLER (Lewis P.⁷), born in Cleveland, O., December 17, 1853; married, March 4, 1877, Charles Lohn, of Madison, O., a farmer. The children were born in Geneva, O. Children:
6752   Inez Lohn, born Feb. 17, 1878.
6753   Ella Lohn, born July 4, 1880.
6754   William James Lohn, born Aug. 13, 1882.
6755   Dora Lohn, born Oct. 16, 1886; died Aug. 25, 1888.
6756   Charles Lewis Lohn, born Feb. 1, 1891.

4435   JAMES W.⁸ TYLER (Lewis P.⁷), born in York-ville, Mich., September 26, 1858; married, October 22, 1888,

Blanche B. Hogle. He is an engineer; in 1898 they lived in North Linndale, O., where the children were born.   Children:
6757   Gertrude Vara Tyler, born July 14, 1889.
6758   Ruth Tyler, born Aug. 8, 1893; died Sept. 18, 1898.
6759   Blanche Elizabeth Tyler, born Nov. 19, 1895.
6760   Clarence Butterfield Tyler, born July 10, 1898.

   4467 JAMES[8] TYLER (Jeremiah[7]), born in 1824; married ——.   Went to Michigan and Illinois with his father; thence to Ventura, Cal.   Children:
6761   John Tyler, lives in Ventura.
6762   William Tyler, lives in Nelson, Neb.

   4472 SARAH HALL[8] TYLER (Cyril S.[7]), born in Hopkinton, N. H.; married James Chase, of Hopkinton, who died in Philadelphia, where she was living in 1896.   He is buried in Hopkinton.   They lived for a time in Cambridge, Mass., and he practiced law in Boston.   He was a captain in the Civil War from New Hampshire, where he recruited his company in Manchester; he served through the war and then moved to Philadelphia where he was a teacher and private tutor.   Children:
6763   Philip Putnam Chase, married; has two children and lived in Philadelphia.
6764   Harry Custis Chase, lived in Philadelphia, unmarried, in 1896.
6765   Reginald Banfield Chase, married, with no children.
6766   Virginia Chase, unmarried; lived in Philadelphia.
6767   Agnes Chase, unmarried; lived in Philadelphia.

   4473 CHARLES H.[8] TYLER (Latimer[7]), born February 7, 1841; married, 1865, Ellen Burley, of Belle Plains, Ia. Children:
6768   Lottie Bell Tyler, born in Clinton, Ia., Sept., 1869.
6769   Milo Eastman Tyler, born Oct., 1871.
6770   John Tyler, born in Tipton, Ia., Sept., 1873.

   4479 CLARA ARABELLA[8] TYLER (Lucius Harvey[7]), born in Hopkinton, N. H., August 3, 1855; died February 2, 1899; married, May 10, 1877, Clarence Foster, a farmer of Warner, N. H., where the children were born.   Children:

6771   Mabel Lillian Foster, born April 26, 1878.
6772   Howard Tyler Foster, born April 22, 1890.

4480   BERTHA SCOTT[8] TYLER (Lucius Harvey[7]), born in Hopkinton, N. H., May 2, 1866; married George Barnard, a farmer of Hopkinton, and lived on the old Tyler homestead for a time.   She is an organist.   The children were born in Hopkinton.   Children:

6773   Raymond J. Barnard, born Jan. 28, 1891.
6774   Perley D. Barnard, born June 6, 1893.

4496   SARAH E.[8] TYLER (Calvin[7]), born in Hopkinton, N. H., December 26, 1833; married, July 31, 1849, Henry D. Page, of Franklin, N. H., born December 5, 1821; died in Dayton, O., in Soldiers' Home, December 5, 1891.   He was in the Mexican, Seminole, and Civil wars.   Children:

6775   Sarah O. Page, born Oct. 27, 1850; married, George A. Rogers, of Manchester, N. H.; they have two daughters and a son (Florence, Winnie, and Harry).
6776   George H. Page, born Sept. 5, 1852; lives in Brookline, Mass., unmarried.

4497   CHARLES RICHARD[8] TYLER (Calvin[7]), born in Hopkinton, N. H., March 31, 1837; died September 2, 1889; married in Georgetown, Mass., January 22, 1871, Elmira M. Tilton, born in Wilmot, N. H., July 6, 1844; daughter of Luther and Susan (Morey) Tilton; she lived in Haverhill, Mass., in 1896.   He was a shoemaker in Haverhill.   The children were born in Georgetown.   Children:

6777   Charles Henry Tyler, born Nov. 5, 1872; works in shoe manufactory.
6778   Annie Laurie Tyler, born Feb. 20, 1883.

4502   ALMENA M.[8] TYLER (Jepthah[7]), born in Lyme, N. H., September 10, 1837; married, February 11, 1866, William Pebbles, of Lyme, where they lived in 1898, and where the children were born.   Children:

6779   Frank G. Pebbles, born Jan. 25, 1867.
6780   Nellie F. Pebbles, born Aug. 13, 1873.

4503   MARY ESTHER[8] TYLER (Jephthah[7]), born in
Lyme, N. H., June 3, 1839; died in Lyme, April 1, 1891; married, December 1, 1858, George W. Runnels, of Lyme.   The
children were born in Lyme.   Children:
6781   Abby Fradilla Runnells, born June 23, 1860.
6782   William Henry Runnells, born Aug. 2, 1862.
6783   Emma Almira Runnells, born June 21, 1866.

4529   ROSANNA[8] TYLER (Orange Brigham[7]), born
in Napierville, Que., June 17, 1824; died May 8, 1888; married,
August 26, 1844, Patrick Murphy, born February 27, 1820;
died September 29, 1866.   Children:
6784   Malvina Murphy, born May 1, 1846; died Feb. 18,
         1893.
6785   Emma Murphy, died.
6786   Charles Murphy, born Sept., 1849; died June 13,
         1869.
6787   Eliza Murphy, born Nov. 16, 1851; died Sept. 1, 1881.
6788   Agnes Murphy, born April 22, 1854; died May 29,
         1877.
6789   Henry Murphy, born July 3, 1856; died Oct. 6, 1896.
6790   Arthur Murphy, born June 15, 1858; died June 14,
         1880.
6791   Ellen Murphy, born May 25, 1860; died Aug. 28,
         1897.
6792   Alice J. Murphy, born July 16, 1862; died 1864.
6793   Alice L. Murphy, born April 22, 1865; in 1897 was
         living in Brooklyn, N. Y.

4532   EDMOND[8] TYLER (Orange Brigham[7]), born in
Napierville, Que., March 30, 1833; married, December 24,
1855, Mary Johnston.   He moved to New York City in 1853,
and resided in Brooklyn, where he died and where his children
were born.   Children:
6794+ Mary Elizabeth Tyler, born Oct. 27, 1856.
6795   Albert Edmond Tyler, born March 29, 1858.
6796   Frank Henry Tyler, born June 2, 1860; married, May
         14, 1884, Louise H. Loughi.   He is in the real
         estate and insurance business in Brooklyn, where
         he resides.
6797   Henrietta Feller Tyler, born June 21, 1863.
6798   Louis Augustus Tyler, born July 26, 1873.

4534 WILLIAM[8] TYLER (Orange Brigham[7]), born in Napierville, Que., June 20, 1836; married, December 24, 1888, Carrie Evans. They live in Bakersfield, Cal. Children:

6799 Charles Edmond Tyler.
6800 George Whitfield Tyler.
6801 Carrie Tyler.

4549 DWIGHT[8] TYLER (Theodore[7]), born in New Braintree, Mass., December 7, 1823; married, March 16, 1848, Harriet Larned, born February 16, 1824. He is a farmer and resides in New Braintree, where their child was born. Child:
6802 Charles Tyler, born July 1, 1849; is a farmer and resides in New Braintree; unmarried.

4550 SUSAN[8] TYLER (Theodore[7]), born in New Braintree, Mass., September 18, 1825; married, May 1, 1851, William Felton, born in New Braintree, Mass., February 13, 1824. He is a retired farmer in New Braintree, and the children were born there. Children:
6803 William Tyler Felton, born Aug. 14, 1852; is a broker.
6804 Henry Felton, born Dec. 17, 1854.
6805 Charles A. Felton, born Dec. 17, 1856; is a farmer in New Braintree.
6806 Susan A. Felton, born March 19, 1865.

4552 GARDNER[8] TYLER (Theodore[7]), born in New Braintree, Mass., February 2, 1829; died January 31, 1884; married, January 1, 1866, Lucy D. Adams, born January 4, 1826; died October 26, 1887. He was a salesman. Child:
6807 Theodore G. Tyler, born in New Braintree, Mass.; died March 5, 1870.

4556 FREDERICK[8] TYLER (Francis Barnes[7]), born in Warren, Mass.; died there, February 14, 1860; married, June 12, 1852, Elenor Button, born in Ware, Mass., April 19, 1838. He was a merchant in Warren and the children were born there. His widow resides there. Children:
6808+ Fanny Eliza Tyler, born May 5, 1853.
6809 Charles Frederick Tyler, born March 23, 1856; mar-

ried in 1880 Ada L. Shueburne, of West Springfield, Mass. He is a railway engineer.

6810+   George Albert Tyler, born Sept. 6, 1858.

4558   JAMES W.[8] TYLER (Isaac[7]), born in West Brookfield, Mass., October 16, 1835; married, January 7, 1873, Fannie B. Howe, born June 6, 1846. He is a mechanic and resides in West Brookfield, Mass. Child:

6811   Sarah E. Tyler, born in West Brookfield, Mass., July 24, 1876; died there April 9, 1896; married George Samson, a farmer; had a daughter (Grace), who died in infancy.

4559   SARAH L.[8] TYLER (Isaac[7]), born in West Brookfield, Mass., March 22, 1838; died December 4, 1864; married, March 24, 1861, John W. Adams. Child:

6812   Mattie Adams, born Feb. 5, 1864.

4569   ABBIE F.[8] TYLER (George F.[7]), born in West Brookfield, Mass., October 10, 1853; married, December 16, 1869, Edwin C. Doolittle, born June 15, 1847. He is a farmer in Ashuelot, N. H. Children:

6813   Frederick M. Doolittle, born Nov. 10, 1870; died in Winchester, N. H., Sept. 28, 1900.

6814   Jennie F. Doolittle, born Sept. 18, 1872.

6815   Emma A. Doolittle, born Jan. 2, 187—.

6816   George E. Doolittle, born Sept. 22, 1883.

6817   Flora C. Doolittle, born March 24, 1886.

6818   Forest E. Doolittle, born Dec. 19, 1888.

4570   GEORGE WARREN[8] TYLER (George F.[7]), born in West Brookfield, Mass., October 10, 1853; married, November 20, 1875, Abbie Elizabeth Cutler, of West Brookfield, born December 29, 1854. He inherited the old homestead in West Brookfield, with his brother, Dwight M.; lives there, a farmer and lumber manufacturer; the children were born there. Children:

6819   Flora Isabella Tyler, born Dec. 18, 1876; died Dec. 21, 1877.

6820   Cora M. Tyler, born Aug. 20, 1878.

6821   Anna B. Tyler, born Oct. 17, 1880.

6822   Arthur W. Tyler, born Feb. 19, 1882.
6823   Herbert F. Tyler, born Dec. 10, 1885.

4571   DWIGHT M.[8] TYLER (George F.[7]), born in West Brookfield, Mass., June 15, 1855; married Theodora E. Woodbridge, born in West Brookfield, March 4, 1858. He is a farmer and lumber manufacturer in West Brookfield, where he inherited the old homestead with his brother George W. and where his children were born. Children:

6824   Clara Louise Tyler, born March 31, 1876; died July 21, 1876.
6825   Lillian May Tyler, born Dec. 28, 1878; died March 3, 1882.
6826   Dwight Louis Tyler, born July 20, 1881.

4573   PHEBE A.[8] TYLER (George F.[7]), born in West Brookfield, Mass., March 19, 1861; married, July 5, 1876, Eugene A. Hack, born in Granby, Conn., November 27, 1856. He lives in West Brookfield, where the children were born. Children:

6827   George H. Hack, born Dec. 21, 1876.
6828   Walter E. Hack, born May 2, 1891.

4574   HATTIE M.[8] TYLER (George F.[7]), born in West Brookfield, Mass., August 19, 1861; married, May 1, 1880, James D. Fellows, born in Hardwick, Mass., August 14, 1851. They lived in Spencer, Mass. Children:

6829   Mabell G. Fellows, born Nov. 27, 1882.
6830   Harrison C. Fellows, born Oct. 1, 1887; died Nov. 1, 1887.

4575   ORIANNA[8] TYLER (George F.[7]), born in West Brookfield, Mass., April 13, 1863; married, October 28, 1891, Eugene A. Kirkland, born in Huntington, Mass., November 14, 1857. He was a contractor and lived in Colfax, Wash. Children:

6831   Helen Irene Kirkland, born April 13, 1895.
6832   Eva Harriet Kirkland, born May 2, 1897.

4588   HARLAND D.[8] TYLER (Dwight[7]), born in South Londonderry, Vt., May 8, 1840; married Miss O. R.

Whitman. He was town clerk for twelve years; a house and carriage painter. The children were born in South Londonderry. Children:

6833   Minnie A. Tyler, born May 13, 1866; she is town clerk.

6834   Frank H. Tyler, born March 6, 1869.

4592 HANNAH[8] TYLER (Joshua[7]), born February 2, 1845; married, March 15, 1868, Matthew Baine, a farmer of Murphysboro, Ill. The children were born there. Children:

6835   Edward Baine, born Nov. 29, 1869; died Dec. 22, 1872.

6836   Celia Baine, born Feb. 11, 1870.

6837   Susan E. Baine, born May 5, 1871; died March 29, 1893.

6838   Martha Ellen Baine, born Aug. 1, 1873; died April 30, 1881.

6839   Laura Baine, born Feb. 21, 1875.

6840   Joshua Baine, born Dec. 19, 1877; died Oct. 19, 1878.

6841   Maggie Baine, born Nov. 27, 1878.

6842   Adam Baine, born Oct. 22, 1880.

6843   Paul Baine, born April 11, 1882.

6844   Fernando Baine, born Jan. 2, 1886.

6845   Eva Baine, born Jan. 28, 1888.

4593 GEORGE[8] TYLER (Joshua[7]), born in Murphysboro, Ill., March 14, 1847; married, September 7, 1869, Mary Sorrels. He enlisted in Company D, 31st Ill. Volunteer Infantry and was mustered out July 19, 1865; is a farmer in Murphysboro, Ill. (Sand Ridge). The children were born in Murphysboro. Children:

6846   Nellie Tyler, born Sept. 7, 1870.

6847+   Edith Tyler, born June 22, 1874.

6848+   Jerusha Tyler, born Oct. 20, 1876.

4595 JAMES[8] TYLER (Joshua[7]), born May 4, 1851; married, August 1, 1875, Martha Hiser. He is a carpenter and resides in Murphysboro, Ill., where the children were born. Children:

6849   Ira Tyler, born Sept. 30, 1878.

6850   Charles Tyler, born March 26, 1882.
6851   John Tyler, born July 26, 1886; died Nov. 1, 1888.
6852   Ellory Tyler, born Oct. 13, 1892.

4596   DANIEL⁸ TYLER (Joshua⁷), born October 12, 1852 (or 1854); married, November 15, 1883, Louisa Thornton. He is a farmer in Pyatt, Ill., where the children were born. Children:
6853   Sadie M. Tyler, born Dec. 28, 1885.
6854   Joshua Tyler, born May 12, 1888.
6855   Harry Oakley Tyler, born June 9, 1890.
6856   Leta Tyler, born Aug. 2, 1892; died March 25, 1898.

4599   LAURA⁸ TYLER (Joshua⁷), born December 15, 1857; married, April 8, 1877, Marcus B. Hawkins, born May 13, 1855. He is in the insurance business in Carbondale, Ill., where the children were born. Children:
6857   Estelle Pearl Hawkins, born Jan. 17, 1878; married, Jan. 22, 1900, George B. Taylor; one son.
6858   Dwight Jay Hawkins, born March 1, 1879; in the Spanish-American War.
6859   Marcus Earle Hawkins, born July 30, 1880; died Aug. 31, 1881.
6860   Lena Frank Hawkins, born Oct. 2, 1881.
6861   Laurie Clay Hawkins, born June 8, 1885.

4600   FRANCES ELLEN⁸ TYLER (Joshua⁷), born in Murphysboro, Ill. (Somerset), November 18, 1859; died April 21, 1882; married, July 27, 1879, Lee Roy Breeden. He was a farmer in Murphysboro, Ill., and the children were born there. Children:
6862   Myrtle Corryta Breeden, born Dec. 24, 1880.
6863   Kenneth Roy Breeden, born March 11, 1882; died May 1, 1882.

4601   EVA LOIS⁸ TYLER (Joshua⁷), born March 5, 1865; married, September 1, 1887, Albert Imhoff, a farmer in Murphysboro, Ill. The children were born in Murphysboro. Children:
6864   Clinton Imhoff, born May 26, 1888.

6865   Clifford Imhoff, born Sept. 14, 1889.
6866   Edna Olive Imhoff, born Aug. 9, 1892.

4605   GERTRUDE MARIA[8] DAVIS (Parkman Tyler[7] Davis), born in Burlington, Vt., February 28, 1847; married in Boston, Mass., March 17, 1869, Abbott T. Maynard; they reside in Allston, Mass. The children were born in Boston. Children:
6867   Fannie Elizabeth Maynard, born Dec. 20, 1869; married, Jan. 13, 1892, George Scott Garritt; one daughter (Helen Maynard, born Nov. 15, 1893).
6868   Alexander Parkman Maynard, born Aug. 5, 1876.

4612   DANA L.[8] TYLER (Samuel King[7]), born in Keene, N. H., September 1, 1845; married, November 8, 1866, Elizabeth H. Whitlock, of West Chester, O., where he lived in 1900 and where the children were born.   Children:
6869   George S. Tyler, born Sept. 19, 1867; in 1900 lived in Cedar Rapids, Ia., unmarried.
6870   Daisy W. Tyler, born April 20, 1875.

4623   JULIA A.[8] TYLER (John Larkin[7]), born in Springfield, Mass., February 2, 1852; married, December 28, 1870, John H. Mathis.   Children:
6871   Eugene Tyler Mathis, born in Fort Wayne, Ind., July 15, 1872; married, Oct. 24, 1894, Minnie M. Hassinger; one son (William E.).
6872   Lillian Adelaide Mathis, born in Springfield, O., July 21, 1876.

4624   MAJOR EUGENE[8] TYLER (John Larkin[7]), born in Harmar, O., July 18, 1854; married, November 19, 1885, Jennie B. Van Cleaf, of Springfield, O.   Child:
6873   Beulah Esther Tyler, born in Detroit, Mich., July 6, 1889.

4625   ALLIEZUMA[8] TYLER (John Larkin[7]), born in Columbus, O., June 12, 1857; married, December 24, 1873, John B. Stroup, of Kenton, O.   All the children were born in Springfield, O., except the third and the youngest. Children:
6874   Florence Iona Stroup, born July 23, 1875; married,

June 29, 1904, Joseph Webster Gilmor, a surveyor of Hardin County, O.; born in Sedalia, Mo., July 6, 1866; was graduated from Ohio Northern University in 1898, A. B. and C. E.; resides in Kenton.

6875   William Burkeley Stroup, born May 9, 1877; married, Oct. 26, 1902, Ethel M. White; was in Camp Thomas during the Spanish War; one child (Tyler, born April 2, 1905).

6876   John Walter Stroup, born in Fort Wayne, Ind., May 29, 1879; married, July 6, 1899, Grace B. Kennedy; was in Camp Thomas during the Spanish War; two children (Blanche I., born Dec. 3, 1903, and Mabel M., born Feb. 27, 1906).

6877   Gertrude Thirza Stroup, born Dec. 18, 1884.

6878   Frederick Howard Stroup, born Jan. 4, 1888.

6879   Warren Douglas Stroup, born Jan. 2, 1892.

6880   Albert Murdock Tyler Stroup, born in Kenton, O., March 30, 1898.

4626   JASON KING[8] TYLER (John Larkin[7]), born in Dayton, O., Dec. 25, 1859; married, July 8, 1881, May Rice, of Springfield, O., where the children were born. Children:

6881   Addie Tyler, born July 11, 1882; died Jan. 11, 1884.

6882   King William Tyler, born Sept. 29, 1883.

4668   EDGAR EDWIN[8] TYLER (Nathaniel[7]), born in Richfield, Ill., November 27, 1842; married in Richfield, December 31, 1865, Lydia F. Mosley, born in Philadelphia, Mo., February 23, 1845. He was in the Civil War under the name of "Edwin," in Company C, 50th Ill. Volunteer Infantry for three years; was at Fort Henry, Donaldson, Shilo, Corinth, etc. Since 1871 he has lived in Great Bend, Kas., where he opened the first store and built the second house; has held numerous town offices. The three younger children were born in Great Bend. Children:

6883   Tray Young Tyler, born in Richfield May 15, 1867; died in Great Bend, Oct. 19, 1880.

6884   Clarissa Tyler, born in Mexico, Mo., Sept. 18, 1868; died in Great Bend, May 15, 1884.

6885   Taylor Barnum Tyler, born in Richfield, Dec. 12, 1870; died in Great Bend, Dec. 22, 1880.

6886   Dora M. Tyler, born May 1, 1874; married, June 25, 1894, Samuel I. Pratt, born in Perciville, Ia.; they reside in Wichita and Great Bend, Kan.; three children (Hallie L., Lydia S., and Lena M.).

6887   Hallie G. Tyler, born Oct. 20, 1877; died in Great Bend, Nov. 14, 1897.

6888   Edwin Tyler, born Oct. 8, 1882; died March 4, 1883.

4688   PERINTHA O.[8] TYLER (Daniel[7]), born in Griggsville, Ill., June 4, 1839; died in Beaver City, Utah, September 19, 1882; married Charles Oakden.   Children:

6889   Olive P. Oakden, born Aug. 11, 1861; died May 12, 1880; married, Feb. 4, 1880, Shepard L. Tanner.

6890   Charles T. Oakden, born Sept. 2, 1864; married, 1885, Anna M. Allred; five children (William C., Stanley, Olive, Mary, and Eva).

6891   Robert E. Oakden, born Oct. 27, 1866; died June 22, 1877.

6892   Ruth E. Oakden, born April 25, 1869; died Dec. 24, 1874.

4692   EMILY P.[6] TYLER (Daniel[7]), born in Council Bluffs, Ia., January 28, 1847; married George W. Adair. The eight elder children were born in Washington, Utah, and the three younger in Arizona.   Children:

6893   Olive P. Adair, born Nov. 27, 1864; died Nov. 28, 1864.

6894   Emily J. Adair, born Dec. 28, 1865; married, Feb. 4, 1885, Edmund Grant; four children (George, Floyd, Emma, and Pansey).

6895   Daniel Tyler Adair, born Dec. 3, 1867; married, June 18, 1895, Florence E. Huntsman; one daughter Tacie V.).

6896   Samuel P. Adair, born March 3, 1870.

6897   William A. Adair, born Feb. 7, 1872; married, July 9, 1894, Mary R. Sawyer; one son (William K.).

6898   John W. Adair, born Feb. 10, 1874; married, March 19, 1894, Cynthia Penrod; one daughter (Cynthia).

6899   George N. Adair, born March 23, 1876; married; one son (George C.).

6900   Ruth A. Adair, born Sept. 16, 1878.

6901   Joseph W. Adair, born June 17, 1881.
6902   Rufus N. Adair, born Sept. 16, 1884.
6903   Edna I. Adair, born Jan. 20, 1887.

4693   DANIEL M.[8] TYLER (Daniel[7]), born in Salt Lake City, Utah, January 27, 1850; died in Harrington, Utah, September 10, 1895; married, August 19, 1872, Sarah E. Pulsipher, born November 6, 1854. The second, third, and fourth children were born in Hebron, Utah. Children:

6904   Barzilla Tyler, born May 18, 1873; died in infancy.
6905   Daniel Tyler, born Oct. 30, 1874.
6906   John P. Tyler, born Aug. 31, 1878.
6907+   Ruth Tyler, born Feb. 25, 1880.
6908   William N. Tyler, born May 31, 1882; died Jan. 7, 1897.
6909   Esther M. Tyler, born Aug. 8, 1884.
6910   Andrews Tyler, born Nov. 7, 1886.
6911   Emily Tyler, born April 19, 1889.
6912   Marion Tyler, born June 3, 1891.
6913   Mary Tyler, twin to Marion; died 1891.
6914   Charles Tyler, born Dec. 24, 1893.

4695   JOHN C.[8] TYLER (Daniel[7]), born in Draper, Utah, November 30, 1857; married, December 19, 1887, Maria L. Billingsley, born January 16, 1867; died in Beaver City, Utah, August 1, 1893. The children were born in Beaver City. Children:

6915   Daniel R. Tyler, born Oct. 9, 1888.
6916   John C. Tyler, born May 8, 1890.
6917   Elsie M. Tyler, born May 1, 1892.

4696   ALICE M.[8] TYLER (Daniel[7]), born in Draper, Utah, May 6, 1859; married in Beaver City, Utah, April 7, 1878, Joseph W. Tanner, born May 19, 1856. The children were born in Beaver City. Children:

6918   Ruth A. Tanner, born Sept. 20, 1879.
6919   Emily F. Tanner, born March 26, 1882; died April 24, 1882.
6920   Jane E. Tanner, born Oct. 29, 1884.
6921   Josie Tanner, born April 18, 1889.
6922   Elfrida Tanner, born Jan. 28, 1892

6923   William J. Tanner, born March 17, 1894; died May 10, 1894.

6924   Hazel Tanner, born May 24, 1895; died Sept. 7, 1895.

4706   JOHN ANDREW[8] TYLER (Henry B.[7]), born in Liberty, Ill., July 1, 1859; married, May 14, 1880, Annie ——, born September 20, 1865. He lives in Ashland, Ill. Children:

6925   Dell Edward Tyler, born Sept. 17, 1881; died Feb. 13, 1882.

6926   Tillis Andrew Tyler, born March 13, 1883.

6927   Cecil Cloid Tyler, born March 9, 1888.

6928   Annie Bell Tyler, born Sept. 20, 1889.

6929   Merry Effie Tyler, born May 12, 1895.

4720   ELTHEA HARDING[8] TYLER (Kimball[7]), born in Haverhill, N. H., February 10, 1830; married in Charlestown, Mass., February 22, 1849, George Lafayette Call, born in Charlestown, February 12, 1825. In 1898 they lived in Stoneham, Mass.   Child:

6930   Ella Frances Call, born in Charlestown, April 10, 1850; married in Lynn, Mass., 1868, John Walden Chase, born in Cambridge Mass., Aug. 27, 1843; died in Lynn, Nov. 8, 1870. In 1898 she lived in Lynn, where her daughter (Maude W.) was born.

4721   FRANCINA[8] TYLER (Kimball[7]), born in Haverhill, N. H., August 15, 1831; died in Lynn, Mass., September 16, 1899; married (1), in Bradford, Vt., January 1, 1850, James Warren Sampson, born in Lyman, N. H., January 7, 1828; died in Washington, D. C., January 13, 1863; married (2), in Lynn, Mass., November 1, 1887, Abiel Sweet Reed, born in Barnet, Vt., August 31, 1821; died in West Bath, N. H., June 27, 1898. All but the eldest child was born in Haverhill, N. H.

CHILDREN, by first marriage:

6931   Elmer Warren Sampson, born in Bath, N. H., Dec. 29, 1850; married, March 22, 1869, Jennie Felton Cox, born in Haverhill, N. H., July 10, 1849; they lived in Lynn; one child (Leola C.).

6932   Alphonsine Hibbard Sampson, born Nov. 4, 1855; married (1), July 3, 1872, Frederick S. Hunt, born in Lynn, March, 1853; died March 17, 1875; married (2), Sept. 2, 1877, Josiah George, born in Lebanon, N. H., March 6, 1854; lived in Lynn; one child (Ralph M.).

6933   Josephine Wetherbee Sampson, born Nov. 3, 1857; married, Nov. 17, 1878, Charles Whipple Abbott, born in North Reading, Mass., July 4, 1857; resided in Lynn; five children (H. Elmer, Josephine M., Lottie F., Beatrice O., and Agnes B.).

6934   John Forest Sampson, born June 17, 1859; died April 22, 1864.

6935   Cora May Sampson, born Nov. 26, 1861; died Oct. 3, 1863.

4722 THADDEUS WARSAW[8] TYLER (Kimball[7]), born in Haverhill, N. H., July 16, 1833; married in Bath, N. H., March 20, 1852, Elizabeth Marie Reed, born in Durham, P. Q., July 18, 1833. In 1898 he lived in Lynn, Mass., where the two younger children were born; the others were born in Bath. Children:

6936+   Sarah Louise Tyler, born Jan. 13, 1853.

6937+   Thaddeus Frank Tyler, born Sept. 20, 1854.

6938   Elmer Ellsworth Tyler, born Feb. 19, 1861; died April 19, 1862.

6939+   Cora Martique Tyler, born April 8, 1865.

4723 MARY JANE[8] TYLER (Kimball[7]), born in Wentworth, N. H., June 25, 1835; married, in 1853, Hiram Hale Poole, born in Haverhill, N. H.; died in Lynn, Mass. Child:

6940   Fred Hiram Poole, born in Boston, Mass., Oct. 21, 1858; married Alice M. Young, born in Washington, Vt.; has one son (Robert), and resides in Lynn.

4724 HARRIET[8] TYLER (Kimball[7]), born in Haverhill, N. H., July 18, 1837; married, in Stoneham, Mass., August 9, 1854, Leonard Franklin Green, born in Billerica, Mass., March 2, 1832; died in Lynn, March 4, 1896. In 1898 she was living in Lynn. Children:

6941   Hattie Ardel Green, born in Stoneham, April 13, 1856.
6942   Thaddeus Warsaw Green, born in Lynn, June 23, 1867.

4725   LYDIA⁸ TYLER (Kimball⁷), born in Haverhill, N. H., July 18, 1837; died in Lynn, Mass., February, 1864; married, April, 1853, Sylvanus Hovey, of Lynn, where the children were born.   Children:
6943   Albini Sumner Hovey, born Jan. 12, 1854; married, Dec. 23, 1875, Henrietta J. Quimby; one son, who is married.
6944   Effie Blanche Hovey, born March 12, 1858; died s. p. April 26, 1891; married George W. Ingalls, of Lynn.

4726   LAURA ANN⁸ TYLER (Kimball⁷), born in Haverhill, N. H., May 1, 1840; married (1), in Stoneham, Mass., June 3, 1855, Charles Phineas Patten, born in Bucksport, Me., November 28, 1829; died in Togus, Me., August 10, 1882; married (2), in Lynn, Mass., December 24, 1892, Hollis Monroe Macdonald, born in Belfast, Me., October 9, 1826; lives in Stoneham.
CHILDREN, by first marriage:
6945   Charles Alphonso Patten, born in Stoneham, Feb. 28, 1856; married, June 12, 1881, Ona Dell Rowe, born in Stoneham, Feb. 6, 1862; lived there in 1898.
6946   Florence Elta Patten, born in Haverhill, N. H., April 16, 1859; died March 16, 1865.
6947   Melissa Belle Patten, born in Lynn, Mass., July 21, 1865; married, Sept. 2, 1884, Richard Anthony Nicholson, born in Lynn, June 12, 1861.   In 1898 they lived in Lynn; three daughters (Laura M., Melissa R., and Marion V.).

4728   GEORGE LAFAYETTE⁸ TYLER (Kimball⁷), born in Bath, N. H., June 18, 1849; married, in Lynn, Mass., July 14, 1867, Rowana Jane Clifford, born in North Haverhill, N. H., March 2, 1847; died in Lynn, January 23, 1893.
Child:
6948+   Ethel Madalena Tyler, born in Lynn, April 17, 1869.

4741 HENRY[8] TYLER (Edwin[7]), born in Benton, N. H., December 14, 1842; married (1), July 29, 1871, Elizabeth Gay, of Indiana, who died September 30, 1874; married (2), August 17, 1885, Mary Jane Elliott; he went to Indiana, but later to Vera Cruz, Mo.; is a farmer.

CHILDREN, by first marriage:

6949 Graham Tyler, died.
6950 Samuel Tyler, died.

CHILDREN, by second marriage:

6951 Sopha Tyler, born Oct. 10, 1886; died July 12, 1888.
6952 Ella Tyler, born June 7, 1891; died Sept. 10, 1891.
6953 Effy Tyler, twin to Ella; died Sept. 20, 1891.
6954 Seth Tyler, born Aug. 28, 1892.

4750 GEORGE B.[8] TYLER (Laban[7]), born in Benton, N. H., May 29, 1841; died April 25, 1894; married, March 25, 1873, Arvilla Southworth; moved to Missouri. Children:

6955 Jessie Tyler, born Aug. 8, 1874.
6956 Albert Edward Tyler, born Nov. 29, 1875.
6957 Ella May Tyler, born Sept. 22, 1877.
6958 Asa Henry Tyler, born May 19, 1882.

4753 FRANK CHASE[8] TYLER (Laban[7]), born in Benton, N. H., March 14, 1854; married in Paw Paw, Mich., Eliza Southworth. Children:

6959 Lewis Laban Tyler, born Nov. 28, 1876; died Nov. 28, 1896.
6960 Lorin Darius Tyler, born Sept. 10, 1879.
6961 Lulu May Tyler, born Jan. 9, 1882.
6962 Lida Elvira Tyler, born Dec. 31, 1883.
6963 Luella Elmira Tyler, born May 17, 1886.
6964 Clara Cecilia Tyler, born Sept. 9, 1889.
6965 Clarence Charles Tyler, twin to Clara.
6966 Alice Eliza Tyler, born Oct. 21, 1893.

4761 IDA[8] TYLER (Moses K.[7]), born in Stoneham, Mass., August 7, 1856; married, May 23, 1878, George Egelens, born December 22, 1845. He is a farmer and they reside in Lacota, Mich., and the children were born there. Children:

6967   Allie Egelens, born April 10, 1879; married, March
        28, 1899, Edward Johnson; one son.
6968   Vie Egelens, born Jan. 15, 1883.
6969   Carl Egelens, born March 22, 1890.

4765 LUCETTA STREETER[8] TYLER (Charles
Carroll[7]), born in Benton, N. H., April 15, 1848; married,
March 20, 1867, Amos Pike. Children:
6970   Alvin D. Pike, born Nov. 16, 1869.
6971   Wilbur F. Pike, born Nov. 7, 1870; married, March
        7, 1893, Edith C. Clark; one son (Forrest M.).
6972   Susan D. Pike, born Oct. 4, 1873; married, March
        24, 1894, James H. Nutter; one daughter (Doris
        L.).

4766   WILDER C.[8] TYLER (Charles Carroll[7]), born
in Benton, N. H., October 28, 1849; married, July 26, 1877,
Hattie E. Hamlin. He is a farmer and resides in Lacota,
Mich., and the children were born there. Children:
6973   Ina D. Tyler, born May 8, 1878; married, Sept. 22,
        1896, Robert Hines.
6974   Sabra Tyler, born Feb. 16, 1880.
6975   Elmer C. Tyler, born June 18, 1885.
6976   Alvin P. Tyler, born Sept. 26, 1889.

4767   FRED M.[8] TYLER (Charles Carroll[7]), born in
Benton, N. H., July 17, 1852; married, March 13, 1873, Ella
Keyser, who died October 16, 1893. Children:
6977   Edna W. Tyler, born Sept. 13, 1876; married, Jan.
        11, 1900, William R. Severance, of Stoneham, Mass.;
        one daughter (Gladys).
6978   Stella C. Tyler, born Feb. 22, 1878; married, Nov.
        26, 1896, Stephen Dexter; resides in Benton, N. H.
6979   Charlena C. Tyler, born Sept. 20, 1879; married,
        Sept. 18, 1897, Clarence Fifield; resides in Benton,
        N. H.
6980   Lewis F. Tyler, born Feb. 11, 1881.
6981   Leon E. Tyler, twin to Lewis.
6982   Scott I. Tyler, born July 11, 1882; died June 17,
        1893.
6983   Roy E. Tyler, born Nov. 15, 1884; died June 3, 1893.

6984   Cora M. Tyler, born Oct. 21, 1886.
6985   Bessie Tyler, born Sept. 1, 1888.
6986   Alice E. Tyler, born Aug. 3, 1890; died June 5, 1893.

4768 ALFRED ELMORE[8] TYLER (Charles Carroll[7]), born in Benton, N. H., April 7, 1854; married (1), October 16, 1878, Mary J. Clark, who died in Benton, June 26, 1894; married (2), August 31, 1898, Bell Muir. He is a farmer and resides in Benton, where the children were born.

CHILDREN, by first marriage:
6987   Charles C. Tyler, born Oct. 26, 1880.
6988   Bernice R. Tyler, born Oct. 7, 1892.

CHILD, by second marriage:
6989   Mary Isabel Tyler, born Oct., 1899.

4770 BYRON M.[8] TYLER (Charles Carroll[7]), born in Benton, N. H., February 22, 1861; married (1), June 7, 1882, Rose B. Clark, who died October 16, 1886; married (2), October 10, 1888, Carrie Spinney, who died August 23, 1897. He is a farmer and resides in Benton, and the children were born there.

CHILDREN, by second marriage:
6990   George B. Tyler, born Oct. 30, 1890.
6991   Arthur Tyler, born April 9, 1894.
6992   Wilder C. Tyler, born May 17, 1897.

4773 LESLIE G.[8] TYLER (Charles Carroll[7]), born in Benton, N. H., November 30, 1865; married, May 30, 1890, Jennie L. French. He resides in Medford, Mass., and the children were born there. Children:
6993   Maurice L. Tyler, born Nov. 28, 1894.
6994   Mildred A. Tyler, born Oct. 11, 1897.
6995   Marjorie D. Tyler, born Oct. 31, 1900.

4774 MAY[8] TYLER (Charles Carroll[7]), born in Benton, N. H., November 30, 1868; married, January 22, 1888, Albert Foss, a farmer of Benton. The children were born there. Children:
6996   Bula L. Foss., born Dec. 10, 1890; died Sept. 2, 1891.

6997   Lawrence A. Foss, born Sept. 12, 1892.
6998   Walter L. Foss, born Nov. 19, 1893.

4784   ABEL MERRILL⁸ TYLER (Charles Augustus⁷),
born in Searsmont, Me., September 25, 1845; married, September 25, 1870, Clara R. Randall. He is a successful inventor of note. Child:
6999   Della E. Tyler, born Feb. 16, 1874.

4785   GEORGE AUGUSTUS⁸ TYLER (Charles Augustus⁷), born in Searsmont, Me., September 2, 1847; died January 30, 1895; married, April 4, 1875, Inez Eliza Lazelle, of California. He went to Graniteville, Nevada County, Cal., where he died. Children:
7000   Inez Mabel Tyler, lives in Graniteville.
7001   Lizzie Irene Tyler.
7002   Blanche Tyler.
7003   Linda Tyler.

4787   MARY AMELIA⁸ TYLER (Charles Augustus⁷), born in Searsmont, Me., January 10, 1852; died September 14, 1878; married, June 4, 1870, George Prescott Packard. Children:
7004   Lester Augustus Packard, born Aug. 24, 1871; married, Dec. 25, 1895, Lizzie G. Oliver; one son (Edward).
7005   Ida May Packard, born March 22, 1875; married, March 30, 1892, Munroe Williams; two children (Frederick and Florence).

4792   RHODA WOODMAN⁸ TYLER (Charles Augustus⁷), born in Searsmont, Me., December 24, 1862; married, October 1, 1882, Samuel Irving Dickerson, and resides in Brockton, Mass., where the children were born. Children:
7006   Myrtle Irene Dickerson, born Jan. 22, 1883.
7007   Harriet Eliza Dickerson, born March 31, 1887; died, Aug. 25, 1888.
7008   Ruth Augustus Dickerson, born June 29, 1891.
7009   Sumner Tyler Dickerson, born Sept. 11, 1896.

4794   ADELAIDE FOSTER⁸ TYLER (Charles Augustus[7]), born in Searsmont, Me., July 2, 1868; married, February 18, 1886, Ernest Perkins, of Bridgewater, Mass., where the children were born. Children:

7010   Ernest Howland Perkins, born Nov. 12, 1886.
7011   John Foster Perkins, born Feb. 26, 1889.
7012   Lucille Jaspar Perkins, born April 20, 1891; died Sept. 1, 1891.
7013   Raymond Stearns Perkins, born June 23, 1894.
7014   Roger Tyler Perkins, born Sept. 12, 1896.

4795 EUGENE[8] TYLER (Abel Dudley[7]), born in Hope, Me., January 12, 1841; married (1), October 3, 1863, Mary A. Walker; married (2), Mary J. Aiken. He was a blacksmith and lived in Brockton; was in the Civil War. The children were born in Abington, Mass.

CHILDREN, by first marriage:
7015   Maud A. Tyler, born Sept. 29, 1864; died, unmarried, March 3, 1884.
7016+   William Eugene Tyler, born Feb. 6, 1866.

4796 ANN SARAH[8] TYLER (Abel Dudley[7]), born in Searsmont, Me., October 18, 1843; married, January 10, 1862, Linus S. Perrault, who lives in Chicago, Ill. Children:

7017   Lizzie Perrault, born March 8, 1864; married Linus Ollendorf.
7018   Charles D. Perrault, born Jan. 10, 1867; died March 12, 1873.

4797 JOHN MORROW[8] TYLER (Abel Dudley[7]), born in Searsmont, Me., August 9, 1846; married, May 16, 1868, Mary F. Bearce; they lived in Whitman, Mass. Children:

7019   Henry Newton Tyler, born Nov. 27, 1870.
7020   Mabel Lavan Tyler, born Oct. 18, 1872; married, Oct. 26, 1892, Joseph Wye.
7021   Charles Dudley Tyler, born March 29, 1874.
7022   Minnie Gertrude Tyler, born May 16, 1875.
7023   Alice Mehitable Tyler, born Oct. 29, 1877.

4798 FRANCES LAVAN[8] TYLER (Abel Dudley[7]), born in Searsmont, Me., August 10, 1849; married (1), No-

vember 23, 1867, Davis H. Packard, of Brockton, Mass.;
married (2), Winchester G. Turner, of Tewksbury, Mass.
The children were born in Brockton.

CHILDREN, by first marriage:

7024   Alice Lucinda Packard, born Aug. 10, 1869; married, June 11, 1890, Adelbert Adams, of Brockton;
four children (Gladys S., Ethel F., Harold D., and
Henry W.).

7025   Ethel Lavan Packard, born March 6, 1873; married,
May, 1898, Cady Kennedy Peck, born in Keokuk,
Ia., Aug. 28, 1862; she is an accomplished actress;
their home is in Chicago; two children (Cady K.
and Helen F.).

7026   Marion Gibbs Packard, born July 5, 1876.

7027   Bertha Moyee Packard, born March 1, 1878.

4799   ABEL D.[8] TYLER (Abel Dudley[7]), born in Camden, Me., May 24, 1852; married, February 8, 1879, Georgi-
etta F. Nash, of Abington, Mass. He became a photographer
and followed that business from 1871-1877; became a model-
maker and the superintendent of the largest shoe-tree manufacturing company in the United States. In 1884 he invented
and patented the shoe-treeing machines now universally used.
He sold out in 1886, and manufactured the Brockton shutter
worker, upon which he had several patents. He worked for a
time in electricity and then became superintendent for some
last manufacturers of Worcester, and has since invented the "Tyler hinged last," which largely revolutionized
the shoe business, being the first great improvement on the
original last. He became president and part owner of the
Mawhinney Last Company. The children were born in Brockton, where he resides. Children:

7028   Annie L. Tyler, born April 15, 1882.

7029   Mildred L. Tyler, born May 31, 1884.

4800   JESSIE BENTON[8] TYLER (Abel Dudley[7]),
born in Camden, Me., August 15, 1856; married, July 2, 1876,
James C. Stannatt, a shoe manufacturer of Brockton, Mass.
Child:

7030   Grace H. Stannatt, born Feb. 3, 1882.

4824 SARAH FIDELIA[8] TYLER (Alden Lorenzo[7]), born in Rockland, Me., August 5, 1848; married, June 13, 1868, David N. Bird, of Rockland, who moved to Belfast, Me., where he is superintendent of the water works. The children were born in Belfast. Children:
7031 Bertha I. Bird, born Jan. 30, 1870.
7032 Tyler H. Bird, born Feb. 8, 1876.
7033 Mary Helen Bird, born Feb. 27, 1883.

4826 JOHN PACKARD[8] TYLER (Alden Lorenzo[7]), born in Rockland, Me., December 12, 1852; married, September 7, 1895, Mary E. Cables, of Rockland, where they live. Child:
7034 Louise M. Tyler, born in Rockland, June 24, 1896.

4827 SAMUEL[8] TYLER (Alden Lorenzo[7]), born in Rockland, Me., January 14, 1858; married, September 24, 1882, Katherine Messenger, of Castleton, N. Y. He is a lawyer and lives in California. Children:
7035 Blanche Tyler, born June 27, 1884.
7036 Mary Helen Tyler, born Nov., 1893.
7037 Claudine Tyler, born June, 1895.

4828 LEMUEL[8] TYLER (Alden Lorenzo[7]), born in Rockland, Me., January 14, 1858; married, November 27, 1881, Annie T. Burpee, of Rockland. He is a mining expert, and his residence is Rockland, where the children were born. Children:
7038 Eva May Tyler, born Oct. 1, 1882.
7039 H. Brown Tyler, born April 2, 1884.

4854 BLANCHE HOWARD[8] TYLER (Simeon Coburn[7]), born in Camden, Me., April 13, 1858; married, December 5, 1874, George Frederick Porter, of Camden. She is divorced and lives in Jamaica Plain, Mass. Children:
7040 Ralph Ross Porter.
7041 George Frederick Porter, Jr.
7042 Infant, died young.

4855 RALPH SUMNER[8] TYLER (Simeon Coburn[7]), born in Camden, Me., July 11, 1860; married, January 31,

1889, Isabelle Josephine Knight, of Camden. He is an architect and resides in West Roxbury, Mass. Child:

7043   Ralph Waldo Tyler, born Oct. 4, 1893.

4856   ANNA EUGENIA[8] TYLER (Simeon Coburn[7]), born in Camden, Me., April 25, 1862; married, July, 1881, Ronello Allison Eldridge, of Camden. She is divorced and lives in Rockland, Me. The children were born in Camden. Children:

7044   Simeon Allison Eldridge, born March 24, 1882.
7045   Ethel Rebecca Eldridge, born Jan. 8, 1884.

4859   BERENICE ANTOINETTE[8] TYLER (Simeon Coburn[7]), born in Camden, Me., June 21, 1868; married, November 28, 1888, Louis Ernest West, of Jamaica Plain, Mass. Child:

7046   Mildred Louise West, born in Jamaica Plain Nov. 5, 1889.

4879   MARIA N.[8] TYLER (Asa Ladd[7]), born in Rutland, Vt., April 14, 1821; married, in Saybrook, O., November 26, 1840, A. Herren, who died May, 1892; he moved to Illinois in 1849, then to Nashua, Ia., in 1865; in 1890 they celebrated their golden wedding, and in 1897 she was residing with her daughter. Children:

7047   Oscar F. Herren, born in Jefferson, O., Feb. 13, 1844; resides in Rogers Park, Ill.
7048   Mary Josephine Herren, born in Chandon, O., Nov. 25, 1847; married, April 28, 1869, Eugene C. Weeks, a dentist, and resides in Nashua, Ia.

4880   ELMIRA S.[8] TYLER (Asa Ladd[7]), born in Rutland, Vt., or Lawrence, N. Y., July 4, 1823; married, in Saybrook, O., November 25, 1841, Avery D. Jackson, who died in Beloit, Mich., September 14, 1893. He was a carpenter and joiner; she lived in Beloit in 1897. Children:

7049   Harriet E. Jackson, born Sept. 1, 1842; married in Belvidere, Ill., Dec. 15, 1864, David Shirrell, who died in Buffalo, N. Y., Oct. 13, 1882.
7050   Frank A. Jackson, born March 12, 1848.
7051   Fred A. Jackson, twin to Frank.

7052   Helen M. Jackson, born Nov. 2, 1858; married, Aug.
        4, 1880, Louis J. Rogers, of Beloit.

4882   SILAS D.⁸ TYLER (Asa Ladd⁷), born in Lawrence, N. Y., August 1, 1831; married, October 17, 1861,
Franciana Blackman, born in Pembroke, N. Y., March 31,
1842; daughter of Walter Blackman, who went to Illinois in
1854.   In 1852 Silas moved from Ashtabula County, O., to
Monroe Center, Ill.   He was a farmer.   Children:
7053   Charles C. Tyler, born Aug. 31, 1862; married, Oct.
        19, 1893, Elizabeth Clover.
7054   William B. Tyler, born Dec. 22, 1863; married, May
        10, 1893, Laura Walch; a storekeeper in Monroe
        Center, Ill.
7055   Adda Tyler, born Nov. 20, 1867; married, July 28,
        1886, Edwin Raup.
7056   Fred Walter Tyler, born May 6, 1869; married, May
        31, 1894, Grace Crill.
7057   Esther May Tyler, born Oct. 27, 1870.
7058   Fannie Ward Tyler, born Aug. 24, 1881.

4883   HORACE C.⁸ TYLER (Asa Ladd⁷), born in Saybrook, O., May 3, 1838; died April 6, 1879; married in Monroe,
Ill., December 23, 1859, Abbie M. Piper, born in West Liberty,
O., February 26, 1841; daughter of Dr. Philip Piper.   He was
a farmer and then a livery man; he went to Monroe in 1852,
where the children were born.   Children:
7059   Harry B. Tyler, born May 21, 1862; died Oct. 7,
        1864.
7060   Ella Ibera Tyler, born March 13, 1864.
7061   Cora Bella Tyler, born Jan. 17, 1866.
7062   Albert Tyler, born Feb. 12, 1868; a druggist in Evans-
        ton, Ill.; is married and has one daughter.
7063   Rosa Mabel Tyler, born Jan. 12, 1870.
7064   Blanche Zera Tyler, born April 18, 1872.
7065   Horace Frank Tyler, born March 18, 1875.

4884   EDMOND⁸ TYLER (George Washington⁷),
born in St. Lawrence County, N. Y., August 11, 1828; married, August 11, 1852, Betsey Elizabeth Brown, who died

December 21, 1883. He lived in Cupertino, Cal., where the children were born. Children:

7066   Truman Edmond Tyler, born May 31, 1853; died Jan. 28, 1858.

7067+   Celia Jennie Tyler, born Aug. 26, 1860.

7068+   Elizabeth Ida Tyler, born Oct. 4, 1864.

4887   THIRZA⁸ TYLER (George Washington⁷), born in St. Lawrence County, N. Y., January 3, 1833; married Samuel Dodge. Children:

7069   Louisa Dodge, married Robert W. Bassett, of Orlonville, Mich.

7070   William Dodge, lives in Lapeer, Mich.

7071   Arnette Dodge, married William Thomas.

7072   Janette Dodge, married —— Davis.

7073   Marette Dodge, married Lewis Bassett; she died.

4888   EDWIN H.⁸ TYLER (George Washington⁷), born in St. Lawrence County, N. Y., May 27, 1835; married, May 27, 1858, Mary M. Richel, of Pennsylvania. He moved to Ashtabula County, O., with his father in 1839, then to Ogle County, Ill., in 1855, thence to Iowa in 1857, and was residing in 1897 in Nashua, Ia., where his children were born. He went through the Civil War, in Company B of the 14th Ia. Volunteers, and was wounded five times in fifteen engagements. Children:

7074   Joseph Tyler, born June 10, 1866; died June 20, 1866.

7075   Edmond Tyler, born Dec. 25, 1867; married and has a family; resides with his father.

7076   George W. Tyler, born Dec. 20, 1868; married and has a family.

4889   AMELIA ELECTA⁸ TYLER (George Washington⁷), born in St. Lawrence County, N. Y., May 1, 1837; married, March 22, 1852, James H. Johnson. In 1868 he moved to a farm near Lansing, Mich. Two sons unnamed, died young. Children:

7077   John Johnson, died young.

7078   Ophelia Johnson, born April 16, 1853; married, 1873,

John Q. Adams; three daughters (Maud, Dora, and Ella).

7079 Maria Johnson, married, 1872, John Hoyt; three daughters (Lou, Loretta, and Ora).

7080 Emma Johnson, born July 25, 1865; married, July 25, 1888, Charles Elsesser; four sons (Lawrence, Albert, Edward, and Howard).

4891 HELEN LOUISE⁸ TYLER (Truman Murray⁷), born in Illinois City, Ill., March 1, 1847; married John R. Benedict, of Galesburg, Ill. Children:
7081 Arthur Clarence Benedict.
7082 Minnie Edith Benedict.
7083 Connie May Benedict.

4942 LAWRENCE STEWART⁸ TYLER (Damon Young⁷), born in Compton, Que., August 19, 1854; married Hattie Blackman, of Merrimack, Wis. He is a prosperous hardware merchant in Salem, S. Dak. Children:
7084 Nellie Leonora Tyler, born in Magnolia, Minn., Nov. 1, 1878.
7085 Grace Tyler.

4943 LEONORA EMMA⁸ TYLER (Damon Young⁷), born in Newport, Wis., June 26, 1859; married in Merrimack, Wis., September 12, 1878, Eugene Ellis Quiggle, of Rapid City, S. Dak. Children:
7086 Bertha Maria Quiggle, born in Merrimack, Dec. 6, 1879.
7087 Alta Maude Quiggle, born in Doland, S. Dak., July 22, 1888.

4960 GEORGE⁸ TYLER (Charles⁷), born in Millbury, Mass., 1837; died in Worcester, Mass., February 17, 1869; married, January 8, 1860, in Worcester, Martha Murphy. Child:
7088 Lizzie Ella Tyler, born in Worcester Aug. 17, 1862; married, Aug. 6, 1884, in Worcester, William H. Sweeney, born in New York City.

4965 HELEN W.⁸ TYLER (William Winter⁷), born

in Lowell, Mass., September 20, 1836; married, June 11, 1856, Erastus H. Barry, of Derby Line, Vt., who lived in Rumney, N. H., and then in Compton, N. H.   He was in Company G, First N. H. heavy artillery, in the Civil War.   Children:

7089   Emma H. Barry, born July 31, 1857; married, 1872, M. J. D. Hooper, of Rumney, N. H.; had seven children, three survive (Thomas, James, and Flora).

7090   Willard E. Barry, born June 5, 1859; married and lives in York Beach, Me.; two daughters (Minnie and Isabella).

7091   Charles F. Barry, born Feb. 28, 1861; married, s. p.

7092   Florence M. Barry, born Aug. 1, 1862; died Aug. 6, 1868.

7093   Caroline A. Barry, born March 3, 1864; married Frank A. Hopkins, of Cliftondale, Mass.; two sons (Leon and Vivien).

7094   Francis C. Barry, born July 13, 1873; unmarried, lived in Cliftondale in 1896.

4966   THOMAS HENRY[8] TYLER (Ebenezer Ballard[7]), born in Haverhill, Mass., October 20, 1832; married, October 9, 1862, Mrs. Mary E. Tenney, of Boston, Mass.; they live in Brookline, Mass., where the children were born. Children:

7095   William Bartlett Tyler, born Oct. 12, 1863; married, Oct. 7, 1890, Carrie N. Bates.

7096+   Thomas Henry Tyler, Jr., born Dec. 8, 1866.

7097   Hellman Barnes Tyler, born Aug. 7, 1870; died Feb. 23, 1871.

7098   Mary Leonice Tyler, born Sept. 1, 1876; died May 6, 1880.

4974   WILLIAM H.[8] TYLER (Thomas[7]), born in Meriden, Conn., September 18, 1835; married, September 18, 1866, Annie M. Kenworthy, of Meriden. He is in the silverware business with the Meriden Brittania Company. Is a prominent I. O. O. F.   The children were born in Meriden.   Children:

7099   Charles H. Tyler, born March 20, 1869; married, Sept. 10, 1891, Lizzie Jane Hively, of Easton, Pa.; a grocer in Wallingford, Conn.

7100   Frank Yale Tyler, born Jan. 16, 1878; died Sept.
          23, 1885.

    4976 EDWARD⁸ TYLER (Job⁷), born in Haverhill,
Mass., 1830; died in Danvers, Mass., August 7, 1871; married
Susan E. Sheldon, born in Beverly, Mass., 1833; died in
Salem, Mass., February 10, 1868; daughter of Abraham B.
Sheldon. She and her husband are buried in Beverly. The
children were born in Salem. Children:
7101   Lucy M. Tyler, married George Glines, of North
          Beverly.
7102   Fannie Tyler, married Benjamin Vickery, of Arlington,
          Mass.
7103   Charles E. Tyler, born Feb. 4, 1868.

    4980 JOHN OTIS⁸ TYLER (Job⁷), born in Haver-
hill, Mass., November 3, 1837; married Minerva W. Dill, born
in Eastham, Mass.; lives in Salem, Mass. The two elder children were born in Lynn; the others in Salem. Children:
7104   Anna Tyler, born July 2, 1867; married, Dec. 22, 1888,
          Eben A. Upton, a musician, son of Henry O. Upton.
7105   Walter Otis Tyler, born April 15, 1869.
7106+   Minnie Williams Tyler, born Feb. 1, 1880; married,
          Nov. 27, 1895, William H. Smith, born 1869 in
          Waterboro, Me.; son of John S. Smith.
7107   Herbert Chester Tyler, born July 18, 1885.

    4995 HARRY W.⁸ TYLER (David Morey⁷), born
April 16, 1863; married, in 1887, Alice I. Brown. He has
been secretary of the Massachusetts Institute of Technology
for many years. The children were born in Boston. Children:
7108   Margaret Tyler, born Oct. 19, 1890.
7109   Elizabeth Tyler, born Oct. 27, 1892.

    5001 WILLIAM HUNT⁸ TYLER (John Laird⁷), born
in Calais, Me., March 13, 1859; married, 1881, Gertrude Spear-
ing, of Calais, where they live and where he is a commission
merchant. Child:
7110   Georgie Tyler, born in Calais, Nov. 5, 1882.

5014   ALVIN[8] TYLER (Ara[7]), born in Staffordville, Conn., February 5, 1825; married, September 10, 1848, Sophia Needham, born December 16, 1828; daughter of Jasper Needham, of Wales, Mass. He was a farmer and mason. The children were born in Staffordville. Children:

7111+   Henry A. Tyler, born July 27, 1849.
7112+   Abbie Sophia Tyler, born Oct. 26, 1853.

5024   CLARISSA HELEN[8] TYLER (William[7]), born in South Otselic, N. Y., September 12, 1830; married there December 23, 1852, Alfred A. Denton, of South Otselic, where the two elder children were born. In 1900 she was residing in Urban, Mich. Children:

7113   Effie Denton, born Aug. 27, 1854; married, March 19, 1891, Matthew Hubbell, of Emmett, Mich.
7114   Alice Denton, born Sept. 2, 1857; married, Sept. 2, 1877, Daniel Hunt, of Columbus, Mich.
7115   Adelia Elvia Denton, born May 7, 1860.
7116   William Tyler Denton, born May 30, 1862; married, March 16, 1892, Viola Springer; resides in Urban, Mich.
7117   Sarah Almeda Denton, born July 15, 1867; married, Dec. 27, 1892, Charles Graham, of Jeddo, Mich.

5025   MARY ANN[8] TYLER (William[7]), born in South Otselic, N. Y., August 21, 1832; married, January 31, 1855, Hosea M. Brown (No. 5028), a farmer and lumberman of New Salem, Mass. They afterward moved to Orange, Mass., where all the children were born, except the eldest. Children:

7118   Edgar W. Brown, born in New Salem, Mass., Dec. 10, 1856; killed by a horse, Aug. 24, 1870.
7119   Oscar S. Brown, born Feb. 28, 1861; killed by boiler explosion, Dec. 8, 1880.
7120   William M. Brown, born March 24, 1862; killed by boiler explosion, Dec. 8, 1880.
7121   George E. Brown, born Jan. 17, 1864; killed by boiler explosion, Dec. 8, 1880.
7122   Hattie H. Brown, born May 30, 1866; married, July 1, 1883, Raleigh E. Morse, who died s. p. 1896.
7123   Minnie A. Brown, born April 6, 1869; is an invalid.
7124   Elvie M. Brown, born March 12, 1871; died Aug. 3, 1872.

7125   Enos H. Brown, born July 4, 1872; married, Lucy
             M. Neece; resides in North New Salem, Mass.
7126   Eva M. Brown, born Sept. 2, 1873.
7127   Ina A. Brown, born May 10, 1875; is a nurse.

    5026 ALMEDA B.[8] TYLER (William[7]), born in
South Otselic, N. Y., October 14, 1843; died July 10, 1889;
married, September 7, 1870, Silas Crumb, who married (2),
Mrs. Henriette Andrews. He resided on the old homestead
in South Otselic, until about 1887, when he moved to McGrawville, N. Y.; but in 1900 he was residing in Otselic. Children:
7128   Son, born July, 1871; died young.
7129   Inez Crumb, born in 1873; died young.
7130   Lettie Crumb, born in 1878; married, Pearl Whitmore;
             has one son (Leon) and resides in Otselic.
7131   Mattie Crumb, born March 14, 1881.

    5027 ANNETTE M.[8] TYLER (William[7]), born in
South Otselic, N. Y., February 24, 1852; married, September
7, 1870, Edwin A. McGraw, born October 6, 1848; resides in
McGrawville, N. Y., until 1887, when he moved to Cortland,
N. Y., where he carries on a large wagon and repair shop.
Child:
7132   Ivan C. McGraw, born Aug. 14, 1871; works with his
             father.

    5038 ASHEL[8] TYLER (William W.[7]), born in Naples,
N. Y., probably about 1820; married Jane Semans. The children were born in Naples. Children:
7133   Willis Tyler, died while in the High School.
7134+   Edith Helen Tyler, born Jan. 5, 1867.

    5040 HENRY[8] TYLER (William W.[7]), born in Naples,
N. Y.; married, October 17, 1861, Martha Corey. He had
a vineyard in Naples, where his daughter was born. Child:
7135+   Carrie Tyler, born Sept. 15, 1863.

    5042 FRANCES M.[8] TYLER (William W.[7]), born in
Naples, N. Y., October 28, 1847; married, August 10, 1870,
T. V. Granby. The children were born in Naples. Children:

7136   Addie M. Granby, born June 10, 1875; died July 23, 1875.

7137   Harriet M. Granby, born June 24, 1877; married, Dec. 9, 1898, Floyd M. De Freest; one son (Francis G.).

5045 BYRON A.[8] TYLER (Asahel Watkins[7]), born in Naples, N. Y., January 18, 1838; married, September 25, 1860, Juliet Henderson, of Cohocton, N. Y., born February 19, 1842; daughter of Rufus Henderson. He is a farmer and lives in Cohocton; he has held town offices. Children:

7138   Hattie Tyler, born Aug. 8, 1861; married, Aug. 25, 1886, George Jackman, Jr., of Livonia, N. Y.

7139   Maggie C. Tyler, born May 26, 1863; died June 15, 1882, unmarried.

7140   Lida E. Tyler, born Oct. 19, 1864.

7141+ Arthur B. Tyler, born Jan. 10, 1871.

5050 CARNOT M.[8] TYLER (Asahel Watkins[7]), born in Naples, N. Y., January 27, 1854; married, November 20, 1873, Adeline M. Clason. (See *Clason Memorial.*) He is a farmer in Cohocton, N. Y., where the children were born. Children:

7142   Julia E. Tyler, born Jan. 21, 1877.

7143   Willet A. Tyler, born March 13, 1879.

7144   Willis W. Tyler, twin to Willet.

7145   Alice A. Tyler, born July 11, 1885.

7146   Agnes C. Tyler, twin to Alice.

5052 HARVEY W.[8] TYLER (Roswell Root[7]), born in Middlesex, N. Y., March 25, 1844; died there December 14, 1897; married, September 26, 1871, Alice Amanda Dintruff, daughter of John L. Dintruff. He was educated at the State Normal School in Albany, N. Y.; was a teacher, farmer, and justice of the peace for twenty years; also a deacon of the Baptist church. His estate was probated in Penn Yan in 1898. Children:

7147   Carrie B. Tyler.

7148   John D. Tyler.

7149   Frank R. Tyler.

5060 LAURA ELVIRA[8] TYLER (Merrill[7]), born in
Fayston, Vt., October 25, 1823; died in Montpelier, Vt., March
11, 1873; married, in Fayston, August 23, 1846, Dr. Gershom
Nelson[7] Brigham, born in Fayston, March 3, 1820; died in
Chicago, Ill., June 21, 1886; son of Elisha and Sophronia
(Ryder) Brigham (Gershom[5] and Sarah [Allen] Brigham;
Benjamin[4] and Hannah [Merrill] Brigham; Gershom[3] and
Mehitabel [Warren] Brigham; Thomas[2] and Mary [Rice]
Brigham; Thomas[1] and Mercy [Hurd] Brigham. See *History
of the Brigham Family*); Dr. Brigham married (2),
Agnes Ruth Walker, daughter of Ephraim Walker, and they
had a family of four daughters and a son, who died in infancy.
Dr. Brigham was graduated from Woodstock Vermont Medical
College in 1845, and later took a course in the College of
Physicians and Surgeons in New York City. He settled in
Montpelier, Vt., where for a quarter of a century was a large
practitioner. He was converted to the theory of Homeopathy,
and was one of five founders of the Vermont Homeopathic
Medical Society of which he was president. In 1875 he moved
to Grand Rapids, Mich., where he was the leading Homeopathic
physician in the city at the time of his death. He was a charter member of the Michigan Hahnemannian Society, of which
he was president; was a member of the American Institute of
Homeopaths and of the International Hahnemannian Association. He published medical works on consumption and
catarrh. He lectured a great deal and contributed to periodicals. The burials of this family are in the Green Mountain
Cemetery, Montpelier. Laura Elvira Tyler was the eldest
born daughter and the first child of her parents who lived to
maturity. She was fair and bright, with golden hair in abun-
dance, and grew up the pride and favorite of the rural district, the scene of her nativity. Not stout and robust, like
most of the Tylers, but naturally delicate and very sensitive,
the cares of life proved untimely heavy to her. Before she
had reached the half-way stone she was relieved of burdens too
onerous for her. Out of devotion to her memory her youngest
son began the work of preparing this genealogy. He too laid
down burdens too heavy for him ere he had lived to reach the
age which his mother attained; but he devoted the last ounces
of strength given him to preparing this wreath of immortelles
to lay upon her grave.

The two elder children were born in Warren, Vt., the next two in Waitsfield, and the youngest in Montpelier, Vt.

CHILDREN:

7150   Julia E. Brigham, born July 29, 1847; died in childhood.
7151   Julia Lena Brigham, born Nov. 10, 1848; made her home in Lowell, Mass., for a number of years.
7152+   Homer Colby Brigham, born July 10, 1851.
7153   Ida Leonore Brigham, born Nov. 16, 1854; died Aug. 13, 1856.
7154+   Willard Irving Tyler Brigham, born May 31, 1859.

5061 CYREN[8] TYLER (Merrill[7]), born in Fayston, Vt., February 2, 1827; married ——. Went to California in " gold times " from New York via Panama; in 1899 lived in Bisbee, Ariz.; was interested in gold mining and lumber.   Child.
7155   Willard Caspar Tyler, born in San Francisco, April, 1873; died unmarried in Bisbee, Ariz., in 1898; was interested in copper in Arizona.

5062 LUCIUS MERRILL[8] TYLER (Merrill[7]), born in Fayston, Vt., July 27, 1832; married (1), February 4, 1856, Eunice Hannah Johnson, of Waitsfield, Vt., who died March 7, 1869; married (2), January 3, 1871, Addie F. Joslin, of Waterbury, Vt., who died January 4, 1884. He was a commission merchant; moved to East Cambridge, Mass.

CHILD, by second marriage:

7156   Willard Lucius Tyler, born March 20, 1874; in 1899 he was in Wear, Alaska, where he married; had a residence in East Cambridge.

5065 JOSEPHINE MARIA[8] TYLER (Merrill[7]), born in Fayston, Vt., December 3, 1841; married, April 1, 1858, Henry Campbell; born in Waitsfield, Vt., April 4, 1837; he is a farmer and lives in Warren, Vt., where the children were born.   Children:
7157   Lois J. Campbell, born Dec. 22, 1858; married, Oct. 2, 1881, Lester Smith; one son (Casper).

7158   Gerald Campbell, born April 26, 1862; married, April
        10, 1889, Lela Drew; one daughter (Ruth).
7159   Merrill Campbell, born Sept. 22, 1873; married, March
        11, 1897, Grace Lamb.
7160   Mildred Campbell, born July 14, 1878.
7161   Bertram Campbell, born March 21, 1880.
7162   Daisy Campbell, born July 30, 1882.

5066   SARAH ELIZA[8] TYLER (Merrill[7]), born in
Fayston, Vt., October 24, 1843; died December 24, 1896;
married, August 10, 1865, Daniel O. Joslyn, a farmer, born in
Waitsfield, Vt., August 30, 1841, where they resided, and where
the children were all born.   Children:
7163   Clayton Tyler Joslyn, born June 27, 1867; married,
        Sept. 29, 1891, Isabella M. Palmer; one son
        (Ralph P.).
7164   John C. Joslyn, born June 28, 1869; lives in Malden,
        Mass.
7165   Clement D. Joslyn, born July 18, 1871; married, Nov.
        24, 1892, Hattie M. Avery; two sons (Earle and
        Olin).
7166   Walter C. Joslyn, born Nov. 18, 1872; lives in Malden.
7167   Bertha Sarah Joslyn, born Dec. 28, 1874.
7168   Blanche Laura Joslyn, born Aug. 29, 1877.

5071   LYMAN[8] TYLER (Hial[7]), born in Hatley, Can.,
June 9, 1830; died in Ayer's Flat, P. Q., February 25, 1888;
married Betsey Meigs, born in 1834 and still resides in Ayer's
Flat, where the children were born.   He was a painter.   Two
children died in infancy, unnamed.   Children:
7169+   Rachel Tyler, born Jan. 17, 1861.
7170+   John Tyler, born Nov. 4, 1863.

5073   SARAH ANN[8] TYLER (Hial[7]), born in Bangor,
Me., September 14, 1833; married (1), April 12, 1850, William
F. Welch; married (2), January 24, 1871, James S. Drew, of
Sheffield, Vt.   He moved to Sheffield in 1861 and later to Stan-
sted, P. Q., and Hatley; resides in Wheelock, Vt.   The children were born in Hatley except the eldest.   Children:
7171   Lelia J. Welch, born in Sheffield, Vt., May 30, 1853.
7172   Lucius F. Welch, born Oct. 14, 1855.

7173   George Welch, born April 15, 1857.
7174   Asenath Welch, born Jan. 21, 1861.

5075   SOPHRONIA A.[8] TYLER (Hial[7]), born in Bernston, P. Q., March 25, 1840; married, October 17, 1859, Hollis Hackett, of Ayer's Flat, Can.; is an invalid from accident; resides in Ayer's Flat. The children were born there.
Children:
7175   Rosa C. Hackett, born Sept. 24, 1860; married, May 4, 1881, James McCoy, a mason of Ayer's Flat, Can.; four children (Irving, Ralph, Sadie, Daisy).
7176   Lucian Hackett, born April 7, 1863; died Dec. 28, 1876.
7177   Gertie Hackett, born Jan. 11, 1868; died Dec. 3, 1876.
7178   Daisy Hackett, born July 25, 1877; died Oct. 15, 1894.

5076   MARION AUGUSTA[8] TYLER (Roswell[7]), born in Hatley, Can., November 10, 1845; died in Lawrence, Mass., March 30, 1893; married (1), 1863, Marcus Magoon, who was killed by a premature blast in a lime quarry in Fitch Bay, P. Q., September 6, 1867; married (2), 1869, Sylvester Lee, who died in Coaticook, P. Q., April, 1893.

CHILDREN, by first marriage:
7179   Arthur Wallace Magoon, born Oct. 4, 1864.
7180   Dora Malvina Magoon, born Feb. 1, 1866.
7181   Marcus Colostine Magoon, born April 7, 1868.

CHILDREN, by second marriage:
7182   Lottie Lee.
7183   Willie Lee, died in infancy.
7184   Elsie Lee.

5077   ERNEST ALBERT[8] TYLER (Roswell[7]), born in Hatley, Can., October 21, 1847; married, December 9, 1873, Jane Bennett. He is a carriage-maker and lives in Hatley, where the children were born. Children:
7185   Carrie Jane Tyler, born Nov. 7, 1874.
7186   Edna Eunice Tyler, born Sept. 12, 1876.

7187   Grover Kenneth Tyler, born April 11, 1881.
7188   Mabel Tyler, born April 22, 1884; died Sept. 1, 1886.

5078   ADELAIDE[8] TYLER (Roswell[7]), born in Hatley, Can., December 20, 1848; married, February 19, 1866,
Stephen Fearon; lives in Whitefield, N. H.   Children:
7189   Marie Adelaide Fearon, born Nov. 10, 1866.
7190   Alfred Edson Fearon, born Aug. 21, 1868.
7191   Enos Edwin Fearon, born Sept. 5, 1870.
7192   Frank Wesley Fearon, born Aug. 6, 1872
7193   Bertie Eugene Fearon, born Dec. 28, 1874.
7194   Lena May Fearon, born April 12, 1877.
7195   Maud Mary Fearon, born Nov. 26, 1879.
7196   Stephen Ernest Fearon, born Aug. 6, 1882.
7197   Percy Fearon, born Oct. 3, 1887.

5079   CAROLINE ELLEN[8] TYLER (Roswell[7]), born
in Hatley, Can., February 3, 1851; died in Compton, P. Q.,
November 14, 1874; married, October 1, 1870, Charles
Demerse, of Compton, P. Q., where the children were born.
Children:
7198   Minnie Alberta Demerse, born Sept. 13, 1871.
7199   Son, died Oct. 8, 1874, in infancy.

5090   WILLIAM O.[8] TYLER (Lyman[7]), born in
Sharon, Vt., March, 1825; died in Rutland, Vt., 1888; married, July 15, 1851, Mary A. Kibling, of Strafford.   Children:
7200   Willie K. Tyler, born 1854; lives in Boston, Mass.
7201   Eddie B. Tyler, lives in Boston.

5100   MARY JANE[8] TYLER (Lucius[7]), born in Strafford, Vt., March 12, 1838; died April 10, 1893; married George
E. Fay, of Sharon, Vt., who died November 26, 1906; a farmer.
The children were born in Sharon.   Children:
7202   Fred Tyler Fay, born July 27, 1863; lives in Lowell,
        Mass.
7203   Minnie Fay, born July 26, 1867; married Albert Chil-
        son; one daughter.
7204   Elwin Fay, born July 9, 1871; died.
7205   Ellen Fay, born May 21, 1877; married —— How-
        land.

5102   LUCIA A.⁸ TYLER (Lucius⁷), born in Strafford, Vt., May 19, 1848; married, January 1, 1868, Rev. Charles Parkhurst, born in 1843; son of Chester and Sarah A. (Barnard) Parkhurst, of Sharon, Vt.   He fitted for college in Meriden, N. H., where Mrs. Parkhurst also was graduated in 1867; he was graduated from Dartmouth College in the Class of 1878. He entered the ministry of the Methodist Episcopal church and served in Hyde Park, Montpelier, and Bradford, Vt., Concord and Dover, N. H., Lawrence and Auburndale, Mass.   In 1889 he was called to the editorship of *Zion's Herald*, published in Boston, the oldest Methodist paper in the world and is one of the most able editors of his church.

CHILDREN:

7206   Charles Erwin Parkhurst, born in Sharon, Vt., Sept. 4, 1871; married, in 1901, Helen A. Chandler, a graduate of Bradford Academy; he was graduated from Boston University in 1894; Harvard Dental School in 1897: a dentist in Somerville, Mass.; two children (Chandler C. and Helen Louise).

7207   Louisa F. Parkhurst, born in Burlington, Vt., Nov. 7, 1874; a teacher of the piano in Lasell Seminary, Auburndale, Mass.

5119   MARIA AMY⁸ TYLER (Osborn Hull⁷), born in Boston, Mass., February 13, 1837; married (1), February 12, 1854, Daniel E. Eaton, of Boston; married (2), June, 1886, James J. Flower, of New York City; married (3), 1892, Chester Parker, of Topeka, Kas.   Her children were born in Boston.

CHILDREN, by first marriage:

7208   Louis Albert Eaton, born July 1, 1855; died Aug. 12, 1857.

7209   Amy Aphia W. Eaton, born Aug. 26, 1858; married Merrill Ray Hinckley, of Boston.

7210   Daniel Osborn Eaton, born Dec. 9, 1861.

7211   Charles Edmund Bartlett Eaton, born Oct., 1863.

5124   LEVERETT WINSLOW⁸ TYLER (Josiah Goodrich⁷), born in New Rowley, Mass., now Georgetown, September 20, 1820; married (1), Maria L. Partridge, of Orland,

Me., who died in 1848; married (2), Lydia Ann Hills, of West Newbury, Mass., who died in Boston, Mass., January 16, 1889. He lives in Bradford, Mass.

CHILD, by first marriage:

7212   Frank W. Tyler, born June 24, 1845; died Sept. 9, 1845.

CHILDREN, by second marriage:

7213   Frank Hills Tyler, born Oct. 3, 1852; died unmarried in Buffalo, N. Y., Oct., 1889.

7214+   Willard Curtis Tyler, born May 2, 1856.

5141 ELLEN W.[8] TYLER (Abraham[7]), born (perhaps in Montgomery, Ala.) May 3, 1829; died August 2, 1894; married, in Montgomery, George Cowles; his family were from Meriden, Conn. A noted Unionist and prominent business man of the South, he sacrificed all his property and, unrequited by the Government, he died in Philadelphia, October, 1883, aged seventy-one; was buried in Meriden. Children:

7215   Laura Cowles, died early.

7216   George W. Cowles, married Lily Blaess; he died; one son (William A., of Philadelphia).

7217   William A. Cowles, assistant examiner in the U. S. Pension Office, Washington, D. C.

7218   Kate M. Cowles, died.

7219   John T. Cowles, married Celia Harrington; lives in Wautogh, L. I.; two daughters (Laura and Edna).

7220   Samuel Cowles, died.

7221   Carrie E. Cowles, lives in New York City.

7222   Nellie E. Cowles, lives in Washington, D. C.

5147 CHAPLIN GREENLEAF[8] TYLER (Caleb Greenleaf[7]), born in Montgomery, Ala., August 10, 1834; married (1), December 25, 1856, Annie E. Bagley, of Georgetown, Mass.; married (2), Ursula Berry. He lived in Georgetown. The two elder children were born in Charlestown, Mass.

CHILDREN, by first marriage:

7223+   Martha Eliza Tyler, born Dec. 30, 1863.

7224   Georgia Rooxbe Tyler, born Jan. 8, 1867; married,

Sept. 16, 1893, Robert P. Butterick, of Salem, Mass., from Toronto.

7225   Harriet Augusta Tyler, born in East Somerville, Mass., Sept. 22, 1871; married, Oct. 2, 1900, Edward Arthur Allen, of Lynn, Mass.

7226   Annie Chaplin Tyler, born in Greenwood, Mass., Dec. 23, 1874.

CHILDREN, by second marriage:

7227   Caleb Berry Tyler, born in Georgetown, April 26, 1880.

7228   Marion Norris Tyler, born in Georgetown, Nov. 25, 1881.

7229   William Greenleaf Tyler, born in West Medford, Mass., July 31, 1883.

5148   CHARLES EDWIN⁸ TYLER (Caleb Greenleaf⁷), born in Boston, Mass., July 7, 1839; married, November 8, 1862, Caroline Harriman, of Georgetown.   He was private in Company K, 50th Mass. Volunteers in the Civil War.   Children:

7230   William Greenleaf Tyler, born Feb. 15, 1865; died Sept. 8, 1868.

7231   Fred Tyler, born Aug. 28, 1867; died Sept. 10, 1868.

5149   GEORGE PRESCOTT⁸ TYLER (Caleb Greenleaf⁷), born in Georgetown, Mass., August 1, 1843; married, October 7, 1868, Irene Spofford, daughter of Harrison Spofford, of Georgetown, where they live.   He is an accountant and a musician; at one time was a member of the military band at West Point; well known as a clarinet player in Essex County, Mass.   Children:

7232+   Irene Chaplin Tyler, born June 26, 1870.

7233   Ellen Spofford Tyler, born Aug. 17, 1873; a graduate of Bradford Academy.

7234   Mary Killam Tyler, born June 2, 1875; an artist.

7235   George Greenleaf Tyler, born June 28, 1876; was in the College of Pharmacy in Boston in 1896.

7236   Caroline Rooxbe Tyler, born April 2, 1880; attended Bradford Academy.

5157 WILLIAM THADDEUS⁸ TYLER (William G.⁷), born in Tylertown, Miss., November 23, 1838; married, December 14, 1869, Mary Elizabeth Quin, daughter of Judge James B. Quin, of Summit, Miss. He entered the Civil War in 1861, in the Confederate Army, Company E, 16th Miss. Volunteer Infantry; mustered out in 1865 at Appomatox Court House, Va.; for a part of the time was on a brigadier-general's staff. In 1868 he settled in Summit, Miss., in mercantile business. September, 1887, moved to Chattanooga, Tenn., where engaged in the manufacture of specialties, and in October, 1898, he moved to St. Louis, to establish a branch of his business, stock and poultry remedies. His children were born in Summit.

CHILDREN:

7237   Mabel Tyler, born Nov. 25, 1870; died Sept. 18, 1872.
7238   James William Tyler, born March 10, 1873; was graduated from the University of Tennessee; with his father in business.
7239   Mary Tyler, born July 2, 1876; died July 24, 1878.
7240   Ethel Margaret Tyler, born July 20, 1879; was graduated in Columbia, Mo., in 1899.
7241   Walter Thaddeus Tyler, born Feb. 11, 1882; died Aug. 18, 1884.

5158 MARY ELIZABETH⁸ TYLER (William G.⁷), born in Tylertown, Miss., July 19, 1840; married, August 30, 1855, D. Newton Ball, who died there December 20, 1897; in that year she was still living in Tylertown, where the children were born. Children:

7242   Mary Eliza Ball, died young.
7243   William Thaddeus Ball, died young.
7244   (Dr.) Jesse Newton Ball, born 1865; married, Jan. 6, 1897, Louise Broomfield, lives in Alexandria, La.; one son (Claudius E.).
7245   Sophia Ball, twin to Jesse; married, Dec. 26, 1889, Rev. W. M. Stevens, of Harriston, Miss.; three children (Willie, Edith, and Clinton).
7246   James Jourdan Ball, born 1867.
7247   Needham Eugene Ball, twin to James; married, Dec. 2, 1897, Effie McDonald; he is sheriff of Pike County, Magnolia, Miss.

7248   Jefferson Davis Ball, born 1869; died 1890.
7249   Fannie Lorena Ball, born 1870; married, Dec. 22,
          1895, Rev. E. L. Alford, of Bonita, La.; one son
          (Alton).
7250   Benjamin Augustus Ball, died in infancy.
7251   Effie Oteria Ball, born 1875.
7252   Emma Louise Ball, twin to Effie, died in infancy.
7253   Walter Howard Ball, died in infancy.
7254   Alma Elizabeth Ball, born 1879.
7255   Minnie Simmons Ball, born 1880.
7256   Robert Tyler Ball, born 1881.

5159 SOPHRONIA MATILDA[8] TYLER (William
G.[7]), born in Tylertown, Miss., September 11, 1846; died
April 24, 1885; married, November 19, 1863, M. R. Conerly,
born in Tylertown, May 30, 1839; died there February 24,
1890; the children were all born there.   Children:
7257   William J. Conerly, born April 17, 1866; married,
          March 16, 1890, Ollie O. Simmons; they live in
          Gloster, Miss., and have three children (Hilda, Earl,
          and William).
7257a Sarah E. Conerly, born Aug. 6, 1867; lives in Wes-
          son, Miss.
7258   Mary F. Conerly, born Feb. 23, 1870; married, April
          25, 1892, Professor J. L. Spence; they live in Monti-
          cello, Ark., and have two children (Lee and Marie).
7259   Thaddeus O. Conerly, born Feb. 4, 1872; a railway
          man in Alexandria, La., in 1898.
7260   Lula C. Conerly, born Feb. 9, 1874; a schoolteacher
          in Monticello, Ark., in 1898.
7261   Myra L. Conerly, born March 9, 1876; married, Aug.
          18, 1897, Allen McLain, a farmer of Gloster, Miss.
7262   Emma Mabel Conerly, born July 15, 1878.
7263   Howard T. Conerly, born Nov. 28, 1880.
7264   Ollie L. Conerly, born March 29, 1884.

5161 FRANCES ANN[8] TYLER (William G.[7]), born
in Tylertown, Miss., November 8, 1852; married, March 6,
1879, Hon. Frank A. McLain, a lawyer of Liberty and Gloster, Miss. He was in the Mississippi Legislature for two
years, 1882-1884; district-attorney for twelve years; member

of the Constitutional Convention; member of Congress in the
55th and 56th terms. The two elder children were born in
Liberty. Children:
7265   Mary L. McLain, born Dec. 14, 1879.
7266   E. B. McLain, born May 4, 1881.
7267   William Tyler McLain, born in Gloster, June 4, 1885.

.5162   HENRY⁸ TYLER (Henry⁷), married Elvira
——. Supposed to have lived in Woburn, Mass. Children:
7268   Edward Tyler, born in Boston, Mass.; died in 1853,
        an infant; buried in North Andover. (This child
        may have been the son of Henry⁷ Tyler. Mr.
        Brigham's notes are confused at this point.—Ed.)
7269   Waldo Tyler.
7270   Elmer Tyler.

5166   LOUISE MARIE⁸ TYLER (Jeremiah⁷), born in
Bradford, Mass., March 10, 1841; married, May 15, 1859,
Lorenzo D. Reed. The children were born in Bradford. Children:
7271   Walter Scott Reed, born March 9, 1860; died Aug.
        29, 1864.
7272   Edward Everett Reed, born July 30, 1862.
7273   May Louise Reed, born Aug. 18, 1863; died Sept.
        6, 1863.
7274   Arthur Leslie Reed, born April 4, 1865; died Aug.
        10, 1865.
7275   Emma Lawrence Reed, born April 6, 1867.
7276   Herbert Sewell Reed, born Nov. 10, 1869; died Aug.
        4, 1870.

5214   NELSON⁸ TYLER (Ira Stickney⁷), born in
Georgetown, Mass., February 17, 1851; married, August 14,
1873, Lillian A. Niles. He moved away from Georgetown
and residence is unknown. Child:
7277   Eva Bertha Tyler, born Feb. 19, 1874; married Walter Tayler, of Bridgton, Me.

5216   WILLIAM BALDWIN⁸ TYLER (Moses Coburn⁷), born in Andover, Mass., August 13, 1832; married

Elizabeth Smith, of Salem, Mass. He lived in Chelsea, Mass., and also in Salem. Children:

7278   Frank Berry Tyler, born Sept. 26, 1859; married June 20, 1894, Minnie Tyler, No. 7401; no children.

7279+   Hattie Osgood Tyler, born in Salem, March 2, 1862.

7280+   Herbert Tyler, born in Chelsea, Jan. 16, 1867.

7281   Parker Tyler, born Sept. 30, 1869; unmarried.

5217   LYDIA MARSHALL[8] TYLER (Moses Coburn[7]), born in Andover, Mass., June 30, 1834; died in Salem, Mass., after a long illness, December 20, 1902; married (1), July 29, 1862, Jerome Carter, born in Harvard, Mass., July 29, 1833; died April 18, 1866; married (2), October 17, 1882, Major Loren Sumner Tyler, No. 5225. She was a very charitable woman, giving freely to churches and organizations.

CHILDREN, by first marriage:

7282   Fannie Carter, born May 22, 1864; died Sept. 20, 1866.

7283   Romie Carter, born Oct 4., 1865; died Nov. 9, 1866.

5221   WILLIAM NICHOLS[8] TYLER (John Abbott[7]), born in Andover, Mass., December 7, 1834; married, November 17, 1859, Mary Ellen Skinner, of Wakefield, Mass., daughter of Thomas B. and Phebe (Smith) Skinner. Mr. Tyler has been clerk of the first district court of eastern Middlesex County. He went to the front with the "Richardson Light Guard" in the Civil War, which became Company B of the 5th Mass. Regiment, and was in the first Battle of Bull Run. The company re-enlisted twice again, finally becoming Company E of the 8th Mass. Regiment and was present at the siege of Fort Hudson. Mr. Tyler was sergeant and later sergeant-major. He was paymaster in the militia, 1876–1879, of the 8th Regiment with the rank of first lieutenant; elected major of the 8th Regiment, and resigned in 1884. He was secretary of the school board of South Reading for a long time; in 1890, elected selectman there where he has lived for many years. When the order of the Grand Army of the Republic was established, Mr. Tyler, as provisional district commander organized several posts and has been commander of posts 4 and 12.

He contributed to local and contemporary publication and is a member of various social, political, and beneficiary organizations. He attended every Tyler reunion, including the sixth, being one of four to have done this.

CHILDREN:

7284 Ellie Mabel Tyler, born Aug. 18, 1862; was clerk of the state board of lunacy and charity.

7285 Wilfred Brooks Tyler, born Aug. 15, 1869; married L. Mabelle Wyman, of Wakefield, Mass.; was assistant clerk of the first district court of eastern Middlesex County.

7286 Frederick William Tyler, born, July 15, 1871; died Aug. 24, 1872.

5222 GEORGE LESLIE[8] TYLER (John Abbott[7]), born in Andover, Mass., November 6, 1835; married, August 25, 1862, Lucy G. Fairbanks, of Wakefield, Mass., born July 18, 1843; died August 10, 1901. Children:

7287 Charles Mullett Tyler, born June 22, 1866.

7288 Ernest Albert Tyler, born Aug. 1, 1871; married, Sept. 9, 1896, Minnie F. Dean, of Brockton, Mass.

7289 Percy Gould Tyler, born Sept. 11, 1874.

7290 John Wellman Tyler, born Feb. 19, 1878; died Sept. 12, 1878.

7291 Lucius Abbott Tyler, born Sept. 6, 1879; was in the Spanish War, in Company A, 6th Mass. Regiment.

7292 George W. Frank Tyler, born Oct. 1, 1882; died March 19, 1883.

5223 MARIAN LUSCOMB[8] TYLER (John Abbott[7]), born in Salem, Mass., March 8, 1838; married, in South Reading Mass., November 30, 1856, Henry Frank Bowers, of Groton, Mass. Children:

7293 John Abbott Bowers, born Feb. 5, 1858; died April 9, 1858.

7294 Ethel Lillian Bowers, born Nov. 14, 1859; died June 12, 1881.

7295 Grace Elizabeth Bowers, born April 9, 1862; died April 16, 1873.

7296   Francis Forestus Bowers, born March 17, 1866; died
         April 26, 1866.
7297   Alice Augusta Bowers, born Sept. 21, 1867; married
         in Waltham, Mass., March 20, 1889, Webster Fisk
         Harrington; two children (Ruth and Paul).
7298   Arthur Wilbur Bowers, born Oct. 10, 1870; married
         in Waltham, March 30, 1892, Kate A. Washburn;
         two daughters (Grace and Marian).
7299   Parker Tyler Bowers, born June 12, 1873; died March
         29, 1889.
7300   Ellen Marian Bowers, born Nov. 2, 1875.
7301   Emily Metcalf Bowers, born Sept. 25, 1878.
7302   Harriet Ruth Bowers, born Nov. 6, 1880; died April
         25, 1889.

    5224 ABIGAIL SUMNER[8] TYLER (Alexander Sum-
ner[7]), born in Buffalo, N. Y., May 22, 1842; married, November 29, 1860, John Milton Bisbee, of Worthington, Mass.,
born September 14, 1833; son of Captain James and Dalouise
(Parish) Bisbee. They live in Keokuk, Ia., where he is a
wholesale grocer, alderman, director of two loan and savings
associations, a member of the Legion of Honor and a Knight
of Pythias. Mrs. Bisbee was graduated from the Bigelow
school in South Boston, Mass., in 1856, where she won the
silver Franklin medal; she has been prominent in Congregational church work and in literary clubs. The children were
born in Keokuk.

CHILDREN:

7303   Frances Harriet Bisbee, born Oct. 9, 1862; died July
         8, 1864.
7304   Sumner Tyler Bisbee, born Oct. 4, 1867.
7305   Nellie Fulton Bisbee, born May 20, 1869.
7306   Lora Louise Bisbee, born Dec. 4, 1873; died Aug. 28,
         1875.
7307   Grace Dalouise Bisbee, born March 20, 1876.
7308   Warren Bisbee, born Sept. 27, 1878.
7309   Henry Parish Bisbee, born Jan. 21, 1881.

    5225 MAJOR LOREN SUMNER[8] TYLER (Alexan-
der Sumner[7]), born in Boston, Mass., April 21, 1845; married (1), in Albany, N. Y., October 17, 1882, Mrs. Lydia

Marshall (Tyler) Carter, of Salem, Mass., No. 5217; died in
Salem, December 20 1902; buried in Greenlawn Cemetery; she
was a most lovable woman and a devoted friend to all who
were in distress; married (2), in Minneapolis, Minn., December 27, 1905, Georgia Wilkins Dutton, born in Littleton,
N. H. When the war broke out, Major Tyler, although under
age, enlisted as a drummer in Company H, 15th Ia. Infantry,
December 21, 1861, his home being Keokuk, and was discharged
December 31, 1863, in Vicksburg, Miss., re-enlisting as a veteran in the same company; was mustered out July 24, 1865,
and discharged August 4, 1865. His regiment (with others)
was formed into Crocker's Iowa brigade, and was the only
brigade organization which held its regiments together all
through the war. Major Tyler was in all the battles, etc.,
in which it was engaged, from Shiloh, Tenn., in 1862, to Ben-
tonville, N. C. Was with the Army of the Tennessee and under
fire eighty-one days out of the eighty-nine of the Atlanta
campaign in 1865. He was on the march to Atlanta and the
sea and on duty in the adjutant's office as headquarter's clerk.
In 1866, he went to Kansas City, Mo., and there engaged in
chair manufacturing. In 1870 he returned to Keokuk and
entered into partnership with his father, in the furniture trade.
From 1875 to 1884 he was the junior member of the firm of
Brown & Tyler, auction and commission merchants. He was
commissioned a major in the militia in 1878 and has held several
high positions. In 1885, on Major Tyler's motion, the 15th
Iowa Veteran Infantry Association was organized. Major
Tyler, one of the three historians of the regiment, compiled
the regimental history at the request of his confrères, and was
highly complimented by General W. W. Belknap. In 1887
Major Tyler made his home in Salem, Mass. He collected
portraits of the 92 officers who served in his regiment during
the war, and completed a collection of portraits of all Iowans
who attained the rank of lieutenant-colonel, colonel and general
—about three hundred in all. It is the most complete collection in existence. In July, 1903, he again returned to Keokuk,
which has since been his home. He has been a well-known
attendant at all the National encampments of the G. A. R.
The winter of 1905-1906 he spent in California with Mrs.
Tyler; they were at the Hotel Netherlands in San Francisco,
April 18, 1906, and were suddenly awakened at 5.14 A. M.

by the great earthquake. Hurrying out to the streets, they went that morning into three cafés and before being able to get even a cup of coffee were ordered out of them, as several large fires were close at hand. At noon an artilleryman with drawn revolver rode up to the Netherlands and ordered every one to move out, as the block was soon to be blown up. With other guests, Major and Mrs. Tyler walked several miles, and for two nights slept out on the vacant sand lots, with occasional cinders and embers falling all over and around them; the air was full of heat, smoke and fine ashes from the miles of burning buildings all over the city. On the 20th, they found the Netherlands a mass of ruins. That night Major Tyler succeeded in getting across the bay to Oakland. Soon after they left for their home in Keokuk. Major Tyler greatly assisted Mr. Brigham in his prepartion for the Tyler genealogy, at the cost of time and money, which he cheerfully gave, and as he himself says, " I took a lot of pride in helping him." He has no children.

5227   JOHN HOLLIS[8] TYLER (Leonard[7]), born in Lowell, Mass., April 30, 1843; married, in Wenham, Mass., September 12, 1865, Mary C. Peabody; born August 13, 1847; died May 21, 1889, in Wakefield, Mass. The second and third children were born in Melrose; the two younger in Wakefield. Children:
7310   Annie R. Tyler, born in Wenham, Mass., Aug. 13, 1866; died young.
7311   Cora M. Tyler, born April 2, 1868; married, Dec. 10, 1889, Amos Sanborn, of Stoneham, Mass; one son (Walter).
7312   Annie R. Tyler, born July 11, 1877.
7313   Lillian M. Tyler, born Nov. 4, 1879; married Henry Tillson; two sons (Harry E. and Harold C.).
7314   Jerome Carter Tyler, born May 15, 1880.

5229   ABBY MARGARET[8] TYLER (Leonard[7]), born in Salem, Mass., September 27, 1849; married in Charles City, Ia., October 12, 1867, Jay S. De Wolf. The four elder children were born in Rockford, Ia., the others in Madison, S. Dak. Children:
7315   Mary Inez De Wolf, born May 7, 1869; married in

Madison, S. Dak., Oct. 12, 1886, Cornelius A. Saxby, born in Bordeauville, Vt., Feb. 1, 1863; three children (Opal S., Hazel A., and Dean E.).

7316   James Clinton De Wolf, born April 7, 1872.

7317   Emma Hattie De Wolf, born May 28, 1877.

7318   Allan Jay De Wolf, born Oct. 29, 1878.

7319   Edith Gertrude De Wolf, born April 23, 1881; died Nov. 8, 1892.

7320   Sylvania Arabella De Wolf, born Jan. 20, 1884.

7321   Florence May De Wolf, born Dec. 25, 1885.

7322   John R. De Wolf, born Nov. 4, 1888; died Dec. 17, 1888.

7323   Nina Bernice De Wolf, born Feb. 15, 1891.

5232   ELLEN A.[8] TYLER (Leonard[7]), born in Janesville, Wis., November 14, 1858; married (1), John E. Curtis, born in Chicago, Ill.; married (2), June 6, 1898, Franklin Vosburg, of Lisbon, N. Dak. The four elder children were born in Janesville; the four younger in Lisbon.

CHILDREN, by first marriage:

7324   Thomas A. Curtis, born March 2, 1876.

7325   George W. Curtis, born Oct. 14, 1877; died Feb. 24, 1891.

7326   Richard A. Curtis, born Feb. 7, 1879; died Jan. 15, 1893.

7327   Lillian M. Curtis, born Nov. 21, 1880.

7328   Franklin W. Curtis, born May 19, 1884.

7329   Charles L. Curtis, born Jan. 4, 1886.

7330   Louis J. Curtis, born Oct. 12, 1887.

7331   Warren P. Curtis, born Sept. 12, 1889; died Dec. 10, 1889.

5234   HARRIET E. JOHNSON[8] TYLER (Leonard[7]), born in Janesville, Wis., September 3, 1861; married (1), October 7, 1877, in Janesville, Robert Marvin Money, born in Janesville, October 9, 1859; killed in a railroad accident in Harvard, Ill., May 15, 1880 (or 1881); married (2), June 17, 1882, Prince Albert Anderson, born in Forestville, Wis., July 4, 1854; died in Janesville, September 5, 1883; married (3), February 12, 1886, Ernest Guernsey Saunders, born in

Stephens' Point, Wis., August 10, 1860. In 1899 she resided in Oak Park, Ill.

CHILD, by first marriage:

7332 Ida May J. Money, born in Janesville, Jan. 9, 1879.

CHILD, by second marriage:

7333 Irene Maud Anderson, born in Janesville, Oct. 13, 1883; died there April 5, 1885.

CHILD, by third marriage:

7334 Lawrence Tyler Bancroft Saunders, born in Madison, Wis., Jan. 2, 1887.

5235 GEORGE W.[8] TYLER (Leonard[7]), born in Janesville, Wis., January 7, 1863; married, September 17, 1885, Ida Phal, born in Horicon, Wis. The children were born in Janesville. Children:

7335 William Leonard Tyler, born July 8, 1886.
7336 Charles Leroy Tyler, born Aug. 2, 1887.
7337 Nettie Genevieve Tyler, born Feb. 18, 1890.
7338 Mabel Henrietta Tyler, born Nov. 24, 1892.

5236 LUCY A.[8] TYLER (Leonard[7]), born in Janesville, Wis., April 5, 1864; married, October 17, 1888, Arthur Haynes. Children:

7339 Mabel Haynes, born Sept. 17, 1889.
7340 Ellen Haynes, born Oct. 8, 1891.
7341 George Haynes, born Oct. 12, 1893.

5251 GEORGE ALBERT[8] TYLER (Charles Kimball[7]), born in Boston, Mass., September 7, 1862; married Mary Martin, of Boston, born there May 26, 1871; daughter of Thomas Martin. The children were born in Boston. Children:

7342 George A. Tyler, born Oct. 4, 1890.
7343 Cyril Tyler, born Sept. 4, 1894; died Dec., 1898.
7344 Abbie E. Tyler, born May 10, 1896.
7345 Harold Tyler, born Jan. 26, 1899.
7346 Walter Tyler, born March 25, 1901.

5255 SARAH[8] TYLER (Moody[7]), born in Leominster,

Mass., January 6, 1822; died in Worcester, Mass., April 4, 1890; married, October, 1843, Albert G. Williams, of Worcester. Children:

7347   Nathan Waldo Williams, died about 1881 in Chicago, aged thirty-one.

7348   Hattie Williams, died in Worcester, aged twenty-three.

7349   Fannie Williams, a schoolteacher in Massachusetts.

7350   Daughter, died aged thirteen months.

5256 MARCUS⁸ TYLER (Moody⁷), born in Union, Me., June 20, 1823; died June 22, 1899; married, December 30, 1848, Esther O. Sawyer, born in Bradford, N. H., November 19, 1824. The second and third children were born in Hampden, Me. Children:

7351   Charlotte F. Tyler, born in Pepperell, Mass., Nov. 16, 1849.

7352+   Marcus K. Tyler, born Dec. 5, 1851.

7353+   Esther E. Tyler, born Oct. 3, 1853.

7354+   Charles A. Tyler, born in Lawrence, Mass., Dec. 14, 1855.

5257 LUCY⁸ TYLER (Moody⁷), born in Union, Me., January 11, 1824; died in Dalton, Mass., April 10, 1890; married, March 26, 1854, Daniel L. Farnum, a farmer living in Lawrence, Mass. Child:

7355   Daisie L. Farnum, born Sept. 13, 1856; married Walter H. Coffin; lived in Aborn, Minn.; seven children.

5258 ALMIRA⁸ TYLER (Moody⁷), born in Gardiner, Me., April 18, 1827; married James D. Ward, born in Pittsfield, Mass., February, 1820; died December 4, 1892. They resided in Dalton, Mass., and moved to Chatfield, Minn., in 1858. Children:

7356   James Brattle Ward, born Jan. 1, 1849; died in Lower California, Dec. 16, 1883; unmarried.

7357   Frank Moody Ward, born Aug. 27, 1854; died Oct. 16, 1881; unmarried.

5261 HENRY KENDALL⁸ TYLER (Moody⁷), born

in Leominster, Mass., April 27, 1832; he married twice, in 1850 and in 1861, but the names of his wives are unknown. He moved south in 1860 and was given the work of making bank-note and cartridge paper, as an expert, for the C. S. A. in a paper mill at Bath, S. C. He was licensed to preach as a Baptist minister in 1884; was ordained in 1890. He resided early in Hampden, Me., and Lawrence, Mass., and in 1901 was in Bath, S. C., where his three youngest children were born.

CHILDREN, by first marriage:

7358   H. M. Tyler, born in Hampden, 1852.

7359   E. M. Tyler, born in Lawrence, 1855.

CHILDREN, by second marriage:

7360   H. W. Tyler, born Dec. 24, 1873.

7361   Fred D. Tyler, born June 21, 1880.

7362   Caritta Tyler, born June 18, 1884.

5262   DANIEL WEBSTER⁸ TYLER (Moody⁷), born in Leominster, Mass., May 5, 1834; died May 23 (or 28), 1878; married, May 17, 1859, Emily Brown, of East Hartford, Conn., born May 28, 1835. He was in the Civil War, enlisting as a private June 21, 1861, in Company D, 10th Mass. Volunteers; was in the battles of Fair Oaks and the Seven Days' Fight; was discharged because of ill health August 13, 1862. He was an invalid for ten years. He died intestate, his widow being appointed administratrix and guardian of the minor children. The children were born in Dalton, Mass. Children:

7363   Alice L. Tyler, born March 1, 1860; died Dec. 25, 1864.

7364   Grace Matilda Tyler, born Jan. 3, 1866; married O. L. Flansburgh.

7365   Jennie D. Tyler, born Nov. 2, 1868; married —— Pierce.

5263   D. WALDO⁸ TYLER (Moody⁷), born in Leominster, Mass., June 22, 1836; married, July 26, 1861, in Saratoga Springs, Minn., Harriet M. Freeman. He is proprietor of the Aurora Flour Mills, and in 1897 lived in Junction City, Kas. The eldest and third child were born in Chatfield, Minn. Children:

7366+ Herbert Ferre Tyler, born Feb. 11, 1865.

7367+ Frederick Waldo Tyler, born in Winona, Minn., Sept. 6, 1866.

7368 Frank E. Tyler, born March 29, 1869; is with his father in the flour manufacturing business.

7369 Wilmina Jessie May Tyler, born in Dubuque, Ia., Sept. 23, 1877.

5264 JANE L.[8] TYLER (Moody[7]), born in Leominster, Mass., August 12, 1838; died in Boise, Idaho, May 3, 1898; married, in Dalton, Mass., February 20, 1867, John W. Maynard, born May 6, 1831. The children were born in Boise. Children:

7370 Hugh Temple Maynard, born April 29, 1869.

7371 Mark Tyler Maynard, born April 10, 1871.

7372 Ruth Maynard, born Dec. 31, 1873.

7373 Kate Maynard, born Feb. 1, 1883.

5269 HARRIET STONE[8] TYLER (Joseph[7]), born in Greenfield, Mass., November 23, 1826; married, April 11, 1848, Charles H. Lusk, of Albany, N. Y., where the children were born. Children:

7374 Carrie Eugenie Lusk, born March 20, 1849; died March 21, 1858.

7375 Charles James Tyler Lusk, born April 8, 1851.

7376 Hattie Theodora Lusk, born Feb. 17, 1863; died April 5, 1866.

5271 GEORGE BURT[8] TYLER (Joseph[7]), born in Greenfield, Mass., April 14, 1830; died in Helena, Mont., October 6, 1881, where he was superintendent of a foundry; married, August 24, 1860, Sarah E. Harrell, born August 26, 1844; she lives in Helena. The children were born in New Boston, Ill. Children:

7377+ Matie Tyler, born May 4, 1863.

7378 Grace Tyler, twin to Matie; married W. R. Schultz, born in Dantzig, Germany; lives in Kelispell, Mont., where he is a furrier.

7379 Edward Joseph Tyler, born June 11, 1873; was petty officer on the *Yale* during the Spanish War, captain of a five-inch gun. Is ex-member of the

Illinois Naval Reserve. He is very strong and can lift four hundred pounds with either hand; standing level can jump ten feet; running high jump 5 feet 8 inches; an amateur athlete. He has been private secretary to the president of the Municipal Voters' League in Chicago, Ill.; he is unmarried.

5273   CORNELIA ANNAH[8] TYLER (Joseph[7]), born May 6, 1838; married, July 18, 1858, Samuel B. Whitaker, of Fulton, N. Y., born July 17, 1834. The children were born in Fulton. Children:

7380   Morris Tyler Whitaker, born Sept. 11, 1869; died Aug. 5, 1891.

7381   Harriet Cornelia Whitaker, born June 8, 1873.

5275   EDWIN[8] TYLER (Phineas[7]), born in Union, Me., October 25, 1826; married, January 15, 1860, in Camden Me., Mary Elizabeth Knight. He was an ordinary seaman in the Mexican War; enlisted in New York City for three years August 14, 1843-May 2, 1846. He was on the U. S. S. *North Carolina, Savannah,* and *Relief.* He applied for a pension, which was rejected on the ground that the service did not amount to sixty days. After discharge he followed the sea until 1849, then he went to California for six years; thence to Rockland and Camden, Me., and about 1865 he went to Boston (See *Pension Book,* p. 70). Child:

7382   Maria Louise Tyler, born in Camden, April 10, 1861; an artist; keeps house for her father.

5276   LOUISA AUGUSTA[8] TYLER (Phineas[7]), born in Thomaston, Me., May 6, 1833; married, April 2, 1855, in Rockland, Me., Charles E. Bliss, of Bangor, Me., born in Bradford, Vt., July 23 1833; son of Doctor Hiram and Polly (Hale) Bliss, of Waldoboro, Me. He is one of the most accomplished telegraphers in the country and one of the first to read by sound. The two children were born in Waldoboro. Children:

7383   Harry Clay Bliss, born June 20, 1856.

7384   Marcia Fessenden Bliss, born March 8, 1858.

7385   Alfred Veasie Bliss, born in Bangor, Jan. 24, 1872.

5286 WILLIAM HENRY[8] TYLER (Laban Ainsworth[7]), born in Boston, Mass., May 18, 1839; married in Boston, Mass., November 19, 1863, Mary Jane Redmond Frellick, daughter of John and Mary A. (Mellman) Frellick, of Boston, an engraver. He was living in 1897 in Chicago. Children:

7386   (Dr.) Harvey Ainsworth Tyler, born in Newtonville, Mass., April 30, 1869.

7387   Spofford John William Tyler, born in Chicago, Jan. 6, 1880.

5307 SARAH FRANCES[8] TYLER (Frederick[7]), born in Foxcroft, Me., December 20, 1837; married, in Huntington, Mass., November 26, 1858, Harry F. Williams, of Northampton, Mass., who died September 6, 1887. In 1897 she lived in Northampton, where her children were born. Children:

7388   Theresa Buell Williams, born 1860; died Jan. 23, 1891, aged thirty-one.

7389   Frederick Bennett Williams, born 1862; died May 3, 1870.

7390   Robert Greely Williams, married Nellie Baird, of Seneca Falls, N. Y.; they live in Northampton; two children.

7391   Frances Tyler Williams, married, Oct., 1895, Frederic W. Smith, of Salem, Mass., who died s. p. May, 1896; lives with her mother in Northampton.

5308 FRANCES HARRIET[8] TYLER (Abel H.[7]), born in South Danvers, Mass., August 13, 1835; married, November 7, 1855, William A. Jacobs, of Danversport, Mass. The children were born in Danvers. Children:

7392   William Henry Jacobs, born May 24, 1856; married, April 21, 1880, Mary L. Stetson; a son died in infancy.

7393   George Allen Jacobs, born Jan. 24, 1858.

5310 ALFRED[8] TYLER (Abel H.[7]), born in Dracut, Mass., February 26, 1842; married, June 23, 1861, Sarah Jane Hall, born in Salem in 1844; daughter of John and Sophronia Hall. The children were born in Salem. Children:

7394   Sarah E. Tyler, born June 30, 1862; died young.
7395   Sarah Elizabeth Tyler, born Jan. 30, 1863; married,
            Jan. 23, 1878, Frank R. Conant, born 1858; son
            of John and Mary C. (Boyington) Conant; sev-
            eral children.
7396   Warren A. Tyler, born Oct. 31, 1863; died young.
7397+   Alonzo W. Tyler, born 1864.

5313   ABEL NORTON[8] TYLER (Abel H.[7]), born in
Danvers, Mass., March 2, 1847; married (1), February 26,
1866, Grace Day; married (2), October 1, 1878, Henrietta
L. Brown, born in Salem in 1853; daughter of Henry H. and
Mary E. (Bartlett) Brown. They live in Salem.

Child, by first marriage:
7398   Hattie E. Tyler, born in Salem; married Albert
            Conant; had a son named for his father.

5316   EDWARD MELVIN[8] TYLER (Abel H.[7]), born
in Danvers, Mass., January 8, 1855; married, May 9, 1881,
Martha J. Sawyer, who was born in Danvers. They live in
Salem, where the children were born. Children:
7399   Arthur Melvin Tyler, born Sept. 6, 1885.
7400   Henry Sawyer Tyler, born March 18, 1892.

5324   ANSEL PEABODY[8] TYLER (Addison[7]), born
probably in Middleton, Mass.; married Ruby A. Estey. He
lived in Middleton. Child:
7401   Minnie Palmer Tyler, married, June 20, 1894, Frank
            B. Tyler, of Salem, Mass., No. 7278.

5325   MAURICE ENDICOTT[8] TYLER (Addison[7]),
born probably in Middleton, Mass.; married Mary H. Estey.
Children:
7402   Marion Endicott Tyler.
7403   Harley Morton Tyler.

5326   WILLIAM HARRISON[8] TYLER (Addison[7]),
born probably in Middleton, Mass.; married Linda Allen.
Child:
7404   Harry Douglas Tyler.

5328 JANE ALMIRA[8] TYLER (Rufus H.[7]), born in Worcester, Mass., April 19, 1843; married, November 26, 1868, John Kirk Somes, of Springfield, Mass., born December 6, 1842. In 1898 they lived in Springfield, where the children were born. Children:

7405 Hattie Tyler Somes, born Jan. 16, 1870.
7406 John Kirk Somes, born Oct. 15, 1874; died Oct. 15, 1875.

5331 RUFUS HENRY[8] TYLER (Rufus H.[7]), born in Worcester, Mass., August 8, 1849; married, May 20, 1876, Edna Wright, of Monroe, Kas., born August 4, 1854. He learned the machinist trade in youth and settled in Kansas in 1867, on the frontier, where he was a farmer, and hunted buffalo and game. He crossed the great American desert in one of his trips west. He went into the cattle business, which resulted disastrously; in 1898 was department county clerk of Wyandotte County, Kas. The youngest child was born in Kansas City and the others in Monroe. Children:

7407 Rufus Henry Tyler, born July 9, 1879; died July 14, 1880.
7408 James Gail Tyler, born Oct. 10, 1880; died Oct. 24, 1887.
7409 Ray Earl Tyler, born Sept. 22, 1885.
7410 Luman A. Tyler, born March 19, 1895.

5332 MARY ELLEN[8] TYLER (Rufus H.[7]), born in Worcester, Mass., June 10, 1852; married, September 19, 1872, William T. D. French, of Springfield, Mass., born June 21, 1849. The children were born in Springfield. Children:

7411 Devonia Stivers French, born June 5, 1873; died July 19, 1873.
7412 Annie Louise French, born May 22, 1877; married, Aug. 14, 1897, Fred O. Seaver, of Brooklyn, N. Y.
7413 Rufus Tyler French, born June 1, 1881.
7414 Jennie Emerson French, born Dec. 6, 1882.
7415 Minnie Helena French, born Aug. 15, 1884; died Sept. 5, 1884.
7416 Lola Fay French, born Jan. 7, 1885.

5354 JAMES ADDISON[8] TYLER (Adolphus[7]), born

in Milford, Mass., October 21, 1853; married, May 21, 1878, Sarah Lee Libby, of Milford, where he resided in 1898 and where the child was born. Child:

7417   Adolphus Lee Tyler, born May 25, 1879.

5380 JOSEPHINE PARKER[8] TYLER (Ancill[7]), born in Lancaster, Mass., July 15, 1846; married (1), December, 1873, W. H. Adams, of Pepperell, Mass.; married (2), November, 1898, Charles H. Damon. She lives in Fitchburg, Mass.

CHILD, by first marriage:

7418   Clesson Tyler Adams, married Blanche W. Larned, of Washington, D. C.; lives in North Leominster, Mass.

5396 FREDERICK BATES[8] TYLER (Abraham[7]), born in Marlboro, Mass.; married (1), January 1, 1877, Flora Elizabeth Bruce, from whom divorced; married (2), 1886, Agnes McCabe, who died, s. p. in 1886; married (3), 1888, Annie May Bennett; no children by third marriage. In 1898 he was a hotelkeeper in North Lancaster, Mass.

CHILD, by first marriage:

7419   Burton Kendall Tyler, died in childhood.

5404 ALBERT A.[8] TYLER (Moses Augustus[7]), born in Woburn, Mass., August 5, 1843; married Lena B. Norton; lives in New Hampshire. Child:

7420   Harry Damon Tyler born in Woburn, Mass., Nov. 12, 1874.

5406 CORA MERRILL[8] TYLER (Moses Augustus[7]), born in Woburn, Mass., May 14, 1859; married, September 36, 1886, William Henry Norris of Epping, N. H. Child:

7421   Elton Tyler Norris, born in Epping, Aug. 10, 1888.

5419 CYRUS H.[8] TYLER (John[7]), is a farmer and in 1897 resided in Westmoreland, N. Y. Children:

7422   John Russel Tyler, married; one son.
7423   Henrietta Tyler.
7424   William Henry Tyler.

7425   Catherine Tyler, married; three children.
7426   Eliza M. Tyler.
7427   Cyrus Winfield Tyler.

5420 HENRY H.[8] TYLER (John[7]), born August 1, 1831; married Elizabeth Stephens, who died in Westmoreland in 1886. He is a farmer and in 1897 was residing in Westmoreland, N. Y. The children were born in Oneida, N. Y. Children:

7428+   Bayard Henry Tyler, born April 22, 1855.
7429+   Fred A. Tyler, born Aug. 22, 1857.
7430   C. Edwin Tyler, born June 21, 1866; resides in Rome, N. Y.
7431   Jesse S. Tyler, born Nov. 6, 1870; resides with his father.

5457 HENRY PARKER[8] TYLER (Aaron Parker[7]), born in Boxford, Mass., February 2, 1846; married, June 17, 1869, Adelia E. Clark. When he was but seven months old his father died, and he lived at his grandfather Tyler's until his mother married again. He is a capitalist and lives in Haverhill, Mass., which has been his residence since 1854. Child:

7432   Henry Parker Tyler, Jr., born in Haverhill, Aug. 18, 1871; died July 3, 1875.

5461 GEORGE FONTENELLE[8] TYLER (Isaac Matson[7]), born in Leominster, Mass., April 25, 1849; married Helen ———. The children were born in Lunenburg. Children:

7433   Willie Fontenelle Tyler, born Dec. 13, 1877.
7434   Florence Bill Tyler, born Sept. 27, 1879.
7435   Helen Cranston Tyler, born April 14, 1882.

5465 ABEL NELSON[8] TYLER (Isaac Matson[7]), born in Lunenburg, Mass., September 9, 1858; married, in Fitchburg, Mass., December 9, 1893, Alma S. Clesson, who died in Leominster, August 9, 1895, aged twenty-six; daughter of Cless and Anna Clesson, of Leominster, Mass. Child:

7436   Clifton Brenton Tyler, born in Leominster, Feb. 13, 1895.

5482   CHARLES PAYSON[8] TYLER (Joseph Augustus[7]), born in Leominster, Mass., September 5, 1865; married, June 23, 1887, Cora A. Derby, of Leominster.   Child:

7437   Ralph Augustus Tyler, born in Leominster, March 5, 1889.

5501   OLIVIA[8] TYLER (Levi Andrew[7]), born in Lyndeboro, N. H., July 15, 1868; married Edwin French, of Wilton, N. H.   Child:

7438   Amy French, born in Wilton, 1894.

5504   MARY GERTRUDE[8] TYLER (Stephen A.[7]), born in Townsend, Mass., November 25, 1868; married, June 26, 1891, Clarence Bohanon, of Petersham, Mass.; they moved to Athol, Mass., where the children were born.   Children:

7439   Clayton Bohanon, born July 26, 1892.
7440   Lawrence Tyler Bohanon, born Dec. 25, 1894.

5505   ALICE F.[8] TYLER (Stephen A.[7]), born in Townsend, Mass., January 14, 1871; married, July 20, 1897, Doctor Elmer H. Cutts, from Chicago to New Boston, Ill. She was graduated from Middlebury, Vt., College in 1896. Child:

7441   Laura L. Cutts, born May 17, 1898.

5509   HARRY ASA[8] TYLER (Aaron Parker[7]), born in Townsend, Mass., January 20, 1877, married, December 31, 1897, in Troy, Idaho, Ethel Bensectu.   Children:

7442   Mary Viola Tyler, born in Kendrick, Idaho, Oct. 10, 1898.
7443   Ada Ethelene Tyler, born in Laprai, Idaho, March 14, 1901.

5511   GEORGE CALVERT[8] TYLER (Phineas Lovejoy[7]), born in Missouri, 1839; died in 1903; married Anna Engs Strobel, daughter of Reverend Williams and Abby A. (Engs) Strobel, of Charleston, S. C.; her people were Alsacetian Huguenots, early residents of Charleston; her mother was of New York City.   Mr. Tyler was educated in Poughkeepsie, N. Y.; became a civil engineer and during the Civil War was on the staff of General McClellan.   Later he engaged in mercantile and building enterprises, and in 1899 resided retired in Bergenfields, N. J. Child:

7444+   William Nathan Tyler, born in Heath, N. Y., Aug. 5, 1864.

5514   NATHAN PEABODY[8] TYLER, M. D. (Phineas Lovejoy,[7]), born in Barrytown, N. Y., October 11, 1848; married, June 16, 1884, Mary W. Miller, of Tarrytown, N. Y., daughter of John (of Scotland) and his wife, Mary (Craigg) Miller (of England). Doctor Tyler was graduated from Yale College in 1876 and from Yale Medical College in 1879. He practiced medicine in New Haven, Conn., until June, 1885; in 1886 he settled in New Rochelle, N. Y., where he practiced until 1907, when he retired, and is now a fruit planter in Manati, Porto Rico. Children:

7444a   Frank Tyler, born July 5, 1885; died Sept. 19, 1885.

7444b   Margaret Eloise Tyler, born Oct. 4, 1886; married, June 26, 1907, Charles Matthew, of Charleston, S. C.; one child (Mary Eloise, born Nov. 5, 1908).

7444c   Lyon Leavenworth Tyler, born March 27, 1889.

5555   REV. ORRIN[8] TYLER (Asa F.[7]), born in Windsor, Me., May 15, 1841; died in Gardiner City, Me.; married (1), Mary Etta Lynn; married (2), Elma T. Searles, daughter of Thomas and Mary (Kidder) Searles, of Chelsea, Mass.; married (3), Adda O. Larabee. He was a minister in the Methodist church.

CHILD, by first marriage:

7445   Nellie Tyler, married —— Fairfield, and lives in Fairfield, Me.

CHILDREN, by second marriage:

7446+   George Leslie Tyler, born Jan. 13, 1870.

7447   Hattie E. Tyler, lives unmarried in Augusta, Me.

7448   Charles Tyler, died young, unmarried.

7449   Frank Tyler, lives in Fairfield, Me.

5561   ELLA MARIA[8] TYLER (Joshua[7]), born in China, Me., July 15, 1853; married (1), in Lewiston, Me., October 26, 1874, Horace J. Hatch, a millman, who died; married (2), in China, Edward Haskel. The two elder and the youngest children were born in China.

CHILDREN, by first marriage:

7450   Clarence Merton Hatch, born Aug. 7, 1875.
7451   Daniel Lester Hatch, born April 5, 1877.
7452   Henry James Hatch, born in Vassalboro, 1879; died aged two weeks.

CHILD, by second marriage:

7453   Elmer Haskel, born July 3, 1883.

5562   HENRY JOHNSON[8] TYLER (Joshua[7]), born in China, Me., July 3, 1857; married, in Skowhegan, Me., September 12, 1885, Laura A. Weston. He was a farmer. The children were born in China. Children:

7454   Alfonso Gilbert Tyler, born July 3, 1889.
7455   Vera Alice Tyler, born April 10, 1892.

5575   ANNIE[8] TYLER (Eleazer[7]), born in China, Me., February 17, 1847; married, July 5, 1866, Rev. George W. Weeks; lives in China, where the children were born. Children:

7456   Mertie L. Weeks, born April 7, 1868; died Oct. 5, 1876.
7457   George F. Weeks, born Nov. 21, 1870.
7458   Harvey J. Weeks, born Dec. 12, 1874.
7459   Edward Tyler Weeks, born Nov. 26, 1878.

5616   MARY ELIZABETH[8] TYLER (Alonzo Chase[7]), born in Boston, Mass., July 1, 1867; married (1), Nelson Powers, of Boston; married (2), in Augusta, Me., October 23, 1893, Frederic William Pen, born in London, Eng., August 8, 1864.

CHILD, by first marriage:

7460   Ethel Tyler Powers, born in Boston.

CHILDREN, by second marriage:

7461   Chauncey F. A. C. Pen, born in Palermo, Me., Oct. 16, 1895.
7462   Spencer Regnal Tyler Pen, born in Augusta, Feb. 5, 1897; died May 6, 1897.

5617 WILLIAM[8] TYLER (John Woodbury[7]), married Emma T. ——, and resides in Greenbush, N. Y. Children:
7463 William Tyler; resides in Greenbush, N. Y.
7464 Phoebe Tyler.
7465 Lottie Tyler.
7466 Emma Tyler.
7467 Woodbury Tyler.

5628 EDITH H.[8] TYLER (George Emory[7]), born December 31, 1863; married, December 12, 1883, Philan D. Fellows, of Charlestown, Mass. In 1900 they lived in Charlestown, where the children were born. Children:
7468 George A. Fellows, born 1886.
7469 Harry W. Fellows, born 1890.

5640 STANLEY CUSHING[8] TYLER (Artemus Stanley[7]), born in Lowell, Mass., June 4, 1857; married, January 31, 1884, Mary Ann Ayres, of Charlestown, Mass., daughter of Oliver and Mary (Hooper) Ayres; her father was chief of police in Charlestown. They live in Zulu, Hansford County, Tex., on a ranch where he has about 2000 head of cattle; he owns several sections and buys grazing rights for miles; he is the county judge. The children were born in Lowell. Children:
7470 Mary Angeline Tyler, born Feb. 4, 1885.
7471 Ethel Maria Tyler, born Feb. 5, 1887.
7472 Oliver Stanley Tyler, born March 4, 1891.
7473 Stanley Cushing Tyler, born May 5, 1888; died Aug. 31, 1888.
7474 Fanny Stanley Tyler, born Oct. 12, 1893.

5641 ARTEMAS LAWRENCE[8] TYLER (Artemas Stanley[7]), born in Lowell, Mass., September 7, 1860; died there December 18, 1897; married, October 1, 1891, Florence Hill Whittier, daughter of Henry Whittier, a manufacturer of Lowell. He was educated at the Massachusetts Institute of Technology and was an assistant there for a time; he was connected with a Boston paper as journalist, and then taught in Lowell in a private school. His widow lives in Colorado Springs, Colo. Child:
7475 Helen Minerva Tyler, born in Lowell, Feb. 28, 1893.

5670 LUCETTE S.[8] TYLER (James[7]), born in Buxton, Me., April 23, 1845; married, November 28, 1864, Nathaniel Sawyer, of Sacarappa, Me. He was in the Civil War, 25th Me. Infantry from the 10th of September to the 10th of July, 1863; in 1900 was residing in Freeport, Me. Child:

7476   Eva E. Sawyer, born in Buxton, Me., Dec. 7, 1866; married in Freeport, Me., Dec. 20, 1888, Arthur C. Bowden; one daughter (Delia S.).

5674 JAMES[8] TYLER, JR. (James[7]), born in Hollis, Me., August 29, 1854; married (1), February 27, 1875, Clara Estelle Johnson, of Hollis, who died December 24, 1893; married (2), May 19, 1896, Edith M. Richardson, of Freeport, Me. He has lived in Biddeford, and Freeport, and in 1900 was living in Hollis. The children, except the youngest, were born in Hollis.

CHILDREN, by first marriage:

7477   Ernest Linwood Tyler, born Feb. 27, 1876; married, Nov. 22, 1899, Charlotte M. Hewitt, of Yarmouth, Me., and resides in Malden, Mass.

7478   Lester Dean Tyler, born Oct. 12, 1877.

7479   Nellie Lila Tyler, born Oct. 6, 1879; married, Oct. 19, 1899, Alton N. Bowder; resides in Freeport, Me.

7480   Georgia Luella Tyler, born Nov. 22, 1882.

7481   Herbert Elroy Tyler, born April 5, 1885.

7482   Harriet May Tyler, born March 21, 1887.

CHILD, by second marriage:

7483   Clementina Dunning Tyler, born in Freeport, Me., Jan. 21, 1899.

5677 LOUISE S.[8] TYLER (Andrew[7]), born in Saco, Me., March 30, 1850; married, September 15, 1869, Alonzo A. Bowdoin, of Hollis, Me. They have a summer home at Old Orchard Beach. Child:

7484   Elizabeth E. Bowdoin, born in Buxton, Me., July 22, 1872; married, May, 1895, Frank H. Colby, a lawyer, of Portland, Me.

5679 EMMA E.[8] TYLER (Andrew[7]), born in Saco,

Me., March 29, 1853; married, January 20, 1885, David S. Stuart, of Portsmouth, N. H.; they live in Saco. Children:

7485   David S. Stuart, Jr., born in Portland, Me., Feb. 6, 1886; died the same day.

7486   Gladys Emma Stuart, born in Biddeford, Me., Aug. 9, 1897.

5681   LUELLA P.[8] TYLER (Andrew[7]), born in Saco, Me., November 7, 1858; married, in Saco, November 11, 1877, W. Gray Rumery. Children:

7487   Harry Willard Rumery, born in Kennebunk, Me., Aug. 13, 1878.

7488   Garnet Wilma Rumery, born in Lynn, Mass., Nov. 4, 1889.

7489   Wilbur G. Tyler Rumery, born in Chicago, Ill., Aug. 9, 1894.

5697   IRVING W.[8] TYLER (Joseph Currier[7]), born in Pownal, Me., 1842; married, September 11, 1872, Helen G. Hubbell, born in Pleasant Valley, N. Y., August 4, 1850. He enlisted July, 1862, in the 20th Me. Volunteer Infantry, and served three years. He is a dentist in Bristol, Conn., where the children were born. Children:

7490+   Arthur Clinton Tyler, born Feb. 7, 1874.

7491   Gertrude May Tyler, born March 20, 1877; is a teacher.

5698   JOSEPH[8] TYLER (Joseph Currier[7]), born in Durham, Me., January 25, 1845; married (1), April, 1870, Sarah E. Watts, of Pownal, Me., who died December 23, 1881; married (2), February 19, 1885, Jennie Cutter Hastings, of Portland, Me. He is a carriage builder and lives in Woodfords (Portland), Me. He was three years in the Civil War, in Company K, 20th Me. Volunteer Infantry. The children were born in Woodfords.

CHILD, by first marriage:

7492   Maud Mildred Tyler, born Oct. 18, 1875; married, July 26, 1900, Alexander H. Gregory.

CHILDREN, by second marriage:
7493 Anna Frank Tyler, born Sept. 8, 1886.
7494 Rose Makee Tyler, born Oct. 14, 1888.
7495 Carroll Hastings Tyler, born Dec. 3, 1891.

5719 GEORGE H.[8] TYLER (Zebulon[7]), born in New Sharon, Me., March 2, 1853; married, 1878, Nellie Ross, of Marshfield, Me. Children:
7496 Nellie J. Tyler, born Oct. 22, 1879.
7497 Alfred Tyler, born April 15, 1881.

5720 SARAH ELIZABETH[8] TYLER (Zebulon[7]), born in New Sharon, Me., October 23, 1854; married (1), July 3, 1879, George H. Braun, who died May, 1889; married (2), November, 1894, Charles H. Ward. In 1897 they lived in Gardiner, Me.

CHILDREN, by first marriage:
7498 Earl R. Braun, born June 20, 1880.
7499 Mazie A. Braun, born Jan. 2, 1885.

5721 MINNIE A.[8] TYLER (Zebulon[7]), born in New Sharon, Me., March 28, 1858; married, December 23, 1877, Albert Arnold, of Farmington, Me., who died November 23, 1895. In 1897 she lived in Gardiner, Me. Children:
7500 Gertrude Arnold, born in Farmington, Nov. 26, 1882.

5723 JOSEPH A.[8] TYLER (Zebulon[7]), born May 3, 1862; married, June 6, 1895, Lephie Kimball, of Boothbay, Me. He was graduated from the Technical College of the University of Maine in 1892; is a civil engineer and lives in Portland, Me., and Boston, Mass. The children were born in Portland. Children:
7501 Dora Frances Tyler, born Oct. 3, 1896.
7502 Randolph K. Tyler, born Aug. 11, 1900.

5725 HATTIE ZORA[8] TYLER (Zebulon[7]), born in New Sharon, Me., September 11, 1867; married, November 25, 1888, Charles H. Braun. They reside in Stark, Me., where the children were born. Children:

7503   Mabel Ahra Braun, born Sept. 5, 1890.
7504   Rosco Henry Braun, born Dec. 23, 1893.

5727   PHILIP J.[8] LARRABEE (Lucy T.[7] Libby), born April 12, 1844; married, January 1, 1872, Sarah L. Ballard, daughter of Joseph D. Ballard.   He was graduated from Tufts College in 1867; is a lawyer in Portland, Me.   Children:
7505   Philip Francis Larrabee, born Oct. 27, 1872.
7506   Emily D. Larrabee, born Sept. 3, 1881.
7507   Helen S. Larrabee, born Dec. 3, 1887.

5748   LETITIA M.[8] TYLER (John F.[7]), born in Hartford, Me., April 19, 1872; married, October 2, 1892, Cyrus T. Bonney, Jr., of Canton, Me., where the children were born. Children:
7508   Alice M. Bonney, born Oct. 1, 1893; died Oct. 14, 1895.
7509   Donald C. Bonney, born July 27, 1895.
7510   Ada C. Bonney, born Jan. 16, 1898.

5753   ARTHUR ULYSSES[8] TYLER (Gilbert[7]), born in Grafton, Me., February, 1868; married, August 12, 1893, Ellen Eudora Curtis.   He was graduated from Hebron, Me., Academy, and in 1899 was residing in South Paris, Me. Children:
7511   Elma Robert Tyler, born Nov. 15, 1894.
7512   Marion Winfred Tyler, born July 21, 1896.

5754   ADDIE MAY[8] TYLER (Gilbert[7]), born in Grafton, Me., February, 1870; married, January, 1893, James Canning.   Child:
7513   Ruth E. Canning, born Nov., 1896.

5780   CHARLES H.[8] TYLER (Henry L.[7]), born in Milford, Mass., April 30, 1848; married ——.   He is a gardener and lives in Chillicothe, Ill.   Children:
7514   Annie Tyler.
7515   Maud Tyler.
7516   Harry Tyler, lives in Peoria, Ill.

5783   WESLEY[8] TYLER (Sylvester[7]), born November

26, 1857; married, January 15, 1885, Josephine M. Gallagher.
Children:
7517   Ernest Tyler, born Aug. 4, 1887; died Aug. 7, 1887.
7518   Edith Tyler, born Sept. 20, 1888.

5786   ADA L.[8] TYLER (William R.[7]), born in Cleveland, O., May 17, 1856; married, January 1, 1877, Harvey A. Lauman, of Niles, Mich.   He moved to Stanton County, Kas., and owns a stock ranch and is county treasurer.   Children:
7519   Clinton Frank Lauman, born Dec. 16, 1877.
7520   William Tyler Lauman, born June, 1889.

5787   LAYTON JAMES[8] TYLER (William R.[7]), born in Decatur, Tex., May 10, 1861; married, in Pleasant Hill, Mo., June 24, 1883, Ruth Vanhoy.   He is a farmer in Vernon County, Mo.   Children:
7521   Ina Tyler.
7522   Willie C. Tyler.
7523   Elton P. Tyler.
7524   Meda Tyler.
7525   Royal Tyler.

5789   JAMES LIBBY[8] TYLER, JR. (James Libby[7]), born in Chelsea, Mass., December 10, 1851; married, July 13, 1885, Sarah Elizabeth Pennock, of Somerville, Mass., daughter of Nathaniel Pennock.   He is a dealer in hardwood lumber in Boston and lives in Somerville.   Child:
7526   Roland Tyler, born in Somerville, March 30, 1890.

5792   CORA L.[8] TYLER (James Libby[7]), born in Somerville, Mass., May 30, 1857; married, July 12, 1881, Lorenzo Dow Carter, Jr., born April 10, 1857; son of Lorenzo Dow Carter, of Somerville; a salesman in Boston; lives in West Somerville.   Child:
7527   Effie Wardwell Carter, born in Malden, Mass., July 8, 1882.

5794   WILLIAM SUMNER[8] TYLER (Charles Abraham[7]), born in East Randolph, Mass., April 14, 1861; married, in 1884, Mary Murphy; resides in Farmington, Ill., where the children were born.   Children:

7528   Charles Sumner Tyler, born in 1888.
7529   Albert Tyler.
7530   Alfred Tyler.

5796   ROYAL HARRISON[8] TYLER (Charles Abraham[7]), born in Newton, Mass., November 23, 1864; married, November 23, 1892, Jennie May Smith.   He lives in Quillayute, Wash., where the child was born.   Child:
7531   Florence Irene Tyler, born Nov. 28, 1894.

5797   JOSEPH ELMER[8] TYLER (Charles Abraham[7]), born in South Weymouth, Mass., August 11, 1867; married, November 17, 1892, Tessa Weldon; resides in Cedar Rapids, Ia., where the children were born.   Children:
7532   Bernice Lorette Tyler, born Sept. 10, 1893.
7533   Charles Tyler, born April 10, 1895.

5798   JOHN MARCH[8] TYLER (Charles Abraham[7]), born in Farmington, Ill., January 6, 1870; married, November 8, 1893, in Patterson, Kas., Nellie May Matlock, daughter of Hon. T. J. Matlock.   His mother died when he was an infant; went west in 1887, where he worked on a cattle ranch, bookkeeping and buying and shipping grain; moved to Butte, Mont., September, 1893, where he began cattle raising.   Child:
7534   Claude Matlock Tyler, born in Butte, May 18, 1896.

5802   DANIEL GAGE[8] TYLER (John Milton[7]), born in Pelham, N. H., February 28, 1844; lives in Lexington, Mass.; married, October 12, 1870, Mary E. Marrett, of Cambridge, Mass.   He is a wholesale merchant in Boston.   The children were born in Lexington.   Children:
7535   Lawrence Milton Tyler, born Jan. 4, 1872; died Sept. 2, 1876.
7536   Winsor Marrett Tyler, born April 28, 1876; in class of 1899 Harvard University.
7537   Eliza Hastings Tyler, born April 19, 1879.

5817   EUGENIA[8] TYLER (George Washington[7]), born in West Newbury, Mass., January 19, 1843; died February 15, 1904; married, January 18, 1866, Charles E. Bailey, of Haverhill, Mass., who died June 23, 1884.   She lived in

Haverhill, and died there, and her children were born there. Children:

7538   Mabel Bailey, born Aug. 29, 1866.
7539   Charles A. Bailey, born April 29, 1868; died in Haverhill, June 30, 1904.

5818   GEORGE GARDNER[8] TYLER (George Washington[7]), born in West Newbury, Mass., October 1. 1844; married (1), October 25, 1868, Kate Rundlet, of Groveland, Mass., who died July 11, 1875; married (2), November 11, 1880, Abbie Tibbetts, of Bradford, Mass.   He lives in Salem, Mass., a conductor on the Boston & Maine Railway.

CHILDREN, by first marriage:
7540   Harvey P. Tyler, born July 6, 1869; married, July 2, 1892, Sarah E. George, of Haverhill, Mass., and lives in Groveland, s. p.
7541+   Fred G. Tyler, born Aug. 9, 1872.

CHILD, by second marriage:
7542   Arthur E. Tyler, born July 18, 1882; died June 27, 1887.

5819   MARY H.[8] TYLER (Charles[7]), born in Newburyport, Mass., November 17, 1839; married, February 2, 1870, D. A. P. George, of Hampton Falls, N. H., who died in West Newbury, May 18, 1904.   She may have died February 25, 1904, but the record is uncertain.   Child:
7543   Sarah Peabody George, born in West Newbury, Jan. 22, 1872; married, Aug. 9, 1892, Myron H. Goodwin, of Baldwin, Me.; lives in West Newbury.

5820   CHARLES A.[8] TYLER (Albert Moses[7]), born in Lowell, Mass., November 7, 1846; married, February 26, 1869, Alice M. Carpenter, of Cleveland, O.   Child:
7544   May C. Tyler, born July 7, 1873.

5823   IDA FLORENCE[8] TYLER (Osgood[7]), born in Bradford, Mass., May 4, 1855; married (1), December 20, 1871, George Bailey, of Lawrence, Mass.; married (2), September 15, 1891, Frank Pashe, of Bradford; lives in New York City.

CHILD, by first marriage:

7545   Frank French Bailey, born May 13, 1873; died Oct., 1875.

5824 CLARENCE EDWARD[8] TYLER (Osgood[7]), born in Bradford, Mass., February 16, 1857; married, August 10, 1878, Angie M. Rowell, of East Kingston, N. H.; lives in Ward Hill, Mass. Child:

7546   Frank Freeland Tyler, born April 7, 1879; died in Bradford, Dec. 19, 1901.

5832 MARY ELIZABETH[8] TYLER (John[7]), born in Barrington, R. I. ("Tyler's Point"), July 28, 1828; died October 1, 1879; married, July 7, 1846, Philip Carr, of Warren, R. I., born February 23, 1823. The children were born in Warren. Children:

7547   John Tyler Carr, born Feb. 22, 1848; died June 8, 1894; married (1), Sept. 28, 1871, Elizabeth, Vaughn Tucker, born April 11, 1851; died July 30, 1881; married (2), Dec. 6, 1882, Emma Elizabeth Carroll; two children.

7548   Annie Major Carr, born Oct. 24, 1850; in 1897 was living in Providence, R. I.

7549   Philip Augustine Carr, born Nov. 14, 1852; married, July 21, 1878, ——; has one son (Ernest Blanchard).

7550   Henry Martin Carr, born Sept. 7, 1854; died May 8, 1856.

7551   Mary Eliza Carr, born Aug. 29, 1856; died April 10, 1863.

7552   Charles Turner Carr, born May 11, 1860; died March 13, 1865.

7553   Joseph Warren Carr, born Sept. 6, 1862; died April 27, 1863.

7554   Frank Taylor Carr, born May 7, 1866; married, Nov. 18, 1890, Lizzie Lincoln Burnham; one child.

7555   William Mauran Carr, born March 5, 1869; died Oct. 1, 1879.

7556   Walter Martin Carr, born Jan. 10, 1872.

5834   MARY S.[8] TYLER (Edward Luther[7]), born in Lexington, Mass., February 7, 1838; married, April 2, 1865, Marshall Leigh, born in Carlisle, Mass., May 31, 1835; son of William and Dorcas (Wheeler) Leigh.   He was a blacksmith.   The children were born in Carlisle.   Children:

7557   Carrie Lillian Leigh, born July 5, 1866.
7558   William Marshall Leigh, born Nov. 18, 1867.
7559   Annie Howard Leigh, born July 18, 1869; died 1873.
7560   Herbert Howard Leigh, born Nov. 23, 1873.

5835   HENRY H.[8] TYLER (Edward Luther[7]), born in Lexington, Mass., November 22, 1840; married, July 3, 1870, Mary T. Spaulding; resides in East Lexington, Mass., where the children were born.   Children:

7561   Edward L. Tyler, born Jan. 8, 1872.
7562   Arthur S. Tyler, born Sept. 9, 1873.

5836   ARTHUR FITZ[8] TYLER (Edward Luther[7]), born in Lexington, Mass., March 12, 1852; married, May 12, 1875, Mary B. Cheney; resides in Athol, Mass., and the children were born there.   Children:

7563   Carrie Dell Tyler, born March 13, 1876.
7564   Almond Wesley Tyler, born Aug. 22, 1877.
7565   Lucien Howard Tyler, born July 11, 1879.
7566   Edward Luther Tyler, born Feb. 26, 1881.
7567   Grace Louise Tyler, born Jan. 7, 1883.
7568   Stella May Tyler, born Feb. 21, 1885.
7569   Arthur Fitz Tyler, Jr., born Feb. 28, 1887.
7570   Wallace Cheney Tyler, born Nov. 2, 1888.

5882   SIDNEY FREDERICK[8] TYLER (George Frederick[7]), born in Philadelphia, Pa., December 21, 1850; married (1), in Providence, R. I., February 10, 1880, Mary Woodrow Binney, born in Providence, December 14, 1856; died in Philadelphia, December 19, 1884, daughter of Hon. William and Charlotte Hope (Goddard) Binney, of Newport, R. I.; descended from Captain John Binney, of Hull, Mass., in 1678; married (2), in Philadelphia, March 8, 1887, Ida Amelia Elkins, born in Philadelphia, August 27, 1859, daughter of William L. and Louise (Broomall) Elkins, of Philadelphia.   He was graduated from Harvard College in 1872; traveled abroad for three years; admitted to the Philadelphia bar in 1878; lived several years in Providence and Boston as agent of the Connecticut Mutual Life Insurance Company, and moved to Philadelphia in 1884; was receiver of the Shenandoah Valley Railway for six years, organized by him in 1886; first president of the Fourth Street National Bank in Philadelphia; was interested in several large corporations. In 1894 was on the reorganization committee of the Savannah and Western Railway of Georgia, of the Philadelphia & Reading Railway Company, and the Choctaw, Oklahoma & Gulf Railway Company of Indian Territory; is a member of many leading clubs and societies.

CHILDREN, by first marriage:

7571   Hope Binney Tyler, born in Boston, Mass., Jan. 5, 1881; married in Philadelphia, Feb. 24, 1902, Robert Leaming Montgomery, born in Philadelphia, March 30, 1879.

7572   George Frederick Tyler, born in Newport, R. I., Aug. 10, 1883.

5883   HON. HARRY BLAKE[8] TYLER (George Frederick[7]), born in Philadelphia, Pa., November 20, 1852; married, in Chelsea, London, England, January 31, 1897, Eleanor O'Donnel. He was graduated from Harvard College in 1874; a member of the common council of Philadelphia, 1885-1886; member of the Pennsylvania Legislature, 1891-1892; director in several financial institutions of Philadelphia; lives in London. Children:

7573   Louise Tyler.

7574   Harry Blake Tyler.

7575   Sidney Frederick Tyler.

5884   MARY LOUISE[8] TYLER (George Frederick[7]), born in Philadelphia, Pa., July 5, 1857; married in Philadelphia, November 12, 1879, John William Brock, born in Philadelphia, November 23, 1854. The children were also born in Philadelphia. Children:

7576   George Tyler Brock, born Oct. 1, 1880; died Jan. 25, 1884.

7577   John William Brock, Jr., born Feb. 14, 1883.

7578   Sidney Frederick Tyler Brock, born May 5, 1885.

7579   Arthur Brock, born Jan. 12, 1887.
7580   Norman Hall Brock, born April 23, 1889.
7581   Louisa Blake Brock, born Sept. 27, 1894.

5886   ROBERT OGDEN[8] TYLER (Edwin S.[7]), born in Hartford, Conn., April 18, 1861; married, in Chicago, Ill., December 22, 1890, Elizabeth Roberts. Child:
7582   Robert Ogden Tyler, born in Chicago, June 1, 1893.

5888   SARAH SOPHIA[8] TYLER (Edwin S.[7]) born in Hartford, Conn., May 26, 1865; died there December 23, 1886; married there, October 21, 1885, George Lockwood Plummer, born in Glastonbury, Conn., January 1, 1860. Child:
7583   Sarah Tyler Plummer, born in Hartford, Dec. 13, 1886.

5890   CAMILLA MATILDA[8] TYLER (Edwin S.[7]), born in Hartford, Conn., November 18, 1870; married in New York City, November 26, 1892, George Pettigrew Bryan, born near York, Pa., September 9, 1865. Children:
7584   Camilla Elizabeth Bryan, born in Brockwayville, Pa., April 18, 1899.
7585   Louise Tyler Bryan, born in Elmira, N. Y., July 26, 1903.

5893   ALFRED LEE[8] TYLER, JR. (Alfred Lee[7]), born in Norwich, Conn., in 1866; married, 1892, Harriet W. Bond. Children:
7586   Annie Scott Tyler, born 1893.
7587   Alfred Lee Tyler, born 1903.

5895   EDITH KERMIT[8] CAROW (Gertrude Elizabeth[7]), born in Norwich, Conn., August 6, 1861; married, in London, England, December 2, 1886, Theodore Roosevelt, twenty-fifth President of the United States of America; born in New York City, October 27, 1858; son of Theodore and Martha (Bulloch) Roosevelt (descended from Claus Martenszen Van Rosenvelt, who came from Zeeland, Holland, and settled in New Amsterdam in 1649; with his wife Janetje Samuels-Thomas); he married (1), October 27, 1880, Alice Hathaway Lee, daughter of George Cabot and Caroline (Haskell) Lee, of Boston, Mass., and had one daughter (Alice Lee) by this marriage. He was graduated at Harvard University in 1880; member of the New York State Assembly, 1882-1883-1884; lieutenant and captain of the 8th Regiment of N. Y. S. N. G., 1884-1888; United States Civil Service Commissioner, 1889-1894; police commissioner of New York City, 1895; Assistant Secretary of the United States Navy, April, 1897-May, 1898; lieutenant-colonel and colonel of the 1st Regiment U. S. V. Cavalry (Rough Riders), which he organized; served with distinction throughout the campaign of Santiago de Cuba, Spanish-American War; elected Governor of the State of New York, November 8, 1898; elected Vice-President of the United States, November, 1900; became President of the United States, through the assassination of President McKinley, September 14, 1901; elected President of the United States, November 5, 1904, by the largest popular majority ever given a candidate for the office. The three elder children were born in Oyster Bay, N. Y.; the two younger in Washington, D. C.

CHILDREN:

7588   Theodore Roosevelt, Jr., born Sept. 13, 1887.
7589   Kermit Roosevelt, born Oct. 10, 1889.
7590   Ethel Carow Roosevelt, born Aug. 13, 1891.
7591   Archibald Bulloch Roosevelt, born April 9, 1894.
7592   Quentin Roosevelt, born Nov. 19, 1897.

5904   JOHN ASAHEL[8] TYLER (Carley[7]), born in Shalorsville, O., May 21, 1821; died August 24, 1871; married, March 9, 1845, Phebe Jane Pearsol, who died January 26, 1873. Children:

7593+   George Durant Tyler, born March 9, 1847.
7594+   William Asahel Tyler, born Sept. 12, 1848.
7595   Adaline Tyler, born Jan. 21, 1850; died in infancy.
7596   Mary Ellen Tyler, born Feb. 10, 1853; married (1), Feb. 21, 1877, William Muhs; married (2), Dec. 14, 1885, George Muhs; no children.
7597+   Amelia Eveline Tyler, born Aug. 3, 1855.
7598+   Charles Edwin Tyler, born Oct. 2, 1861.
7599+   Henry Franklin Tyler, born June 23, 1864.

5907   POLLY RAHAMA[8] (Carley[7]), born in Shalorsville, O., December 27, 1829; married, July 12, 1848, Nicholas Walrod, a merchant, who died June 5, 1897. Children:

7600   Lucretia Ann Walrod, born April 3, 1849; married (1), Sept. 18, 1866, Andrew J. Staggs; married (2), John J. Huebner, a merchant; two sons by second marriage.

7601   Ellen Eady Walrod, born Jan. 27, 1851; married, April 18, 1867, Alden O. Mudge, a dentist; three children.

7602   Electa Elizabeth Walrod, born Feb. 27, 1853.

7603   Horace Herman Walrod, born Oct. 24, 1854; married Amelia McConnell; he is a merchant; one daughter (Lela).

7604   Ruhama Viola Walrod, born July 14, 1858; married Dr. L. E. George, a dentist.

5908   NANCY[8] TYLER (Carley[7]), born in Shalorsville, O., June 8, 1835; married, 1851, John Walrod. Children:

7605   Frank Walrod, born Aug. 9, 1852; died leaving two children.

7606   Riley Walrod, born Sept. 9, 1854; married Philena Bardwell; nine children.

7607   Thalia Walrod, born Jan. 24, 1857; married Charles Howson; one daughter (Leola).

7608   Martha Walrod, born Aug. 19, 1863; died Aug. 19, 1872.

7609   Ward Walrod, born Oct. 19, 1873; married Ona Knight; one daughter (Melba).

5915   SARAH DRUSILLA[8] TYLER (Asahel[7]), born in Canandaigua, N. Y., May 18, 1823; married in Ravenna, O., September 10, 1844, Linus Ely, born in Deerfield, O., March 18, 1821, son of Ashley Ely (see *Ely Genealogy*). He is a bookkeeper and resides in Chicago, Ill.; resided a while in Alliance, O., where the children were born. Children:

7610   Frank Ashley Ely, born Jan. 1, 1855.

7611   Ralph Asahel Ely, born Aug. 22, 1861.

7612   Mary Ely.

5920   RUBY[8] TYLER (John Hazen[7]), born in Yates,

N. Y.; married, 1850, Silas Stevenson, of Kenton, O. Children:

7613 Hazen J. Stevenson; married and had a family; children married and had families living near Kenton.
7614 Charles Augustus Stevenson.
7615 Selina Levinia Stevenson.
7616 Horace Allen Stevenson.
7617 William Ward Stevenson.
7618 Laura Ella Stevenson.
7619 John Wright Stevenson.
7620 Margaret Stevenson.
7621 Frank Stevenson.

5921 LAURA EMMA⁸ TYLER (John Hazen⁷), born in Yates, N. Y., March 7, 1846; married, March 7, 1867, Thomas P. Evans, a farmer of Kenton, O.; son of David and Lavina (Price) Evans. The children were born in Kenton. Children:

7622 Soma Lydia Evans, born Dec. 14, 1867; married, Dec. 24, 1891, John E. Hanna, of Hardin, O.; two daughters and a son.
7623 Arthur Thomas Evans, born Feb. 7, 1869; married, Oct. 18, 1893, Avice Gary; one son.
7624 Loa Estelle Evans, born June 2, 1871; married, Oct. 15, 1896, Elmer B. Elsey, of Columbus, O.; one son.
7625 Asher Tyler Evans, born Aug. 17, 1872; married, Oct. 14, 1896, Minnie Ansley.
7626 Gertrude Laura Evans, born Sept. 11, 1874; died April 16, 1889.
7627 Alta Maud Evans, born Aug. 7, 1880.

5922 LYDIA ELLA⁸ TYLER (John Hazen⁷), born in Yates, N. Y., August 29, 1847; died in Yakima, Wash., August 20, 1895; married, April 10, 1869, Morris N. Mansfield, of Buchanan, Mich. Went to Yates, then to Ohio, thence, in 1884, to Yakima. Children:

7628 Dalton Mansfield.
7629 Minnie Mansfield.
7630 Myrtle Mansfield.
7631 Ralph Mansfield.

5923   JOHN JAY[8] TYLER (John Hazen[7]), born in Yates, N. Y., March 2, 1850; married (1), Ella Barnum, who died early in Yates; married (2), Annie Martin, of Yakima, Wash., from whom separated; married (3), Kate ——, of Yakima. He inherited his father's homestead in Yates, but on the death of his wife he moved to Yakima; after the separation from his second wife she took the children and he went to Central America, where he was engaged in mining three years; returned to the United States and in 1898 was engaged in developing mines in British America; his post office address is Portland, Ore.

CHILD, by first marriage:

7632   Burrie Tyler, born in Yates; died there aged five years.

CHILDREN, by second marriage:

7633   Willard Thurston Tyler, born in Yakima.
7634   Gilbert Martin Tyler, born in Yakima.

5930   D. ALONZO[8] TYLER (Royall[7]), born in Lake Mills, Wis. He is a farmer, living in Morningside, Sioux City, Ia. His wife (maiden name unknown) is a state evangelist of the M. E. Church. This record is from a letter dated in 1900. Children:

7635   Rosa Tyler, married Rev. A. S. Dean, of Harris, Ia.; is a singing evangelist.
7636   Jason Tyler, stenographer and bookkeeper in Sioux City.
7637   Gertrude Tyler, married C. H. Hall, a carpenter in Arthon, Ia.
7638   Meta Tyler, in college, in 1900.

5934   MAROSIE F.[8] TYLER (John Alfred[7]), born in Northfield, Vt., September 10, 1853; married, May 8, 1873, Eugene Smith. Children:

7639   Fred Smith, born April 22, 1874.
7640   Albert F. Smith, born Nov. 26, 1878.

5936   DELLA MAY[8] TYLER (John Alfred[7]), born in Northfield, Vt., November 8, 1858; died in Concord, N. H., September 30, 1892; married, September 4, 1884, George E. Tilton. Children:

7641   Sadie Dell Tilton, born Aug. 3, 1885.
7642   Rolla B. Tilton, born April 8, 1887.

5937   FRANK E.⁸ TYLER (John Alfred⁷), born in Northfield, Vt., January 4, 1862; married, June 27, 1891, Mabel E. Trask, of Bethel, Vt. Child:
7643   Evelyn A. Tyler, born Aug. 1, 1896.

5945   JOHN B.⁸ TYLER (Hazen⁷), born in Strafford Hollow, N. H., 1850; married, in Concord, N. H., November 26, 1874, Mary J. Breserahan, born in Concord in 1852; daughter of John Breserahan. The children were born in Concord. Children:
7644   Edward Hazen Tyler, died Sept. 28, 1882, aged over nine months.
7645   Charles H. Tyler, died Aug. 12, 1889, aged one month.
7646   Clarence E. Tyler, died Aug. 19, 1893, aged over three months.

5949   CHARLES COIT⁸ TYLER (Elisha⁷), born in Griswold, Conn., December 30, 1830; died in Cincinnati, O., May 5, 1865; married, 1858, Elizabeth Cogswell, stepdaughter of Hon. Roger Coit, and daughter of Osmand Cogswell, of Cincinnati; she died May 11, 1866. From his fourteenth year he was in mercantile business in Detroit, first as an employée; when he came of age he entered business on his own account. He became a prominent merchant, active in social, religious, and commercial affairs; he was particularly devoted to works of benevolence. Perhaps no one was ever better loved within his own sphere. Children:
7647   Anna Cogswell Tyler, born in Cincinnati, O., Oct. 4, 1859; was unmarried in 1898, living in Ithaca, N. Y.
7648   Osmand Cogswell Tyler, born Jan. 15, 1863; died Oct. 20, 1863.

5952   PROFESSOR MOSES COIT⁸ TYLER, LL. D. (Elisha⁷), born in Griswold, Conn., August 2, 1835; died in Ithaca, N. Y., Delember 28, 1900; married, October 26, 1859, Jeannette H. Gilbert, daughter of Jesse Gilbert, of New Haven, Conn. He was a descendant of several of the earliest and most conspicuous families of Connecticut. He was graduated from Yale College in 1857, and there began a course in theology which he concluded in Andover Theological Seminary. He preached 'for a few months in Owego, N. Y., and was pastor of a Congregational church in Poughkeepsie, N. Y., from 1860 to 1862. He went abroad for health, and returning in 1866 was called to the chair of English literature at the University of Michigan, where he remained until 1881, when he took the professorship of American History at Cornell University. In 1881 he entered the Protestant Episcopal church. His published writings are as follows: *Brawnville Papers*, 1869; *History of American Literature During the Colonial Time*, in two volumes, 1878; *Manual of English Literature*, 1879; *Life of Patrick Henry*, 1887; *Three Men of Letters*, 1895; *Literary History of the American Revolution*, two volumes, 1897; *Glimpses of England*, 1898. He has been a contributor to contemporary literature, and especially to *The Independent* and *The Nation*. In 1896 he declined a call to the head of Yale's English department. The *Literary Digest*, at the time of his death, called him " The leading historian of American Literature." It is said that if he had lived a few days longer, he would have been elected president of the American Historical Society, of which he was the founder. In the early days of *The Christian Union*, he was the literary editor. " Whether in the pulpit, in his responsible chair of the faculty, or writing with that delightful simplicity of style of which he was a master, he was guided by a lofty and unerring sense of duty, speaking with the aid of profound knowledge and exhaustive research. To sit under his teachings was an inspiration to the best that can be made of life." At the meeting of the 'Tyler family in Andover, Mass., in 1896, Professor Tyler was elected president of the Association. Degree LL. D. Wooster University, 1875; L.H. D. Columbia University, 1888.

CHILDREN:

7649   Jessica Tyler, born in Poughkeepsie, N. Y., Aug. 9, 1860; married, June 20, 1898, Willard Austen of Ithaca, N. Y.; he was graduated from Cornell University and became assistant librarian.

7650+   Edward Tyler, born in Boston, Mass., Jan. 3, 1863.

5953 OLIVE COIT[8] TYLER (Elisha[7]), born in Marshall, Mich., July 3, 1837; married, September 15, 1856, Professor Albert Miller, of Thuringia, Germany, who died March 20, 1896, aged seventy-five years; he was a teacher of Music and German in State Normal School, Ypsilanti, Mich. The children were born in Ypsilanti, except the two younger. She lives in Detroit, Mich. Children:

7651   Clara Miller, born Dec. 4, 1857; resides at home.

7652   Albert Edward Miller, born Sept. 21, 1861; married, Nov. 11, 1896, Bessie George Wilkinson, of Marquette, Mich., daughter of James M. and Harriet (Conklin) Wilkinson; resides in Marquette.

7653   Charles Tyler Miller, born Sept. 18, 1865; married, Aug. 30, 1898, Pauline Pope, of Detroit, Mich.; daughter of Willard S. and Julia B. Pope; lives in Detroit.

7654   Mary Greene Miller, born Aug. 8, 1868; died Aug. 20, 1868.

7655   Wilhelm Miller, born in Virginia, Nov. 14, 1869.

7656   John Tyler Miller, born in Detroit, Mich., March 15, 1872; died Sept. 18, 1881.

3

5955 MAJOR JOHN[8] TYLER (Elisha[7]), born in Burlington, Mich., July 19, 1841; died in Dearborn, Mich. (near Detroit), August 3, 1889; married, 1864, Fanny Barrows, daughter of Hon. Isaac Barrows, Mayor of Detroit; she died March 4, 1882. He entered Company A, 1st Mich. Infantry, as a private, for three months' service, May, 1861; mustered out August 7, 1861; first lieutenant 17th Infantry, June 17, 1862; captain, January 24, 1863; he was in the first Battle of Bull Run, and in the battles of South Mountain, Antietam, and Fredericksburg, and engaged in the siege of Vicksburg, capture of Jackson, Miss., and the Battle of Campbell's Station, where he lost his left arm; after that he was made captain of the Veteran Reserve Corps, and, March 13, 1865, was brevetted major, U. S. Volunteers, " for gallant and meritorious service at the Battle of Campbell's Station, Tenn."; was first lieutenant 43d U. S. Infantry, July 28, 1866; brevetted captain U. S. A., March 2, 1867, " for gallant and meritorious services in the Battle of South Mountain, Md."; brevetted major U. S. A., March 2, 1867, for his services in the " attack upon Campbell's Station." He was transferred to the 1st Infantry, April 8, 1869; retired, May 29, 1874.

CHILD:

7657   Francis John Tyler, born in Buffalo, N. Y., May 14, 1878.

5960   MARY JANE[8] TYLER (William Belcher[7]), born in Tunbridge, Vt., March 19, 1823; married ―― Dimick. Children:

7658   Kate Dimick, born Dec. 25, 1848; married ―― Bucklin; lives in Bayard, Ia.

7659   Nate L. Dimick, born April 30, 1861; lives in Chicago.

5962   GEORGE W.[8] TYLER (William Belcher[7]), born in Tunbridge, Vt., January 16, 1827; died in Alameda, Cal., April 9, 1895; married ―― Frazer. Children:

7660   W. B. Tyler.

7661   George Tyler.

7662   Alla J. Tyler.

7663   Maud Tyler.

5963   SUSAN[8] TYLER (William Belcher[7]), born in Tunbridge, Vt., April 9, 1829; married, November 9, 1850, Thomas B. Thurston. Children:

7664   Frances Thurston, born April 14, 1852; died April 24, 1854.

7665   Marcia Thurston, born Dec. 17, 1853; died May 26, 1857.

7666   James Tyler Thurston, born Sept. 12, 1855; married, Feb. 22, 1882, Mattie Lyon; lives in Waterbury Center, Vt.; two sons (Howard and Henry).

5964   MARCIA[8] TYLER (William Belcher[7]), born in Tunbridge, Vt., September 18, 1830; died February 6, 1895; married ―― Morse. Child:

7667   A. C. Morse, born Oct. 31, 1857; a farmer and lives in Burke, N. Y.

5977   WILLIAM BARNEY[8] TYLER (John B.[7]), born in Liverpool, O., February 20, 1840; married, July 24, 1859, in

Ada, O., Susan Cahill, born November 10, 1840. In 1898 he lived in Benton Harbor, Mich., and is a fruit grower. The three elder children were born in Ada. Children:

7668   John Tyler, born April 13, 1860; died May 29, 1860.
7669   Sarah Eliza Tyler, born June 26, 1862; married, Dec. 5, 1880, Wendell P. Emery, of Bainbridge, Mich.
7670+   Iva Marie Tyler, born June 10, 1866.
7671   Ida Viola Tyler, born in Bainbridge, Mich., June 8, 1871; lived in South Bend, Ind., in 1898.
7672   Melvin Dunning Tyler, born in Riverside, Mich., July 21, 1877; employed on the railway in Anderson, Ind.

5979 EMILY JANE[8] TYLER (Benjamin[7]), born in Tunbridge, Vt., September 2, 1835; married James A. Cook, of Preston, Conn. Children:

7673   Jennie T. Cook, born in Preston; married, Aug. 3, 1893, John E. Thomas; a daughter (Hannah L.).
7674   Sarah C. Cook, born in Preston.

5980 LEVI ECKFORD[8] TYLER (Benjamin[7]), born in Tunbridge, Vt., June 13, 1837; died in Prescott, Conn., 1885; married ——. He was a lieutenant in the 1st Conn. Cavalry, in the Civil War; had two bad wounds and drew a pension. Child:

7675   Eckford W. Tyler, lives in New York City.

6009 JOSEPHINE[8] TYLER (Frederic William[7]), born in Griswold, Conn., February 11, 1841; died December 25, 1900, in Ravenswood, Ill.; married, May 1, 1866, Bradford H. Rogers, of Norwich, Conn., who died November 4, 1895. The children were born in Norwich. Children:

7676   Annie Rogers, born Oct. 3, 1867; died Jan. 22, 1871.
7677   Carl Bradford Rogers, born April 11, 1875; living in Ravenswood with mother in 1896.

6014 FRANK[8] TYLER (Frederic William[7]), born in Griswold, Conn., May 7, 1856; married Emma Beebe. He is a farmer, living in Norwich, Conn. Child:

7678   Caroline Elizabeth Tyler, born Sept., 1880.

6046 JOSEPH[8] TYLER (Joseph Cogswell[7]), born in

Griswold, Conn., May 20, 1852; married (1), March 6, 1871, Sarah Elizabeth Main, daughter of Charles E. and Sarah (Crary) Main, of Voluntown, Conn., from whom he was divorced; married (2), November 5, 1894, Louise Mary Strout, daughter of Elisha and Sarah (Haskell) Strout, of Standish, Me. The two younger children were born in Voluntown.

CHILDREN, by first marriage:

7679   Elmer J. Tyler, born in Griswold, June 14, 1876; was living in Voluntown in 1896.

7680   Mary E. Tyler, born Nov. 12, 1880; died Aug. 20, 1889.

7681+   Carrie Tyler, born Jan. 5, 1883.

6048   EMMA ISORA[8] TYLER (Dwight Ripley[7]), born in Cleveland, O., October 5, 1855; married, March 6, 1877, Rufus Winslow Walton, born in Walton's Mills, O., May 19, 1843. The children were born in Uhrichsville, O. Children:

7682   Joseph Dwight Walton, born April 13, 1880; married, June 3, 1905, Mrs. Margaret Emma (McCoy) Bocatius, who was born in Charleston, W. Va., Nov. 20, 1878.

7683   Mary Tyler Walton, born Oct. 8, 1883.

6049   EDWARD DWIGHT[8] TYLER (Dwight Ripley[7]), born in Uhrichsville, O., June 8, 1875; married, August 28, 1902, Gertrude Florence White, born in Chicago, Ill., September 3, 1882. Child:

7684   Alice Gertrude Tyler, born June 16, 1905.

6050   FLORENCE IRENE[8] TYLER (Dwight Ripley[7]), born in Uhrichsville, O., May 22, 1878; married, September 26, 1905, James M. Evans, born in Bolivar, O., September 25, 1877. Child:

7685   Elizabeth Tyler Evans, born in Beloit, Wis., Dec. 7, 1906.

6051   FRANK JOHNSON[8] TYLER (George[7]), born in Griswold, Conn. July 7, 1863; married, January 24, 1894, Isabel Palmer, born August 16, 1869; daughter of Edwin A. Palmer, of Warren, O. He was interested in the manufacture of agricultural implements until 1900 when he retired, but at the present time is actively interested in the manufacture of automobiles. He resided in Waltham, Mass., until 1898, when he removed to the Aberdeen district of Boston. Children:

7686 Philip Palmer Tyler, born in Waltham, Mass., Nov. 15, 1895.

7687 Arthur Bromley Tyler, born in Boston, Mass., May 12, 1897.

6082 WALTER BANCROFT⁸ TYLER (Charles⁷), born in Baltimore, Md., March, 1870; married, October 20, 1891, Ida Etheridge Ferguerson. The children were born in Baltimore. Children:

7688 Helen Marquis Tyler, born Feb. 19, 1893.

7689 Virginia Etheridge Tyler, born Sept. 23, 1894.

7690 Charles Tyler, born June 27, 1896.

7691 Walter Bancroft Tyler, born July 10, 1897.

6157 LUTHER E.⁸ TYLER (Elijah⁷), born in Savoy, Mass., December 31, 1851; married Hattie Dickinson, of Florida, Mass. He is an engineer and electrician; in the city council and resides in Northampton, Mass. Children:

7692 Edward E. Tyler.

7693 Isabel Tyler, married Robert Risley, a plumber, in Northampton, Mass.; s. p. in 1900.

7694 Minnie Tyler.

7695 Arthur Tyler.

7696 Eugene Tyler.

7697 Clifton Tyler.

6171 WILLIAM HENRY⁸ TYLER (Henry P.⁷), born in Savoy, Mass., about 1845; died aged about thirty-two in Baltimore, Md.; married Fidelia Jane Bardwell, of Shelburne Falls, Mass. He was general manager in Baltimore for the Southern and Middle States for the Remington Typewriter. Children:

7698 William Henry Tyler, died aged eleven years.

7699 Paul Tyler, died aged six months.

7700 Margaret Elizabeth Tyler, born in Elizabeth, N. J., Sept. 4, 1872; in 1900 was living in Boston, unmarried, at Willard Settlement.

6207   WILLIAM DOWLIN[8] TYLER (Leander Ansel[7]), born in Oil City, Pa., June 24, 1865; married, October 23, 1892, Mattie Hopkinson, of St. Clair, Pa. He was graduated from Lafayette College in 1888; a member of the D. U. Society; took charge of engineer corps as mine inspector, and assistant land agent with Flat Top Coal Company, Bramwell, W. Va., where his children were born. Children:

7701   Joseph Hopkinson Tyler, born and died July, 1893.
7702   Stuart Croasdale Tyler, born June, 1894.
7703   William Dowlin Tyler, born 1895 or 1896.
7704   Edgar Phillips Tyler, born 1897.

6232   ALBERT WINSLOW[8] TYLER (Albert Winslow[7]), probably born in Washington, D. C.; died there June, 1893; married May Van Arnum, who married again after his death. He was employed as an engineer in the United States Navy in Washington. He was a fine pianist and composer. Child:

7705   Ralph Van Arnum Tyler, born in Washington, D. C.; died Feb. 16, 1892, aged sixteen months.

6234   REV. C. W.[8] TYLER (William P.[7]), born in Dimock, Pa., August 2, 1861; married in Rochester, N. Y., October 12, 1895, Laura Hoag; was residing in 1901 in West Sparta, N. Y. Child:

7706   Ralph Tyler, born in North Collins, N. Y., Feb. 4, 1897.

6235   EDITH[8] TYLER (William P.[7]), born in Dimock, Pa., July 9, 1863; married, December 1, 1887, W. H. Everett, of Binghamton, N. Y. The children were born in Binghamton. Children:

7707   Clare Everett, born Nov. 5, 1889.
7708   Leon Everett, born Oct. 5, 1892.
7709   Lena Everett, twin to Leon.

6281   WINNIFRED PEARL[8] TYLER (Rush H.[7]), born in Wadsworth, O., June 21, 1876; married, December 25, 1895, De Forrest R. Wall, a teacher in Sharon Center, O. Children:

7710   Laura La V. Wall, born Aug. 9, 1896.

7711   Harold M. Wall, born May 1, 1898.
7712   Hazel M. Wall, born Oct. 5, 1900.

6307   HENRY JUDSON[8] TYLER (Jared[7]), born in Harford, Pa., February 24, 1832; died December 7, 1878; married, September 28, 1857, Julia A. Coughlan, born June 30, 1838; daughter of Obed G. and Hannah (Guild) Coughlan (see *Guild Genealogy*). Child:
7713   Mary Emeline Tyler, born Aug. 5, 1862; married Dr. William W. Fletcher.

6308   JOHN WADSWORTH[8] TYLER (Jared[7]), born in New Milford, Pa., July 6, 1834; died in Rutherford, N. J., February 15, 1898; married, August 19, 1860, Alpha D. Waldron, born in Harford, Pa., March 9, 1835. He lived in New Milford and Scranton, Pa., and in Rutherford, N. J. The three elder children were born in New Milford, the others in Scranton. Mr. Tyler was in the Erie Railway mileage office in Jersey City for seventeen years previous to his death. Children:
7714   Daughter, born July 15, 1861; died the same day.
7715   Arthur Edward Tyler, born Feb. 23, 1863; died in Scranton, March 22, 1869.
7716   Charles Henry Tyler, born Aug. 14, 1866; an electrician; was for several years a clerk in the offices of the Erie Railway.
7717   Ray Waldron Tyler, born March 24, 1870; was a printer; now with the Prudential Insurance Company.
7718   Sally Bradford Tyler, born Aug. 13, 1875; died in Rutherford, April 24, 1893.

6310   EDWARD JOB[8] TYLER (Jared[7]), born in Harford, Pa., April 13, 1841; married (1), September 11, 1865, Caroline Stanley Miller, born February 19, 1842; died March 21, 1872; married (2), Mrs. Susan (Hill) Morris. He lives in New Milford, Pa. Children:
7719   Hannah Miller Tyler, born June 23, 1866.
7720   Albert Wadsworth Tyler, born June 19, 1868.
7721   Fanny Augusta Tyler, born March 8, 1872.

6313   COLONEL MASON WHITING[8] TYLER (William Seymour[7]), born in Amherst, Mass., June 17, 1840; died in New York City, July 2, 1907; married, December 29, 1869, Eliza Margaret Schroeder of New Milford, Conn., born in New York City, February 8, 1834; died in Plainfield, N. J., October 14, 1906; daughter of Rev. John Frederick Schroeder, D. D., an able and learned minister of Trinity Parish, New York City. Mrs. Tyler's mother was Caroline Maria Boardman; daughter of Hon. Elijah Boardman, of New Milford, Conn. (a Revolutionary soldier and United States senator; he was grandson of Rev. Daniel Boardman, one of the earliest graduates of Yale College, and the first minister of New Milford. Mrs. Elijah Boardman was Mary Anna Whiting, sister of Mason Whiting, whose noted ancestry has been mentioned under the title of Professor W. S. Tyler).

Colonel Tyler prepared for college at Amherst Academy and at Williston Seminary, Easthampton, Mass. He entered Amherst College in 1858, where he was a member of the Psi Upsilon fraternity, to which his father, his three brothers, and his two sons have also belonged, and in which he always took the greatest interest, being prominent in its councils, and earnestly active in its welfare. In scholarship he stood well. He was Commencement orator, and a member of the Phi Beta Kappa Society. From 1860 to 1862 he was also class president. On July 10, 1862, he was graduated with the degree of A. B., and three years later received the degree of A. M.

Immediately on graduating, July 30, 1862, he entered military service in the Civil War, and was mustered as second lieutenant 36th Mass. Volunteers. On August 13, 1862, as first lieutenant, he was transferred with the company which he had recruited and which became Company F, to the 37th Mass. Volunteers. With this regiment he served with distinction until the end of the war. This regiment was attached to the Sixth Army Corps, then in the Army of the Potomac, which was detached to serve under Sheridan in the Shenandoah Valley. He was commissioned captain in this regiment January 17, 1863; brevetted major of U. S. Volunteers, September 19, 1864, for distinguished gallantry in the Battle of Winchester, Va.; made major of the regiment, March 4, 1865, commissioned by the Governor as its lieutenant-colonel, May 4, 1865, and as its colonel, June 26, 1865, but could not be remustered, although in command of the regiment because the losses had depleted the ranks below the numbers required by the U. S. Government for those appointments. He was mustered out and honorably discharged, July 1, 1865. He took part in the following engagements; operations of Fredericksburg, December 11 to 14, 1862; Burnside's "Mud Campaign," January 20 to 23, 1863; second Fredericksburg and Marye's Heights, May 2 and 3, 1863; Salem Church, May 3 and 4, 1863; Gettysburg, July 2 and 3; Funkstown, July 11; Rappahannock Station, November 8; Mine Run, November 29; Wilderness, May 5 to 9, 1864; Spottsylvania, May 12 to 18, 1864; North Anna, May 24 and 25; Cold Harbor, June 2 to 4; Petersburg, June 15 to 19; Weldon Railroad, June 21; Reams Station, June 29; Fort Stevens, July 11 and 12; Charlestown, August 21; Opequan, September 19; Cedar Creek, October 19; Hatcher's Run, February 6, 1865; Dabney's Mills, February 7; Forts Stedman and Wadsworth, March 25, 1865. These with several skirmishes numbered thirty in all.

Colonel Tyler's regiment had an enrollment of 1324 men, and lost 588 killed or wounded and 169 killed or died of wounds (12.7%). It was one of the *Three Hundred fighting Regiments* enumerated in Colonel Fox's *Regimental Losses in the American Civil War*. Colonel Fox names twelve battles as the bloodiest of the war. Colonel Tyler was engaged in seven of these twelve. He was wounded in the chin September 19, 1864, and March 26, 1865, in the right knee. He served on General Neill's staff from May 15 to June 30, 1864, and was Provost Marshall at Winchester, Va., from September 19 to December 18, 1864. His regiment was the first to arrive in New York City to quell the draft riots.

At the Battle of Spottsylvania Colonel Tyler's regiment supported the salient of the Bloody Angle twenty-two consecutive hours during which time "all Grant's toilers in the ditch were relieved except the 37th Massachusetts" (*Massachusetts Historical Society, Military History of the War*, Vol. 4, p. 66). Fifty volunteers were called for to "rush inside the angle and drive the enemy from the traverses." Colonel Tyler volunteered to lead the party, but the order was countermanded just as the assault was starting. In the Russo-Japanese War such parties were frequent and were regarded as details for death. So, in this instance, it was considered by every man who volunteered.

Colonel Tyler studied law in Columbia College Law School 1865-1866; was admitted to the bar in 1866, after which he practiced three years in the law office of Evarts, Southmaid and Choate. In 1869, he formed a partnership with General Henry Edwin Tremain, under the firm name of Tremain & Tyler. In 1893 he formed a new partnership under the name of Tyler and Durand, and in 1903 that of Tyler & Tyler, consisting of himself and his two sons, William S. and Cornelius B.

He conducted many important cases, one of the most famous of which was the suit of Marie vs. Garrison, resulting in the recovery of over a million dollars. Tremain and Tyler were attorneys for the importers in the famous " hat trimmings " cases—Hartranft vs. Langfeld (*125 U. S. 128*) ; Robertson vs. Edelhoff (*132 U. S. 614*) ; Cadwalader vs. Wanamaker (*149 U. S. 532*) ; Walker vs. Seeberger (*149 U. S. 541*), and Hartranft vs. Meyer (*149 U. S. 544*), resulting in the recovery by his firm of several million dollars from the government. They were the counsel in the sugar importation cases, Whitney vs. Robertson (*124 U. S. 190*). He was also prominent in the Removal Cases (*100 U. S. 457*), and as counsel in Pacific Railroad vs. Ketchum (*101 U. S. 289*). He was connected with important business enterprises. He was president of the Cumberland Coal and Iron Company, and director of the Columbus and Hocking Coal and Iron Company. He was many years director and vice-president of the Rossendale, Reddaway Belting and Hose Company. But he was most active in public enterprises and benevolences, particularly in Plainfield, N. J., where he made his home from 1870 until his death in 1907. He was instrumental in founding the Plainfield Public Library and Reading Room in 1880, the second to be founded in the State of New Jersey, and of this he was president until his death. He was promoter and first president of the Organized Aid Association of Plainfield and North Plainfield. He was also one of the early trustees of the Muhlenberg Hospital, president of the Music Hall Association, and president of the Anti-Racetrack Association of New Jersey. No matter of public interest in Plainfield, where he resided went without his support. He was also one of the trustees of Amherst College. His former law partner, General Tremain, says of him:

" His was one of those rare natures who, in business or in social life radiates the benevolences of humanity and goodness and peace, that dispel the shadows of evil. He was a patriot-soldier, an honored citizen, a beloved husband and father."

He was a member of the society of the Mayflower Descendants in New York and New Jersey and governor of the New Jersey society, and of the societies of the Sons of the Revolution, Colonial Wars, and Colonial Governors, and a member of the N. Y. Commandery of the Loyal Legion, and numerous other societies and clubs. The children were born in Plainfield.

CHILDREN:

7722   Mason Whiting Tyler, born July 24, 1872; died Aug. 17, 1872.

7723+   William Seymour Tyler, born Oct. 18, 1873.

7724+   Cornelius Boardman Tyler, born Nov. 15, 1875.

6314 WILLIAM WELLINGTON[8] TYLER (William Seymour[7]), born in Amherst, Mass., October 24, 1841; died in Plainfield, N. J., at the home of his brother Mason, May 4, 1903; married (1), September 12, 1872, Sallie Brakeley Sherrerd, born September 22, 1851; died September 18, 1882; daughter of Dr. John B. Sherrerd, of Scranton, Pa.; married (2), October 15, 1885, Nellie Ramburgher Bickings, born April 5, 1860; daughter of John Bickings, of Norristown, Pa. He prepared for college at Amherst Academy and Williston Seminary and was graduated from Amherst College A. B. in 1864. He learned the machinist trade and worked as hydraulic engineer with the Ames Manufacturing Company, Chicopee, Mass., 1864-1870; was engineer and member of a firm of manufacturers of turbine water wheels, Mt. Holly, N. J., 1870-1878. He moved to Dayton, O., and again to York, Pa., where he spent the last two years of his life. He was authority on hydraulic and mechanical engineering and was employed as an expert in the litigation over the water rights connected with the Chicago drainage canal and other important cases. His paper on the "Evolution of the American Type of Water Wheel," read before the Western Society of Engineers in Chicago, 1898, received high commendation. He was deeply interested in religious work and the Y. M. C. A., and had considerable local reputation for his talks before Sunday schools. The two elder children were born in Mt. Holly, N. J.

CHILDREN, by first marriage:

7725   Amelia Whiting Tyler, born Jan. 17, 1875; was graduated from Smith College A. B. 1895; resides with
Professor Henry M. Tyler.

7726   John Sherrerd Tyler, born Nov. 17, 1881; married,
May 25, 1905, Daklah Irene Fruhauf; daughter
of Alfred A. Fruhauf; one daughter (Amelia Whiting).

CHILD, by second marriage:

7727   Nellie Edwards Tyler, born in Dayton, O., Sept. 10,
1889; is a student at Smith College, class of 1912.

6315 PROFESSOR HENRY MATHER[8] TYLER,
D. D. (William Seymour[7]), born in Amherst, Mass., November
18, 1843; married, July 30, 1872, Mary Frances Disbrow, of
Galesburg, Ill., born January 7, 1843; daughter of Henry Van
Dyke and Harriet (Cummings) Disbrow. In 1860 he entered
Williston Seminary to fit for college and was graduated from
Amherst, A. B. 1865, A. M. 1868, and D. D. 1902; he was
teacher at Williston Seminary 1865-1866; studied at the University of Halle and traveled in Greece 1866-1868; Walker
instructor in Latin at Amherst 1868-1869; was professor of
Greek and German at Knox College, Galesburg, 1869-1872;
was ordained May 6, 1872, and pastor of the Calvinistic church
in Fitchburg, Mass., 1872-1877; has been professor of Greek
at Smith College, Northampton, Mass., since January 1, 1877,
and is Dean of the faculty; trustee of Williston Seminary;
member of the managing committee of the American School of
Classical Studies at Athens, Greece, and member of the Archeo-
logical Institute in America. He edited, with introduction and
notes, selections from the Greek lyric poets; re-edited and
revised William Seymour Tyler's edition of the Germania and
Agricola of Tacitus, 1878, and Plato's Apology and Crito,
1887; he wrote " a Greek play and its presentation," in 1891,
and is an occasional contributor to periodicals and prominent
as a leader in town and church. The children were born in
Northampton, except the eldest who was born in Fitchburg.

CHILDREN:

7728   Henry Disbrow Tyler, born Aug. 24, 1875; was graduated from Amherst College A. B. 1896; is a member of the New York bar.

7729 Marjorie Edwards Tyler, born Oct. 3, 1877; died Aug. 16, 1878.

7730 Donald Whiting Tyler, born July 5, 1879.

6317 PROFESSOR JOHN MASON[8] TYLER, M. A., PH. D. (William Seymour[7]), born in Amherst, Mass., May 18, 1851; married, July 12, 1883, Elizabeth Smith, born August 30, 1855; daughter of William Smith, of La Harpe, Ill. He fitted for college at Williston Seminary, Easthampton, Mass.; entered Amherst College in 1869, and was graduated A. B., and as valedictorian of the class of 1873; A. M. 1876. He was teacher at Phillips Academy, Andover, Mass., 1873-1874; was a student at the Union Theological Seminary in New York, 1874-1876. He then went abroad and was at Göttingen University, Germany, 1876-1878; at Leipsic, 1878-1879. Returning home in 1879 he became instructor in biology at Amherst, 1879-1881; in zöology and botany, 1881-1882, and has been professor of biology at Amherst since 1882. He received the degree of Ph. D. at Colgate University, Hamilton, N. Y., in 1888. In the spring of 1895 he was invited to deliver the Morse lectures at the Union Theological Seminary, and these were afterward, with some additions, published in book form under the title " The Whence and Whither of Man." He is prominent as a lecturer on the development and education of children, and the author of " Growth and Education," 1907; " Man in the Light of Evolution," 1908.

CHILDREN:

7731 Mason Whiting Tyler, born Oct. 28, 1884; was graduated from Amherst College A. B. 1906, and is a student of history at Harvard University.

7732 Elizabeth Stearns Tyler, born Jan. 17, 1888; was graduated from Smith College A. B. 1909.

6319 ARTHUR WELLINGTON[8] TYLER (Wellington Hart[7]), born in Pittsfield, Mass., March 14, 1842; died March, 1906, of pneumonia. He was graduated from Amherst College A. B. 1867; he then engaged in journalism in

New York City until 1870, then was editor of a newspaper in Meadville, Pa., for one year; he was assistant librarian at Astor Library, New York City, 1871-1876, and second librarian there in 1876. He was first librarian at Johns Hopkins University until 1879; in that year he was elected librarian of the public library at Indianapolis, Ind., and for four years was in charge of an institution doing the seventh largest work of any public library in America. From 1883-1885 he was engaged in cataloguing and classifying in the state library at Topeka, Kan., and the State University Library at Lawrence, Kan. In the fall of 1885 he took charge of the organization work of the public library in Plainfield, N. J., and in two years started it on a very successful career. In 1888, in the formation period of what is now Teachers' College, New York City, he was the first Dean of the faculty, and had charge of the executive work during the absence of the president in Europe. The next four years he spent in Quincy, Ill., developing an old subscription library into a free library. In 1893, after six months of special cataloguing of sixteenth and seventeenth century pamphlets at Columbia University, New York, he was employed at Wilmington, Del., in doing a work similar to that which he had recently completed in Quincy. In the fall of 1895 he organized from its foundation the public library of Branford, Conn., which had an endowment of $700,000, and continued to be its librarian until 1898. After traveling extensively in Europe he was assistant librarian of the new public library in Washington, D. C. (whose building was the gift of Andrew Carnegie), from 1902 until a short time before his death. Mr. Tyler was a devoted Bible student, and was particularly learned in the literature relating to the ancient codices of the Scriptures. He frequently delivered lectures on this subject. In 1871 and 1873 he did some important work upon the text of the Greek testament, the results of which were published in several numbers of the *Bibliotheca Sacra*, and were received with marks of strong commendation by literary newspapers in England as well as in America. "He was a fine Greek scholar, indirectly assisted the New Testament revisers, and published a book on *Studies in the Greek Testament*. For nearly forty years he had been a quiet but faithful and useful worker in the service of libraries and Christian scholarship." Mr. Tyler was unmarried.

6320 CAROLINE CARPENTER[8] TYLER (Wellington Hart[7]), born in Pittsfield, Mass., February 15, 1844; married, August 24, 1869, Rufus Pratt Lincoln, M. D., of New York City, born in Belchertown, Mass., April 27, 1841; died in New York City, November 27, 1900. Dr. Lincoln was graduated from Amherst College A. B. 1862, and Harvard College M. D. 1868. He was a boyhood friend and college classmate of Colonel Mason Whiting Tyler, with whom he had the closest friendship throughout life. Their Civil War Records in the 37th Mass. Regiment were substantially the same until they separated as colonels. He enlisted as second lieutenant of the 37th Mass. Volunteers, July, 1862; commissioned, August 27, 1862; captain, October 15, 1862; major, March 4, 1865; lieutenant-colonel and colonel, May 19, 1865; was wounded in the side at the Battle of the Wilderness, May 6, 1864; was also at Spottsylvania. In 1869 he began practice as a throat specialist in New York City, and became one of the most eminent in his line in the United States. After his death Mrs. Lincoln moved from New York City to Plainfield, N. J., where she built a house near that of Colonel Tyler. She is a person of great activity and executive ability and has always been prominent and generous in religious and philanthropic work. The children were born in New York City.

CHILDREN:

7733   Carrie Anna Lincoln, born Nov. 7, 1872; died April 25, 1873.
7734   Rufus Tyler Lincoln, born Feb. 8, 1874; died in Winnepeg, Manitoba, July 15, 1890, while on a pleasure trip to Alaska.
7735   Helen Lincoln, born Dec. 30, 1877; married in Plainfield, October 11, 1902, Frederick Herrick Schauffer, born Aug. 24, 1872. (Children: Caroline, born Jan. 11, 1905, and Frederick Herrick, born April 22, 1906.)

6332 MARY ELLA[8] TYLER (Ebenezer Denison[7]), born in Ararat, Pa., February 26, 1869; married, July 17, 1889, Fred B. Reynolds, of Binghamton, N. Y. In 1899 lived in Scranton, Pa., where the children were born. Children:

7736   Helen Mary Reynolds, born Feb. 14, 1892.

7737   Lilian Morris Reynolds, born Dec. 17, 1896.
7738   Henry Julian Reynolds, born Sept. 5, 1898.

6347   MALVINA[8] TYLER (Ralph[7]), born in Perry, O.,
June 16, 1833; married, December 1, 1853, R. E. Allison, a
farmer of Perry, where the children were born. Children:
7739   Genevieve Allison, born Dec. 28, 1864.
7740   Gertrude Allison, born Jan. 23, 1872.

6350   ANNA O.[8] TYLER (Ralph[7]), born in Perry, O.,
December 25, 1843; married, November 9, 1870, E. S. Belknap,
a farmer of Perry. The children were born there. Children:
7741   Ralph S. Belknap, born Aug. 14, 1871.
7742   Eliza M. Belknap, born May 21, 1875.
7743   John G. Belknap, born Jan. 29, 1884.
7744   Harry T. Belknap, born Oct., 1885.

6351   JARED H.[8] TYLER (Ralph[7]), born in Perry,
O., August 31, 1847; married, November 18, 1873, Carrie J.
Blair. The children were born in Perry; he is a farmer. Children:
7745   Frederick J. Blair Tyler, born June 15, 1875; was
            educated at the State University of Ohio.
7746   Florence Julia Tyler, born Sept. 15, 1882.

6354   JOHN H.[8] TYLER (Jared Whiting[7]), born in
Marcellus, N. Y., December 5, 1846; married, October 4, 1871,
Fannie M. Broughton, daughter of Samuel R. Broughton. He
lives in Jordan, N. Y., where he is the manager of the large
malt house of C. M. Warner Malting Company. Before this
he was with the firm of Peck & Tyler, manufacturers of engines
and agricultural implements in Jordan. He has been trustee
and member of the board of education and an elder in the
Presbyterian church. The children were born in Jordan. Children:
7747   Grace A. Tyler, born April 27, 1873.
7748   Bertha M. Tyler, born March 17, 1877.

6355   GEORGE S.[8] TYLER (Jared Whiting[7]), born in
Marcellus, N. Y., August 17, 1851; married, October 20, 1880,
Jennie Ray, of St. Louis. He was educated in the seminary

in Cazenovia, N. Y. He has been in the railway business since 1872, and in 1896 was assistant general freight agent of the C. & A. Railway, with a residence in St. Louis, where the children were born. Children:

7749 Alvaretta Tyler, born July 14, 1882.
7750 Simeon Ray Tyler, born Oct. 10, 1883.
7751 Jared Whiting Tyler, born Sept. 15, 1884.

6359 KATE VIRGINIA[8] TYLER (James M.[7]), born in Vicksburg, Miss., in 1853; married there, February 11, 1874, John R. Childress, born in Tuscaloosa, Ala., in 1847; son of Colonel James Childress. Was in the Commissary Department during the Civil War and later a railway man. She assisted in establishing the Mississippi State Normal School for girls, and is a proficient musician; in 1900 was residing in New Orleans. Children:

7752 John Read Childress, born in Canton, Miss., in 1878; is in the fire insurance business; unmarried in 1900.
7753 Kate Tyler Childress, born in New Orleans, Dec. 20, 1875; received diploma at the World's Fair in the Educational Department.

6364 CLARENCE ROLLIN[8] TYLER (Charles Rollin[7]), born in Bay City, Wis., July 5, 1859; married Martha G. Miller, of Prescott, Wis. Children:

7754 Dottie J. Tyler, died early.
7755 Rollin Tyler, died early.
7756 Fay Tyler.
7757 Clinton Tyler.
7758 Ruby Tyler.

6366 WILLARD GREENFIELD[8] TYLER (Charles Rollin[7]), born in Bay City, Wis., September 7, 1865; married Elsie Mealy, of Maiden Rock, Wis. The children were born in Bay City. Children:

7759 Clyde Tyler.
7760 Glynn Tyler.

6475 JAMES D.[8] TYLER (Danford[7]), born in Richmond, N. H., June 15, 1848; married, January 11, 1888, Anna S. Bassett, born June 28, 1856; daughter of Elisha Bassett, of

South Berlin, Mass.   He was educated in the Institute of Technology in Boston; is a farmer, land surveyor, and director in the Hudson (Mass.) National Bank, residing in Berlin, Mass. The children were born in South Berlin.   Children:

7761   Emily Grace Tyler, born Dec. 23, 1889.

7762   Danford Bassett Tyler, born Aug. 23, 1893.

6479   GEORGE WENDALL[8] TYLER (David[7]), born in Dedham, Mass., April 10, 1857; married, October 25, 1887, Lilla C. (Sibley) Wilton, born July 10, 1852; daughter of Kneeland Sibley, of Lawrence, Mass.   He is a farmer in South Berlin, Mass., where the children were born.   Children:

7763   David Sibley Tyler, born Sept. 29, 1889.

7764   Marion Sibley Tyler, born May 20, 1891.

7765   Charlotte Sibley Tyler, born March 10, 1893; died March 11, 1893.

6496   FRANK N.[8] TYLER (Oscar[7]), born in Washington, Utah, August 26, 1860; married, September 20, 1882, Adelia P. ――――, born in North Harmony, Utah, September 18, 1864; resides in Thatcher, Ariz., where the children were born. Children:

7766   Lucinda Tyler, born April 4, 1888.

7767   Ellen Tyler, born Aug. 18, 1894.

7768   Delbert F. Tyler, born Dec. 14, 1896.

7769   Jesse L. Tyler, born Aug. 5, 1899.

6497   OSCAR[8] TYLER (Oscar[7]), born in Washington, Utah, May 22, 1870; married, July 24, 1889, Mary A. ――――, born in Hardman, Tenn., October 25, 1870.   He resided in Washington, Utah, and later in Central, Ariz., where the children were born, except the youngest.   Children:

7770   Amanda B. Tyler, born Jan. 16, 1892.

7771   William O. Tyler, born Nov. 21, 1893.

7772   Willford Tyler, born Aug. 6, 1895.

7773   Gena M. Tyler, born in Washington, U., Aug. 20, 1897.

6503   WILFRED RICHMOND[8] TYLER (William Leigh Richmond[7]), born in Jacksonville, Fla., in 1873; married, 1897, Mabel Margaret Christian.   He lives in Jacksonville, where he owns a house. The children were born there. Children:

7774   Margaret Christian Tyler.
7775   Dorothy Irene Tyler.

6586   EDWARD JUDSON⁸ TYLER, JR. (Edward Judson⁷), born in Enosburg Falls, Vt., October 30, 1873; married, September 26, 1895, Ada Leone Chamberlain, born in Sheldon, Vt., July 2, 1874; daughter of Arthur W. and Cynthia (Chadwick) Chamberlain. He is editor of the Enosburg *Standard*. The children were born in Enosburg Falls. Children:

7776   Edward Judson Tyler, Jr., born Nov. 28, 1897.
7777   Hildreth Chadwick Tyler, born June 27, 1899.

6598   LEON F.⁸ TYLER (George W.⁷), born in Licking County, O., January 2, 1869; married, May 27, 1895, Eva E. Warner, born in Pueblo, Colo., July 23, 1874. In 1897 he was living in Granite, Colo., where he was a railway agent. Child:
7778   Lucile Tyler, born in Sellar, Colo., April 25, 1896.

6646   WILLIAM DEXTER⁸ TYLER (William F.⁷), born in Mansfield, O., February, 1852; married ——. He was a grain merchant in Wooster, O. Children:
7779   Jacob F. Tyler.
7780   Walter Tyler.

NINTH GENERATION

6662 JOHN AUGUSTUS^9 TYLER (George W.^{8}), born in Warren, Mass., October 24, 1832; died in Nevada, Mo., May 8, 1895; married (1), in Belton, Tex., April, 1861, Adelaide Smith, a native of New York City; she died in Bell County, Tex., in 1863; married (2), in Pleasant Hill, Mo., in 1866, Maggie A. Thomas. He moved to Bell County about 1857 and thence to Missouri, where he settled in Nevada in 1865. The children of the second marriage were born in Nevada.

CHILD, by first marriage:

7781   Nellie Tyler, born in Bell County, Tex., 1862; married in Nevada in 1885, Charles Thorn, and they lived there in 1907.

CHILDREN, by second marriage:

7782   George Richard Tyler, born Jan. 8, 1869; died in Nevada, Nov. 10, 1897; married Nettie Jones, of that place; no children.

7783   John Augustus Tyler, born Nov. 15, 1877; married, July 16, 1908, in Nevada, Ettie Vatelle James, daughter of James Edward and Elizabeth Eleanor James. They live in Nevada.

6663 HON. GEORGE W.^{9} TYLER (Orville Thomas^8), born in Coryell County, Tex., October 31, 1851; married, February 7, 1878, Sue Wallace, daughter of Dr. D. R. Wallace, of Waco, Tex., Mrs. Tyler being a native of Texas. Mr. Tyler was graduated from Salado College (Texas) in 1871; attended the University of Virginia, 1871-1872; was graduated at Lebanon Law Schools (Cumberland University) in 1874, with the degree of A. B. He began the practice of law in Belton, Tex., in 1874, and has been actively engaged in the profession in that place since that time, having a large civil practice. In 1906 his son Wallace became associated with him under the firm name of Tyler & Tyler. He was chosen presidential elector in 1884 on the Cleveland and Hendricks ticket; was elected State senator in 1888 and served in the Senate during the 20th and 21st Legislatures. He was elected Grand, Master of Masons in Texas by the Grand Lodge of Texas in 1890. He has a handsome house in Belton, a large plantation near the city and other important interests in the town and community. Children:

7784   Belle Hodges Tyler, born in Belton, Tex., Oct. 31, 1882; attended school at Baylor Female College, Belton, Randolph-Macon Woman's College, Lynchburg, Va., and Chicago Art Institute.

7785   Wallace Tyler, born in Belton, May 7, 1884; was graduated at Belton High School with first honor in 1900; after attending Randolph-Macon Academy, Bedford City, Va., he was graduated in the Law Department of the University of Texas in Austin, June, 1906; after two years of academic work there became his father's partner.

6667 ORVILLE THOMAS[9] TYLER, JR. (Orville Thomas[8]), born in Coryell County, Tex., March 9, 1861; married, October 5, 1887, Travis O. Strong. He lives in Belton, Tex. Children:

7786   Frederick Louis Tyler, born July 10, 1888; died Aug. 6, 1900.

7787   Carrie May Tyler, born April 29, 1890.

7788   Orville Thomas Tyler, Jr., born June 13, 1894.

6668 ANNIE CAROLINE[9] TYLER (Orville Thomas[8]), born in Coryell County, Tex., January 31, 1864; married, March 17, 1886, Andrew J. Embree, who is manager of the Embree Printing Company, of Belton, Tex., where they reside. Children:

7789   Louine Pearl Embree, born May 5, 1887; died Dec. 18, 1897.

7790   Evelyn Tyler Embree, born June 28, 1891.

7791   Andrew Tyler Embree, born May 28, 1902.

7792   Annie Caroline Embree, twin to Andrew.

6670 LOUINE CHILDERS[9] TYLER (Orville Thomas[8]), born September 15, 1866; married, March 28,

1888, Hon. Robert Lee Henry. Mr. Henry was assistant attorney-general of Texas from 1891-1895, and is now and has been since 1896 a member of Congress and a member of the Judiciary Committee. They live in Waco, Tex. Children:

7793   Orville Tyler Henry, born Feb. 13, 1889.
7794   Lelia May Henry, born Sept. 28, 1893.
7795   Robert Lee Henry, Jr., born Feb. 17, 1902.

6679 LOUIS SAMUEL[9] FISKE (Maria Louise[8] Hodges), born in Southbridge, Mass., February 14 or 15, 1844; married (1), April 24, 1883, Mary Dobson, born December 22, 1855; died February 28, 1886; married (2), May 10, 1894, Katherine Holmes Tucker. He fitted for Harvard College, but changed his plans for life and learned woolen manufacturing; after a time he formed the wool house of Louis S. Fiske & Co., in Philadelphia, Pa., a successful and progressive firm which has a world-wide reputation for honorable dealings. He is a member of prominent clubs and associations in Philadelphia and New York. (See *Fiske Genealogy.*)

CHILD, by first marriage:
7796   Sarah Dobson Fiske, born Feb. 11, 1886.

6687 EMMA AUGUSTA[9] TYLER (John[8]), born in Detroit, Mich., December 29, 1850; married, January 25, 1869, Lyman Gunn, of Amherst, Mass. In 1900 they lived in Palmer, Mass., where the children were born. Children:

7797   Charles Tyler Gunn, born May 17, 1879; lives in Palmer.
7798   Fred Lyman Gunn, born Dec. 16, 1873; lives in Palmer.

6690 FRANK EASTHAM[9] TYLER (Wilson Makepeace[8]), born in Vincennes, Ind., January 25, 1859; died in Alpine, Colo., October 29, 1899; married in Kansas City, Mo., November 22, 1881, Clara Danforth McLean, born in Randolph, N. Y., November 30, 1854; daughter of Benjamin and Ellen (Rumsey) McLean, of Warsaw, N. Y.; her father was a Canadian Scotchman. Mr. Tyler was graduated from Northwestern University in 1879. From 1882 to 1893 he was in the hide and wool business in Kansas City, where he carried on nearly the largest business of the kind in the United States.

Later he engaged in mining in Colorado. The children were born in Kansas City.

CHILDREN:

7799   Marguerite McLean Tyler, born May 24, 1883.
7800   Frances Ellen Tyler, born March 13, 1890.

6794   MARY ELIZABETH[9] TYLER (Edmond[8]), born in Brooklyn, N. Y., October 27, 1856; married, August 10, 1881, Frederick H. Vail, of Brooklyn. Child:
7801   Florence Tyler Vail, born in Brooklyn, Aug. 2, 1887

6808   FANNY ELIZA[9] TYLER (Frederick[8]), born in Warren, Mass., May 5 1853; married, 1871, Truman O. Stevens, of Turner's Falls, Mass.; he is a conductor on the San Lui Patosi Railway in Mexico. Children:
7802   Ernest Stevens.
7803   Eva Stevens.

6810   GEORGE ALBERT[9] TYLER (Frederick[8]), born in Warren, Mass., September 6, 1858; died in North Adams, Mass, August 13, 1897; married, November 27, ——, Alida E. Tylor, of Zoar, Mass. He was a railway man. The child was born in North Adams. Child:
7804   Lewis Frederick Tyler.

6847   EDITH[9] TYLER (George[8]), born in Murphysboro, Ill., June 22, 1874; married, February 4, 1892, S. B. McNeill, of Murphysboro, where the children were born. Children:
7805   Homer McNeill, born Dec. 5, 1892.
7806   Mary C. McNeill, born Oct. 22, 1894.
7807   Benjamin Tyler McNeill, born Oct. 14, 1896; died May 9, 1899.
7808   Laura C. McNeill, born Feb. 13, 1898; died Oct. 14, 1899.
7809   John McNeill, born June 10, 1900.

6848   JERUSHA[9] TYLER (George[8]), born in Murphysboro, Ill., October 25, 1876; married, May 19, 1891, J. N. Butcher, a merchant of Sato, Ill., where the children were born. Children:

7810   George Butcher, born March 15, 1892.
7811   Goldia A. Butcher, born Aug. 18, 1894.
7812   Bessie Butcher, born Jan. 16, 1897.

6907   RUTH[9] TYLER (Daniel M.[8]), born in Hebron, U., February 25, 1880; married Phineas W. Cook, of Harrington, U.   Child:
7813   Elzina Cook, born in Harrington, Dec. 18, 1896.

6936   SARAH LOUISE[9] TYLER (Thaddeus Warsaw[8]), born in Bath, N. H., January 13, 1853; married, in Lynn, Mass., October 3, 1877, Frank Soule, born in Lynn, October 13, 1855.   In 1898 they lived in Lynn.   The children were born in Nahant.   Children:
7814   Benjamin Floyd Soule, born Feb. 26, 1884.
7815   Frank William Soule, born Dec. 6, 1885; died Sept. 9, 1886.

6937   THADDEUS FRANK[9] TYLER (Thaddeus Warsaw[8]), born in Bath, N. H., September 20, 1854; married, in Mass., February 26, 1885, William Story Doah, born in Lynn, Lynn, Aug. 30, 1855.   Child:
7816   Shirley Holmes Tyler, born in Lynn, March 22, 1879; married, March 22, 1899, Dr. Frank J. Babbitt, born in Taunton, Mass., Nov. 26, 1869; they live in Lynn.

6939   CORA MARTIQUE[9] TYLER (Thaddeus Warsaw[8]), born in Bath, N. H., April 8, 1865; married, in Lynn, Lynn, Mass., July 12, 1877, Caddie Sophronia Breed, born in October 3, 1863.   In 1898 they lived in Wolfboro, N. H. Child:
7817   Charlotte Elizabeth Doah, born in Haverhill, Mass., April 6, 1887.

6948   ETHEL MADALENA[9] TYLER (George Lafayette[8]), born in Lynn, Mass., April 17, 1869; married, October 23, 1895, Walter Alden Washburn, born in Lawrence, Mass., March 4, 1872.   They live in Lynn, where the child was born. Child:
7818   Priscilla Rowena Washburn, born Aug. 28, 1896.

7016 WILLIAM EUGENE⁹ TYLER (Eugene⁸), born in Abington, Mass., February 6, 1866; married, October 16, 1894, Ella Jane Hutchinson. He lives in Brockton, Mass. Child:

7819   Gertrude Lavan Tyler, born in Brockton, Jan. 23, 1897.

7067 CELIA JENNIE⁹ TYLER (Edmond⁸), born in Cupertino, Cal., August 26, 1860; married, March 18, 1879, George W. Valentine, born April 1, 1855. Children:

7820   Pearl E. Valentine, born June 28, 1880; married, July 4, 1899, William H. Wilcox; one son (Edward).
7821   Orville E. Valentine, born Sept. 1, 1885.
7822   Guy A. Valentine, born Dec. 15, 1889.
7823   Harvey Valentine, born June 27, 1892.
7824   Ruby Valentine, born May 11, 1894.
7825   Leula Valentine, born Jan. 12, 1897.

7068 ELIZABETH IDA⁹ TYLER (Edmond⁸), born in Cupertine, Cal., October 4, 1864; married, July 20, 1887, Edwin H. Baker, a druggist in San Jose, Cal. Child:

7826   Elwin H. Baker, born Aug. 2, 1898.

7096 THOMAS HENRY⁹ TYLER, JR. (Thomas Henry⁸), born in Brookline, Mass., December 8, 1866; married, January 5, 1892, Florence E. Farquhar. He is a merchant in Boston. Child:

7827   Samuel Farquhar Tyler, born in Brookline, May 13, 1893.

7105 WALTER OTIS⁹ TYLER (John Otis⁸), born in Lynn, Mass., April 15, 1869; married, May 15, 1889, Addie B. Plaisted, born in Danvers, Mass., 1869; daughter of Edwin Plaisted. Child:

7828   Harry Russell Tyler, born in Salem, Mass., May 2, 1890.

7111 HENRY A.⁹ TYLER (Alvin⁸), born in Stafford, Conn., July 27, 1849; married, 1870, Etta Maine, of Willington, Conn. He lived in Florence, Mass., in 1899. Child:

7829   Marshall Henry Tyler, born in Stafford, June 12,

1873; married, June 28, 1899, Edwina Mabel Richardson, daughter of Edwin Richardson, of Cumberland Mills, Me. He was graduated from Amherst College, and in 1899 was a teacher in the Agricultural College, Kingston, R. I.

7112   ABBIE SOPHIA[9] TYLER (Alvin[8]), born in Stafford, Conn., October 26, 1853; married, October 26, 1869, George Thompson Fiske, a farmer and clerk in Staffordville, Conn., son of Calvin and Nancy (Young) Fiske. The children were born in Stafford. Children:

7830   May Fiske, born June 13, 1872; married William Clayton, of Stafford; a teacher in Ipswich, Mass.

7831   Belle A. Fiske, born Jan. 15, 1874; died, unmarried, October 18, 1896.

7134   EDITH HELEN[9] TYLER (Ashel[8]), born in Naples, N. Y., January 5, 1867; married, January 26, 1887, John S. Buck. The children were born in Naples. Children:

7832   Willis Ashel Buck, born Oct. 11, 1889.

7833   Laura Agnes Buck, born Aug. 15, 1891.

7834   Laurence R. O. Buck, born Oct. 1, 1893.

7835   Janeva Tyler Buck, born July 16, 1895.

7836   Carolyn Seamans Buck, born Feb. 5, 1901.

7135   CARRIE[9] TYLER (Henry[8]), born in Naples, N. Y., September 15, 1863; married, October 17, 1882, Albert Dunton, a musician. The children were born in Naples. Children:

7837   Gertrude Delia Dunton, born July 9, 1883.

7838   Carolyn Tyler Dunton, born July 14, 1887; died March 1, 1901.

7141   ARTHUR B.[9] TYLER (Byron A.[8]), born in Cohocton, N. Y., January 10, 1871; married, July 18, 1891, Mary A. Corey. He lived in Atlanta, N. Y., where the children were born. Children:

7839   Gordon Arthur Tyler, born Sept. 12, 1892.

7840   Leland C. Tyler, born Jan. 9, 1896.

7152   DOCTOR HOMER COLBY[9] BRIGHAM (Laura

E.[8]), born in Waitsfield, Vt., July 10, 1851; married (1), Nellie Atherton, of Waterbury, Vt.; married (2), Harriet Ferrin; daughter of Honorable Whitman Ferrin, of Montpelier, Vt. He was graduated from the New York Homeopathic College in 1872, and has practiced in Montpelier, Grand Rapids, Mich., and New York City; has been president of the Vermont Homeopathic Society, and vice-president of the Michigan State Homeopathic Society; also United States pension examiner; resides in Montpelier and New York City. The children were born in Montpelier.

CHILDREN, by first marriage:
7841   Roy Brigham; died aged about one year.
7842   Conrad Brigham; died aged about one year.
CHILD, by second marriage:
7843   Laura Brigham; died aged about one year.

7154 WILLARD IRVING TYLER[9] BRIGHAM (Laura E.[8]), born in Montpelier, Vt., May 31, 1859; died s. p. in Auburn, Cal., September 26, 1904; married, March 22, 1893, M. Hazel Morse, born in Concord, Vt., who married after his death, her cousin, Edwin E. Nelson, and resides in Texas. Willard was a natural leader in the local grammar school, and class orator of Grand Rapids, Mich., High School, 1878. He taught a year, then entered the University of Michigan, class of 1883; elected Freshman historian, principal contributor to the Sophomore *Oracle*, corresponding secretary Alpha Delta Phi; for his excellence in Greek and Natural History was advised by the professor of each to adopt that branch of teaching for his life work. Leaving college through ill health, he studied law in Grand Rapids, also, a year with the leading practitioner of Petosky, Mich., where, for services rendered the Pottowatomie Indians, he was adopted by the tribe under the name of " Kenoshaus " (Pickerel, big-mouth—hence orator).

Long a student of Shakespeare and excelling as a reader and amateur actor, he now accepted a flattering offer from Thomas Keene, the tragedian. The next five years were spent in touring the United States with such eminent players as Booth, Barrett, Sheridan, Haworth, Marie Prescott, and under " the Frohmans." He became a B. P. O. E. and a recognized " leading heavy," with bright prospects; but finding

the life too exacting for his nervous type, he returned to practice at Grand Rapids, incidentally writing the chapter " Bench
and Bar," for Baxter's *History of Grand Rapids.* In 1890
he removed to Minneapolis, where he continued in the law, and
was a chief assistant in the preparation of Judge Atwater's
excellent history of that city. He removed to Chicago in
1893 and continued there until 1901, when ill health sent him
to Phoenix, Ariz. During this period he was attorney for the
state board of dental examiners and interested also in important cases, one being a division suit among minors of the real
estate of his deceased father, valued at $100,000. He went to
Auburn in September, 1904.

He was descended from eighty different immigrants to Amer-
ica, among the earliest being Richard Warren, 1620, on the
Mayflower; Robert Bartlett, 1623, on the *Ann;* Governor
Simon Bradstreet, Governor Thomas Dudley, 1630, Cambridge,
Mass.; Thomas Brigham, 1635, on the *Susan and Ellen;* Job
Tyler, Rhode Island, 1638, Andover, 1640; Edmund Rice, Sud-
bury, 1638; the latest dates noted being those of George Geer,
New London, Conn., 1651; Walter Taylor, Amesbury, 1659;
and Francis Davis, Amesbury, 1673. Of the other immigrants
from whom he was descended, a few may be named: Robert
Allyn, Walter Allen, Thomas Brown, Aquila Chase, David
Fiske, Jacob Farrar, Edward Garfield, Thomas Hatch, George
Haywood, Robert Jennison, Thomas Loring, Simeon Mills, John
Prescott, Samuel Ryder, William Simonds, Henry Tewksbury,
Ralph Wheelock, John Whitcomb, Dr. Thomas Wells, John
Webster, Edward Woodman, etc. It will thus be noted that
he was descended from a large number of the important men
of the earliest colonial days. He had two lines of descent from
Thomas Brigham, the immigrant, of 1635—through Thomas[2]
on his father's side, and through John[2] on his mother side.

He interested the Tyler family to form a family association,
which first met in North Andover, Mass., September 2, 1896.
Other meetings followed,—New Haven, Conn., August 25, 1897;
Boston, Mass., September 7, 1898; Washington, D. C., September 13, 1899; Philadelphia, Pa., September 12, 1900, all
arranged and carried through with consummate skill by Mr.
Brigham, who was the secretary and historian of this organization. Meanwhile, he was gathering Tyler records as fast as
possible for the purpose of publication.

In 1893, he became the historian of the Brigham Family Association, formed that year, and he served this organization faithfully in this capacity until 1900, when he was made its secretary-historian. He published a report of seven meetings, replete with historical matter involving years of labor and invaluable to the family. In 1901 he was formally engaged to write *The History of the Brigham Family*, and was aided to some extent by records already gathered in considerable quantity. Scarcely had the arrangements for this work been completed, when Willard had occasion to go to a physician one day in Chicago, and to his utter consternation he was told he must leave Chicago at once and go to the far south-west and stay there indefinitely. His wife was told that he was a doomed man, but this he did not know. Leave Chicago! Think what that meant to him! There he had certain sure sources of income. He was a lawyer, with a special genius in certain lines of his profession, which was recognized by his brother lawyers, and it was an easy matter for him to earn good money for a comparatively small expenditure of time. He was attorney for a corporation; he was employed by a publishing house as a writer of biographies for a number of years. His father had said of him that Willard's talents would always procure him a competency, and acting upon this idea, the old doctor, leaving about a hundred thousand dollars, and having a second wife and young daughters, settled the fortune upon them. Like a brave fellow he settled his father's estate for the heirs, and went back cheerfully to his own business. When he went into exile, he had the Tyler genealogy well advanced and he carried, with his burden of ill health, material for completing two large family histories. With but small means the outlook was anything but cheerful. His faithful wife disposed of their effects in Chicago, and followed him. Mrs. Brigham had a genius for finding a silver lining to her clouds. She looked about her in Arizona—and promptly set up a chicken yard. Picture him now, if you can, with two histories on his hands, on each of which money had been pledged and paid, dependent on the small and irregularly paid income from the Brigham work, such sums as interested Tylers might advance him, and—his wife's chicken yard. If you know anything of the constant small demands on the pocketbook in genealogical work, you will recognize that it was something like the old tale of bricks without straw. Had health been given him, and life spared, think not but that every obligation he had made would have been met. Willard Irving Tyler Brigham was a high-minded, honorable man—but misfortune came to him from out of a clear sky, in a form which it was impossible for him to foresee or to provide against, and it found him at a point in his work where he needed health and a prolongation of life to fullfil the obligations resting upon him. *He did the best he could.* No one conversant with *all* the circumstances can doubt this. How bravely he battled for life that he might finish his noble tasks can never be sufficiently known to his kinsmen. His editors marvel at his erudition and industry. He toured New England and New York State on his bicycle more than once, going to large and small places for records. One summer he traveled in this way more than two thousand miles. The summer of 1900 he spent in Great Britain and France in researches. In fact, he contracted the disease from which he died in the damp stone buildings of London, searching for Tyler origins. The pathetic story of the later days of his life, when he kept at his work while struggling with the treacherous disease which conquered his brave spirit at last, is known to but few. With joy he recognized that the early symptoms of his disease disappeared under the influences of good care and climate; but with equal sorrow and depression he found that the attack was begun in another part of his system, and learned, at last, that hope must be given up. Not the least of his burdens at this time was that relating to the obligations he had incurred in the course of this work which had been so sadly hampered. The Tyler genealogy, begun that he might honor his mother's memory, was his undoing, but he made a brave fight, and what he completed was well done. Mr. Brigham was a member of the New England Historic Genealogical Society, Southern History Association, Society of Colonial Wars, Sons of the Revolution, British Record Society; also corresponding member of the New Hampshire and Maine Historical societies. His record as a genealogist rests on the two histories of the Tyler and Brigham families which he left ready for compilation, and the excellent work he did places him in the front rank.

7169   RACHEL[9] TYLER (Lyman[8]), born in Ayer's Flat, P. Q., January 17, 1861; married, January 1, 1879,

Willis H. Whipple, born November 27, 1856; a farmer and resides in Magog, P. Q., Canada. The children were born in Magog. Children:

7844 Ira L. Whipple, born Nov. 1879; died Feb. 11, 1900.
7845 Ida C. Whipple, born April 22, 1882.
7846 Alice H. Whipple, born Nov. 4, 1884.
7847 Ivers W. Whipple, born July 8, 1887.
7848 Fred E. Whipple, born June 15, 1890.
7849 Bessie E. Whipple, born July 26, 1893.
7850 Claude D. Whipple, born Oct. 10, 1896.
7851 Mable R. Whipple, born April 10, 1899.

7170 JOHN[9] TYLER (Lyman[8]), born in Ayer's Flat, P. Q., November 4, 1863; married, May 19, 1885, Blanche Morisett, born August 30, 1866. He works on the railroad and resides in Ayer's Flat, where the children were born. Children:

7852 George Tyler, born Sept. 16, 1886.
7853 Rose Tyler, born Oct. 21, 1888.
7854 Bertha Tyler, born March 24, 1892.
7855 Clarence Tyler, born July 19, 1894.
7856 Harold Tyler, born June 21, 1897.
7857 Blanche Tyler, born April 6, 1900.

7214 WILLARD CURTIS[9] TYLER (Leverett Winslow[8]), born May 2, 1856; married, November 7, 1882, Emma Jane Pulsifer, of Charlestown, Mass., where the children were born. Children:

7858 Emma Bickford Tyler, born Aug. 18, 1883; married in Brookline, Mass., Aug. 20, 1908, Louis Boussy Leonard.
7859 Marion Willard Tyler, born Dec. 19, 1885.

7223 MARTHA ELIZA[9] TYLER (Chaplin Greenleaf[8]), born in Charlestown, Mass., December 30, 1863; married, November 16, 1893, Edward A. Bassett, of Salem, Mass., son of John F. Bassett. He is an electrician. Child:

7860 Helen Chaplin Bassett, born in Lynn, Mass., Feb. 8, 1896.

7232 IRENE CHAPLIN[9] TYLER (George Prescott[8]),

born June 26, 1870; married, April 16, 1897, Tamotsu Fuwa, born in Kurume City, Fukuoka Province, Island of Kiushu, Japan; son of Yozo Fukushima, but was adopted when six years of age by a Buddhist priest by the name of Fuwa. He was educated in the Buddhist faith and in the Confucian schools and when sixteen years old he entered Chinzai Seminary, Nagasaki, mainly for the study of English, this being a Methodist Episcopal mission school. He was graduated there and spent some years in the study of Christian theology and was a local preacher in a Kumai church for a few years. In 1896 he came to America to study law and was graduated from the law department of Howard University, Washington, D. C., in 1898. Before her marriage, Mrs. Fuwa was librarian of Howard University. In 1898 her husband intended to enter the diplomatic service of Japan, but expected to practice law in Tokio before doing so. In 1899 Mrs. Fuwa joined her husband in Japan. Child:

7861   Hamao Fuwa, born in Washington, D. C., March 28, 1898.

7279   HATTIE OSGOOD[9] TYLER (William Baldwin[8]), born in Salem, Mass., March 2, 1862; married, October 26, 1889, Lewis Nason, of Danvers, Mass. The children were born in Salem. Children:

7862   Gladys Louise Nason, born Jan. 9, 1890.
7863   Osgood Tyler Nason, born Aug. 16, 1891.

7280   HERBERT[9] TYLER (William Baldwin[8]), born in Salem, Mass., January 16, 1867; married, November 10, 1892, Mattie Jane Kincaird, of Chelsea, Mass. Child:
7864   Mildred Allen Tyler, born in Salem, Feb. 12, 1894.

7352   MARCUS K.[9] TYLER (Marcus[8]), born in Hampden, Me., December 5, 1851; married, June 12, 1889, in White Plains, N. Y., Maria Ellis. In 1899 they lived in White Plains, where the child was born. Child:
7865   Ernest Ellis Tyler, born June 22, 1890.

7353   ESTHER E.[9] TYLER (Marcus[8]), born in Hampden, Me., October 3, 1853; married, August 2, 1885, George T. Earhart. The children were born in Hamilton, O. Children:

7866   John Carlisle Earhart, born Jan. 5, 1887.

7867   Georgia Earhart, born June 23, 1890.

7868   Robert Shenk Earhart, born April 8, 1889; died May 6, 1889.

7354   CHARLES A.[9] TYLER (Marcus[8]), born in Lawrence, Mass., December 14, 1855; married, October 15, 1885, in Salisbury Mills, N. Y., Lulu Clark.   Children:

7869   Esther Louise Tyler, born Jan. 23, 1888.

7870   Grace Helene Tyler, born July 13, 1894.

7366   HERBERT FERRE[9] TYLER (D. Waldo[8]), born in Chatfield, Minn., February 11, 1865; married ——.   He is in the flour mills with his father in Junction City, Kan.   Child:

7871   Donald Marsh Tyler, born in Marion Junction, S. Dak., Nov. 7, 1888.

7367   FREDERICK WALDO[9] TYLER (D. Waldo[8]), born in Winona, Minn., September 6, 1866; died in Dubuque, Ia., May 18, 1893; married ——.   The children were born in Epworth, Ia.   Children:

7872   Majorie Tyler, born Nov., 1887.

7873   Harold Tyler, born in 1889.

7377   MATIE[9] TYLER (George Burt[8]), born in New Boston, Ill., May 4, 1863; married John H. Hibbard, who went from Harvard, Ill., to Helena, Mont.; he is a topographer and made the official map of Montana.   The children were born in Helena.   Children:

7874   Mattie Florence Hibbard, born June 22, 1887.

7875   Alfred Tyler Hibbard.

7876   Harrell Harris Hibbard.

7397   ALONZO W.[9] TYLER (Alfred[8]), born in Salem, Mass., in 1864; married, March 29, 1886, Ada I. Adams, born in Harrison, Me., in 1866; daughter of Horace E. and Emily H. Adams.   He is a compositor.   Child:

7877   Mabel Chandler Tyler, born Jan. 20, 1889.

7428   BAYARD HENRY[9] TYLER (Henry H.[8]), born in Oneida, N. Y., April 22, 1855; married, October 3, 1883,

Charlotte Elizabeth Wiltsie, of Yonkers, N. Y., daughter of John A. Wiltsie, a banker of note of Yonkers. He began the study of art in 1877, in Syracuse University; in 1878 was admitted to the National Academy of Design in New York City; in 1879, at the close of his first year he won the class medal, The Elliott Bronze; he was graduated in 1882 and won the first prize, a silver medal, for drawing of full length figure; had a studio in New York City from 1882-1893; then at his residence in Yonkers, where he is a portrait painter and where his children were born. He exhibits annually at the New York Academy and had three exhibits at the World's Fair in 1893.

CHILDREN:

7878   Mary Spofford Tyler, born Feb. 10, 1887.
7879   Myra Joslin Tyler, born Feb. 9, 1891.
7880   Bayard Hermance Tyler, born Aug. 24, 1898; died Nov. 3, 1899.

7429   FRED A.[9] TYLER (Henry H.[8]), born in Oneida, N. Y., August 22, 1857; married ———. He is a member of the Pease Furnace Company in Syracuse, N. Y. Children:
7881   Bessie Eliza Tyler.
7882   Miriam Emelia Tyler.
7883   Frederick Harold Tyler.
7883a   Donald Tyler.

7444   WILLIAM NATHAN[9] TYLER (George Calvert[8]), born in Heath, N. Y., August 5, 1864; married Emma Helen Hoffman, born September 17, 1872; her family came from Belgium to Ulster County, N. Y. He was graduated from the Rhinebeck (N. Y.) De Garmo Institute; studied civil engineering; engaged in newspaper work for a time; was manager of the largest tobacco trade journal in the world. In 1899 was general agent of the National Acetylene Gas Company of Cleveland, O. Children:
7884   Arthur Stroebel Tyler, born Oct. 18, 1896.
7885   Leavenworth Hoffman Tyler, born July 29, 1899.

7446   GEORGE LESLIE[9] TYLER (Orrin[8]), born January 13, 1870; died July 31, 1899; married, January 6, 1896, in Farmingdale, Me., Lucretia H. Ring. He lived in Gardiner

City, Me., where he kept a gentlemen's furnishing store.   Child:
7886   Beatrice E. Tyler, born April 8, 1898.

7490   ARTHUR CLINTON[9] TYLER (Irving W.[8]),
born in Bristol, Conn., February 7, 1874; married, September,
1894, Stella M. Delavan, of New Haven, Conn.   He is in the
hardware business.   Child:
7887   Joseph Delavan Tyler, born May 25, 1896.

7541   FRED G.[9] TYLER (George Gardner[8]), born
August 9, 1872; married, September 2, 1893, Fannie A. Richardson, of Groveland, Mass., 'where they live and where the
children were born.   Children:
7888   Hazel Katherine Tyler, born July 17, 1894.
7889   Helen Osgood Tyler, died young.
7890   Vera Frances Tyler, born Oct. 6, 1899.
7891   Mary B. Tyler, born Dec. 13, 1903.

7593   GEORGE DURANT[9] TYLER (John Asahel[8]),
born March 9, 1847; married, July 16, 1882, Jennie Bowman.
Children:
7892   Tracey T. Tyler, born June 9, 1885.
7893   Charles Howard Tyler, born Sept. 19, 1888; died Feb.
           1, 1891.

7594   WILLIAM ASAHEL[9] TYLER (John Asahel[8]),
born September 12, 1848; married, September 14, 1869, Huldah M. Stafford.   He is a farmer.   Children:
7894   Kittie Maud Tyler, born July 17, 1870; married, May
           31, 1894, John W. Livingston; two children (Ruth
           R. and Helen M.).
7895   Clara Eva Tyler, born April 6, 1872.
7896   Bruce Tyler, born June 3, 1874; died May 2, 1878.
7897   Fanny May Tyler, born Feb. 14, 1877.
7898   Mary Josephine Tyler, born July 17, 1879.
7899   Georgia Edna Tyler, born Oct. 29, 1881.
7900   Harry Asahel Tyler, born Dec. 31, 1883.
7901   William Richard Tyler, born May 25, 1886.
7902   Raymond Tyler, born July 8, 1890.

7597   AMELIA EVELINE[9] TYLER (John Asahel[8]),

born August 3, 1855; married, November 20, 1872, Charles Roman, a steamboat captain. Children:

7903   Minnie Haha Roman, born March 7, 1874.
7904   Irvie Holly Roman, born March 19, 1877.
7905   Charlie Loyd Roman, born Sept. 3, 1879.

7598   CHARLES EDWIN[9] TYLER (John Asahel[8]), born October 2, 1861; married, March 17, 1883, Mary Newell. He is a railway engineer. Children:

7906   Phebe Ellen Tyler, born Jan. 6, 1884.
7907   Verna Tyler, born Sept. 19, 1886.

7599   HENRY FRANKLIN[9] TYLER (John Asahel[8]), born June 23, 1864; married, February 27, 1886, Kate E. Willet. Children:

7908   Elsie Grace Tyler, born April 15, 1888.
7909   Robert John Tyler, born July 6, 1889.
7910   Florence Amelia Tyler, born Sept. 24, 1891.
7911   Willard Willet Tyler, born Oct. 6, 1893.
7912   Freddie Willet Tyler, born March 12, 1897.

7650   EDWARD[9] TYLER (Moses Coit[8]), born in Boston, Mass., January 3, 1863; died in New York City, August 18, 1901; married, March 4, 1889, Susana Emilia Den, daughter of Don Nicholas Augusto Den, of Santa Barbara, Cal. Children:

7913   Ricardo Juan Den Tyler, born Jan. 26, 1890.
7914   Ynés Margarita Francisca Tyler, born Nov. 3, 1891.
7915   Rosita Maria Josefa Tyler, born March 24, 1893.
7916   Eduardo Arturo Coit Tyler, born July 7, 1894.

7670   IVA MARIE[9] TYLER (William Barney[8]), born in Ada, O., June 10, 1866; married, May 4, 1882, William H. Merrill, of Bainbridge, Mich. She travels for a publishing house and they reside in Riverside, Mich., where the children were born. Children:

7917   Mary Jane Merrill, born Nov. 12, 1884.
7918   William Loyd Merrill, born Jan. 27, 1886; died July 23, 1887.
7919   Child, born Oct. 12, 1890; died Oct. 20, 1890.

7681 CARRIE[9] TYLER (Joseph[8]), born in Voluntown, Conn., January 5, 1883; married, October 9, 1905, Maurice C. Stuart, born in Lord's Cove, King's Island, N. B., December 25, 1872. The children were born in Voluntown. Children:
7920 Howard Holmes Stuart, born Nov. 11, 1906.
7921 Harold Jennings Stuart, twin to Howard.

7723 WILLIAM SEYMOUR[9] TYLER (Mason Whiting[8]), born in Plainfield, N. J., October 18, 1873; married there, November 23, 1899, Ethel Van Boskerck, born February 5, 1879; daughter of George W. and Elizabeth (Rowe) Van Boskerck. He prepared for college at Williston Seminary, Easthampton, Mass.; was graduated from Amherst A. B. 1895; traveled in Europe in 1894; studied in Germany and traveled in Egypt and Palestine 1895-1896; studied in Columbia University Law School, 1896-1899; was graduated LL. B. 1899. He was admitted to the New York bar in 1898; practiced law with Evarts, Choate & Beeman one year; in 1903 formed a partnership with his father and brother under the firm name of Tyler & Tyler, which has continued since his father's death under the same name at 30 Church Street, New York City. Mr. Tyler has been a member of the Common Council of the city of Plainfield 1902-1908, and of the Board of Education since 1908, is Secretary of the Charity Organization Society of Plainfield and North Plainfield, and a director of the Rossendale Reddaway Belting and Hose Company of Newark. In New Jersey he is a member of the Mayflower Society. In New York City he is a member of the Bar Association, Military Order of the Loyal Legion, University Club, Phi Delta Phi Club, Psi Upsilon Club, New England Society and Railroad Club. The children were born in Plainfield.

CHILDREN:
7922 Margaret Rowe Tyler, born April 8, 1901.
7923 William Seymour Tyler, born May 16, 1904.
7924 Edith Edwards Tyler, born July 31, 1905.

7724 CORNELIUS BOARDMAN[9] TYLER (Mason Whiting[8]), born in Plainfield, N. J., November 15, 1875; married, December 29, 1908, at Pittsfield, Mass., Susan Tilden

Whittlesey, born November 21, 1883, at Florence, Wis.; daughter of William Augustus and Caroline Benton (Tilden) Whittlesey, of Pittsfield. He prepared for college at Williston Seminary, Easthampton, Mass.; was graduated from Amherst College A. B. 1898; studied at Columbia University Law School 1898-1901, and was graduated LL. B. and admitted to the New York bar in 1901. He was one of the founders of the *Columbia Law Review* in 1901, and treasurer of the first board of editors. He practiced one year with the firm of James Schell and Elkus. In 1903 he formed a partnership with his father and brother under the firm name of Tyler & Tyler, which has continued since his father's death under the same name at 30 Church Street, New York City. He traveled in Europe in 1894, in Japan in 1900, in Alaska in 1901, and in Central America and the West Indies in 1909. He is president and director of the Liberty Realty Company of Seattle, Wash.; secretary and director of the West Canada Land and Development Company; secretary, treasurer and director of the Jaffray Realty Company. He is one of the trustees of the Plainfield Public Library and Reading room, and director of the Plainfield Trust Company; a member of the Commandery of the District of Columbia, of the Military Order of the Loyal Legion, and in New York City he is a member of the Bar Association, Psi Upsilon Club, Phi Beta Kappa Alumni, Phi Delta Phi Club, Mayflower Society, New England Society, and Railroad Club.

INDEX

Bigelow, Nathaniel Perkins, 516
Bill, Hannah, 54
  Mary H., 354
Billings, Abigail, 172
  Elizabeth, 427
Billingsley, Maria L., 679
Billington, Rachel, 551
Bingham, ——. 107
  Byron, 576
  Mary, 576
Binney, Charlotte Hope (Goddard), 738
  John, 738
  Mary Woodrow, 738
  William, 738
Bird, Bertha I., 689
  Charles, 224
  David N., 689
  Hannah, 224
  Henry, 224
  Loretta, 224
  Mary Helen, 689
  Tristram, 224
  Tyler H., 689
Birdsall, Ernest, 454
  Esther, 454
  Frederick, 454
  Jennette, 454
Bisbee, Dalousie (Parish), 712
  Dolly K., 548
  Frances Harriet, 712
  Grace Dalousie, 712
  Harriet, 296, 316
  Henry Parish, 712
  Horatio, 548
  James, 712
  John, 296
  John Milton, 712
  Lora Louise, 712
  Nellie Fulton, 712
  Sarah Philbrick, 296
  Sumner Tyler, 712
  Warren, 712
Bishop, Almira, 605
  Diana, 470
  Hester, 93
  Irene, 244
  Paul, 133
  Rhoda, 272
Bissell, Asahel, 366
  Mary, 366
  Polly, 366
Bither, Benjamin, 154
Bixby, Albert R., 410
  Allen Tyler, 409
  Charles N., 410
  Esther, 410
  Franklin, 410
  George, 409
  Haley, 409
  Henry Hudson, 409
  James, 409

Bixby, Joseph H., 410
  Loring, 410
  Mary E., 410
  Moses, 409
  William H., 410
Black, Josiah, 308
Blacker, Catherine, 484
  David, 484
  Jack, 484
  Lelia, 484
  Muzetta, 484
Blackington, Anna, 106
  Pentecoast, 106
Blackman, Franciana, 691
  Hattie, 693
  Walter, 691
Blackstone, Carrie, 663
Blaess, Lily, 705
Blair, Carrie J., 762
Blaisdell, J., 267
  James, 132
Blake, Dorothy, 17
  George, 17
  John Lauris, 578
  Jonathan, 578
  Louisa Richmond, 578
  Mary Howe, 578
  Prudence, 17
  W., 164
Blakeley, George, 361
  Mary, 218
Blakeslee, Alonzo, 375
  Sarah, 375
Blalock, Sarah Esther, 625
Blanchard, Maria R., 244
Blanding Simeon, 202
  Spencer, 202
Blenthen, John, 309
  Joseph, 309
  Washington, 309
Blick, Mary H., 536
Bliss, Alfred Veasie, 720
  Charles E., 720
  Elias, 411
  Emeline J., 411
  George, 241
  George Willard, 652
  Harry Clay, 720
  Hiram, 720
  Loren Wallace, 652
  Lydia, 263
  Marcia Fessenden, 720
  Martha, 426, 432
  Nancy, 396
  Norman Willard, 652
  Polly (Hale), 720
  Timothy, 422
  Willard Flagg, 651
Blodgett, Joseph, 385
  Margaret (Rockwell), 70
  Zenas Arthur, 454
Blood, Bessie, 524

Cushing, Edward R., 665
  Ethalinda, 554
  Ethalinda (Edwards), 554
  Fannie, 665
  Joseph, 554
  Matthew, 554
  Peter, 554
  Samuel G., 665
  Stephen, 554
  Thomas, 554
  William Tyler, 665
Cushman, ——. 586
  Alpa, 240
  Daniel W., 240
  Eunice, 240
  Isaac, 166
  Jane, 240
  John, 240
  Lucretia, 240
  Porter, 240
  Sarah, 345
Custer, ——, 415
Cutler, Abbie Elizabeth, 672
  Abigail, 227
  Bethiah, 226
  Ebenezer, 227
  Flora I., 665
  Henry S., 630
  James, 227
  Joseph, 227
  Maria, 630
  Mary Ann, 482
  Mary J., 630
  Rensselaer, 629
Cutting, James, 261
Cutts, Elmer H., 726
  Laura L., 726

D

Daboll, Emily, 534
Dada, Mr., 627
Daggett, Mrs., 220
Daily, ——, 378
Dake, Helen W. B., 605
  John, 605
Dalbee, Willard Franklin, 633
Damon, Charles A., 429
  Charles H., 724
  Clarissa, 267
  Edward J., 429
  Frances L., 429
  George, 429
  Harrison S., 429
  Isaac Tyler, 429
  Jerome B., 429
  John, 429
  Martha Tyler, 429
  Mary E., 429
  Mary T., 429
  Thomas Henry, 429
  William C., 429

Dana, Charles, 497
  Charles C., 497
  Ellen L., 498
  Frank, 497
  Hiram, 497
  L. Frances, 498
  Louisa, 498
  Nellie, 497
  Ransom Stephen, 497
  Reed, 497
  Rodney, 497
  Ruth E., 498
  Stephen, 497
  William, 497
Danby, ——, 628
Dane, Emerson, 244
  George Willis, 244
  Joseph, 243
  Lucy Ann, 244
  Rebecca, 244
  Stillman Ayres, 244
  Warren, 245
Danforth, Calvin, 485
  Charles, 271
  Eben, 485
  Emily, 485
  Samuel, 130
Daniels, John, 176
  Loyal, 215
Davidson, Lyman, 646
  Peter E., 519
Davis, ——, 123, 294, 500, 549, 692
  Amanda, 263
  Amy, 323
  Anna E., 263
  Clara Emma, 560
  Cora A. B., 560
  Daniel, 246
  Della J., 491
  Dennis D., 468
  Ella Maria, 560
  Ellen A., 557
  Eliza C., 467
  Elmer, 549
  Emeline M., 330
  Fannie Elizabeth, 452
  Francis, 774
  Frank, 549
  George C., 468
  Gertrude Maria, 452, 676
  Grace, 549
  Helen, 493
  Henry R., 535
  Herbert C., 491
  Irene, 263
  Isaac, 491
  Jeremiah B., 467, 468
  Jonathan, 263
  Joseph, 504
  Joseph Henry, 560
  Joshua, 265
  Judith, 128

Finch, Flora, 493
  Nathaniel, 493
  Ruby, 493
  Vincent, 493
Fish, Susanna, 104
Fisher, Barney, 214
  Calvin, 214
  John, 66
  Sarah, 424
  Sunsanna, 104
Fisk, Daniel, 100, 101
  Della D., 457
  Ebenezer, 100
  Hannah, 100
  John, 100
  Josiah, 451
  Julia A., 500
  Martha, 17, 21
  Mary V., 451
  Robert, 100
  Samuel, 100
  Simon, 100
  Submit, 101
  Symond, 99
  William, 100
  Zilpha, 100
Fiske, Abigail, 100
  Arthur Tappan, 660
  Belle A., 772
  Calvin, 772
  David, 774
  Dorcas, 100
  Ebenezer, 100
  Elizabeth, 100
  Frank, 660
  George Thompson, 772
  John, 100
  John Quincy, 660
  Jonathan, 100
  Levi, 100
  Louis Samuel, 660, 768
  May, 772
  Moses, 100
  Nancy Young, 772
  Sally, 660
  Sally (Lyon) 660
  Samuel, 660
  Samuel Lyon, 660
  Sarah Dobson, 768
  Simeon, 100
  William, 660
Fitch, Daniel, 32
Flagg, Mary, 249
Flanders, Albert Vernon, 499
  Alice, 469
  Arthur C., 469
  Bessie, 469
  Charles, 469
  Elmer J., 499
  Emily, 499
  Fred H., 469
  George W., 499

Flanders, Herbert A., 499
  Joseph B., 499
  Lorenzo D., 499
  Mary Ann (Downs), 465
  Newton, 499
  Nora, 469
  Roscoe H., 469
Flansburgh, O. L., 718
Flavill, David, 471
Fletcher, Annie Y., 562
  Bertha M., 563
  Betsey, 234
  Betsey Tyler, 439
  C. C., 562
  Edward F., 641
  Elizabeth, 439
  Ellen C., 391
  Eva, 439
  Grace (Benton) 439
  Hattie, 439
  James Tyler, 439
  John A., 562
  Jonathan, 234
  Laura Ann O., 439
  Leonard, 439
  Leonard Benton, 439
  Lucinda, 439
  Nettie J., 562
  Royal Benton, 439
  Sarah, 69
  Sarah Candace, 439
  William W., 753
Flint, Charles N., 323
  George W., 323
  Hannah, 140
  Willie Tyler, 323
Flower, James J., 704
Fogg, Albert H., 562
  Carroll, 562
  Cyrus, 318
  Jacob, 154
Follansbee, Alice Cushman, 570
  Benjamin A., 570
  Helen L., 570
  William Tyler, 570
Follet, Molly, 201
Folsom, Mary C., 547
Forbes, Asa, 551
  Charlotte, 387
  Herbert, 551
  John, 596
  Malcolm, 596
  Oliver Tyler, 596
  Rachel (Deane), 203
Forbush, Isaac, 490
  Lottie H., 490
  Peter, 100
  William H., 490
Ford, Mercy, 567
Fordham, Sybil, 196
Forney, Alice, 594
Forrest, Christina Caroline, 615

Tyler, Henrietta, 223, 520, 724
Henrietta Feller, 670
Henrietta Maria, 167
Henrietta O., 480
Henriette L., 529
Henry, IV, 188, 218, 259, 276,
282, 342, 350, 413, 416, 423,
427, 444, 446, 468, 495, 505,
529, 534, 602, 653, 661, 683,
709
Henry A. 696, 771
Henry Addison, 435
Henry B., 250, 464
Henry Bates, 382
Henry Brooks, 188
Henry C., 223, 366
Henry Carroll, 443
Henry Cass, 369
Henry Clay, 367-368, 605-606
Henry Coit, 178, 350
Henry Disbrow, 758
Henry Franklin, 741, 782
Henry Dunreath, 322
Henry Edward, 245
Henry Erastus, 392
Henry H., 375, 476, 530, 573,
585, 610, 725, 738
Henry J., 488
Henry Johnson, 543, 728
Henry Judson, 617, 753
Henry Kendall, 515, 717-718
Henry L., 319, 320, 565
Henry Leavenworth, 539
Henry M., 15, 16, 233
Henry Mather, 622, 758-759
Henry Newton, 687
Henry Oscar, 539
Henry P., 366, 603
Henry Parker, 533, 725
Henry Pierce, 516
Henry Putnam, 143
Henry Rollins, 518
Henry S., 223
Henry Sawyer, 722
Henry Walton, 626
Hepsibah, 137
Hepsibeth, 125, 252-253
Herbert, 489, 602, 710, 778
Herbert Chester, 695
Herbert Elroy, 730
Herbert F., 673
Herbert Ferre, 719, 729
Herbert H., 535
Herbert Milton, 399, 633-634
Herbert N., 531
Herbert William, 643
Hermione, 496
Hetty, 415
Hespiah, 71
Hester, 93
Hial, 259, 271, 483, 498
Hildreth Chadwick, 765

Tyler, Hiram, 195, 197, 209, 250,
374, 380, 395
Hiram L., 258
Hiram M., 499
Hiram Walter, 609
Hiram Ward, 195, 374
Hitty, 169
H. M., 718
Homer C., 197
Hope Binney, 739
Hopestill, 6, 14, 16, 18, 20, 25-
32, 59-60, 89, 356
Hopestill, Jr., 29, 31, 32
Horace, 411
Horace C., 155, 481, 691
Horace Frank, 691
Horace P., 194
Horace Upton, 666
Horatio, 226, 423-424
Hosea B., 260
Howard, 259, 366, 559
Howard Benson, 527
Howard J., 234
Howard Tyler, 669
Hubbard, 128, 259
Hugh Arlington, 654
Hugh Claverly, 655
Huldah, 67, 109, 110, 197, 353
Huldah Maria, 270
Humphrey, 85, 253
Humphrey M., 223, 421
Humphrey Perley, 251, 465
H. W., 718
Ida, 470, 534, 602, 683-684
Ida A., 666
Ida Florence, 571, 736-737
Ida J., 377
Ida May, 465, 643
Ida Melissa, 565
Ida Viola, 749
Ignatius, 148, 149, 303-304, 555
Immigrants, III-X
Ina, 734
Ina D., 684
Inez Mabel, 686
Ira, 250, 261, 461, 462, 463-464,
674
Ira B., 283
Ira Stickney, 277, 509
Irena, 301
Irene, 214, 236, 238, 346
Irene Chaplin, 706, 777-778
Irene Graves, 310, 559-560
Irene Heaton, 235, 236
Irving C., 638
Irving W., 559, 731
Isaac, 70, 113, 116, 126, 135, 160,
161, 226-227, 230, 233, 242, 255,
274-275, 426, 427, 448-449, 468
Isaac Allen, 425, 663
Isaac Barker, 275
Isaac Bartholomew, VI

59, 60, 63-64, 75, 76, 81-82, 86,
94-95, 97, 98, 99, 102-103, 104,
108, 125, 128, 131, 146, 147, 156,
161, 169, 172, 174-175, 180, 186-
187, 193-194, 195, 197, 204, 257-
258, 259, 264, 265, 278, 301, 319,
330-331, 381, 452, 516, 559, 594,
692, 731-732, 749-750
Joseph, Jr., 97, 146, 174, 348, 352-
353
Joseph A., 561, 732
Joseph Allen, 541
Joseph Alonzo, 187, 189, 365
Joseph Alva, 297
Joseph Augustus, 289, 535-536
Joseph C., 146, 250, 297, 460
Joseph Cogswell, 351, 594
Joseph Coit, 178, 349
Joseph Currier, 310, 559
Joseph Curtis, 194, 373
Joseph Curtis, Jr., 373
Joseph Delavan, 781
Joseph E., 312
Joseph Edwin, 354, 595-596
Joseph Elmer, 567, 735
Joseph F., 564
Joseph H., 331, 556
Joseph Henry, 356, 599
Joseph Hopkinson, 752
Joseph Howe, 326, 568
Joseph Keyes, 425
Joseph M., 346
Joseph Pride, 352
Joseph Punderson, 175
Joseph Stickney, 135, 276-277
Joseph Warren, 121, 246-247
Joseph Woods, 279
Josepha, 398
Josephine, 353, 529, 590, 749
Josephine Amelia, 412, 653
Josephine E., 308
Josephine Maria, 497, 701
Josephine Mehitable, 479
Josephine Parker, 527, 724
Joshua, 23, 43, 49-50, 71, 72, 79,
117, 119, 120-121. 136, 139, 140,
245, 283-284, 295, 300, 452, 543-
544, 552, 675
Joshua, Jr., 139, 239-240, 284-285,
451-452
Joshua B., 264, 487-488
Joshua Dudley, 487
Josiah, 155
Josiah Goodrich, 274, 503
Josiah S., 482
Josie Alberta, 382
Josie R., 615
Juda Ann, 404, 642
Judith, 121, 129, 245-246
Judson, 109, 217
Julia, 216, 256, 366, 378, 394,
452, 479, 613

Tyler, Julia A., 456, 676
Julia Ann, 230, 231, 255, 296, 303,
424, 426, 432-433, 434, 478, 546,
555
Julia Antoinette, 599
Julia Caroline, 517
Julia E., 431, 668, 698
Julia Ellen, 290, 537
Julia F., 256, 405
Julia Huntington, 571
Julia Pierce, 407, 645-646
Julia Treadwell, 578
Juliet, 343
Julius, 391, 411
Justin, 365
Kate, 400, 468, 504, 634, 636, 655
Kate Browning, 595
Kate Virginia, 628, 763
Katherine Douglas, 599
Katura, 134
Kelita, 105, 195
Kelita R., 194
Keyes, 227, 425
Kimball, 125, 251-252, 253, 466-
467
King William, 677
Kittie Marie, 661
Kittie Maud, 781
Laban, 252, 468-469
Laban Ainsworth, 278, 517-518
Lafayette, 222
Larissa Clark, 502
Larkin W., 246
Latimer, 236, 440
Laura, 141, 143, 232, 245, 379,
395, 452, 497, 552, 559, 675
Laura Ann, 467, 682
Laura Elizabeth, 632
Laura Elvira, 497, 699-700
Laura Emma, 582, 743
Laura Griswell, 260
Laura J., 404, 641
Laura M., 538
Laura Whitman, 655
Lauraette, 559
Laurens, 209
Lavinia, 111, 208, 219, 275, 346,
503-504
Lavinia Draper, 222
Lawrence E., 375
Lawrence Milton, 735
Lawrence Stewart, 486, 693
Layton James, 565, 734
Leafa, 214
Leaffie Pauline, 629
Leah, 91
Leander, 111
Leander Ansel, 371, 608
Leavenworth Hoffman, 780
Le Grand, 436
Leland C., 772
Lelia, 364

Tyler, Lelia May, 601
Lemuel, 198, 383, 476, 689
Lena, 378, 611
Lendell, 155, 314
Lendell, Jr., 314
Leo Orville, 644
Leon E., 684
Leon F., 651, 765
Leon Meredith, 487
Leonard, 277, 512
Leonora Emma, 486, 693
Lepha, 437, 667
Leroy Herbert, 643
Leslie, 685
Leslie G., 470, 685
Leslie Pierce, 537
Lester Dean, 730
Leta, 675
Letitia M., 563, 733
Leverett Winslow, 503, 704
Levi, 141, 291
Levi Andrew, 291, 537
Levi Eckford, 587, 749
Levi Y., 437
Levinia, 342
Levinus A., 256, 479, 480
Lewis, 231, 279, 294, 367, 519-520, 542-543, 609
Lewis, Amos, 486
Lewis Cutler, 245
Lewis F., 684
Lewis Frederick, 769
Lewis Harrison, 520
Lewis Laban, 683
Lewis Orlin, 408, 649
Lewis P., 233, 436
Lewis W., 638
Lida, 662
Lida E., 698
Lida Elvira, 682
Lidia, 366
Lillian M., 714
Lillian May, 673
Lillian Stallo, 491
Lillie A., 666
Lillie M., 470
Linda, 686
Liza, 394
Lizzie, 324, 492
Lizzie Ella, 693
Lizzie Irene, 686
Llewellyn Starbord, 561
Logan Osceola, 372
Lois, 592
Lois Cornelia, 530
Lora, 207, 380, 396
Lora Elizabeth, 399, 633
Loren, 270
Loren Butler, 412
Loren E., 412
Loren Francis, 404
Loren Sumner, 512, 710, 712-713

Tyler, Loretta, 482
Lorin, 216, 411-412
Lorin C., 413
Lorin Darius, 683
Lot, 319
Lottie, 729
Lottie Bell, 668
Louine Childers, 659, 767
Louis Augustus, 670
Louis Hodges, 659
Louisa, 140, 150, 157, 214, 242, 245, 269, 343, 366, 378, 494
Louisa Augusta, 517, 720
Louisa Blake, 578
Louisa Elvira, 222, 420
Louisa Emeline, 412, 652
Louisa M., 479, 480, 689
Louisa Maria, 406
Louisa R., 222, 223, 420
Louisa Southwick, 196, 376-377
Louise, 739
Louise Elizabeth, 634
Louise Marie, 506, 709
Louise Mabel, 500
Louise S., 557, 730
Lovina, 218, 415
Lucenia, 192
Lucetta, 252
Lucetta Streeter, 470, 684
Lucette S., 557, 730
Lucia A., 463, 500, 704
Lucia J., 496
Lucian C., 499
Lucien Howard, 738
Lucile, 765
Lucilla Dix, 59
Lucina, 270, 495
Lucinda, 111, 204, 219, 220, 221, 231, 234, 271, 276, 297, 417, 418, 419, 438, 439, 496, 506, 764
Lucius, 261, 272, 499
Lucius Abbott, 711
Lucius Harvey, 237, 441
Lucius Merrill, 497, 700
Lucius Spaulding, 595
Lucretia, 71, 93, 98, 117, 182-183, 344
Lucretia Ellen, 378
Lucretia George, 517
Lucretia J., 239, 444, 445
Lucy, 70, 78, 79, 91, 97, 110, 115, 125, 130, 132, 142, 154, 168, 171, 215, 218, 233, 239, 251, 252, 253, 300, 312-313, 331, 352, 416, 492, 515, 552, 717
Lucy A., 512, 716
Lucy Ann, 232, 245, 255, 261, 292, 355, 478, 596
Lucy B., 316
Lucy Bancroft, 356, 597
Lucy Belcher, 350, 592
Lucy Brooks, 230, 431-432

Tyler, Melville H., 565
Melvin Dunning, 749
Mercy, 35, 42, 128, 134, 140, 144, 201, 293-294, 384-385
Mercy Ann, 249
Mercy Wood, 122
Merriam Coleman, 369
Merrill, 271, 497
Merrill Judson, 435, 666-667
Merry Effie, 680
Merton Griswold, 650
Meta, 744
Michael, 261
Mildred A., 685
Mildred Allen, 778
Mildred Edith, 537
Mildred L., 688
Milo, 260
Milo E., 434
Milo Eastman, 668
Milo Hildreth, 519
Milton R., 407
Minerva, 199, 367, 383
Minerva A., 605
Minnehaha Eloise, 632
Minnie, 437, 485, 751
Minnie A., 561, 674, 732
Minnie G., 655
Minnie Gertrude, 687
Minnie Palmer, 722
Minnie R., 653
Minnie S., 438
Minnie Williams, 695
Mira, 279
Mira Eliza, 281, 527
Miriam, 116, 141, 235-236, 290-291
Miriam Emelia, 780
Miriam L., 321
Molly, 72 92, 118, 119-120, 135, 170, 171, 240-241, 273, 335-336, 600
Moody, 278, 515
Morgan Carpenter, 624
Morris Philip, 643
Morseen G., 312, 562
Moses, 6, 12, 13, 14, 15, 16, 17-23, 40, 41, 43, 51, 52, 55, 59, 67, 70-71, 72, 79, 82, 88, 89-90, 92-93, 102, 109, 113, 115-116, 120, 136-137, 146, 149, 160, 161, 162-163, 173, 176, 190-191, 212-213, 225, 227, 237, 243, 244, 253, 255, 256, 321, 344-345, 423
Moses, Jr., 149, 404
Moses Augustus, 282, 529
Moses Coburn, 135, 277, 509-510
Moses Coit, 585, 745-746
Moses Coleman, 191, 367-368
Moses Cyril, 443
Moses K., 252, 470
Moses Kimball, 264, 488

Tyler, Moses M., 227, 429-430
Moses Merrill, 233, 435
Moses Osgood, 510
Moses Reed, 639
Moses S., 196, 376, 430
Moses W., 126, 193, 255, 373
Mylon J., 496
Myra Joslin, 780
Myrtle, 634
Nabby, 72, 116, 136, 232
Nahum Amos, 263
Nancy, 71, 108, 111, 123, 175, 203, 204, 211, 213, 215, 222, 237, 240, 253, 281, 308, 323, 388, 410, 441-442, 493, 580, 617, 742
Nancy A., 308, 366, 603
Nancy B., 310
Nancy H., 564
Nancy Jane, 443, 650
Nancy M., 291, 618
Nancy Mariah, 301
Nancy Ober, 189
Nancy Roselia, 399
Nanne, 106, 202
Nannie, 116
Nanny, 201, 386-387
Nat, 667
Nathan, 34, 35, 60-62, 63, 67, 72, 79, 82, 98-99, 110, 119, 134, 136, 137, 147-148, 183-184, 185, 187-188, 218, 231, 281, 366, 433-434, 602
Nathan, Jr., 149, 302
Nathan C., 427
Nathan Elmore, 360
Nathan Peabody, 143, 292-293, 540, 727
Nathan R., 531
Nathan Southwick, 611
Nathan Web, 101, 189
Nathaniel, VI, X, 23, 44, 75, 81, 116, 124-125, 144-145, 232-233, 250, 294, 436, 461-462
Nathaniel, Jr., 145
Nathaniel Bayley, 329
Nathaniel Hiram, 294
Nathaniel S., 557
Nellie, 127, 415, 538, 674, 727, 766
Nellie Edwards, 758
Nellie G., 480
Nellie J., 556, 732
Nellie L., 639
Nellie Lila, 730
Nellie Leonora, 693
Nellie Osgood, 579
Nelson, 509, 709
Nelson G., 666
Nelson W., 582
Nettie, 380
Nettie Genevieve, 716
Nettie M., 437
Neva, 635

www.ingramcontent.com/pod-product-compliance
Lightning Source LLC
Chambersburg PA
CBHW050642270326
41927CB00012B/2834